FIRSTING AND LASTING

Indigenous Americas

Robert Warrior and Jace Weaver SERIES EDITORS

FIRSTING AND LASTING

Writing Indians out of Existence in New England

Jean M. O'Brien

Indigenous Americas Series

University of Minnesota Press
Minneapolis
London

Portions of chapters 3 and 4 were published in "'Vanishing' Indians in Nineteenth-Century New England: Local Historians' Erasure of Still-Present Indian People," in Sergei Kan and Pauline Turner Strong, eds., *New Perspectives on Native North America: Cultures, Histories, and Representations* (Lincoln: University of Nebraska Press, 2006), 414–32.

Published by the University of Minnesota Press
111 Third Avenue South, Suite 290
Minneapolis, MN 55401-2520
http://www.upress.umn.edu

Library of Congress Cataloging-in-Publication Data

O'Brien, Jean M.
    Firsting and lasting : writing Indians out of existence in New
England /   Jean M. O'Brien.
        p. cm. — (Indigenous Americas)
    Includes bibliographical references and index.
    ISBN 978-0-8166-6577-8 (acid-free paper) —
    ISBN 978-0-8166-6578-5 (pbk. : acid-free paper)
    1. Indians of North America—New England—History—19th century.
2. Indians of North America—New England—Historiography. 3. New
England—History—19th century. 4. New England—Historiography.
5. New England—Race relations. I. Title.
E78.N5O35 2010
974'03—dc22
                                                            2010003781

Printed in the United States of America on acid-free paper

The University of Minnesota is an equal-opportunity educator and employer.

30 29 28 27 26 25 24 23 22   14 13 12 11 10 9 8 7

For Tim

Contents

Author's Note on Sources

I used several principles of inclusion and exclusion in identifying the texts on which this book rests. I started by creating a comprehensive bibliography of local histories of all the towns and cities of Connecticut, Massachusetts, and Rhode Island published between 1820 and 1880, using the indispensable volumes produced by the Committee for a New England Bibliography.[1] I decided not to confine my search solely to volumes that announced themselves as histories of particular localities in single or multivolume form, but also included pamphlets that contained historical orations, Fourth of July orations, publications that grew out of local commemorations, and the like. I included in my bibliography the few items I found that were published before 1820, and I added some texts published after 1880, especially if there were no other texts available for that particular town, for places located near nineteenth-century Indian communities, or if the titles intrigued me.

Once I settled down to read the texts I noticed some patterns and further modified my list. Fairly early on I concluded, for example, that church histories, manuals, and anniversaries rarely included Indians; sermons or historical discourses delivered at churches also likely did not. I did include some of these, but for the most part I omitted them from consideration. I excluded genealogies (no real narratives there, except the implicit argument of the depth of non-Indian lineages in particular places); newspaper, journal, and periodical literature (far too much of it, usually topically aimed); publications devoted to topical themes that weren't likely to include Indians (for example, a history of the copper mines in Granby, Connecticut); histories of wars, unless they involved Indians (I discovered early that even accounts of the Boston Massacre, in which Crispus Attucks was killed, did not talk much about his Native descent); missionary histories, specifically Indian missionary histories (of course they include Indians); and the dedication of buildings (although I did include a few of these).

Two more items to note: At a certain point I culled out the towns that were incorporated after the seventeenth century, because few seemed to include Indians at all and because most grew out of older towns that somehow included these places in their story of colonialism. And by no means did I look at every Forefathers' oration delivered at Plymouth (although I did consult many of them).

In the end, there were a number of local texts from my bibliographies that I never managed to track down, perhaps a couple of dozen. I finally decided these few texts would not alter the story I saw emerging from the texts I already had consulted.

Introduction   Indians Can Never Be Modern

The Story

On June 3, 1856, Harvard legal scholar Emory Washburn, fresh from a brief term as governor of the Commonwealth of Massachusetts, stood to address the people of Bridgewater on the two hundredth anniversary of its legal incorporation.[1] They were gathered, he proclaimed, "to lay the offerings of cherished memories and honest pride upon altars which our fathers reared here in years that are past."[2] Washburn's account participated in a robust tradition of southern New England ancestor worship, and it grounded that story locally. The original inhabitants of the land that became Bridgewater barely registered in his address, although the way they did turn up is telling. Their first mention came when he named the committee that was appointed "to obtain the requisite title-deeds from the good old Massasoit, within whose jurisdiction this territory was situated."[3] Washburn went on to note:

> Tradition points out the spot where this act of purchase was completed, which once bore the name of "Sachem's Rock." But it is sad to think, that, of all that race who then peopled this region, nothing but tradition now remains. It is sad to recall in how short a time not a drop of the blood of the Sachem of Pokanoket, whose hand of friendship welcomed our fathers to these shores, was to be found in the veins of any living being.[4]

After having turned over legal possession of their lands to the newcomers, Indians receded from the scene in Washburn's account. Indians, he asserted, had so thoroughly vanished from the region that no physical trace of them survived in any living person. Mournful though it may be, Bridgewater people would have to settle for place-names and traditions when it came to knowing about the Indians their ancestors encountered.

We can only imagine how the hundreds of Indians who remained in their southern New England homelands might have received this sweeping claim.

In spite of more than two centuries of English colonialism that worked to displace them and make them disappear, New England Indians remained in their homelands. We know they were there because of a report produced by John Milton Earle, special commissioner to the Indians in Massachusetts in the 1850s, who enumerated Indian families and communities throughout Massachusetts.[5] We know they were there because Connecticut, Massachusetts, and Rhode Island maintained bureaucracies for Indian affairs at the time Earle was writing that offered additional archival evidence. We know they were there because their descendants are still there.

How could Emory Washburn have overlooked them? How could he have failed to know the larger and far more complicated story of Indian survival? These are not trivial questions: they get to the heart of crucial aspects of the racial dynamics of southern New England and indeed of the United States. The text that contained Washburn's historical account was one of hundreds that participated in the larger ideological project that this book takes up. My aim is to understand how non-Indians in southern New England convinced themselves that Indians there had become extinct even though they remained as Indian peoples—and do so to this day. I argue that these processes can be best understood by getting at the mind-set of ordinary non-Indians.

But why should we pay attention to southern New England, arguably the most overstudied area of the United States for matters ranging from history to literature to national identity and beyond? First, that region took the lead in this genre and writers there produced an enormous body of literature in the nineteenth century. New Englanders dominated this culture of print, obsessed over its self-fashioned providential history, and defined itself as the cradle of the nation and seat of cultural power. Part and parcel of this self-fashioning is the genre of local history writing that became crucial in defining Indians out of existence. Second, these histories narrate a rich Indian history for which they took some pains to account, though the histories they constructed fell short of full comprehension. Indians mattered to these authors because they were central to telling the story they wanted to tell. Third, the collective narrative these texts assert of Indian extinction is demonstrably false: Indian survival in New England (which sometimes appears as ruptures in these texts) makes it imperative to raise the question of how these local narrators could have gotten it so wrong.

Southern New England is the ideal place to locate this study because it was there that people made the boldest claims to "firsting," a central thematic of this book that in essence asserts that non-Indians were the first people to erect the proper institutions of a social order worthy of notice. Plymouth—

and southern New Englanders tied to that place in their imaginary—insisted on origin stories of the nation that were rooted in that place and its Indian history. Indeed, this body of literature is so vast, and the stories they had to tell so complicated, that I've chosen to focus on southern New England: Connecticut, Massachusetts, and Rhode Island even though similar conclusions could be drawn for northern New England.[6] Besides limiting the source material to a manageable size, this bounding of the project also limits the number of stories that I need to account for: while the strains of settler colonialism I find in southern New England resonate throughout the region, bringing in the north would entail even more peoples, places, and origin stories. The local historians of southern New England brought into being a practice of historical writing that historians from elsewhere drew upon, customized for their locality, and replicated across the landscape of the nation.

These dusty old volumes, so attuned to the minute unfolding of seemingly obscure stories, demand our attention because they constitute a vital vernacular history that shaped the ideological predispositions of nineteenth-century New Englanders. While the historical, ethnological, and literary output of the literati—Francis Parkman, George Bancroft, Henry Rowe Schoolcraft, Henry Louis Morgan, James Fenimore Cooper, Lydia Maria Child, and others— deeply influenced the thinking of the time, the local texts that I analyze in this book reached large audiences as well. More important, while the emergent national literature that these luminaries produced certainly gave shape to an understanding of American history, culture, and identity, local texts grounded those stories in the concrete. Local narrators took up the histories of the exact places their audiences lived, and they rooted stories about Indians in those places. The overwhelming message of these narratives was that local Indians had disappeared. These local stories were leashed to a larger national narrative of the "vanishing Indian" as a generalized trope and disseminated not just in the form of the written word but also in a rich ceremonial cycle of pageants, commemorations, monument building, and lecture hall performance. They both served as entertainment and they inscribed meanings in particular places. More specifically for my purposes, these scripts inculcated particular stories about the Indian past, present, and future into their audiences. The collective story these texts told insisted that non-Indians held exclusive sway over modernity, denied modernity to Indians, and in the process created a narrative of Indian extinction that has stubbornly remained in the consciousness and unconsciousness of Americans.

In making this argument, I do not claim that this is an exclusively New England project. In fact, much of the narrative construct about Indians in New

England can be found in local histories elsewhere. Many local histories from New York to Minnesota and as far away in place and time as California and Washington would fit comfortably on bookshelves alongside those of New England in their inclusion of stories about firsts and lasts.[7] And the entire construct of firsting and lasting that I posit in this book can be found everywhere—in tourist sites and public history venues, and in news stories of all sorts. But certain aspects of this story certainly are unique to New England. In particular, New Englanders insisted they commanded cultural power in the nation, and were morally superior vis-à-vis Virginia and the slaveholding South in general. Both of these assertions are rooted in New English claims about their modernity.

These obscure, largely forgotten authors engaged in an ideological project that involved working out a vision of American Indians that continues to shape, limit, and inhibit views of Indians even today. They inculcated on the microlevel a paradigm about the place of American Indians in U.S. history and the ongoing future of the United States that remains deeply influential. These texts help us understand how it is that a powerful mind-set of non-Indian modernity and Indian extinction unfolded in the mundane ideological transactions of the everyday world, and that this level of understanding is every bit as important as—if not more important than—the grand narratives of a Parkman, Cooper, or Child. I want to argue that the *local* gave particular valence to the twinned story of non-Indian modernity and Indian extinction. Romanticized constructions of generalized Indians doomed to disappear were one thing; it was quite another thing to contemplate the "extinction" of Indian peoples who might instead have been your very neighbors. At the local level the problem of *recognizing* Indians played out as tangible reality for non-Indians and Indians alike.

The idea of "recognition" of Indians is central to my project in two fundamental ways. First, I am concerned with Indians in southern New England, some of whom are—and others who are not—at present recognized as tribal nations by the U.S. government. Most tribal nations in the former English colonies occupy a different position than those who engaged in treaty making with the United States that recognized their nation-to-nation relationship. The state governments recognized tribal nations in New England where their homelands were located during most of the chronological scope of this book, but the process of establishing recognition by the federal government had to wait until the late twentieth century. This is of enormous consequence, though the contemporary federal recognition process itself is not what this book is about. Second, I focus on the processes whereby non-Indians in the nineteenth century failed or refused *to recognize Indian peoples as such.* Even though non-Indians had Indian neighbors throughout the region, and even when they acknowledged that these neighbors were of Indian *descent,* they still denied that they were authentic Indians. A toxic brew of racial thinking—steeped in their understanding of history and culture—led them to deny the Indianness of Indians. In other words, I am trying to sort out how it is that non-Indians convinced themselves that New England Indians had become extinct even though they had not, and how those who made the claim should have come to other conclusions if it were not for their assumptions that foreclosed full understanding.

In taking up this second sort of "recognition," I analyze the ways in which local texts narrated Indian history and "extinction" in Massachusetts, Connecticut, and Rhode Island roughly between 1820 and 1880. I examined some six hundred local texts—broadly defined—roughly three-quarters of which contain material about Indians and Indian history. These include everything from standard single- or multivolume treatments, to smaller texts, even pamphlets, published in the wake of historical commemorations of all sorts. My aim is to analyze the narrative strategies that New Englanders used regarding the Indian past and that attempted to put Indians themselves in the past by asserting their extinction in subtle and not so subtle ways. Central to all of this is the construction of an origin myth that assigns primacy to non-Indians who "settled" the region in a benign process involving righteous relations with Indians and just property transactions that led to an inevitable and (usually, drawing on the Romanticism that conditioned nineteenth-century sensibilities) lamentable Indian extinction. Thus, the "first" New Englanders are made to disappear, sometimes through precise declarations that the "last" of them has passed, and the colonial regime is constructed as the "first" to bring "civilization" and authentic history to the region. Non-Indians stake a claim to being native—indigenous—through this process. In stark contrast to the narrative construction, New England Indians actually "last," and remain vibrant peoples into the future.[8]

This book is also about how Indians have resisted their effacement, as they continue to do to this day.[9] A rich and growing literature on Indian New England provides a different vantage point on the past than was available to nineteenth-century local historians. Crucial work has been happening within the tribes themselves, and a burgeoning community of Native and non-Native scholars promises to recast our understanding of this pivotal time and place.[10] Emanating from a range of disciplinary perspectives, from archaeology to anthropology, ethnohistory, literary criticism, history, and more, this literature has transformed our understanding of the past and it will continue to do so in the future. Throughout this book I interweave stories about Indian resistance and survival drawing from this rich and emergent body of scholarship.

I do not, however, attempt to include a point-by-point refutation of the extinction claim by presenting a detailed demographic reconstruction of Indian communities. Instead, I opt for an analysis of the ideological construct. I have made this choice for three reasons. First, there are no comprehensive accounts of nineteenth-century Indian New England to draw on: reconstructing this history is very much a work in process. Second, I want to avoid the trap that I think much of the literature falls into: giving credence to "census taking" as survival and going to "cultural retentions" as evidence of Indianness. A faithful demographic reconstruction of nineteenth-century Indian New England is impossible given the state of the archival record, and hewing too closely to a project of identifying "cultural retentions" carries the danger of insisting on cultural stasis that is so centrally embedded in the New England project of modernity. And third, finding a way to finally displace the stubborn, erroneous, and harmful myth of Indian extinction is essential to understanding Indian New England. In seeking to move the conversation into an entirely different direction, I am resisting making declarations about what is "true" because this whole project is really about contesting the "truth" that New Englanders are trying to make.

My position is in agreement with that of other scholars who have observed that demographic methods have historically been tools of colonialism used against New England (and other) Indian peoples. Ruth Wallis Herndon and Ella Wilcox Sekatau found that in the Revolutionary era Rhode Island officials ceased identifying Indians as such in their dealings, instead "designating them as 'Negro' or 'black,' thus committing a form of documentary genocide against them."[11] Thomas Doughton points out a "discourse of disappearance" in forging an "official story" that erroneously declared that Nipmuc people had vanished from central Massachusetts.[12] More recently, Amy E. Den Ouden has pointed out that by "*counting Indians* living within the bounds of reservation land as a means of evaluating that community's social viability," colonial officials in nineteenth-century southern New England objectified Indian bodies in insidious ways and undermined their land rights. This discourse linked the idea of eventual Indian "extinction" to land rights. Further, the practice of focusing their enumerations on Indian men failed to understand female presence and authority as well as ignoring the mobility of Indian men, who participated heavily in the newer Indian economy of military service, whaling, and wage labor.[13] The surveillance of racialized Indian identities and communities in connection with ideas about blood purity and the supposed "degeneration" of Indians as of "mixed ancestry," Den Ouden argues, "emerged as a governmental tactic of control in the late eighteenth century."[14]

Local Texts as (Unlikely) Sources

For all the preceding reasons, I rely principally on what might seem like an unpromising archive for Indian history: local texts produced mainly but not exclusively by male, non-Indian antiquarians who were generally preoccupied with forging dense chronicles of the origins and historical happenings of mostly small towns and often with connecting these small places with the project of forging Anglo-Saxon nationalism.[15] As Michel-Rolph Trouillot has argued, to understand the relations of power in the *process* of historical production, we need to account not just for professional historians but also for "artisans of different kinds, unpaid or unrecognized field laborers who augment, deflect, or reorganize the works of professionals."[16] Local historians included scions of the Boston elite such as Edward Everett and Joseph Story, whose polished publications reflect their social position. But rural ministers such as Joseph B. Felt of Salem, and amateur history buffs such as Frances Manwaring Caulkins, whose family ran a female academy in eastern Connecticut, dominated the medium. These mostly middle-class authors participated in the institutionalization of the historical society movement, and they far outranked elites in the production of local literature.[17] Their publications formed a vernacular historical sensibility of enduring influence, as their work, however fanciful or downright erroneous, became blueprints for understanding the past. They frequently shared their work with one another, and it circulated throughout the nation as historical societies proliferated and collected these publications. They served as local experts where consolidated versions of the past were disseminated in print and in periodic public celebrations that included historical orations as a central feature of public entertainment. Local histories broadly conceived participated importantly in this project as locations of ideological production and consolidation.

Preoccupied as they generally were with the Anglo-Saxon origins of the nation, how can these texts serve as source material for Indian history? Because asserting a break from the past demanded the inclusion of stories about Indians, these texts operate as source material on multiple levels. They narrate events about Indians. They include Indian historical figures. They make judgments about the morality of their colonial history. They chronicle—often in great detail—the history of land transactions on which they based their claim to a benevolent and just colonialism. They make claims about Indian fates and especially about Indian disappearance. And in the way they construct narratives about non-Indians, they implicitly make arguments about what counts as legitimate history, and who counts as legitimate peoples. Thus, even when the subject matter of local texts is not explicitly about Indians, it is frequently implicitly so. The implicit arguments of local narration will be a crucial theme in this book. These texts help us understand a larger narrative that cannot be dislodged from nineteenth-century sensibilities about Indians, race, and modernity. The texts themselves helped create a particular reality, but not one that adequately accounted for Indian lives, survival, or history.

Contemporary concerns with issues such as shifting patterns of immigration, industrialization, urbanization, abolitionism, and Indian affairs nationally were occasionally explicit reference points for local narrators, but even when such issues were not specifically referenced, their influence on perceptions are often in evidence. Of great importance in these local accounts was the massive out-migration of New Englanders to all points, and the rapid demographic, economic, and social transformations they witnessed—and frequently feared and lamented.[18] Even while they anxiously asserted their centrality to the nation, New Englanders in the nineteenth century harbored fears about their declining power and influence, in part accounted for by the very out-migration that fueled Indian dispossession across the continent in the service of American nationalism. These narratives must be understood in this context, as cultural elites and local farmers alike desperately argued for the enduring importance of New England in defining the nation.[19]

As Lucy Maddox has argued about American literature, the policy of Indian removal as a solution to the "Indian problem" loomed large as a moral issue in the minds of nineteenth-century writers who "removed" Indians from their stories because of their supposed incompatibility with "civilization."[20] For New Englanders, Indian removal had special resonance, given the prominent role its congressmen took in opposing the legislation on the basis that it would stain the honor of the nation. This prominence gave rise to the charge, "What happened to your Indians?" a challenge local historians generally took up with some degree of enthusiasm. The notion of forced removal of Indian peoples became the focus of vigorous debate by the 1820s, was first planned and imposed on the Five Tribes of the Southeast in the 1830s, then was reformulated and replicated across the continent, culminating in the 1890 massacre at Wounded Knee.

Although it is not initially why I settled on the chronological bounding of this project, this broader preoccupation with the forces of Indian removal, westward expansion, and national innocence between 1820 and 1880 stands as a crucial though largely implicit unifying theme of local texts in southern New England. I started by trying to take stock of the genre as a whole, noting that many local texts contained valuable material about Indians that either did not exist elsewhere or could be difficult to locate. After several years of collecting local texts in fits and starts, I spent almost a year systematically reading mainly in the unparalleled collections of the American Antiquarian Society and the Newberry Library, with side trips to the Massachusetts Historical Society, the Minnesota Historical Society, the Beinecke Rare Book and Manuscript Library at Yale University, and, later on, a four-month stint at the Library of Congress. The sheer number of these texts available across the United States (and elsewhere) suggests the reach of this phenomenon. Over the course of several years, I have looked at every local text I could find that was published between 1820 and 1880 about Connecticut, Massachusetts, and Rhode Island, as well as many that were published in the last two decades of the nineteenth century.[21]

I begin in 1820 because even though there are a few brief locally focused publications from before 1820, that date roughly coincides with the beginnings of what would quickly become a vibrant enterprise (see Table 1).[22] As has been frequently pointed out, cultural production beginning around 1820 participated in the assertion of American nationalism. Americans anxiously demonstrated their fitness as a separate and legitimate nation in the production of a uniquely American body of cultural work: language, art, literature,

Table 1. Local histories by decade (selective)

YEARS	CONNECTICUT	MASSACHUSETTS	RHODE ISLAND	TOTAL
1810s	1	3	0	4
1820s	1	16	0	17
1830s	7	34	2	43
1840s	10	33	2	45
1850s	18	50	5	73
1860s	9	37	1	47
1870s	29	87	19	135
1880s	6	45	8	59
1890s	4	18	2	24
(number of histories)	85	323	39	447

Note: This represents the numbers of local histories that contain Indian materials. The numbers from the 1880s and 1890s do not represent an exhaustive search of all published materials: I looked at titles in these decades selectively, especially including texts for places that did not have published accounts previously and texts that were located near ninteenth-century Indian communities.

history, and more. Also, the technology and distribution systems made possible the production of cheap books that could be printed and circulated broadly.[23] The explosion in local history writing fits squarely within this context. The year 1880 is a logical point to end, both because the genre itself transformed in that decade as local histories (and other sorts of local publications like histories of industries) lost their truly local flavor, through becoming standardized and commercialized, and because of the changing character of the increasingly industrialized, urbanized nation and shifting patterns of immigration.[24] As well, this end date provides for the inclusion of the great many publications that followed the U.S. centennial in 1876, partly due to a presidential proclamation that urged localities to publish their histories, and several historians paused to reflect on events during the bicentennial of King Philip's War in the same year. The year 1880 also marks Rhode Island's legislation terminating that state's official recognition of the Narragansett Nation, the culmination of the mythology-steeped political project that sought to legislate the tribe out of existence.

Within this sixty-year span, momentous historical events rocked the United States, with the Civil War standing at the center of this chronology. In spite of massive changes in the social, cultural, political, economic, gender, ethnic, and racial order of the United States, the local histories produced in this span of time read similarly in topic and intent, especially as they pertained to Indians. The events included obviously depend on the year of publication, but beyond the topical variation thus manifested, I do not analyze this material according to finer grains of time. In my reading of these texts, the larger narrative thread pulls through these years fairly consistently regarding the central theme of my book, namely, the production of modernity through purification of the landscape of Indians. Ironically, even as New Englanders were building an argument about Indian timelessness they were creating a timeless narrative of their own about Indians; that narrative doesn't change, really, until the late twentieth century and even then it isn't entirely effective in understanding Indians *in* time.

Because local texts form the core source material for this book, it is essential to note the ways in which they are conceptualized and used. Like all sources, these texts are both richly informative and limited in their utility. They frequently reproduce, in whole or in part, rare and sometimes lost documents that contribute significantly to the evidence of the past. Many of them collect in one volume much of the source base for early (especially non-Indian) history of a place for convenient access and dissemination. The best of them rely on meticulous archival research, even beyond the locality, that at times compares favorably to newer social history in methodology. Their flaws begin with the racial (and other) biases that the authors brought with them and used to shape their narratives, and range widely across a spectrum of issues.

As Michel-Rolph Trouillot has pointed out, "Historical narratives are premised on previous understandings, which are themselves premised on the distribution of archival power."[25] I understand local texts to compose an archive that "set[s] up both the substantive and formal elements of the narrative" of Indian extinction in New England.[26] The archival power of local texts transformed what happened (a long and continuing process of colonialism and Indian survival) into that which is said to have happened (Indian extinction).[27] Local texts have been a principal location in which this false claim has been lodged, perpetuated, and disseminated. The extinction narrative lodged in this archive has falsely educated New Englanders and others for generations about Indians, and it has been—and is still—used as an archival source itself, sometimes to be taken as factual evidence of Indian eclipse. Still, we cannot and should not simply toss out this colonial archive. Instead, we need to find ways to use it judiciously. I hope this book will help with that problem.[28]

Indians Can Never Be Modern

Why did local narrators tell Indian stories at all? Indeed, operating within relations of power would have permitted them to elide Indian history entirely. Drawing on the insights of Bruno Latour's *We Have Never Been Modern*, I argue that New Englanders embraced Indians because doing so enabled them to establish unambiguously their own modernity. Non-Indians narrated their own present against what they constructed as the backdrop of a past symbolized by Indian peoples and their cultures. The master narrative of New England was that it had made a stark break with the past, replacing "uncivilized" peoples whose histories and cultures they represented as illogically rooted in nature, tradition, and superstition, whereas New Englanders symbolized the "civilized" order of culture, science, and reason. Modernity is predicated on exactly this sort of rupture.[29]

The narration of Indian extinction in local texts proceeded along two important avenues. Insistence on "blood purity" as a central criterion of "authentic" Indianness reflected the scientific racism that prevailed in the nineteenth century.[30] New England Indians had intermarried, including with African Americans, for many decades, and their failure to comply with non-Indian ideas about Indian phenotype strained the credence for their Indianness in New English minds. Non-Indians thought about race and blood according to a colonial calculus in which the possession of even a single drop of African American "blood" relegated one to the status of "Black" and "slave," whereas it demanded of Indians evidence of just the opposite: purity of blood. This calculus operated within the colonial order, on the one hand securing a labor supply in hereditary bondage, and on the other justifying the seizure of Indian lands on the basis of Indian "disappearance." This penchant for Indian purity as authenticity also found essential expression in the idea of the ancient: non-Indians refused to regard culture change as normative for Indian peoples. Thus, while Indians adapted to the changes wrought by colonialism by selectively embracing new ways and ideas, such transformations stretched beyond the imaginations of New Englanders: Indians could only be ancients, and refusal to behave as such rendered Indians inauthentic in their minds. Indians, then, can never be modern.[31] These ideas provided fertile ground for the idea of extinction, a mythology that obliterated the fact of Indian survival and fostered the dominant ideology about racial formation in nineteenth-century New England and informed a developing national ideology about Indians.

In the process of asserting their modernity, local writers worked mightily to root the New English social order deeply. In effect, they claimed to be the first people who established cultures and institutions worthy of notice, thereby subtly declaring the invalidity of Indian ways of life. Indians serve the larger story line of establishing the primacy of the New English social order. Collectively, the effect of their ideological labor is to appropriate the category "indigenous" away from Indians and for themselves. They subtly argue for the sole legitimacy of New English ways, as the institutions and practices of non-Indians are posited as the epitome of modernity.

Further building on Latour, these constructs served to purify the landscape in particular ways. Not only did ideas about racial and cultural purity disqualify Indians of mixed descent for Indianness in the New England imaginary, but legal and bureaucratic processes operated against Indian "recognition" as well. Connecticut, Massachusetts, and Rhode Island all—in complex ways—took measures to "terminate" their recognition of the political status of tribes within their boundaries in the mid- to late nineteenth century. This drive for terminating the political status of the tribes can be best understood, I argue, as bringing racial expectations into alignment with political processes. New Englanders did not recognize the Indianness of Indians there, and they attempted to terminate their political existence to harmonize these racial and political expectations. This can be seen as completing what I have come to think of as the New England replacement narrative. They effect a stark break from the past, with non-Indians replacing Indians on the landscape. These are processes of purification that are central to the ongoing production of modernity. These are also claims about purification that failed even while they were being made. This failure translates into the inconsistency and uncertainty of nineteenth-century narratives about Indians and has produced the historical backdrop for contention over New England Indianness into the present.

By taking up the narrative construction of Indian history in local accounts, this book aims to undermine its collective claim that modern New Englanders had replaced ancient Indians on the landscape. I hope to show the ways in which non-Indians actively produced their own modernity by denying modernity to Indians. I also want to expose the futility of these claims, as New England Indians continued to resist their effacement as tribal nations in the nineteenth century and beyond. It is this long-term ideological construct, I would argue, that shapes contemporary debates and confusion over the "authenticity" of New England Indians. I hope that by exposing these constructions, I can shed light on larger issues about Indianness, "authenticity," recognition, and modernity in the United States.

This book is composed of four chapters that explore crucial dimensions of this ideological process. These artificial categories, constructed to bring a semblance of organization to a mass of material, constitute a thematic ordering in order to make sense of the construction of the myth of New England Indian extinction, and the centrality of Indians to the New England project of modernity. Chapter 1, "Firsting," examines claims that local texts make about the primacy of English culture, institutions, and lifeways in the production of modernity in New England. I look at the precise ways that the production of local histories participates in the creation of modernity as the exclusive purview of Anglo Americans, and asserts the production of a new social order built on the ideas and practices of modernity. Local histories claim Indian places as their own by constructing origin stories that cast Indians as prefatory to what they assert as their own authentic histories and institutions.

Chapter 2, "Replacing," looks at the construction of what I call the New England "replacement narrative." The erection of monuments, the mounting of historical commemorations, local interest in amateur archaeology and place-names as well as claims to rightful ownership of the land show how local histories built a collective case that they had replaced Indians on the landscape of New England. Monuments to Indians propose their eclipse, and are juxtaposed with monuments to non-Indians that are intended to assert English origins. Historical narratives and relic collecting place Indians in the past, and selective retention of Indian place-names is meant to commemorate Indian peoples and practices that are asserted as extinct. These elements of the replacement narrative participate in the purification of the landscape of Indians in the production of New English modernity.

"Lasting," chapter 3, takes up the narrative construct of Indian extinction through what I call the "last of the [blank]" syndrome, whereby local historians occasionally tell stories about people they identify as the last Indian who lived in places they claimed as their own. I analyze this ideological construct with reference to ideas about race, blood, and culture that fueled and rationalized these assertions. I also show how they used the construct of "lasting" to talk about other peoples, institutions, and practices in the ongoing production of New English modernity. This chapter ends with an overview of the various ways local texts made Indians disappear to complement the more extreme claim of the "last of the [blank]."

Chapter 4, "Resisting," focuses on the contradictions that are found even in single texts about Indian extinction and Indian fates. Because non-Indians failed to recognize the Indianness of New England Indians, and because they denied that Indians could be part of modernity, they produced narratives that failed to understand and account for Indian persistence. They displayed uncertainty about Indian fates, exposing cracks in their façade of New England modernity purified of Indians. Local texts reveal performances of this uncertainty when they included Indian participants at historical commemorations that purported to explain Indian extinction, and they collectively report an Indian geography of survival even if only incompletely. In this chapter I also take up the writings of the remarkable William Apess (Pequot) to look at the ways he wrote and talked back against colonialism and the ways that non-Indians sought to make Indian peoples and Indian versions of history disappear. Apess embodies the futility of the project of purification, defying non-Indian constructions of Indians as ancient in his writings, speeches, actions, and everyday life as a modern political thinker and activist. Finally, this chapter looks at the processes whereby New Englanders sought to "terminate" the ongoing political existence of Indians and how Indians resisted this process.

In the many years that I have been at work on this book, one image has long stood out as emblematic of the process I've been trying to understand. The frontispiece to Alonzo Lewis's *History of Lynn* (1829) is a finely honed etching in a coastal setting of a well-heeled Englishman handing over a set of garments to a feathered Indian man clothed in skins with a quiver of arrows

BLACK WILLIAM selling NAHANT
to Thomas Dexter for a Suit of Clothes.

Figure 1. *Black William Selling Nahant to Thomas Dexter for a Suit of Clothes.* This lithograph, prepared for an 1829 history of Lynn, Massachusetts, encapsulates a replacement narrative, conveying the notion that non-Indians compensated Indians for their homelands, from which they then departed. Pendleton's lithograph, Boston. Frontispiece for Alonzo Lewis, *The History of Lynn* (Boston: J. H. Eastburn, 1829). Courtesy of the Newberry Library.

on his back. This illustration is titled "BLACK WILLIAM selling NAHANT to Thomas Dexter for a Suit of Clothes" (see Figure 1).[32] Here is the replacement narrative in its most encapsulated form. Culture meets nature, culture replaces nature, and the landscape is purified of Indians in a stark break with the past. This illustration goes to the heart of colonialism and the replacement narrative by directing the viewer's focus squarely on the issue of whose land this is. This problem, as subsequent history and present-day circumstances tell us, could not be resolved as neatly as that.

Chapter 1 Firsting
Local Texts Claim Indian Places
As Their Own

From Its First Settlement

Enoch Sanford named his 1870 narrative *History of Raynham, Massachusetts, from the First Settlement to the Present Time.*[1] Sanford's title for his fifty-one-page survey of local history resembled those given many other histories. Slight variations on this formulaic approach to naming abounded in nineteenth-century local texts. Take, for example, Myron O. Allen's *The History of Wenham, Civil and Ecclesiastical, from Its Settlement in 1639, to 1860,* Abiel Abbot's *History of Andover, from Its Settlement to 1829,* Elias Nason's *A History of the Town of Dunstable, Massachusetts, from Its Earliest Settlement to the Year of Our Lord 1873,* and Sidney Perley's *The History of Boxford, Essex County, Massachusetts, from the Earliest Settlement Known to the Present Time, a Period of about Two Hundred and Thirty Years.*[2] Although they differ in subtle ways, each of these titles reveals much about the assumptions about Indians and non-Indians, "history" and "settlement" its author brought to his project. Adding two more titles to the mix provides additional perspectives on often unspoken assumptions that drove the implicit narratives these texts framed. Instead of leaving the reader guessing about when these places "first" came to be (as some of the aforementioned titles do), John Murdock Stowe's *History of the Town of Hubbardston, Worcester County, Mass., from the Time Its Territory Was Purchased of the Indians in 1686, to the Present with the Genealogy of Present and Former Resident Families* and David Wilder's *The History of Leominster, or the Northern Half of the Lancaster New or Additional Grant, from June 26, 1701, the Date of the Deed from George Tahanto, Indian Sagamore, to July 4, 1852* offer indispensable clues as to their perspectives on origins.[3]

More is at stake in the naming of these texts than mere marketing. Although these histories of small places likely were intended for local and limited audiences, the project in which they participated was grand and helped produce grave consequences for Indian peoples whose places they claimed as

1

their own. The claiming is present in the very process of naming. The histories of Raynham, Wenham, Andover, Dunstable, and Boxford argue implicitly that authentic history begins with the arrival of English people in the place that came to be called New England, and further, they might even be taken to suggest that these places remained unpeopled until these momentous "settlements" came to be. The histories of Hubbardston and Leominster announce through their titles that the relevant accounts of those places begin with the "legal" transfer of land title from Indian to English hands. Even though Indian peoples are acknowledged as historical actors in these formulations, their possession of their homelands is mundanely dispensed with as prefatory to the real history that began with the advent of English transformation of the land. Nowhere is this semantic maneuver more direct than in an 1880 history of Derby, Connecticut. In this volume, the authors used roman numerals to distinguish the Indian history of the town, and expressed surprise that this story was so rich and extensive it needed xcvii pages to tell.[4] Conflict, colonialism, and contestation are subtly elided in the benign establishment of New English places on Indian homelands, at least as far as can be detected from these titles.

Other local narrators acted more imaginatively in naming their works, and some even acknowledged Indians in their titles, such as Josiah Howard Temple and George Sheldon in their *A History of the Town of Northfield, Massachusetts for 150 Years, with an Account of the Prior Occupation of the Territory by the Squakheags: and with Family Genealogies.*[5] This inclusion helps make the point: Indians were "prior occupants"—their supposed disappearance constituted a preface to the authentic history of Northfield, a place that claimed to participate in the production of New English modernity. Reflecting back, the vast majority of local historians saw a process of Indian decline and extinction that paved the way for the replacement of "traditional" Indian peoples with modern New English people. Indeed, operating within relations of power would have permitted them to elide Indian history entirely. Instead, New Englanders embraced Indians and used them to establish unambiguously their own modernity.

In spite of New English claims about being "first," indigenous peoples in New England lived rich and complex lives long before the English and other Europeans arrived. By the time Europeans stumbled on to the eastern seaboard of North America—the Norse around the year 1,000 and then other Europeans in the late fifteenth century—New England Indians had been forging their own histories and destinies for tens of thousands of years. The Wampanoag, Massachusett, Nipmuc, Pocumtuck, Pequot, Mohegan, Schaghticoke,

Paugussett, Niantic, Narragansett, and other indigenous peoples shared closely related Algonquian languages and northeastern woodlands cultures, and their village-based geographies were defined by both alliances cemented through strategic intermarriage and occasional enmity. Their sociopolitical systems were village-based chieftainships that operated in diplomatic relations with one another. Rather than exerting coercive power, Indian leaders—called sachems in New England—led by persuasion and displays of generosity. Intermarriage between high-status families facilitated alliance building and helped weave the sociopolitical fabric.[6]

Indian peoples reaped the riches of the northeastern woodlands in seasonally mobile and gendered economies that embraced female agriculture and gathering of wild foodstuff with male hunting and fishing in the interior and coastal waterways. Dense networks of trade connected them to each other and to Native peoples from elsewhere. Common group ownership of the land helped define Native senses of identity and of place, and a complex usufruct system whereby needs shaped land usage without conveying outright ownership of the land to individuals. Indians possessed deeply rooted histories transmitted principally in the oral tradition that tied them to their homelands, elaborate cultures that made them distinctive, and a rich spiritual and ceremonial calendar that defined their place in the created world.[7]

But even when elements of this longer and complex history are included in local narratives, the larger argument displaced Indians in favor of a landscape that is exclusively claimed by non-Indians. At work in these constructions is the collapsing and selective telling of thousands of years of human history in what came to be called New England. Narrating the story of modernity in New England required the inclusion of an Indian presence. The collective argument of local narratives asserted a stark break with a past rooted in nature, tradition, and superstition symbolized by Indian peoples and their cultures. The master narrative of New England, based on the minute evidence of local narration, involved the replacement of "uncivilized" peoples whose histories and cultures they interpreted as illogically rooted in nature, tradition, and superstition, whereas New Englanders symbolized the "civilized" order of culture, science, and reason. According to Bruno Latour,

Modernity comes in as many versions as there are thinkers or journalists, yet all its definitions point, in one way or another, to the passage of time. The adjective "modern" designates a new regime, an acceleration, a rupture, a revolution in time. When the word "modern," "modernization," or "modernity" appears, we are defining, by contrast, an archaic and stable past. Furthermore, the word is always being thrown into the middle of a fight, in a quarrel where there are winners and losers, Ancients and Moderns. "Modern" is thus doubly asymmetrical: it designates a break in the regular passage of time, and it designates a combat in which there are victors and vanquished.[8]

The modernity New Englanders claimed as their hallmark depended upon breaking with an Indian world they interpreted as rooted in nature, tradition-bound, and confounded by superstition. The dramatic tensions between Indians, resisting English incursions, and the English, heroically struggling to triumph over their "savage" foes, stood at the center of local narration in the nineteenth century. In this narrative the English triumphed and the Indians were vanquished and replaced on the landscape.

Furthermore, and still following Latour, asserting modernity involved a process of "purification"—clarifying the advent of modernity by negating the continuing presence of tradition as so perfectly symbolized in North America by Indians. As the residents of Stamford, Connecticut, heard during the bicentennial celebration of the incorporation of the town, "They came— and a wilderness was changed into the abode of civilized man."[9] William Cothren's history of Woodbury, Connecticut, said more:

Less than two hundred years ago, these pleasant hills and sunny valleys, now teeming with life, intelligence and happiness, were one vast solitude, unvisited by the cheering rays of civilization. . . . Everything now is changed. The desert waste that met the first gaze of our pioneer forefathers, has been made to bud and blossom as the rose. Where once were but scattered huts of the former race, are now enterprising and busy villages.[10]

This mind-set lent itself perfectly to the construction of a myth of Indian extinction that bolstered the heroic claims of New English modernity.[11] In their minds, in the histories they constructed, and in the stubborn reproduction of ideology, Indian peoples became forever ancient—mired in the static past. Deemed inauthentic if they did not comply with the expectation that they be persistently ancient, the collective project of local narrations cast Indian peoples as teetering on the brink of extinction if they did not relegate them explicitly to the past by declaring them extinct.

The scripting of "inauthenticity" of New England Indians operated most boldly in two critical dimensions. Relying on the scientific racism that posited separate and pure races organized in a strict hierarchy, non-Indians invoked notions about "blood purity" as essential to "authentic" Indianness. This constituted a literal embodiment of the obsession over purification Latour associates with the production of modernity. Because of a long history of intermarriage for New England Indians, they did not all "look Indian" to those who interpreted the racial terrain according to stereotypical notions of "pure races." Likewise, the obsession over purification found expression in ideas about change. New England Indians had dramatically altered their lifeways in dialogue with the new peoples and cultures brought by English colonialism. As they had for centuries before, Indian peoples changed over time. However, invoking ideas about a stable and indelible culture for the ancient peoples of the Americas, New Englanders refused to regard culture change as normative for Indian peoples. Indians who changed did not comply with non-Indian expectations of their authenticity. These ideas produced a lethal brew: non-Indians insisted that Indians could only be ancients, they could never be modern. This ideological construct produced the idea of Indian extinction as critical to racial formation in New England.[12]

The extinction narrative emerged out of the collective process of storytelling at the local level and participated in broader ideas about blood purity and cultural stasis. The texts drew upon these notions that were in common circulation and they rooted them in particular places. The minutiae of individual community stories thus coalesced into a master narrative of New England Indian extinction that became overwhelmingly pervasive and persuasive. Ordinary New Englanders who learned about their local history from these narrators were instructed that Indians had vanished from their vicinities. The collective end product purified New England of its Indian past on the imaginative level.

In addition to their dependence on Indians to establish themselves as modern, New Englanders posited a stark break with the irrational feudalism of Europe as a bedrock of their claims to be modern. As David Noble has argued, historical narration between 1770 and 1830 became crucial in asserting "the vision of history as progress, of history as a ritual of purification. . . . These historians were celebrating the liberation of their nations from the suffocating complexity of the medieval world."[13] Following their invasion of Indian places, the English equated Indians with the medieval world of Catholics and Jews, living in traditional worlds based on generational transmission. English individualism rejected the medieval world of reciprocity that rooted the social order in personal exchanges, and enshrined the marketplace as the epitome of modernity. Bourgeois nationalism rejected feudal orders as irrational and transformed subjects into citizens operating in new states of nature governed by Newtonian physics, Protestant theology, and citizenship in nations whose cultural and physical boundaries coincided in harmony and uniformity. "Each nation's middle class had symbolically replaced the homes of peasants and aristocrats and the homes of indigenous peoples with its own home."[14]

In the process of asserting their modernity, local writers performed the political and cultural work of rooting the New English social order deeply, which is visible in the very structuring of historical accounts and the claims they make. Indians, a necessary presence in the vast majority of local texts, advance the argument that the New English social order is primary. Indeed, these texts go even beyond this presumptuous claim: the result of this political and cultural work is to appropriate the category "indigenous" away from Indians and for themselves.[15] The overarching device in this construction is what I will call "firsting," a straightforward scripting choice that subtly argues for the sole legitimacy of New English ways. Furthermore, the practice of firsting implicitly argues for the inherent supremacy of New English ways, as the institutions and practices of New Englanders are posited as the epitome of modernity.

What is firsting, and how does it work? An 1882 history of Northampton, Massachusetts, offers a compelling example. Chapter 6 of Rev. Solomon Clark's volume is titled "Some of Northampton's First Things." The chapter begins, "The first settlement commenced 1654," and proceeds to instruct the reader about its first name (Nonotuck), marriage, meetinghouse, birth, death, minister's house, court, temperance measures, minister, accidental death, militia, bridge, interment, school, public highway, Indian attack, death at the hands of an Indian, college graduate, and prison, among other things: "The foregoing are some of the First Things of Northampton during the first fifty years of its history."[16] Clearly, the "first settlement" Rev. Clark has in mind is English, not Indian, and even its previous Indian appellation has been supplanted. Further, this construction implicitly argues that Indian peoples never participated in social, cultural, or political practices worthy of note, and that history began only with the gathering of English people in a place they renamed "Northampton." And although some of the notable firsts included here involve calamities and even Indian hostilities, most of them suggest that Northampton steadily and mightily built institutions of value that constituted the modernity of a place that could not have reached its pinnacle of rationality under Indian regimes of tradition and nature.

Although mainly devoted to a listing of Civil War soldiers, *Foundation Facts Concerning Its Settlement, Growth, Industries, and Societies*, published by the town of Haverhill, Massachusetts, begins with a fascinating four-page exercise in firsting. On this list, the only items that are not firsts concern Indians, specifically, the purchase of the land from Indians in 1642, the capture of famous captive Hannah Duston in King Philip's War, and a 1708 "massacre" by Indians.[17] These firsts served to bolster Haverhill's modernity (imposing English rules for property ownership) and highlight Indian "savagery" (warfare and captivity). The title of the thirty-nine-page text sums up the impulse and intent of firsting nicely: a chronicling of the steady and sure production of modernity through its social development and the entrenchment of capitalism from colonialism toward the industrial age.

Few historical accounts devote a separate chapter to firsting. Instead, most use the device as the most natural framework for a survey stretching from the past to the present, and some texts are laced through from beginning to end with firsting. Texts that take up the annals format do not lend themselves to "firsting," cataloging as they do a year-by-year accounting of peoples and events, but even this format implicitly builds a story about the forging of modernity.[18] And while not all historical texts engage in firsting, the vast majority do (see Table 2).

No place could rival Plymouth in the process of firsting, as is abundantly evident in James Thatcher's *History of the Town of Plymouth, from Its First Settlement in 1620, to the Present Time: With a Concise History of the Aborigines of New England, and Their Wars with the English, &c*, reprinted and expanded in 1835 after the 1,250 copies of the 1820 edition quickly sold out.[19] As the place that could make a generally accepted claim about primacy in the "permanent establishment" of New England, Plymouth could boast a plethora of firsts vis-à-vis any other New English place.

Some of these firsts could be unique to Plymouth: where else could a contest ensue over whose was the first foot of the first white person to land in the first permanent English settlement in New England? Descendants of John Alden and Mary Chilton quarreled over the distinction in the nineteenth century.[20] Thatcher's volume detailed the dramatic event of the first landing and

Table 2. Themes appearing in local histories (by number and percentage)

	CONNECTICUT	MASSACHUSETTS	RHODE ISLAND	TOTAL
Epidemics	5 (6%)	86 (27%)	9 (23%)	100 (22%)
Firsting	53 (62%)	245 (79%)	20 (51%)	318 (71%)
Indian landscapes	55 (65%)	189 (58%)	23 (59%)	267 (60%)
King Philip's War	40 (47%)	192 (59%)	27 (69%)	259 (58%)
Land transfers	70 (82%)	213 (66%)	32 (82%)	315 (70%)
Missionary outreach	30 (35%)	126 (39%)	11 (28%)	167 (37%)
Pequot War	34 (40%)	63 (19%)	7 (18%)	104 (23%)
Other conflicts	60 (71%)	217 (67%)	16 (41%)	293 (65%)

went on to claim that "this, then, is to be considered as the first stepping on the Rock of the Pilgrims from the shallop belonging to the Mayflower, and this is the *birth day of our nation,*" a claim that certainly might have been contested—and was—by Jamestown.[21]

But wait. Much later in Thatcher's volume, the issue of first landings reemerged:

> *Clark's Island* is the first land that received the footsteps of our fathers who formed the exploring party from Cape Cod. It received its name from Clark, the master's mate of the Mayflower, who first took possession of it with the shallop, December 8th, 1620. There is a tradition that Edward Dotey, a young man, attempted to be the first to leap on the island, but was severely checked for his forwardness, that Clark might be the first to land and have the honor of giving name to the island, which it still retains. My authority for this tradition is Mr. Joseph Lucas, whose father was the great-grand-son of Edward Dotey. The anecdote has been transmitted from father to son, so tenaciously that it need not be disputed.[22]

What can account for relegating the exploring party to the end of the narrative, which clearly made it secondary to the Alden and Chilton dispute? I would suggest that this more transient landing could not fully symbolize the permanency that lay at the roots of firsting. Exploring is not settling. Plymouth, not Clark's Island, was destined to attain primacy in the mythology of the nation. It is interesting that this narrative scripted competition over primacy of people and place as part of the actual events rather than a contest of memories. Further, the authorities invoked in both disputes are oral history—memory transmitted from generation to generation—here endorsed as reliable beyond dispute, an endorsement Indian oral traditions never received. The stakes in this special first are evident in other narratives; although they could not enter the contest for first setting foot on Plymouth Rock, one historian asserted that "we are not sure but *Falmouth* may yet claim the honor of being the first spot on the main land of America on which an Englishman ever trod."[23]

Plymouth, too, could claim "the first English child born in New England" (the formerly famous Peregrine White),[24] and could muse over the March 6, 1621, encounter with Samoset, who purportedly greeted the new arrivals "cheeringly in broken English—'Welcome Englishmen, welcome Englishmen.'" Samoset reputedly learned some English from fishermen in what was to be renamed Maine, which calls into question the novelty of the encounter. Thatcher tells us that "this was the first savage with whom the whites had obtained an interview," at least in Plymouth.[25] Less amiable encounters mounted by Captain Myles Standish ensued later, yet peace with the Indians came to prevail. A map of Plymouth Village in 1832 forms the frontispiece to this volume, on which Watson's Hill is depicted as the place where the first Indian treaty was made (about which, more later). This location apparently remained an important landmark for Plymouth, a place to be remembered as significant throughout time: "The stone arch bridge was erected over the Town brook in the year 1812, at Spring hill, precisely at the spot where the colonists had their first interview with Massasoit, in 1621. The hill where the sachem with his train of 60 men appeared, was called Strawberry hill by the first planters, now Watson's hill" (see Figure 2).[26]

Figure 2. *A Map of Plymouth Village, 1846.* This map of Plymouth Village posits the exact location where the first treaty between Massasoit and the English was negotiated. Pendleton's lithograph, Boston. Frontispiece for James Thatcher, *History of the Town of Plymouth, from Its First Settlement in 1620, to the Present Time: With a Concise History of the Aborigines of New England, and Their Wars with the English, &c,* 2nd ed. (Boston: Marsh, Capen & Lyon, 1835)

Interestingly, although they did not name this place "Massasoit hill," they could still locate the place where the "first interview" occurred. And momentously, Plymouth could claim the Mayflower Compact and insist it constituted the "first essay in the civilized world to found a republican constitution of government." This entitled Plymouth to make the claim of establishing "the foundation of all the democratic institutions of America," thus engaging in a dubious reading back of history.[27]

Other firsts noted by Thatcher included the first Sabbath, "first English town built in New England," "first offence committed and punished," "first prison," "first marriage ever solemnized in New England" (Susannah White and Edward Winslow), first record of horses, first division of lands, "first notice of a bell . . . probably the first used in New England," first church, Ralph Smith, first pastor of the first church, and the first mention of a wharf (see Figure 3). All of these firsts relate in one way or another to the establishment of institutions New Englanders regarded as central to their identity, and as essential elements in the modernity of their social order. Whether it be institutionalized religious practice, the implementation of legal codes governing everything from marriage to civil and criminal offenses, economic development, or political establishments, New Englanders scripted themselves as modern people looking to the future, creating order out of chaos and forging modern societies and cultures that broke from the past. This story implicitly argued that Indians and Indian ways could not be acknowledged as legitimate, ongoing, and part of the landscape of the future.[28]

Such is the message of the scattered etchings of places and events that found their way into some local texts. A Truro, Massachusetts, text included perhaps the most fascinating of these, a fine etching with the caption "The First Washing-Day at Cape Cod" (see Figure 4).[29] Here, English women stoically go about the process of laundering clothes while armed men stand guard, presumably awaiting Indian foes that might put a halt to these domestic activities. A poem by Margaret J. Preston accompanied the illustration:

And there did the Pilgrim mothers,
    "On a Monday," the record says,
Ordain for their new-found England,
The first of her washing-days.

And there did the Pilgrim fathers,
    With matchlock and axe weil slung,
Keep guard o'er the smoking kettles
    That propt the croches hung.

For the trail of the startled savage
   Was over the marshy grass,
And the glint of their eyes keep peering
   Through cedar and sassafras

For the earliest act of the heroes
   Whose fame has a world-wide sway,
Was—to fashion a crane for a kettle,
   And order a washing-day.

Such depictions suggest that the English brought cleanliness and domesticity with them to a place where they never existed before, and these illustrations inscribe a particular gender order of femininity and masculinity that is being initiated through their mundane activities. So too is gender inscribed in the etching of the mythological "First Thanksgiving," which depicts English and Indian men at table being served by English girls (see Figure 5).[30] Taken together, such depictions suggest that the very institution of home life properly ordered by gender never existed prior to the arrival of the English.

If they couldn't match Plymouth's precise catalog of firsts, other places could still replicate the practice of firsting by merely qualifying events as firsts for that particular locality. Even if Woonsocket, Rhode Island, could not claim the Mayflower Compact as a local event, it could point out that its "first public demonstration in Woonsocket, that is worthy of mention, took place in 1833," and thus assert its political activism while it celebrated the centennial of the nation.[31] And the firsting script mutated constantly, as particular localities chose different firsts to note, though the most common included first settlers, births of first white children (especially males), first marriages, first town meetings and town officers, first meetinghouses and ministers (numbered on into the present), first divisions of land, first newspapers, first schools, first bridges, mills, and other public works that symbolized modernity. Many communities also carefully detailed their first actions in the American Revolution, the quintessential break from the past (and the irrationality of Europe), especially participation in the first battle with the British at Lexington and Concord, and interestingly, citizens of Concord expended much ink in attempting to wrest primacy of their place over Lexington as the place of first bloodshed.[32] Lexington, sure of its firstness, did not reciprocate.

Some narratives that engage in firsting densely weave the themes into richly descriptive paragraphs. A thumbnail sketch from Rev. Myron Dudley's *History of Cromwell: A Sketch* blends present and past in a picturesque commentary on a momentous and inevitable trajectory toward modernity:

FIRST CONGREGATIONAL MEETING-HOUSE, NATICK

Figure 3. *First Congregational Meeting-House, Natick.* This etching erroneously asserts that this building represented the first congregational meetinghouse in Natick, Massachusetts. The actual first congregational meetinghouse was built entirely by Indians, who officially gained congregational status in 1660. Unknown engraver. Frontispiece for Oliver N. Bacon, *A History of Natick, from Its First Settlement in 1651 to the Present Time; with Notices of the First White Families* (Boston: Damrell and Moore, 1856).

THE FIRST WASHING-DAY AT CAPE COD.

Figure 4. *The First Washing-Day at Cape Cod.* Note the armed men standing guard over the women as they engage in the supposed first washing day on Cape Cod. Unknown engraver. From Shebnah Rich, *Truro—Cape Cod; or, Land Marks and Sea Marks* (Boston: D. Lothrop & Co., 1883), [57].

The first English explorers, in passing up and down the river, saw upon the high ground, not far from the corner of Washington and High Street in Middletown, the Castle of Indian Sachem Sawheag, chief of a tribe who occupied the surrounding hills in Maromas, Durham, Middlefield, Westfield, Cromwell, Chatham and Portland, then known by the Indian name Mattabesett, afterwards included within the limits of Middletown. . . . Chief Sawheag was unfriendly to white strangers.

These two reasons, the pre-occupancy of this region by unfriendly Indians and the low swampy condition of the alluvial, delayed settlement something like twenty years or more after the regions above had been occupied.

This is the first picture of life in this section. . . . The first settlements by the ancestors of the present occupants were made in 1650. This date is pretty sure. There may have been a few pioneers two or three years earlier, but this present year of 1876 marks the two hundred and twenty-sixth anniversary of the white man's permanent establishment upon these lands.[33]

Dudley explicitly asserts that Indian possession of their homelands constituted a "pre-occupancy" of the lower Connecticut River Valley, and thus suggests that it is a lesser sort of ownership. (Could it be that Dudley was importing Anglo-American legal language from the 1823 U.S. Supreme Court case

Figure 5. *The First Thanksgiving.* This depiction of the supposed first thanksgiving inscribes an English gender order on the proceedings. Unknown engraver. From Shebnah Rich, *Truro—Cape Cod; or, Land Marks and Sea Marks* (Boston: D. Lothrop & Co., 1883). [77].

Johnson v. M'Intosh that characterized Indian land tenure as "mere occupancy" rather than outright ownership?) Further, he anachronistically superimposes present-day markings of Indian lands by using New English street and town names in describing the area. And the advent of permanent English presence on the land marks the "first picture of life in this section." This semantic maneuver effectively scripts all previous human history in this place as a dead end—as incongruent with the modern Euro-American order that now begins as English pioneers begin the heroic process of erecting English institutions in the region.

Particular "firsts" became occasions for public gatherings devoted to historical commemoration. On June 11, 1855, for example, citizens of Charlemont, Massachusetts, gathered to commemorate a special first in the town's history. Joseph White provided the centerpiece of the occasion by delivering his oration, later published, *Charlemont as a Plantation: An Historical Discourse at the Centennial Anniversary of the Death of Moses Rice, the First Settler of the Town.* Near the beginning of his oration, White offered up the story line in this pithy passage, which neatly summarizes the common thread of nineteenth-century firsting narratives:

This quiet valley, now so beautiful with its garniture of green, and these guardian hills, still bore up the ancient forest. But the time appointed for a wonderful change was at hand. The axe was now to be laid at the root of giant trees; the blue smoke was now to curl from the low cabin of the pioneer; and the voice of industry, and the notes of prayer and praise, were now to arise; and the long, dark reign of wild beast, and wilder man, not without a bitter struggle, was soon to cease forever. The first settler—the patriarch of the valley—was on his way. In the spring of 1743, if not, indeed, in the previous autumn, Moses Rice of Rutland, in the County of Worcester, removed with his family to the town, and settled upon the tract which he had previously purchased.[34]

Like Dudley in the case of Cromwell, this author waffles over dates even while he strives for precision in the mapping of origins. With Moses Rice's arrival in 1743, or perhaps even 1742, the modern order was set in motion, initiated by his manly boldness in venturing out to the wild beyond populated by nameless Indian foes whose violent resistance was destined to fail, and preceded by his presumptively lawful yet unspecified purchase of Indian lands.

White's listeners then heard rich descriptions of the bloody incursions, as "the little band of hardy adventurers" felled the forests and turned them into fields, even while they coped with "the hardships of frontier life,—the fear of the tomahawk and scalping knife," with local Indians regularly joining forces with Canadian Indians in their forays.[35] Yet the title of White's account completely obscured the drama that was to come. Having fled from Charlemont during King George's War (1744–48) only to return and rebuild his farm, which had been destroyed, Rice finally met his fate in 1755 while plowing in a cornfield along with his son, grandson, and other men from the town.[36] A small party of Indians attacked them, scalping and mortally wounding Rice, and carrying his grandson into captivity in Canada, which ended six years later with his ransom. Moses Rice was buried on a hill near his dwelling. White expressed the hope that the town "will see to it that the sacred spot, set apart by him as a burial-place forever, and the hallowed depository of his mortal remains and those of his children's children, shall be guarded by an appropriate enclosure, from the intrusive ploughshare, and the unhallowed feet of cattle and swine."[37] His rhetoric effectively canonized Rice, who was elevated to esteemed status by his very firstness, and the ground that held his remains recommended to the populace as a sacred site. Anonymous Indian resistance to English incursion is scripted in this rendering as irrational, savage, and doomed.

This episode closed the chapter on Indian conflict, and constituted the final mention of Indians in White's forty-eight-page sketch. He ends by musing on the importance of history and its preservation, even while lamenting the startling lack of early records for the town. His final paragraph is a classic expression of the ancestor veneration that is so typical of nineteenth-century narratives and a richly subtle example of firsting:

> We are descended from men of no common mould. They were worthy sons of the men who first landed on these shores. These fathers of our fathers, were indeed a peculiar people. They were the seed-wheat, sifted by the winds of persecution from the chaff of the old world, and wafted across the sea, to be sown broadcast on the virgin soil of the new world. They were educated men. . . . They acknowledged the claims of the future, and manfully strove to pay the debt. And, as were the fathers, so also were the sons whom we this day commemorate. . . . True, also, to the future, they sowed that we might reap; they labored, that we might enter into their labors; they purchased with blood, that we might inherit in peace. May ours be the high privilege, as it is the solemn duty, to transmit this rich inheritance, unimpaired, to the generations to come. So shall we best honor the memory of the Fathers.[38]

From generation to generation, the principled, educated men who had been driven from a backward old world—a world mired in tradition—engaged in a masculine struggle to forge the foundations of the modern world. The denizens of present-day Charlemont owed it to their honorable ancestors to maintain those ideas and values and secure their transmission into the future.

Originary Places

Others shared the angst over lost or incomplete records of origins expressed by the residents of Charlemont as well as the reverence they attached to their ancestors and their originary deeds. Although frequently frustrated by fragmentary and disorderly archives, local historians nonetheless worked diligently to document precisely the people and events that set their modernity in motion. As an account of North Providence posed the issue, "It is pleasing to be able to answer the questions, Who felled the first trees of the primeval forests within its borders? Whose plowshare turned the first furrow? Whose hoe broke the first sod? Whose cabin sheltered the first residents?"[39] In Medford, Massachusetts, "the records of the first forty years are lost," and so its first major historian reconstructed the evidentiary base from other sources: General Court records, town histories, and circulars returned by town residents who provided genealogical information. He fretted over the indifferent results of the project, lamenting that "these registers of early families in New England will contain the only authentic records of the true Anglo-Saxon blood existing among us; for, if foreign immigration should pour in upon us for the next fifty years as it has for the last thirty, it will become difficult for any man to prove that he has descended from the Plymouth Pilgrims."[40]

Of course Plymouth served (and for many continues to serve) as the quintessential originary place, the birthplace of the nation. Many other localities in addition to Medford, however geographically or genealogically distant, joined Medford in connecting their story to the "Plymouth Pilgrims."[41] By the 1770s, New Englanders invented the tradition of Plymouth Rock as the mythic site of origins, and organized themselves into New England societies that proliferated throughout the nation.[42] Their annual Forefathers' Day celebrations, complete with historical orations by famous dignitaries, spawned a large body of texts lauding the rock as the originary place of the nation.[43] As claimed by William S. Russell:

> Forefather's Rock, so attractive to the curiosity of visitors, excepting that part of it which is now enclosed within the railing in front of Pilgrim Hall, retains the same position it occupied two hundred and thirty years ago, when the founders of New England first landed on our shores, and introduced the arts of civilization, the institutions of religion, civil government and education, upon the basis of just and equal rights, which from that memorable day to the present time, have secured the general good of the whole community, to an extent probably unexampled in any equal period of human experience.[44]

Thus could Plymouth Rock as an originary place symbolize modernity and become a place of pilgrimage throughout the nineteenth century and into the twenty-first.

Local historians found plenty of other larger themes of colonialism with which to frame their narratives. Christopher Columbus is frequently featured, and some writers push further: "it is now definitely settled that a bold and hardy Norwegian seaman crossed the stormy Atlantic to colonies in Greenland, in the year 985, discovering Nantucket on that voyage, naming it *Nauticon*," thus preceding Columbus by centuries.[45] Luminary antiquarian Samuel Gardner Drake offered a thorough discussion of European forays to North America before arriving on page 12 at the story of Captain Bartholomew Gosnold, "the first Englishman who had come in a direct course to this part of the continent, and the first of any nation who thus reached any part of what is now the United States, except Verazzani."[46] This firstness is called into question by the description that followed: Gosnold encountered "eight Indians, two of whom were dressed partly in European costume. These Indians came from a rock, which, from this circumstance, was called Savage Rock; the first spot on the shores of New England that received an [ironic] English name."[47] (Where did they get those European costumes?) Prominently featured also is Captain John Smith, who named New England.[48] Prior to that time, a historian of Gloucester tells us, "our Cape still remained without a name"—a dubious proposition given the rich Native nomenclature of Indian New England.[49] Not until chapter 8 did Drake arrive at the subject of his 840-page volume: Boston. At the bicentennial celebration of the arrival of Governor Winthrop held in Charlestown in 1830, Edward Everett paused to remember the exile of Puritans to Leyden.[50] Towns in Connecticut occasionally referenced the Dutch who preceded them.[51]

Those narrators who reached back to these early interactions between Indians and non-Indians hinted at a long and complex story that more recent scholarship tells us transformed New England even before the more dramatic changes that followed the permanent arrival of Europeans. Beginning in the late fifteenth century, periodic encounters occurred between Europeans exploiting the Grand Banks and other fisheries. Eventually explorers and traders began to make incursions into Indian New England and points north and south. By their nature fleeting and episodic, such interactions did not necessarily entail major disruptions for indigenous peoples. Rather, mutually beneficial trade relations rooted in Native notions of diplomacy tapped into existing networks of exchange that emerged from nonpermanent European ventures. Indians exchanged furs, pelts, and other Native goods for metal, cloth, and assorted trade goods, incorporating these items into their lives in Indian ways. As a result, Indian material culture and artistic expression changed through the inclusion of new items—though not necessarily in the ways Europeans might have expected. For example, Indians pounded out kettles to make arrowheads, and Native jewelry crafted out of metals appeared as grave goods alongside glass beads and Indian goods such as wampum (made out of quahog shells). Native clothing styles changed as woolen jackets and shirts that came through the trade complemented the leather leggings and moccasins of Indian origin and design.[52] Such changes attest to the dynamic nature of Indian cultures just as the relations of trade that underwrote these transformations are evidence of a complex international diplomacy at work for more than a century before the English arrival at Plymouth.

Other authors rejected the very murkiness of much of this early history in favor of a vastly circumscribed precision. Wallingford, Connecticut's historian, Charles Henry Stanley Davis, started right off in chapter 1 with the "Purchase of Indian Lands." He then expounded on the exceptional nature of the defendable claims of precise origins that set the nation apart:

> There is nothing in which our nation is more peculiar, than that it records its own origins. There is no other nation that does this, the Jews excepted. No one of the present nations of Europe can tell in a word of their earliest ancestors, or even specify the century in which their territory was first taken possession of by them; but all is involved in obscurity, as are the years before the flood. But it is far different with our early history as a nation. We know the men who said they would be free, and who laid the foundation of this mighty republic. We know whence they came, the object for which they came, the spot to which they came, and the year, the month, and the day they took possession. Our nation owes a lasting debt of gratitude to our ancestors for their fidelity in recording the incipient steps taken by them in settling this new world.[53]

This passage stakes a claim to American exceptionalism (excluding the Jews) about the exact moment of origins as well as the actual names of those who arrived in order to forge a free republic down to the very day they "took possession" of the land. Davis made a virtue of the clean break rooted in precise origins that marked the colonial state. The ability to clearly demarcate the beginnings of what came to be the nation is celebrated, juxtaposed with the shadowy origins of Europe's time immemorial. Davis elevated the very act of writing about those very first actions—of producing the records that enabled the claim—to heroic feats for which posterity owed its ancestors a debt of gratitude.

Judge Joseph Story shared this mind-set. In his oration celebrating Salem he declared, "Our history lies far within the reach of the authentic annals of history."[54] The origins of the modern nation—a free republic—could be dated to the day of taking possession of "the spot to which they came." James Dimon Green pushed the point further in addressing the questions of origins:

> No cloud of uncertainty envelopes the subject. As a people, a constituent part of a commonwealth, or a community of nations, we have not to go back for our origins to a period of ignorance and semi-barbarism, when there were no letters, no records, but such as existed in the memory of uncivilized men,—vague and varying traditions handed down from father to son, through successive generations. We have our literal records,—family, town, and state records,—of all transactions interesting and important.[55]

The nation is distinguished from unnamed ignorant and semibarbaric others by a precise documentary record that symbolizes civilization. The unreliable foundation of tradition and memory—of oral history—could not support a modern, civilized nation.

Implicit in the foregoing constructions is the contrast between non-Indians and Indians, who one can only imagine were readily invoked in discussions of semibarbarism and the lack of "civilization." A historian of Manchester, Massachusetts, brought Indians explicitly into the picture and rooted his originary claims in the idea of how history is made:

> The history of America begins with the advent of Europeans in the New World. The Red Men in small and scattered bands roamed the stately forests and interminable prairies, hunted the bison and the deer, fished the lakes and streams, gathered around the council-fire and danced the war-dance; but they planted no states, founded no commerce, cultivated no arts, built up no civilizations. . . . *They made no history.*[56]

And in Lynn: "The history of the red men remains in impenetrable obscurity. They had no books to contain their laws, exhibit their polity, or record their achievements; no written language."[57] Both of these constructions conjured up the stereotype of lazy, wandering, ignorant Indians living in lawless chaos and confusion without a written language with which to record their feats on a land they could not truly claim to own. According to this calculus, Indian peoples did not make history and therefore could not become the foundation of modern nations.

Famous First Indians

These notions about origins called into being a peculiar phenomenon: famous first Indians. Originary places depended on famous first Indians to authorize their origins and inaugurate the production of modernity. Plainly, the only thing that makes these Indians "firsts" is their role in a narrative whereby they are to be replaced. Here is where first Indians depart dramatically from their non-Indian counterparts. Rather than gaining their fame as firsts who will be a part of an enduring modernity, they are famous because they set into motion the processes that are the beginning of their end. Most notable in this respect are Indian leaders who entered into diplomatic relationships with the English, thus in one way or another authorizing the English presence in Indian homelands. Even though part of non-Indians' claims to Indian places rested in the argument that Indians "made no history," in their depictions of famous first Indians we learn that Indians *did* do diplomacy.

Trade, diplomacy, and conflict over power and land followed the arrival of the English, with different groups assessing the motivations and power of the others and attempting to forge alliances within the new geopolitical realities. Indian sachems such as Massasoit negotiated terms of coexistence with the newcomers at Plymouth, concluding a treaty with Plymouth in 1621.[58] The Narragansett sachems Canonicus and Miantonomi likewise treated with Roger Williams for peaceful coexistence following Williams's banishment from Massachusetts Bay in 1636.[59] At the same time, the enigmatic Mohegan sachem Uncas engaged in diplomacy with everyone in order to secure his own ends.[60] All of these figures became the subject of narrative after narrative, securing their positions in history as famous first Indians.

Not surprisingly, stories about Plymouth and its pivotal figures attained a centrality in this firsting process. The primary and secondary source matter for narrating Plymouth's story is relatively abundant, and the frequency with which localities from all over southern New England linked their stories to Plymouth meant these stories found wide circulation. Of the iconic figures of early Plymouth, the trio of Samoset, Massasoit, and Squanto gained the most notice as firsts. The life stories of these individuals signify a particular story of colonialism.

Witness Rich's account of Truro, Massachusetts:

> Another circumstance as clearly providential as any event in history, and without which we cannot see how the Pilgrims could have survived, was the friendship of Samoset, Squanto, and Massassoit [sic]. As subjects of rare historical interest, honesty and nobility of character, they are an honor to their race, and worthy a niche in the temple of fame. From savage tribes, thinned by pestilence, and basely betrayed by the white men, came these three men from different channels, and differing widely in offices, yet with a unity of purpose to serve the Englishman in his weakness and necessity.[61]

Rich singled out this trio because of their "honesty and nobility of character," because of their concerted efforts to "serve the Englishman," which secured them a spot in "the temple of fame." The base white men in question included Englishman Thomas Hunt, who seized twenty-seven Pokanoket (or Wampanoag) men and women in 1614 and sold them as slaves in Malaga in an episode that would carry long-standing implications for Indians and Europeans alike. Most famous of the enslaved was none other than Squanto, who made his way back to his homeland in the company of Thomas Dermer only to discover that his village had disintegrated in the wake of a disastrous epidemic. Squanto became a cultural broker between the powerful Wampanoag sachem Massasoit and the English before meeting his demise under shadowy circumstances in 1622.[62]

In February 1621, weeks after the first landing, the English had failed to establish relations with Indians. By then, "a general meeting was called to establish some military arrangements, and Myles Standish was chosen Captain."[63] But it was not until the sixteenth of March that

> much surprise was excited by the appearance of an Indian who boldly walked to the rendezvous, and cried out cheeringly in broken English—"Welcome Englishmen, welcome Englishmen." This was Samoset, a Sagamore, who had come from Monhiggon, (District of Maine,) where he had learned something of the English tongue from the Captains of the fishing vessels, on that shore, and he knew by name most of those commanders. This was the first savage with whom the whites had obtained an interview. No incident could have diffused greater joy in the hearts of the disconsolate . . . He said that the place they now occupy is called Patuxet, and that about four years ago all the natives died of an extraordinary plague; that there was neither man, woman, nor child remaining in the territory, of which the English had now possessed themselves.[64]

The remarkable providence of an Indian hailing the English *in* English (however halting) bode well for the English. Intermittent visits and exchanges with other Indians ensued after this "first interview," which paved the way for something much more momentous. Samoset returned to the fledgling settlement on April 2 with other Indians, including Squanto, "the only surviving native of Patuxet," in tow. They came to trade and to announce the imminent arrival of "their great Sagamore, Massasoit . . . with Quadequina, his brother, and all their tribe." With Squanto acting as intermediary, Massasoit and Edward Winslow exchanged preliminaries on Watson's Hill, which included greetings from the king of England, and overtures for trade and peace extended by each side. With military precautions also taken on each side, Myles Standish guided Massasoit and a contingent of his group to Governor Carver, after which a treaty was negotiated.[65]

Leaving aside the terms of the "treaty" and the degree to which a thorough and shared understanding governed its negotiation, the author of this account inserted this footnote to the proceedings: "This treaty, the work of one day, being honestly intended on both sides, was kept with fidelity as long as Massasoit lived, but was afterwards (1675) broken by Philip, his successor," a quote taken from Jeremy Belknap's *American Biography*.[66] Others put it differently:

> With him [Massasoit] their first treaty was concluded. In an unfinished building near Plymouth, the floor spread with a rug and cushion to give dignity to the proceedings, were conducted the simple negotiations which are memorable as the beginning of American diplomacy. The treaty was one of alliance, and not one of subjection . . . He lived to see his territories melt away before the steady inroad of the whites . . . But he remained to the last true to the compact he had made.[67]

Even before a proper building could be finished to dignify the negotiations, the English entered into a treaty of alliance (not subjugation) with the Indians. Thus did the trio of Samoset, Squanto, and Massasoit set into motion the grand tradition of American diplomacy and set the stage for more than fifty years of peaceful relations horribly violated by Massasoit's own son, King Philip. And in this single family Plymouth scripted both the noble and the ignoble savage, the excellent and friendly Massasoit, whose dignified commitment to amiable interaction and exchange was destined to be betrayed by his ignoble son. One history summed up the first part of the story succinctly in its index, which included an entry for "Friendly Indians—Massasoit, Samoset, and others."[68]

William Shaw Russell's *Guide to Plymouth, and Recollections of the Pilgrims* began with "Introductory Lines" in the form of a lengthy poem "designed to form a general outline of the work, and briefly to describe the most interesting localities rendered memorable by the early and intimate connection with the pilgrims."[69] The poem contained the following central plot lines of Indian history:

The rising Hill, upon whose brow,
Was first exchanged the solemn vow,
When Massassoit [sic] the Indian Chief,
So promptly tendered kind relief,
And by whose early proffered aid
A lasting peace was firmly laid.
While Carver, Winslow, Bradford stand,
Time honored Fathers of our land,
This Chieftain too shall homage claim,
Of praise far more than princely fame,
True-hearted, gentle, kind and brave,
Unfading honor crowns his grave.

The path through which Samoset came,
And boldly welcomed them by name,
Whose practised skill and counsel sage,
Inscribed appear on history's page,
That tells his worth and friendship true,
And yields the praise so justly due,
His comely form and features stand,
Portrayed by Sargent's tasteful hand,
Besides the Groupe of exiled name
Who pressed the *Rock* of endless fame.[70]

In this poem, Massasoit took his proper place alongside the English "Fathers of our land" because of his peaceful embrace of the English, and Samoset's linguistic skills in the service of friendship also earned him a place in the annals of history. Squanto and other first Indians were relegated to a much smaller role in this appreciation. In a later edition of the volume, Russell offers an account of the "First Celebration of the Landing of our Forefathers," held on Friday, December 22, 1770. During the festivities, those gathered participated in a lengthy round of toasts, beginning with "the memory of our brave and pious ancestors, the first settlers of the Old Colony." Massasoit ranked number five in order: "To the memory of Massasoit, our first and best friend, and ally of the Natives." No other Indians rated at all.[71]

Rather than "welcome, Englishmen," Roger Williams was purportedly greeted to what became Providence, Rhode Island, with "an animating salutation, *Whatcheer, Netop, Whatcheer*" in 1636, fifteen years after Samoset made his appearance in Plymouth.[72] The identity of the supposed greeter is nowhere specified in the local narratives of the origins of Providence. One local historian attributes this story to

> tradition [which] says that they first landed on "the Slate rock" on the bank of the Seekonk river, near the residence of his Excellency Governor Fenner. . . . That there is some foundation for the tradition appears from the fact, that a tract of land adjoining this rock, has ever since borne the name of "what cheer." Under this name, it was assigned to Mr. Williams in the first division of lands among settlers.[73]

Williams's arrival, supposedly heralded by an anonymous first Indian in a hearty greeting of welcome, authorized his appropriation of Indian lands, and the first encounter became enshrined in memory in the rock where this event supposedly took place.

Banished from Massachusetts Bay and Plymouth for his writings that insisted that the king of England could not empower settlers through the Massachusetts Patent to occupy Indian lands without compensating them, this story argues that Williams was embraced by the Indians of Narragansett Bay. What gained him the currency for such a robust welcome in this narrative?

> A knowledge of their language, a just notion of their rights, and the means which he employed to gain the affections of the natives, enabled him to procure from Canonicus and Miantinomo, the Chief Sachems of the Narragansetts, the land which first constituted the Providence colony. In a deed of confirmation of these lands to his associates, dated 20th December, 1661, and now on the Providence records, he says, that he "was by God's merciful assistance the procurer

of the purchase, not by monies, nor payment, the natives being so shy and jealous that monies could not do it, but by that language, acquaintance and favor with the natives, and other advantages which it pleased God to give him."[74]

Providence's peaceable origins are sanctified in this story. Williams's just and honorable negotiations with chief sachems Canonicus and Miantonomi, presumably conducted in Algonquian rather than English, authorized his possession of Indian land through the "language, acquaintance, and favor with the natives" rather than any base monetary transaction. These two Narragansett leaders in turn gained fame as firsts in historical accounts as the peaceful negotiators who legitimated colonialism on Narragansett Bay. Indeed, "the early history of Rhode Island could almost as well be written without allusion to Roger Williams as Canonicus. . . . Miantinomo was the complement of Canonicus, and neither can be separated from the other."[75] In addition, the claim about diplomacy allowed Providence to assert primacy vis-à-vis Plymouth and Massachusetts Bay, as "neither of these colonies deemed it important to obtain from the Indians a title to the soil, before they commenced their plantations. They relied, in the first instance, either upon their own actual possession, or a grant from the king, as sufficient to confer a title to the soil they occupied."[76] Furthermore, justice and honesty continued to govern relations between Canonicus and Roger Williams for the rest of their lives. "From what we know of this old Indian King, there does not appear a grander character in our colonial history."[77]

Towns in Connecticut could distill no similarly comforting stories about first Indians embracing them with open arms and unbridled affection. With the stain of the violent Pequot War of conquest to contend with, local narrators looked in vain for a Massasoit, Miantonomi, or Canonicus. Instead they were inclined to settle on Uncas as an enigmatic signifier of their origins. In the words of one narrator:

> After the destruction of the Pequot fort at Mystic by Major Mason, in 1637, Uncas seems to have been so impressed by the bravery and power of the English, and to have felt so strongly that if he had their friendship, they could defend him against any enemy, he ceded, from time to time, to his many friends among the white settlers, and to the colony of Connecticut, all his lands and possessions, reserving to himself certain rights and privileges.[78]

New London historian Frances Manwaring Caulkins similarly expressed ambivalence about Uncas, noting that "it can not be denied that in all controversies between the Mohegans and other Indian tribes, the colonial authorities were inclined to favor Uncas. This chief, by the destruction of his enemies, and the gratitude of the English, was daily rising in importance."[79] Given the martial origins of their claim to place—much of the land in Connecticut they claimed through right of conquest in the wake of the war—Connecticut had little choice but to embrace Uncas, to whom they erected a monument in 1842 bearing the simple inscription "UNCAS."[80] A monument to Major John Mason, leader of the English militia in the Pequot War, took nearly fifty years more. At the dedication an orator declared, "It may be mentioned in passing that Mason's friendship for Uncas continued unbroken till his death in 1672. Uncas survived him ten years, and with his tribe was always a loyal friend and faithful ally of the whites."[81]

Even given the ambivalence evident in depictions of Uncas, these famous first Indians signify essential elements in the project of modernity. Iconic Indians are meant to project the notion of a pacifist colonialism in which friendly Indians invited the English to settle among them. The English reject the medieval order of aristocracy and land grants from kings in favor of a new American diplomacy that involved negotiations with Indians for the peaceable occupation of their homelands. First Indians gain their fame by authorizing these transactions; their ancestors then give way to the processes of replacement in their homelands through the production of modernity.

The Script

For the vast majority of authors the story of modernity they wanted to tell depended upon the inclusion of Indian history, and further, Indians provided dramatic material that Americanized their narratives. The central story line of the colonial past for New Englanders involved the heroic overcoming of the "savage foe" in a valiant struggle to make the wilderness "blossom as the rose," a phrase that is repeatedly invoked as the metaphor for subduing the land in English ways. This biblical phrase from Isaiah 35:1, which prophesied the recovery from a country made a ruin and a wilderness because of wickedness, provided a metaphor for the distinction between nature and culture that so preoccupied the assertion of modernity.[82] In many narratives, this story is quickly and tersely dispensed with, including a few sentences or paragraphs that offer little of substance beyond a few basic points. In others, however, whole chapters or sections are devoted to Indian history, or Indian history is woven throughout the structure of the text.

Although widely ranging in the density of its presence, Indian history appears in local narratives in fairly patterned ways. These are the predominant themes: epidemics; missionary outreach; the Pequot War; King Philip's War; other Indian conflicts (including other wars, raids, and fears about

Indians); Indian landscapes (including place-names, relics, graves and other sites); and Indian land transfers of all sorts to the English.[83] While these categories do not exhaust the topics local narrators considered, they do summarize the majority of Indian material. These themes are not present uniformly, and there are variations among Connecticut, Massachusetts, and Rhode Island in their presence (see Table 2). Furthermore, including the Pequot War and King Philip's War is somewhat problematic, given the rhythm of town founding and the regional specificity of these conflicts—many towns came into existence long after the conflicts had ceased. It is interesting to note, however, that even places that had not yet come into being while these conflicts were being waged sometimes connect their history to one or both of them, either because earlier, larger borders of places would have connected them, or because the migration of combatants or their descendants brought them to newer places, or because narrators deemed these events as pivotal in the story they had to tell of modernity's origins.

All of these themes speak to the issue of purification—of distinguishing between nature and culture. Instead of acknowledging them as defensive actions to protect their homelands against English invasion, wars are typically scripted as savage and heathen, initiated by furious assaults by Indians on innocent "settlers." Stories about Indian men attacking English men in their fields and women being seized into captivity in their homes frequently appeared. Indian cultures are cast as primitive, and Indian bodies—horrifically subject to imported diseases—as inferior. Indian social and political orders, if acknowledged at all, are either described as formless and irrational or equated with feudalism—Indian sachems become kings over their vassals. Indian economies and land use are depicted as equally irrational; rarely is the complexity of Indian seasonal economies acknowledged. Instead, Indians are generally cast as aimless wanderers over a wilderness landscape. Narrators describe Indian religions, if they describe them at all, as heathenish devil worship, or worship of nature, purely superstitious and irrational.

After more than a century of sporadic interaction between European fishermen, traders, and explorers and Indians, the English made what would become a permanent incursion at Plymouth in 1620 and then Boston in 1630. The still-unidentified epidemic of 1616–19, which ripped through Squanto's village and much of the coastal region twenty to thirty miles inward and then stopped at Narragansett Bay, reduced the Native population by perhaps 50–90 percent, disrupting Indian lives in ways we will never fully understand. This demographic catastrophe facilitated their incursion and assured the English, who fled England from religious persecution and in pursuit of commercial gain, that divine providence had favored them by reducing the Indians to make room for them. Smallpox followed in 1633, and other more locally contained epidemics periodically decimated Indian peoples well into the eighteenth century. English families reproduced rapidly, additional migrants arrived in waves through much of the rest of the seventeenth century, and English colonizers encroached onto Indian lands as far as the Connecticut River valley and then southward, as well as to Narragansett Bay and what would become Rhode Island.[84]

This story of disease became a minor theme in local narratives and carried with it either explicit declarations of Indian demographic decline or the underlying implication of population loss. Histories from Massachusetts and Rhode Island contained more material on epidemics than those from Connecticut, which makes sense given the geography of pestilence in the colonial period. The two most devastating epidemics that predominated in these histories—the epidemic of 1616–19 that preceded the permanent English incursions at Plymouth, and the 1633 smallpox epidemic that raged throughout the region—did not affect Connecticut in the same way as they did Rhode Island and especially Massachusetts. More locally confined epidemics at Natick (1745–46 and 1759) and Nantucket (1763–64) gained notice in those places.[85] Like many others, James Thatcher's history of Plymouth adopted a divinely ordained interpretation of the earliest epidemic, telling his readers that "this Providential event [the landing of the *Mayflower* at Plymouth rather than Hudson's River] . . . proved auspicious to their enterprise and future prosperity, as the native inhabitants of the place had been destroyed."[86] This characterization simultaneously acknowledged the presence of Indians and suggested their imminent demise, thus paving the way for Plymouth people to erect modern societies properly ordered in their place. Bringing attention to Indian population loss through epidemic diseases underscored a larger story of Indian demise and argued for the inferiority of Indian bodies as unsuitable to participate in modern societies.

As early as the 1640s, missionaries such as Thomas Mayhew and John Eliot found some Indians willing to listen to their messages, at least some of whom did so in order to secure a place within their own homelands in the context of aggressive English expansion. Under Eliot's auspices, fourteen Praying Towns were founded, although only four of them survived the horrors of King Philip's War. In spite of English demands that Indians take up English ways, Indians shaped their own destinies by selectively borrowing English beliefs and practices.[87] In places such as Natick and Mashpee, and on Martha's Vineyard in Massachusetts and Charlestown, Rhode Island, the Indian meetinghouse became important and enduring foci for community life. Elsewhere, Indians remained hostile to Christianity and maintained Native ceremonial life. Moravians made their way to a Schaghticoke village in the mid-eighteenth century, where their leader, Gideon Mauwee, invited them to stay. The Moravians encouraged Schaghticoke people to continue producing material culture in order to accommodate to the colonial economy and adjust to changing circumstances, but the Schaghticoke resisted the Moravians when urged to alter their lifeways.[88]

Total cultural transformation stood at the center of English expectations about conversion, although they seldom succeeded in this goal. The Indian College at Harvard, founded in 1656, famously educated a handful of Indians in the classical tradition and then turned its back on Indian education until the late twentieth century.[89] Indians took up literacy in the colonial context and forged distinctive identities.[90] In the mid-eighteenth century, Eleazar Wheelock educated Indian girls and boys in Lebanon, Connecticut, for a decade and a half before removing his operation to Hanover, New Hampshire, as the newly founded Dartmouth College. Wheelock forged troubled relationships with a number of Indians, most famously the Mohegan missionary Samson Occom.[91]

Local historians took up the story of proselytization with some degree of enthusiasm. Given the meager efforts at converting Indians to Christianity throughout New England, this seems rather surprising. Failure to make the effort to convert Indians, an espoused justification for colonialism in the first place, composed an important critique mounted against New Englanders in the seventeenth and eighteenth centuries. In part, these extensive assertions about missionary outreach can be accounted for because the most famous missionary, John Eliot, traveled throughout eastern and central Massachusetts (and into Connecticut), and met with at least modest (although frequently ambiguous) success in fourteen different places local narrators could later point to as evidence of proselytizing. Others, such as Sarah Loring Bailey in her history of Andover, Massachusetts, included material about Eliot on the grounds that the Praying Town Wamesit was "near to them."[92] Other places could link their histories to proselytizing through genealogy. Glastonbury, Connecticut, could boast that the granddaughter of John Eliot, "Apostle to the Indians," married Rev. John Woodbridge, a seventh-generation minister in West Springfield because his father served as minister in Glastonbury in the late seventeenth century.[93] Four of seven histories of Providence make reference to the missionary outreach of Roger Williams (without commenting on the contradiction between his proselytizing of Indians and their claims about his role in establishing religious liberty, another dubious reading back of history), which helped inflate the numbers for Rhode Island.

Franklin, Connecticut, listed thirty-two missionaries "raised up in Franklin," most of them in the nineteenth century, who did their work with Indians from elsewhere (such as the Oneida and the Choctaw); the majority of them worked at locations across the globe. Included in their list was the famed eighteenth-century Mohegan missionary Samson Occom.[94] Indeed, nearly one-third (ten of thirty-five) of all Connecticut local histories made at least passing reference to Occom—claims quite possibly made plausible because of his itinerant career. In a manner parallel to the mobile lifeways of New England Indians in general, Occom moved frequently. He traveled throughout Connecticut, spent several years as a missionary to the Montauk on Long Island, and eventually moved to Oneida in New York in connection to his efforts to build the Brothertown community.[95] He also made a fund-raising trip to England that precipitated his break from patron Rev. Eleazar Wheelock (also among missionaries who received notice in local histories). In addition to Franklin, six more histories of localities surrounding the Mohegan community featured Occom: Columbia, Lebanon, and Norwich (four different texts).[96] Other town histories took note of his missionary activity among the Nipmuc in northeastern Connecticut (Thompson), his sermon on the occasion of the execution of Indian Moses Paul that became a popular selling item (Waterbury), the removal of Indians from Connecticut, to Stockbridge, Massachusetts, then Stockbridge, New York, where they joined Occom and the Brothertowns—and then later moved on to Wisconsin (Windsor).[97]

It is interesting to note the extent to which Samson Occom received notice in local histories, particularly compared with Pequot minister William Apess (1798–1839), author of five published books in his lifetime. Like Occom and many other New England Indians, Apess's life story involved struggling with making Christianity meaningful to Indian peoples, as well as tremendous itinerancy—both preceding and following his conversion to Methodism.[98] Apess eventually made his way to Mashpee, Massachusetts, where he found himself embroiled in a battle between the Mashpee Wampanoag and their corrupt overseers. The "Mashpee Revolt" that successfully led to the upheaval of the guardianship system became the focus of one of Apess's five books, *Indian Nullification of the Unconstitutional Laws of Massachusetts Relative to the Marshpee Tribe; or, The Pretended Riot Explained* (1835). Apess, however, did not find his way into any local history in Connecticut, and only one *county* history in Massachusetts mentioned him.[99]

In spite of a history of diplomacy that local historians frequently noted to authorize their claims to the land, conflict broke out regularly over everything from English theft of Indian corn to English settlers' cattle tramping through Indian cornfields.[100] But it was the catastrophic Pequot War of 1636–37, ending with the massacre of between four hundred and seven hundred Pequot men, women, and children at Mystic Fort, that truly taught Indians a lesson about the lengths to which the English would go to secure their invasion. The Treaty of Hartford of 1638, negotiated not with the Pequot but instead with the Mohegan, Niantic, and Narragansett tribes who had allied with the English, purported to obliterate the Pequot nation. By the terms of the treaty, Pequot survivors were prohibited from returning to their villages and banned from using the name Pequot, and noncombatant Pequots were divided among Uncas, Miantonomi, and the Niantic sachem Ninigret.[101] But the Treaty of Hartford and the assertion of English hegemony failed to restrain Pequots from returning to their homelands and regrouping. Official acknowledgment of this fact included the creation of a reservation in 1651 for the Mashantucket Pequot at Noank, and in 1683 at Stonington, in an area still held by today's Eastern Pequot Tribal Nation. Pequots continued their resistance to colonialism on these homelands and defended them as the rightful possession of Pequots into the future.[102]

Because the Pequot War was waged in 1636–37, long prior to the establishment of most New England towns, it was possible for most localities to omit mention of this brutal conflict. Still, as it is arguably the most important Indian event in the colonial history of Connecticut, it seems surprising that the war is mentioned in fewer than half of local accounts. It is perhaps less notable that Massachusetts and Rhode Island mostly elided this brutal conflict, although Massachusetts was deeply implicated in provoking and waging the war.[103] One is tempted to conclude that discomfort with the undeniable brutality of the conflict factored into its marginalization in local narration. Many of those who did include accounts of the Pequot War decried the horrific resort to massacre on behalf of the English.

But others took pains to justify the actions of their ancestors, including an orator who stood at great length to memorialize Major John Mason during the Norwich, Connecticut, jubilee in 1850. His bottom line? "Major Mason indulged in no indiscriminate hostility to the Indians. He was as just and moderate and discriminating, as he was vigorous and firm in his dealings with them."[104] Rejecting the lamentations of those who exuded sympathy upon the "poor Indians" from the luxury and comfort of their homes, the speaker asked:

Were they to allow themselves to be exterminated by this savage tribe? The infant colony numbered less than 800 persons, with less than 200 able to bear arms. They settled in their new homes on the invitation of the Indians occupying and claiming the territory. They had been there less than two years. They had done no acts of wrong toward the Indians, and lived remote from the territory of the Pequots, who intermitted their causeless wars with the more powerful tribes only to commence one of extermination against the settlers of Connecticut river. Thirty of their number, including women and children, had been slain under circumstances of the grossest barbarity and insult. . . . There was no remedy but by a sudden, sharp and terrible vengeance, severely to punish this band of pirates, and destroy them in their den.[105]

This justification turned the tables on intended extermination and defended the actions of Mason as the only possible response to the threats posed by barbarous Indians who had invited the English to settle among them. This orator admitted that the burning of the Pequot fort at Mystic resulted in the deaths of as many as seven hundred Pequots, leaving few survivors. Such an incommensurate response to the claimed violence against the English in Connecticut ("thirty in number" slain) constitutes the "just and moderate and discriminating" response of Mason and his men. The dedication of a monument to Mason in 1889 both affirmed the ultimate justification of his actions to those responsible for the erection of the monument and provided an occasion for the orator of the day to wrestle with precisely that problem. He concluded ultimately that the land thus "reclaimed from savagery and waste" all the way to the Pacific "for the occupation of sixty million people" and the "growth and development of the nation" overrode any moral qualms that might be raised.[106]

Nearly four decades after the Pequot War, Massasoit's son, the Wampanoag leader Metacom, led a pan-Indian resistance movement that sparked what came to be called King Philip's War, which for a time it appeared would successfully rid Indians of the English. Fueled by decades of anger and frustration over English encroachment, this conflict has been called the deadliest war proportional to population in U.S. history. By the time it ended in 1676, twenty-five English towns had been destroyed—more than half of all their settlements—and the English had been driven back nearly to the Atlantic coast.[107] But instead of Indian triumph, the war ended in Indian defeat, with many survivors enslaved and shipped off to the West Indies, a fate many Pequots suffered in 1637 as well.[108] Still, the English only turned the war to their advantage by enlisting Indians to their cause and taking up Indian warfare techniques well into the deadly conflict. After the death of Philip in August 1676, the

English decapitated and quartered him, putting his head on display at Plymouth, where it remained for years.[109] More than two dozen accounts of this conflict were published in the immediate aftermath, including Mary Rowlandson's *The Soveraignty & Goodness of God.* This account of her captivity among the Nipmuc established a genre and become a foundational text of American literature.[110]

Unlike the Pequot War, which largely awaited its historians, this literary output ensured that King Philip's War gained instant fame.[111] At least twenty-one accounts of this conflict appeared in print within seven years of the outbreak of the war, which helped secure its notoriety for the moment and provided ample material for local narrators.[112] It took its place in most narratives as the foremost threat to "civilization" in the history of New England. Treatments of the conflict ranged widely, with some accounts merely mentioning the war as a milestone or marker in the past in a paragraph or even less,[113] and others devoting multiple chapters to the events, embracing the full chronological and geographical scope of the conflict rather than confining their vision to the local.[114] Some places organized commemorations of particular battles, or erected monuments, which resulted in the publication of historical addresses solely devoted to the war.[115]

Military resistance to the English and other Europeans continued in the northeast, but King Philip's War closed the door on armed resistance for Indians from southern New England. The English continued to be embroiled in colonial and imperial wars throughout the eighteenth century, including the multitribal Deerfield Raid of 1704, and the French and Indian War of 1754–63, but Indians who remained in southern New England and participated in these conflicts did so on the English side.[116] These conflicts, as well as Lovewell's Fight, Father Ralle's War, and others that involved Indians from northern New England, Canada, or elsewhere as the principal combatants, found their place in local texts, especially but not exclusively when they directly affected localities. So too did local historians memorialize generalized violence involving generic Indians, faceless foes who posed a constant threat spurring perpetual fear. Plotlines included raids for captives, the burning of farms and fields, and portrayals of terror assumed to be continuously imminent, a constant threat to orderly life mounted by the irrational fury of Indians. The audience who heard the history of Haverhill, Massachusetts, at the celebration of the U.S. centennial heard their orator tell them, "The laborer in the field had his gun near at hand, and the Sunday worshipper carried his loaded weapon to the house of God, and grasped it while engaged in prayer."[117] Including Indian hostilities in local histories underscored the heroic nature of colonial histories, which featured constant vigilance against a "savage" foe who stood as the most fundamental threat to the establishment of "civilization" in the fearful wilderness.

In the wake of King Philip's War, English officials created the category "Friend Indians" to distinguish between allies and enemies. Indians who had allied themselves with the English in King Philip's War and after made claims on English authorities for their rightful ownership of remaining homelands. Although they acknowledged this moral imperative, English legal protection did not forestall continuing land loss for Indians. What's more, through periodic legislation and in their day-to-day dealings, English officials attempted to regulate Indian lifeways and mobility. They categorically treated those Indians they thought they could geographically bound and control differently from those they still regarded as enemies. In other words, they continued to treat Indians as separate peoples. And while such regulations might make it seem like English officials tightly scrutinized and regulated Indian lives, Indians exercised much autonomy in practice.[118]

English encroachment on Indian homelands prior to these catastrophic wars paled in comparison to what came afterward. The English seized massive swaths of Indian homelands, citing right of conquest and other pretexts, which compounded the problem of English invasion for Indian people. Indian mobile economies, which the English interpreted as wasteful and savage, suffered disruption in the process. Indians adjusted to the English presence in myriad ways throughout the seventeenth and eighteenth centuries, taking up everything from fixed agriculture and pastoral ways, to wage labor.[119] Beginning in the eighteenth century, Indian men routinely participated in the dangerous whaling industry, and many women became itinerant peddlers of Native crafts such as baskets and brooms.[120] The military itself became an important economic pursuit throughout the colonial period and beyond, as southern New England Indians took part in future conflicts at least in part as a way to get a living. Through indebtedness, English perfidy, orphanhood, or other misfortune, Indians also found themselves trapped in the oppressive English practice of indentured servitude. John Sainsbury estimated that in Rhode Island in 1774, 35.5 percent of Indians were to be found residing in non-Indian families as indentured servants.[121] Ruth Wallis Herndon and Ella Wilcox Sekatau found that more than 42 percent of all children indentured in Rhode Island between 1750 and 1800 were Indians.[122]

After taking some account of the brutal history of violent encounter and Indian land loss, local narrators typically considered the Indian plotline to have played out. Indians received far less attention living their lives as "Friend

Indians," and few authors bothered to take up this complex and important story of Indian survival and resistance that is manifest in their changing ways under settler colonialism. A few did indeed make note of surviving Indian communities (see chapter 4), but the vast majority either explicitly or implicitly wrote Indians out of existence (see chapter 3).

But Indian history and culture did find other ways into the story lines of New England places. Local historians regularly included an Indian presence woven into the landscape, especially in the form of retained Indian place-names and in an intense interest in Indian relics and remains. Like much of local history writing, such portrayals situate Indians securely in the past, separating them neatly as part of nature instead of culture.

Yet selective retention of Indian place-names also highlighted the unique Americanness of New English places, and some authors lamented the relative paucity of Indian names that had been retained. In his account of Easthampton, Massachusetts, Luther Wright tells his readers that "two portions of the town were named by them, and these names have been transmitted to modern times. Would that we had more of these Indian names; for instance, that we knew the Indian name of our noble mountains, so that we might no longer detract from its dignity."[123] In Wright's account, this lack is especially lamentable because the town was "once the favorite resort and dwelling place of the Indian race, now long since gone from this valley."[124] Like so much of local writing, this sort of observation fed off the romanticism so pervasive in nineteenth-century writing.

In many local histories, an abiding interest in what might be thought of as amateur archaeology reminded New Englanders of an Indian past they romanticized as the end of Indian history. In his history of Medford, Massachusetts, Charles Brooks observed that "remnants of the Indian tribes were common till the beginning of the present century. . . . So late even as our day, farmers in Medford have ploughed up stone arrow-heads, stone drills, and other Indian weapons and tools. No Indian necropolis has yet been discovered, though one probably exists on the borders of our pond."[125] A new edition of this text, revised by James Usher, confirmed his suspicions: miraculously an Indian necropolis had indeed been found in 1862! Harvard professor Louis Agassiz subsequently examined its contents and included the skeletal remains in his museum. Agassiz's letter of acknowledgment of the remains remarked that "every bone, arrow-head, pipe, and the like, is valuable as part of the history of a race already gone from this part of the continent."[126] Charles Brooks had published a report on this exciting discovery and suggested somewhat

hopefully that the skeletal remains might be those of the important Pawtucket sachem Nanepashemet.[127]

The obsession with Indian relics participated in the project of purification
by literally burying Indians, and it interacted with another essential colonial
move: nothing symbolized modernity more powerfully for New Englanders
than their imposition of their own system of ownership over Indian homelands. Thus it is not surprising that all variety of land transactions accounted
for the most frequent item in the script of Indian history.

Charles Henry Stanley Davis was not alone in foregrounding the history
of Indian lands by placing the story front and center in his *History of Wallingford, Conn.* His first chapter is titled "Purchase of Indian Lands," and its
detailed exposition of the theme included reprints of multiple deeds upon
which Wallingford could rest its claim of honorable transfer of Indian lands
to New Englanders.[128] The frequency with which local narrators focused on
the details of the bureaucracy of land transfer reveals a preoccupation with
establishing the justness of their occupation of Indian homelands. A Springfield, Massachusetts, history reproduced a facsimile of a 1636 deed, allowing
readers a virtual encounter with the historical document that authorized its
origins (see Figure 6). And a Windsor, Connecticut, history included a map
that delineated all of its Indian purchases, suggesting that not one inch of
land came into the town's possession without a legal transaction (see Figure
7).[129] Deeds and other documents regarding land transactions took on a reverential character, as is evident in the following passage, taken from Charles
Francis Adams's address at the opening of the new town hall in Braintree,
Massachusetts:

> Fellow citizens, I now hold that deed in my hand . . . it is in the nature of a quit-
> claim to eight persons in behalf of the inhabitants of Braintree of all the Indian
> title, not before granted, to the lands within the township bounds—reserving
> however the right of hunting and fishing, provided no harm be done to the En-
> glish. Consideration, twenty-one pounds, ten shillings. Signed, sealed and deliv-
> ered on the fifth day of August, one thousand six hundred and sixty-five, by
> Josiah, alias Wampatuck, Sagamore, and his six wise men—Squamog, Old Naha-
> tun, Manunion, Noistenus, Mamuntago, and Hahatun.
>
> This deed came into my possession with other family papers. How we came
> by it, I know not, but I am sure it has been held for at least two generations. . . .
> My inference is that at a former time, when much less value was attached in
> towns to old documents than is the case now, this was placed in the hands of
> John Adams for safe keeping. But I do not think he or his successors ever
> regarded it in any other light than as a trust. And now that this town has

erected so noble a depository for it, I purpose to restore it; and after repairing it and putting it in a suitable frame, to cause it to be placed in the care of the officers of Braintree, for the benefit and for the edification of all future generations of the people of the three towns.[130]

The opening of the new town hall in Braintree offered a perfect opportunity to enshrine one of its foundational documents, a quitclaim relinquishing outright ownership of remaining Indian lands in Braintree (with reserved rights) that also secured their peaceful occupation. Adams took the trouble to note each of the Native signatories to the deed, to laud their wisdom in partaking in this transaction, and to elevate the document by pointing out that it had passed through the hands of none other than his esteemed ancestor John Adams, thus linking it to the founding of the nation. These documents established a history of just property relations with Indians as foundational to the town, a break from the notion of tradition determining property rights, and they scripted some of the very first actions of New Englanders as they establish their modernity in the wilderness.

The Larger Context

What conditioned the selection principles for inclusion in the script of the prefatory Indian history of New England? Only rarely did local narrators explicitly make reference to ideas, events, or themes that shaped the construction of their narratives about Indians. When they did, however, authors shed light on the larger intellectual milieu in which they forged their texts. In addition, some recurrent themes hint at nagging concerns regarding the Indian history of New England localities and, by extension, New England as a region that made bold cultural claims about its particular place in the origins of modernity in what became the United States.

Many local narratives reflected the romanticism that prevailed through much of the nineteenth century, and as has been frequently observed, Indians were a stock in trade of the Romantic movement. On occasion towering literary figures found their way into local accounts, such as this 1859 history of Norwich, Connecticut:

> Legends enough are extant to celebrate each hill and plain in Norwich. Wawequa's hill, Fort hill, Little Fort hill, Sachem's plain, Trading cove, the Indian burying ground, each has its interesting story. Would that some skillful hand would weave the scattered threads, and do for Norwich what Cooper has so aptly done for another portion of the country![131]

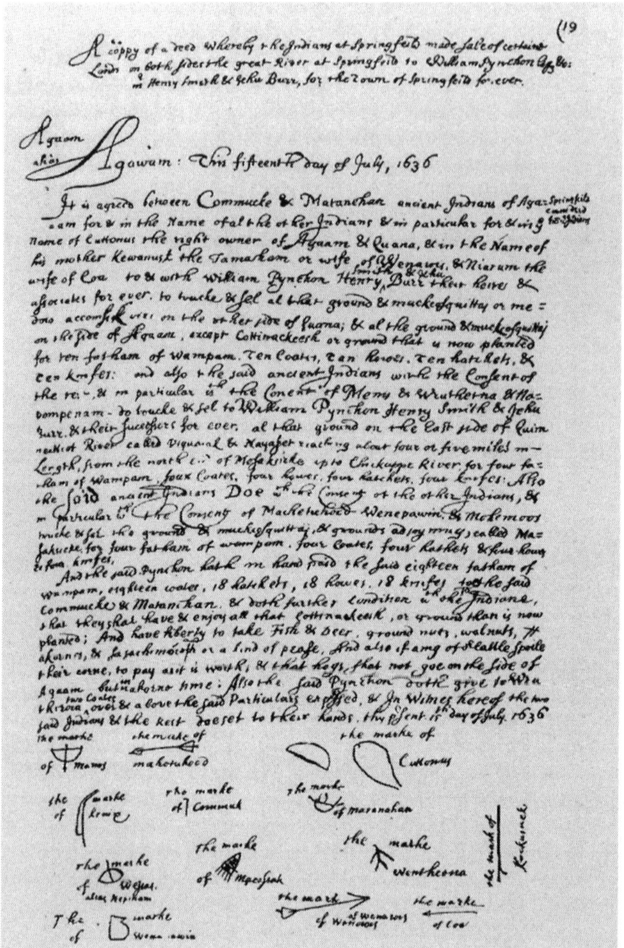

OLD INDIAN DEED.

Figure 6. *Old Indian Deed.* This facsimile of a 1636 deed constitutes tangible evidence of the transaction on which Springfield based its claim of just possession of the land. The deed is headed: "A coppy of a deed whereby the Indians at Springfield made sale of certaine Lands on both sides the great River at Springfield to William Pynchon Esq &: mr Henry Smith & Jehu Burr, for the Town of Springfield forever." The text transcribes the difficult-to-decipher document on the opposite page. The terms of the sale for three lots of land were "eighteen fatham of Wampam, eighteen coates, 12 hatchets, 18 howes [hoes], 18 knifes." From Mason A. Green, *Springfield, 1636–1886: History of the Town and City Including an Account of the Quarter-Millennial Celebration at Springfield, Mass., May 25 and 26, 1886* (Springfield: C. A. Nichols and Co., 1888), 13.

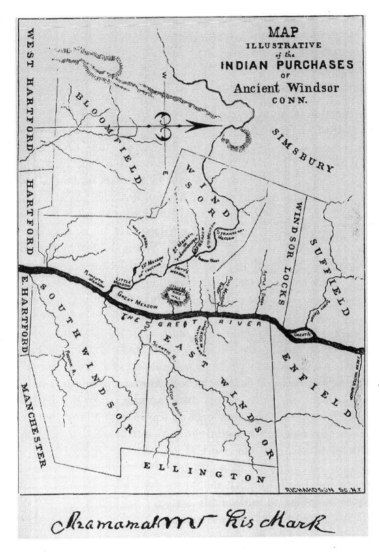

Figure 7. *Map Illustrative of the Indian Purchases of Ancient Windsor, Conn.* This map
shows the exact bounds of the Indian transactions encompassed by town boundaries in
the vicinity of Windsor, Connecticut. The author credits Jabez H. Haden of Windsor
Locks, Connecticut, with research for the map, prepared by "Richardson." From Henry
Stiles, *The History of Ancient Windsor, Connecticut, Including East Windsor, South Windsor,
and Ellington, Prior to 1768, the Date of their Separation for the Old Town; and Windsor,
Bloomfield and Windsor Locks, to the Present Time. Also the Genealogies and Genealogical
Notes of Those Families Which Settled within the Limits of Ancient Windsor, Connecticut,
Prior to 1800* (New York: Charles B. Norton, 1859), [103].

This snippet, in which the author pines for a skillfully rendered treatment of his locality such as James Fenimore Cooper had become famous for in New York, makes claims for a rich tapestry that is heavily reliant on Indian history for its texture. He enumerates places of significance within Norwich that blend Indian and English nomenclature, but all of which entail Indian stories. These implicit stories involve conflict and trade (Fort hill, Little Fort hill, and Trading cove), acknowledge Indian ownership of land as prefatory to the existence of Norwich (Wawequa's hill and Sachem's plain), and that subtly put an end to an Indian future in Norwich (the Indian burying ground).

Another literary luminary, Washington Irving, occasionally turns up in local accounts. His musings on New England Indian history made him a natural point of reference, which makes it seem odd that it is only infrequently that he is specifically referred to. An 1845 account of Warren, Rhode Island, argues that Irving's brilliance secured the preservation of this Indian history, which otherwise might well have been lost to posterity:

> Philip, hunted down like a stricken deer, at last fell a victim to the treachery of one of his own people: and thus sunk the last of a noble race, whose melancholy fate would even now have been almost forgotten and unwept forever, but for the imperishable interest associated with his memory, by the brilliant genius of Irving. "With heroic qualities and bold achievements, that would have graced a civilized warrior, and have rendered him the theme of the poet and the historian: he lived a wanderer and a fugitive in his native land, and went down, like a lonely bark, foundering amid darkness and tempest—without a pitying eye to weep his fall, or a friendly hand to record his struggle."[132]

Irving's "Philip of Pokanoket" from his *Sketch Book* is the source for this account, as it is for many other portrayals of Philip.[133] King Philip is scripted here as the last of his race, done in by the hands of one of his own, which makes the issue of his lastness confusing indeed. (What, then, became of his slayer?) None are left, in this sampling from Irving, to write the history of his resistance.

Irving's blistering 1820 commentary on the history of Indian affairs, "Traits of Indian Character," also published in the *Sketch Book*, was deliberately invoked (although without specific attribution) in an 1876 tract. A chronicle of Sudbury's history prepared for its bicentennial celebration took on Irving's argument directly even though anonymously in assessing the various positions people took on Indian history:

> There have not been wanting those who declare that the Indians have from the beginning received nothing but wrong at the hands of the white men; that they have first been dispossessed of their hereditary possessions by mercenary and

wanton warfare, and then that their characters have been vilified by the misrepresentations of hostile writers. Their great chieftains, it has been said, have been persecuted while living, slandered and dishonored when dead. On the other hand there are those who exonerate the founders of New England altogether, denounce the aborigines as savages and pagans, and affirm that they deserved their fate.

It is never safe for us to form our estimate of any class of men from the romancers and poets. They idealize and embellish. . . . This has been our experience in regard to the Indian.[134]

Irving's "Traits" constituted a searing indictment of Euro-Americans that singled out New Englanders for particular rebuke in their history of Indian affairs. This passage echoes the language of Irving's critique so closely that the source is unmistakable.[135] This author contrasts Irving's position with those who would justify New Englanders in their treatment of Indians but in the end he dismisses any interpretation that emanates from romanticism.

An appendix to Leonard Bacon's *Thirteen Historical Discourses, on the Completion of Two Hundred Years, from the Beginning of the First Church in New Haven* directly addressed the "treatment of the Indians," and in the process Bacon offered a revealing analysis of the ideological climate surrounding the discourse about Indians:

There are two sorts of people who habitually represent the New England fathers as having treated the Indians with great injustice.

First, we have the sentimentalists, to whom the Indian is an object of poetic interest. They feel that the wigwam by a waterfall was a far more romantic sight than a five story cotton mill on the same spot. . . . And to their mind's eye a "feather-cinctured chief," like Sassacus, is a much more imposing figure than Roger Sherman or Oliver Ellsworth. The melancholy fate of the wild tribes, disappearing with the forests they once inhabited, and leaving the graves of their fathers to be turned up by the white man's ploughshare, affects these sentimental readers or makers of poetry so deeply, that they cannot but take it for granted that the poor Indian was the victim of Puritan oppression.

Secondly, we have those who think to silence all remonstrance and argument against some recent proceedings in respect to the Indians, by asking, Where are the Indians of New England; and who have a political interest to maintain by making themselves and others believe that there is no precedent, and therefore no warrant for justice in dealing with the native proprietors of the soil.[136]

Much is entailed in these brief passages tacked on toward the end of Bacon's four-hundred-page tome, but his two main themes are especially pithy. First, he divides critics of New Englanders with regard to their Indian history into two camps: "sentimentalists," who are moved by the "melancholy fate" of vanishing Indians rather than by the wonder of industrialization, symbolized by the cotton mill that replaced Indian wigwams.[137] Second (and only by implication), he indicts proponents of Indian removal policy, who advanced their own political interests in backing the abrogation of Indian treaties in order to expel them from the southeast by asking New Englanders to explain their own Indian history. Where, critics pointedly asked, are your New England Indians? What in your history of Indian relations could defend opposition to a policy so clearly designed to sustain the advance of civilization over savagery? The claimed melting away of the tribes with the forest, as Bacon portrays matters here, does not amount to a ruthless history of expulsion or unjustified conquest but a natural outcome in the production of modernity.

Although published thirty-seven years later, Lucius Barber might have been directly responding to Leonard Bacon. His address, delivered at the commemoration of the bicentennial of the burning of Simsbury, Connecticut, during King Philip's War, contained an extraordinary imagining of an Indian version of the history of New England. His characterization of the justification that is "the boast of our New England historians" contained language very similar to Bacon's assertion of justice and proper land transactions, apart from the conquest of the Pequot. "But could we read," Barber continued, "the story of the settlement of New England, written by the pen of an Indian,—could we view these scenes as painted by a *'native,'* artist, what different impressions would they leave upon our minds!"[138] Here, he pined for a *Native* version of history and artistic production to place alongside the emerging non-Indian body of work. Barber expounded on this theme for fifteen pages, fully half of the entire address. In the process, he critiqued the justice of land transactions, exposed the theft of Myles Standish and his party from Indians in 1620, lambasted the New English for their conquest and massacre of the Pequot (which he cites as an example of warfare for Indians to adopt in King Philip's War), and critiqued the supposed causes of the conflict. Philip's crime? "To resist the rising power of the English, and to fight in defence of Indian rights."[139] In the conflict itself, Barber tells his listeners that butchery reigned on both sides.

Barber's address closed with musings on the "destiny of the Indian race":

> There has never been an Indian war, from the "Pequot" to the "Modoc," which was not commenced by aggression on the part of the whites. To-day Sheridan is carrying on the work which Endicott commenced at Block Island two hundred and forty years ago. Witness his report of an "engagement" with a band in

Montana: "one hundred and seventy-three Indians were killed, three hundred horses captured, and the village and property of the band totally destroyed," . . . [Among these were] *"fifty children under twelve years of age."*[140]

Barber's analysis—to this point—resonates startlingly with prose one might expect out of the twenty-first century, including his problematization of the term "engagement" to characterize a massacre. He sees a continuous story of Anglo aggression and brutality, from the first major conflict (the Pequot) to the present, rather than asserting that such dishonorable dealings occurred later and elsewhere. His address alluded to the massacre on the Marias River, a brutal slaughter of a peaceful Blackfeet village of 173 composed mostly of elderly men, women, and children that occurred just six years before in Montana. Even more startling was what immediately followed this lamentation:

Thus, "manifest destiny" points to the speedy extinction of the race. We may mourn over their decay and final disappearance; but who would call them back? Who shall say it is not better that the Pequots, the Narragansetts, and the other Indian tribes, that once roamed over the hills, and fished along the streams of New England, have disappeared, and given place to a better race? Who shall say it is not better that our brave and sturdy John Mason, and his companions in arms, who achieved such feats of valor at Fort Mystic, though stained with marks of cruelty, should be victorious; than that our infant colony should be cut off, and the march of improvement and civilization be stayed?

From that victory, what immense good has resulted! How incalculable the benefits, from the burning of that Indian fortress! The Christian home, the school-house, and the church—instead of the Indian trail, the railway; instead of the Indian canoe, the steamboat.[141]

This passage illuminates the limits of Barber's Indian imagining and it even helps to explain it. From the first to the most recent, even though Indian wars were all caused by Anglo aggression, they all are part of the culmination of the modern. "*We* can afford to be just to his [Philip's] memory," because in its aftermath "the once powerful nation of the Narragansetts was blotted out for ever!"[142] In their place came a "'tidal wave' of a better population."[143]

Occasionally, local narrators cast their eyes across the hemisphere in shaping their story:

Was it chance that led to these shores the Briton and not the Spaniard; the Protestant and not the papist; the man of integrity and godliness rather than the greedy unprincipled adventurer; that peopled these rugged hills with an upright and pious population, so that in every hamlet should rise the house of prayer, and in every cottage should be erected the domestic altar . . . We have but to cast our eyes over this continent, we have but to compare North with South America, to contrast the social conditions of Mexico with that of New England, in order to estimate how much depended upon the character of the early colonists—how deeply the welfare of unborn millions was involved in the mould into which the infant state should be cast.[144]

Although Indian peoples are not explicitly included in this sweeping claim about properly ordered societies, the reference to the "social conditions of Mexico" carries implications about race in addition to the broad-brush detractions of the Spanish. Their inherent backwardness and superstitious Catholicism rooted in the medieval order stood in stark contrast to the enlightened modernity of the New English.

In an address commemorating the Battle of Bloody Brook in King Philip's War, Edward Everett was even more direct about the racial implications of the long history of settler colonialism. His sweeping conclusions about colonialism in North America speak tellingly to the processes of purification and modernity:

In Spanish America, a wild and merciless crusade will be waged against [the Indians]; they will be hunted by the war-horse, and the bloodhound; vast multitudes will perish, the residue will be enslaved, their labor made a source of profit, and they will thereby be preserved from annihilation. In the Anglo-American settlements, treaties will be entered into, mutual rights acknowledged; the artificial relations of independent and allied states will be established; and as the civilized race rapidly multiplies, the native tribes will recede, sink in to the wilderness, and disappear. Millions of Mexicans, escaping the exterminating sword of the conquerors, subsist in miserable vassalage to the present day;—of the tribes that inhabited New England, not an individual, of unmixed blood and speaking the language of his fathers, remains.[145]

Everett's hemispheric analysis invokes the Black Legend of the Spanish in condemning their methods of colonialism, mired in a feudal world of violence and slavery, so different from the Anglo-American enshrinement of treaty relations in dealing with Indians that evidenced their modernity purified of the ancient in every way. Importantly, Everett claims that the pacific and rights-based colonialism of the English resulted in the disappearance of Indians in Anglo-America, whereas the martial order of the Spanish ironically preserved Mexicans into the present even if as only vassals. In New England, none remain who are of pure blood and speakers of their own language. In this rendering, the massive vassalage of Mexico can survive the sword of extermination in the archaic order of the backward Catholic regime, but even though the English used enlightened methods of diplomacy and acknowledged Indian rights, Indians there are portrayed as mixed and receding. Everett also laid the base acquisitiveness of the Spanish alongside the "prospects of political aggrandizement and commercial profit" that motivated Virginia planters, thus rendering their role in subduing the wilderness less honorable and laudatory than that of New England.[146]

It is not surprising that larger concerns about Indian history, Indian policy, and Indian affairs condition the way authors shaped their works. Local narrators periodically referred to issues such as the "treatment of these 'wards of the nation'" as moral issues, as they did in Providence at the dedication of the Canonicus memorial. On that occasion they admitted that "as a people we have been, and still are, not without guilt."[147] This orator suggested that "Faith in God, kindness, charity, honor, nobility, manhood and Christian character" constituted the central virtues that would provide for "the solution of the Indian question."[148] In contrast, in Norwich, Connecticut, while celebrating their jubilee, the people rejoiced that "the citizen of Norwich need not blush at recalling the early relations of the town to this aboriginal tribe," in contrast to the painful story of fraud and oppression elsewhere, which "have provoked the indignant rage of the red man, and then the explosion of his wrath has been the signal for indiscriminate vengeance and prompt extermination."[149] Such comparative constructions of the history of Indian relations—quite apart from their veracity—undergirded a structuring that placed New England above the rest of the nation in terms of justice and morality.

As suggested by Leonard Bacon's analysis of the climate of opinion on Indians, the important role played by New Englanders in debates over Andrew Jackson's policy of Indian removal made it a natural touchstone for local narrators. Edward Everett, a central player in the debates, weighed in on this subject in an address he delivered in 1830—the year the Indian Removal Act narrowly gained passage—on the bicentennial of the arrival of John Winthrop at Charlestown. Everett admitted that Indian affairs did not always transpire with perfect justice and harmony in New England:

> In allusion to these actions, and in vindicating the course, which during the past year, has been pursued toward the tribes of civilized Indians, resident within the United States, it has been argued, that they have not been treated with greater severity, by the Government of the United States, or of any of the separate States, than they were treated by the fathers of New England. But it would seem not enough for an age, which is so liberal of its censures of the puritans, to show itself *only not more* oppressive than they. Has civilization made no progress, in two hundred years?[150]

Even if New Englanders might be vulnerable to critiques over their Indian past, Everett argued that their treatment of Indian peoples ought to be placed in historical context. The passage of two hundred years should witness the enshrinement of more enlightened views and actions.

Other narratives referenced particular events or scandals in their claims for the virtuousness of New England's Indian history. In Braintree, a narrator asserted that "in 1679, there evidently being no 'Indian Ring' in operation in those days, an agreement was made with Wampatuck, the first tribal sachem of this region, for certain lands," which constituted a commentary on the corruption of present-day Indian affairs.[151] A historian of Marlborough, Massachusetts, did not claim an unblemished record of Indian land transactions for his ancestors, but he did compare them favorably to "those of us at the present day, who run wild in pursuit of California gold, or who embark in every vain scheme of speculation, to accuse them of selfishness."[152] Though not perhaps as scrupulous as they might have been, still Marlborough people could celebrate that they were mostly honorable, particularly in comparison with forty-niners who ruthlessly pursued their own self-interest. George Armstrong Custer came off badly at the U.S. centennial celebration at Roxbury, where the orator stretched exceedingly to place favorite son John Eliot's story alongside Custer's:

> It is sad to think that Eliot's Indian policy would have saved poor Custer's life and prevented most of our Indian wars. Mr. Eliot would never have made the Indian a fiend, and then whined over a fair, square Indian fight and terrible victory as a "massacre." He thought that *one* "season of hunting" undid his missionary work. He would have the Indians forced into some kind of civil society, and taken from their wild ways of living. "One season of hunting makes them complete Indians." Our Congress has begun at the wrong end.[153]

Here, the orator critiqued present-day Indian policy and used contemporary events—the Battle of the Little Big Horn where Custer and the Seventh Cavalry met their demise at the hands of Lakota warriors and their allies—in order to insist on the superiority of New Englanders. He mused on the peacefulness of their early encounters figured through the missionary program of "civilization" and conversion, eliding the long history of conflict and bloody warfare that characterized that history.

At the 1887 celebration of the two hundredth anniversary of the incorporation of Falmouth, Massachusetts, the orator acknowledged a less than pristine history of Indian relations in Massachusetts, but he argued that the Quaker influence in Falmouth translated into just and humane relations there:

Massachusetts has many black marks against her for dealing with the savage upon a martial rather than a merciful basis. Of late the State has sought to offset its harsh and sometimes cruel record in this particular. Massachusetts, a few years ago, did much to condemn the cold-blooded policy of an American Secretary of the Interior in his inhuman dealings with the Poncas. Now her senior senator is the recognized champion of the rights of the Indians, and he is regarded as high authority upon what may be deemed one of the most important of our public questions.[154]

Even though not all transpired perfectly in the past, Massachusetts played a role in shaping affairs justly in the present by condemning Indian policy when appropriate and by formulating policy as well. This passage invoked Massachusetts senator Henry Dawes, architect of the turn-of-the-century allotment policy, which carried devastating consequences for Indian peoples, and which, in particular, resulted in the loss of one-third of all remaining land in Indian hands.

Several historians made William Penn their touchstone in significant and telling ways.[155] Indeed, the story of William Penn negotiating the first ever treaty with Indians in 1701 appears to have rankled many New Englanders, striking as it did at the core of New England's claim for primacy in the race to modernity. Instead, New Englanders disputed the notion, popularized both in the new nation and in Europe (especially France), that William Penn could be credited as inaugurating and enshrining peaceful relations with Indians on the basis of treaty making and just property transactions. Plainly perturbed, Sylvester Judd took up this concern in his 1863 history of Hadley, Massachusetts:

> Some European writers have been strangely ignorant of the fact, that most of the early settlers of New England occupied their lands by actual bargain with the Indians. These writers have represented that William Penn was the first to purchase a conveyance from the Indians, and have bestowed much praise upon him for doing what had been done a hundred times in New England, before Penn came to America.
>
> Penn is said to have completed his bargain or treaty with the Indian chiefs under an elm tree near Philadelphia, and the transaction has been rendered famous by the historian and the painter. Yet it would be difficult, perhaps, to tell why the purchase of Indian lands in Pennsylvania by Wm. Penn, is more worthy of renown, than the purchase of Indian lands in Northampton or Hadley by John Pynchon, 20 years before. Both bought as cheaply as they could.[156]

Judd reclaimed the origins of modern property relations rooted in honorable dealings with Indians and gestured toward land transactions as treaty making and diplomacy in his critique. He even casts doubts on the story of Penn's treaty. He references the 1771 Benjamin West painting of the transaction, commissioned by Thomas Penn, which gained wide circulation and even found its way to the Capitol Rotunda in Washington. Judd wondered why Penn should gain such fame when hundreds of just yet "cheap" transactions of Indian land in New England preceded Penn's treaty.

Thomas Russell's oration at the two hundredth anniversary of the incorporation of Middleborough echoed Judd's critique, implicating a famous Enlightenment thinker in the error:

> Voltaire has said, and even juvenile histories have repeated, that the treaty of William Penn was the first treaty ever made without an oath, and the only one never broken. . . . But on the hill beyond Town Brook, in Plymouth, our fathers made a treaty with Massasoit, not confirmed by an oath, and never violated.[157]

Russell pushed his story of the origins of treaty making all the way to Massasoit and Plymouth in 1621. In his narrative, he admitted that the treatment of Indian captives in the wake of King Philip's War could not stand up to scrutiny without shocking humanity, but these brutalities were perpetrated by descendants of the Pilgrim fathers, not the Pilgrim fathers themselves. Further justifying the behavior of those involved, he declared that even the king of England sold his countrymen into bondage. Penn's heirs and other Americans fared worse in his moral calculus: "even these outrages upon enemies fall short of those committed at a later period upon the friendly Indians of eastern Pennsylvania. . . . and even now our own dealings with the Indians of the far west should make us pause before we utterly condemn our fathers."[158] On a different point of comparison, local historian of Roxbury Charles Ellis pointed out that John Eliot "was more than a laborious missionary, more than such as Penn."[159]

The New Social Order

Judge Joseph Story's centennial oration on the "first settlement" of Salem, Massachusetts, included an extended consideration of the question, "How far was it lawful to people this western world, and deprive the Indians from that exclusive sovereignty over the soil, which they had exercised for ages beyond the reach of human tradition?"[160] Story attacked this essential question by examining the broad principles upon which Europe began its incursions into Indian America. In pursuing their intense ambition, he tells us, Europeans seized upon the "flexible and convenient" idea of "first discovery" of the continent to convey exclusive rights to "sovereignty and settlement" as the ethical code regulating European "acquisitions." But what about lands inhabited by Native peoples? Already possessing these lands by "prior discovery," Native rights to possession and sovereignty could not be discarded. Yet "ambition and lust of dominion" spurred Europeans to argue that Indians could be expelled on the basis of their "infidelity and barbarism." "Ample compensation" would still be held out to them in the form of religious instruction in Christianity, and "admission into the bosom of European society with its privileges and improvements." This, Story argues, is how royal ambition disguised its true objectives and justified their "spirit of conquest."[161]

Not so Story's forefathers: "Our forefathers did not attempt to justify their own emigration and settlement, upon the European doctrine of the right of discovery." While the English Crown did grant this right in their patent, still they probed more deeply: Here "savage people" ruled over extensive lands "without title or property," so why could not Christians take up their "waste lands" and live among them? Story invoked God's granting of natural and civil rights to the land as distinct. Natural right describes common ownership of land, while enclosing and improving that land conferred civil right. In New England, an abundance of land presented itself to the English because "God hath consumed them with a miraculous plague, whereby the greater part of the country is left void of inhabitants." Furthermore, the English arrived "with the good leave of the natives," and were motivated by "higher considerations" of religious conversion. Unlike the pretentious displacement of Natives elsewhere on the continent, Story's forefathers only "occupied and cultivated" what Indians granted to them or they found vacant. They respected Indian settlements and land claims, provided protection to them from their enemies, and engaged in "no wars for their extermination." Story rejected contemporary criticisms mounted by philosophers or theologians regarding injustices toward Indians as appropriate to New Englanders. Even though perhaps "private hostilities and butcheries" may have transpired, they found no sponsorship or sanction in the government.[162]

Even while he lamented the melancholy history of "these unfortunate beings," Story mused on what he saw to be a fundamental incompatibility between Indians and his forefathers: "By a law of nature, they seem destined to a slow, but sure extinction. Every where at the approach of the white man, they fade away."[163] What's more:

> Philosophy may tell us, that conquest in other cases has adopted the conquered into its bosom; and thus at no distant period given them the common privileges of subjects;—but that the red men are incapable of such an assimilation. By

their every nature and character they can neither unite themselves with civil institutions, nor with safety be allowed to remain as distinct communities. . . . A wilderness is essential to their habits and pursuits.[164]

In the end, one might conclude, it mattered little whether New Englanders bought into the dubious notion of "first discovery," since the laws of nature doomed Indians to an inevitable extinction. Indians have been shown to be incapable of assimilation as subjects. Their nature and character prevented their incorporation into civil institutions, and they could not be permitted to remain as distinct peoples "with safety." Indians by natural law belonged in the wilderness, not as participants in modernity.

New Englanders repeatedly scripted this story as an inevitable trajectory. Such story lines formed the foundation of their social order. On the one hand, they posited a break with misguided European ideologies of conquest in which "first discovery" constituted a feeble façade concealing naked ambition in seizing Indian lands. On the other hand, enlightened New English ideas about acknowledging Indian land ownership and sovereignty marked them as rational thinkers even while their laudatory attempts to convert Indians were doomed because the natural inferiority of Indian peoples condemned them to extinction. In spite of their rational ordering of relations with Indians, Indians remained rooted in nature. Throughout New England, local narrators expounded on related themes, foregrounding their enshrinement of treaty-based relations with Indians and their complex history of land transactions as authorizing their replacement of Indian peoples and their cultures.

Enshrining treaty relations as the basis for a rational ordering of Indian affairs constituted a rejection of the feudal history of Crown grants as an authentic basis for the nation. Some authors articulated this persistent theme in local narration by explicitly asserting that treaty making in New England constituted "the beginning of American diplomacy."[165] Along with the loud chorus that stressed the piecemeal yet ever honorable purchase of Indian homelands—which moved past pretentious European claims that Crown grants could justly be relied upon as the basis of colonialism—the elevation in retrospect of the idea of Indian treaties argued for a break from the European world of feudalism and tradition as well as the rational reordering of property relations in the tradition-bound world of Indians mired in the ancient. And as Judge Joseph Story's musings on the question of colonialism also make clear, Indians—if they demonstrated themselves capable—were to receive the blessings of Christianity in exchange for the necessary loss of their land and diminishment of their sovereignty in the service of modernity.

Sadly, they demonstrated themselves incapable of survival outside of the wilderness. In their place came Anglo Americans, including Mason Noble's "grandfather, David Noble, who planted himself immediately on the banks of the Hoosic [in Williamstown, Massachusetts], in a house which stood on the spot where the new factory company are now erecting their principal dwelling house."[166] On this spot, Noble fashioned a story of the making of modernity scripted on a single piece of land.

In the process of constructing their stories, local narrators engaged in a subtle process of seizing indigeneity in New England as their birthright, which is the coded message of the entire enterprise of "firsting." Along the way, "Native" insidiously took on the meaning "non-Indian." New Englanders elaborated on the colonial claim for indigeneity in myriad ways. Thus could a Truro narrative assert that Peregrine White "was the first native New Englander, the original Yankee if not the original native American,"[167] and a Dunstable, Massachusetts, history could assert that after Lovewell's War in 1721, Indians "gradually withdrew from their ancient haunts and hunting-grounds in New England. . . . [and Dunstable] has never [since] been invaded by a hostile savage."[168] (How could indigenous peoples conduct invasions?)

Many local narratives incorporated family histories throughout their texts, weaving them into the landscapes as they asserted their propriety: "On the site of the house built by the late Francis Fisher, stood a large old-fashioned house, known as the Ackers house. John Ackers was a resident of Muddy River in 1656, and for more than two hundred years his descendants, to the sixth generation, have lived on or near that spot."[169] A Plymouth history offered a different way of scripting antiquity in the landscape: "The apple tree [depicted in an illustration] was planted by Peregrine White, the first Englishman born in New England, about the year 1648, who died in 1704, in the 84th year of his age. It still produces apples, and the orchard in which it grows is now owned by his descendants, near the lot which he occupied, in Marshfield."[170] Many also discuss local cemeteries, repositories for those who bolster their claims of antiquity in New England places:

> Our ancient burial place claims, at least a passing notice . . . Beneath the turf, our feet has pressed; under this sacred house, in which we are now assembled; have long since been deposited the mortal remains of those who encountered, and began the subjugation of the forest that once waved in unbroken grandeur over these hills and dales. A few humble monuments remain to remind us of them; let those dilapidated, moss covered stones be cherished as mementos of the past, and as we tread the soil that rests upon the unmarked graves of others. . . .
> But those are not all whose remains have been deposited. Their children,

and their children's children unto the sixth and seventh generation, together with the stranger that has come within their gates, and humble African, once held in bondage under their roofs; here, have rested from their labors, and together await a resurrection day.[171]

This passage, including its not uncommon confession that Africans had previously been enslaved in New England, situates the Suffield, Connecticut, cemetery as a sacred site containing the remains of generations who sub-. dued nature.[172] This story is scripted as "ancient," but in a very different way than Indian cultures are associated with the ancient.

In related ways, genealogy serves as a perfect metaphor for the process of "firsting" in New England, and for the casting of a new social order in New England. New Englanders asserted a stark break with feudal England by rejecting monarchy and the feudal order more generally. They rejected a hierarchical ordering of society based on a particular rendering of the divine order, and instead obsessed with documenting the founders of families that rooted themselves deeply in New English places. In this new order, lineage trumped hierarchy in determining one's place in the social order. New Englanders expended tremendous energy, not in arguing for the precise ranking of individuals in a divinely mandated hierarchy, but in anxiously demonstrating the depth of their lineages in New England. In so doing they did not reject religion as determining social order; rather they persistently noted that English persecution drove their ancestors to New England, where they constructed religious liberty as the rational bedrock of modernity. There, they heroically built the modern order. So successful were they in reproducing themselves, they in turn populated the nation—through massive out-migration in the nineteenth century, New England is claimed as the birthplace, literally, of the nation. In the words of the eminent nineteenth-century historian George Bancroft, "The pilgrims were destined, in the purpose of God, to be pioneers in the great work of planting in this country the seminal principles of republican freedom and national independence."[173] His reflections on New English demography bore repeating in an 1855 Billerica text: "'I have dwelt . . . the longer on the character of the early Puritans of New England, for they are the parents of one-third of the whole white population of the United States.'"[174] At the celebration of the centennial of Princeton, Massachusetts, the imperative of demographic reproduction took a humorous note, when the dinner attendees toasted "*Bachelors*—left alone, as they *wish*, will not have history in the next celebration"—a toast to which "there was no response."[175]

The end product of "firsting," then, is the successful mounting of the argument that Indian peoples and their cultures represented an "inauthentic" and prefatory history. The New English break with the traditional world of Indians (building upon their break with feudal Europe) made possible the insidious claim that New England erected the first houses, institutions, polities, and economies—the first social order—in the modern world. In this construct, even when local narrators took note of Indian peoples, villages, cultures, polities, economies, and religion, such aspects of Indian life did not represent a rational and thus authentic ordering of the social order. By their persistent arguing for a prefatory Indian history of New England, local narrators participated in a seizure of indigeneity from Indians and for themselves. This seizure in turn depended upon an insistence that incompatible Indian peoples had disappeared—or would do so in the near future.

Chapter 2   *Replacing*
Historical Practices Argue That
Non-Indians Have Supplanted Indians

Replacement Narratives

Local narrators in New England simultaneously embraced and replaced Indian peoples in shaping their story about New England history, collectively arguing for the primacy of the new modern social order they claimed as their hallmark. Their accounts of the past, present, and future entailed a process of physically and imaginatively replacing Indians on the landscape of New England. That is, they formulated a history that negated previous Indian history as a "dead end" (literally), supplanting it with a glorious New England history of just relations and property transactions rooted in American diplomacy that legitimated their claims to the land and the institutions they grounded there. In the process, they rationalized their history of settler colonialism and claimed New England as their own.

Local narrators substituted one (Indian) history with another (their own), sometimes collapsing the story into a few terse yet evocative phrases:

> The dark tangled forests have gone; the wild beasts which prowled there for prey are gone likewise; the Indians with their canoes, wigwams, council-fires and terrific war-whoops have also disappeared; and in their place we have fertile fields, smiling gardens, tasteful commodious dwellings, a civilized community, and the temples of the living God. . . . the locality is the same. Time, culture, and science, alone, have wrought the transformation.[1]

This stark rendering of history argues for a rupture: Indians, cast as anonymous savage denizens of the forest, have been replaced by God-fearing farmers who have tamed the wilderness and erected framed buildings that composed "civilized" communities. The lengthy, complex, and contested history of Indian relations is dispensed with in a series of sweeping assertions that dismiss Indians as long gone, replaced by non-Indians who are making modernity. Scripts such as these serve as what I call "replacement narratives." Firsting alone did not finish the work of claiming Indian places. Instead, local texts both narrated a process by which non-Indians replaced Indians in their home-lands, and attested to a wide range of cultural practices that contributed to the larger message of replacement. The creation of replacement narratives perme-ated the very process of literary and historical production, but the message of replacement can also be read in other venues—in historical monuments and commemoration, relics and ruins, place-names, and in the land itself.[2] Ideas surrounding these acts of memory making and place making participate in the production and reproduction of assumptions about Indians, New England, and modernity, and they constitute an implicit argument of replacement.

As Michel-Rolph Trouillot has pointed out about commemorations, they "contribute to the continuous myth-making process that gives history its more definite shapes: they help to create, modify, or sanction the public meanings attached to historical events deemed worthy of mass celebration."[3] Such cel-ebrations, he observes, "impose a silence on the events that they ignore, and they fill that silence with narratives of power about the event they celebrate."[4] Much the same might be said of other public dimensions of history making that participate in subtle and not so subtle ways to make meaning on—and out of—the landscape. Monuments, in particular, both often inspired com-memorative events and served similar ends in shaping and sanctioning mean-ings surrounding historical figures, places, and events. In perhaps less obvious ways, the fascination with ruins and relics unearthed throughout the region also became a site for the creation of replacement narratives. Non-Indians frequently paused to consider the stories behind the artifacts they so enthusi-astically collected, musing about the peoples they insisted they had replaced.

Place-names do important cultural work regarding history as well. In his superb study of landscape and language among the Western Apache, Keith Basso has observed:

> Because of their inseparable connection to specific localities, place-names may be used to summon forth an enormous range of mental and emotional associ-ations—associations of time and space, of history and events, or persons and social activities. . . . And in their capacity to evoke, in their compact power to muster and consolidate so much of what a landscape may be taken to represent in both personal and cultural terms, place-names acquire a functional value that easily matches their utility as instruments of reference. . . . place-names provide materials for resonating ellipses, for speaking and writing in potent shorthand, for communicating much while saying very little.[5]

Although Basso's study focuses on the intricacies of Apache place making, his observations about place-names and meaning are broadly useful in thinking about landscape and language. Non-Indians devoted much energy to pondering the Native nomenclature of New England, sometimes even searching for the stories encapsulated by the names. Local narrators took different positions on the value of Native place-names, but those who favored their retention because of their rich symbolic meaning generally lost out to those who argued for the systematic renaming of the landscape. This too constituted a replacement narrative, as place-names argued for the privileging of non-Indian stories to inscribe on the land. This claiming of Indian landscapes found even more tangible expression in stories local narrators told about the land itself, in particular, in the painstaking reconstruction of the "legalities" surrounding the land transactions that undergirded their claims to Indian homelands.

In this chapter, I focus especially on these five locations where we can read the replacement narrative of New England: the erection of monuments to Indians and non-Indians, the celebration of historical commemorations of various sorts, the enterprise of excavating Indian sites, the selective retention of Indian place-names, and claims Non-Indians made to Indian homelands. These bodies of cultural production all attest to the simultaneous presence of Indian history in New England places even while they declare that Indians themselves were only to be found in the past. Collectively they argue for the justice of the replacement of ancient Indians by modern New Englanders.

Monuments

In the 1866 edition of her popular history of Norwich, Connecticut, Frances Manwaring Caulkins followed her rather full treatment of the troubling death of the Narragansett sachem Miantonomi at the hands of the Mohegan sachem Uncas with a revealing discussion of memory and place. In this account, she called into question claims that the location of the spot of Miantonomi's death could be precisely determined. This judgment reversed her own assertion in the first edition of her history, which was "based upon tradition rather than coeval testimony." In particular, she disputed the contention of the eminent historian of Connecticut John Hammond Trumbull that Mohegans, directed by Uncas, "buried the victim at the place of his execution, and erected a great heap or pillar upon his grave; adding that this memorable event gave to the place the name of Sachem's Plain."[6]

Even so, as the location that Miantonomi was first captured (though not yet executed), Sachem's Plain retained its interest as a commemorative place. Caulkins argued that the heap of stones was doubtless in its origins a Mohegan pile,—a martial trophy erected upon the spot where the tribe had been victorious. But the place of sacrifice in the woods of Windsor,—the spot where the helpless chief received the fatal blow,—was left unmarked and unvisited. There, perchance, the carrion fowls fed upon his flesh, and his bones were left to bleach and decay.[7]

Caulkins's explication of Indian ways of commemoration offered an alternative explanation for the memory heap that had taken such a hold in local tradition. As the site was located near an Indian trail, she suggested that passing Indians—friends and foes—added to a small original mound as they passed by, with Narragansetts wailing in lamentation over what had occurred on that spot while Mohegans celebrated the capture that signified their victory. English observers of such actions, she suggested, "would easily credit the report, however vague its authority, that here lay the remains of the great Miantonomo."[8] Caulkins's analysis of the competing interpretations of the precise events that transpired on Sachem's Plain thus included a concise description of this widespread New England Indian way of marking memory and place.[9] Indians paid tribute to places of historical significance by creating piles of stones and other materials, adding to them when they passed them and pausing to tell the stories that had happened at those places. Caulkins's account also suggested that those heartfelt commemorative practices had ceased to take place, implicitly arguing that no Indians remained to continue to inscribe their histories on the landscape.

But what became of the memory heap? Caulkins tells her readers that eventually the non-Indian owner of the land, "perhaps ignorant of the design of the stones, removed the greater part of them to use in the undersetting of a barn he was erecting in the neighborhood," thus engaging in an appropriation of Indian commemoration in the service of modernity by replacing this monument with a wood building. The rest of the pile gradually disappeared, the oak trees that framed the memory heap decayed, and "nothing was left to designate the spot where the flying chieftain yielded to his foe, until the 4th of July, 1841," when some stalwart citizens of Norwich erected a new and quite different monument to Miantonomi. A five-foot-square granite block placed on a pedestal that raised it to eight feet tall overall, the monument bore the simple inscription "Miantonomo. 1643," thus refusing to boil down their commemoration to a single event in the great sachem's life (or death).[10]

As Robert S. Nelson and Margaret Olin have observed (following Bruno Latour), "Monuments are examples of a premodern cultural hybrid that modernity in its most powerful phases attempted to purify and neuter. Denying their composite character strips monuments of their animism, so redolent of 'primitive societies,' and makes them civilized but dead." For monuments to animate the past they need to be embedded in social networks. Monuments engage both the past and the present to make claims about the future. The Miantonomi monument erected by the people of Norwich replaced a dynamic Indian site that inspired Indian ways of remembering their history from their own points of view with a fabricated and static New English memorial that flattened historical interpretation.[11] The people of Norwich infused the new Miantonomi monument with their own meanings, divorced from Indian ways of marking history.

By placing the monument at Sachem's Plain two years prior to the bicentennial of Miantonomi's death, the people of Norwich intriguingly commemorated an event that most local narrators characterized as the culmination of perfidious *English* actions. Uncas, after all, had killed Miantonomi, with the full knowledge and sanction of the commissioners of the United Colonies. The commissioners consisted of representatives of the colonies of Plymouth, Massachusetts Bay, Connecticut, and New Haven, and they aimed to secure martial order in the region. In this dispute, they backed Uncas.[12] And, one might wonder, what about Uncas? As the perpetrator of the murder sanctioned by the English, where was his monument?

Plans had already been well laid for commemorating Uncas: "The first step toward the accomplishment of the object was taken in the summer of 1833, during a visit to Norwich by General Andrew Jackson, then President of the United States, who assisted in laying a corner stone. On that occasion an address was pronounced extemporaneously by General Cass, Secretary at War."[13] Funds were lacking, however, until the women of Norwich took action, drummed up the financing, and orchestrated the erection of "a granite obelisk, of respectable height and proportions, to be reared upon the chieftain's grave, bearing the simple inscription, in relief,—UNCAS."[14] Thus did the mastermind of removal policy for American Indians participate directly in placing a memorial to the controversial Mohegan leader who had departed nearly one hundred and fifty years before (in 1684). Even as he visited Norwich, removal policy pressed full speed ahead. It had commenced with the 1830 Treaty of Dancing Rabbit Creek that forced the Choctaw from their homelands on to Indian Territory, and of the Five Tribes of the southeast specifically targeted, all but the Cherokee had been coerced into signing away their homelands at the time of Jackson's visit. Jackson's Indian removal policy constituted an overt and aggressive campaign of replacing Indian peoples on a grander scale with Anglo Americans than the seemingly less violent

project of the replacement narrative. Still, the Uncas monument both invoked
the memory of violence in the past and represented a different sort of removal. The people of Norwich placed the greatly symbolic granite obelisk
commemorating Uncas over his grave in the "royal burying-ground" of the
Mohegans, a parcel of Indian homeland retained by the Mohegans for the exclusive use of the Uncas family.[15] What could better spell the end than the
burying ground?

In the fourth and fifth decades of the nineteenth century, local narrators
took note of several actual or proposed monuments to Indian people in Connecticut. William Lester's 1833 sketch of Norwich mentioned Miantonomi's
memory heap on Sachem's Plain, and also a monument to be erected to
Samuel Uncas: "The corner stone was laid by Andrew Jackson, President of
the U.S., assisted by Lewis Cass, during their late visit to New England," which
raises the question of whether Lester was confused about who was to be commemorated or if Jackson and Cass were kept busy during their sojourn to
Norwich.[16] In a discourse delivered in Hartford in 1843, Thomas Day took
note of the deed that conveyed land to "the first permanent settlers of Hartford . . . [from] Sunckquasson, Sachem of Suckiauge," a relative of Miantonomi and alternately rival and ally of Uncas. While Uncas had his "stately
monument, erected on the soil which was once his own . . . not even a rude
head-stone has ever told us where the bones of Sunckquasson repose. He,
and his subjects, and their descendants, have vanished from his dominions.
May not the majestic pile across the street, standing on the soil over which he
once bore sway, constitute his cenotaph!"[17]

All of these early monuments to Indians in Connecticut found their symbolic location on or near the sites of real or supposed graves of particular famed
Indian leaders. Farmington's 1840 memorial both shared this powerful imaginary and broke new ground in Indian commemoration. There, the School
Society of the town arranged for a block of red sandstone to be placed in the

new burying ground. . . . The spot is one of sad historical interest as the following inscription on one side of the monument explains:

IN MEMORY OF THE INDIAN RACE; ESPECIALLY
OF THE TUNXIS TRIBE, THE ANCIENT
TENANTS OF THESE GROUNDS[18]

This inscription, though attuned specifically to the local Tunxis people, boldly
proclaimed *all* Indians to reside only in the memories of the peoples who had
replaced them. Although Noah Porter described it as a new burying ground,
he explained that the discovery over many years of skeletal remains suggested

this indeed had been "formerly an Indian burying place." Further, tradition "declares" that an important battle between the Tunxis and Stockbridge had been waged on the site, where some of their remains reposed.

This expansively cast memorial to Indians also broke ranks with other early Connecticut monuments in its inscription on the reverse side, which encompassed the message of New England Indian commemoration at the time:

Chieftains of a vanished race,
In your ancient burial place,
By your fathers' ashes blest,
Now in peace securely rest.
Since on life you looked your last,
Changes o'er your land have passed;
Strangers came with iron sway,
And your tribes have passed away.
But your fate shall cherished be,
In the strangers' memory;
Virtue long her watch shall keep,
Where the red-man's ashes sleep.[19]

Rather than allow a simple inscription of the name of a particular famous Indian to interpret a monument, this piece of local narration spelled out the meaning intended for the observer. The Indian race had passed, including the local Tunxis Indians, and it behooved those people who have replaced Indians to enshrine them all in memory. This monument stood, the orator tells us, as "the silent and the only witness that they ever were here."[20] By the 1880s, the silence threatened to overtake even this terse remembrance, as the inscription "is becoming rapidly obliterated."[21] No wonder, since the people of Farmington had chosen sandstone for their canvas in depicting their tribute.

These monuments, like those proposed or erected to Masconomo (Manchester, Massachusetts, proposed 1895), Canonicus (Providence, Rhode Island, dedicated 1883), and Passaconaway (Lowell, Massachusetts, dedicated 1899), commemorated famous Indians in New England who symbolized a previous history no longer looking to the future.[22] Others included specific assertions of Indian extinction, echoing the message of the Farmington monument. In Medford, Massachusetts, Francis Brooks collected and carefully reinterred the skeletal remains that had been such a source of excitement when discovered in 1882. Two years later, "with characteristic reverence for the old traditions, he placed a monument on the spot, bearing the date-marks, 1630–1884, and with an inscription dedicating it to Sagamore John and to the memory of the Indians who lie buried there."[23] This oddly precise dating of imprecise remains correlates with the origins of nearby Boston on the one hand, and with the reburial on the other, thus erasing millennia of Indian history on one side and declaring its end on the other. This statement of chronology suggests that even Indian history began only with the origins of Boston, and that it came to a neat conclusion with the reinterment of human remains unearthed two years before. An 1870 history of Middleborough, Massachusetts, brought the story of endings down to the level of lineage. It noted a "small granite obelisk" in the Lakeville cemetery with the inscription: "In memory of Ben. Simons, the last male of the native Indians of Middleborough. He was a revolutionary soldier. Died May, 1831, aged 80 years."[24] Having helped secure independence for the United States, Benjamin Simons apparently waited out his last years peacefully before his compliant retiring, thus obliterating the possibility of perpetuating his line. Or so we are meant to believe.

As was the case for monuments to non-Indian New Englanders, the fund-raising campaigns for Indian memorials could take decades to reach fruition.[25] The drive for a monument to the Wampanoag sachem Massasoit, in Warren, Rhode Island, commenced with a single donation of a small sum in 1880. But the Massasoit Monument Association did not reach its goal until 1907, when it erected a bronze marker on the site of Massasoit Spring.[26] In the association's 1893 event aimed at fund-raising, the audience heard addresses, poems, and music on themes relating to Massasoit's life and legacy, and "three tableaux were presented, representing Massasoit's childhood; Massasoit and Roger Williams[;] and the end of the Wampanoag nation."[27] While the tableaux tersely encapsulated the Massasoit story that Warren people were likely to find meaningful, Governor D. Russell Brown asserted in his address that "at the critical moment in the birth hour of this new settlement, afterwards to grow into a mighty nation, his loyal and unselfish assistance was a godsend to our pioneer fathers and the liberty loving founder of this dear old commonwealth, his memory deserves a lasting monument."[28]

A statue to Massasoit in Plymouth, a place that firmly rooted its origin story in its relations with the quintessential First Indian, awaited events surrounding the tercentenary celebration of Plymouth in 1921 when a full-length sculpture in bronze designed by famed sculptor Cyrus E. Dallin and sponsored by the Friends of the Indians organization the Improved Order of Red Men was dedicated. Meanwhile, the treaty with Massasoit that emerged as significant to Pilgrim claims of pacifism toward Indians and the inauguration of the practice of American diplomacy found its place in the design for the

National Monument to the Forefathers at Plymouth.[29] This monument, conceived of in 1820 and committed to in 1850, was not finally dedicated until 1889.

When it finally took its place among other monuments that narrated Pilgrim history in particular ways, the Massasoit statue stood gazing across the bay at the monument in Duxbury to (the ruthless) Myles Standish.[30] Rising to prominence in American iconography as the subject of Henry Wadsworth Longfellow's long poem *The Courtship of Myles Standish* and in the wake of the Civil War, for non-Indians Standish powerfully symbolized the resolute military spirit that secured the future of the republic.[31] Recruited for the Plymouth venture to be their military commander, Standish pursued an Indian policy of brute force. He wasted little time in establishing his bellicose ways, stealing Indian corn supplies his men claimed they "found" on their very first expedition and two years later killing seven Indians on trumped-up charges of Indian conspiracy against the English.[32]

The Standish monument depicted him atop a one-hundred-foot tower (perhaps to compensate for his legendary diminutive stature) with his hand on his sword—standing guard (see Figure 8).[33] In 1871, an elaborate gathering took place for the "consecration" of the ground on which the monument eventually would arise, the site of the "old Standish Farm, at Duxbury, where Captain Standish lived and died" (perhaps the site was chosen because the location of his gravesite remained unknown).[34] The event demonstrated that memorializing Standish "has properly taken the subject from the hands of a few of his immediate descendants, and placed it in charge of the American people at large . . . The military of the United States very naturally claim a large share in perpetuating the memory of the first commissioned military officer of the new world."[35] For those present, at least, Standish symbolized morality and force "perpetuated in their descendants," who inaugurated a proud New English ancestry forged in the "frozen, barren shore, with privations and sufferings before them."[36] For Indians, one can imagine Standish symbolized a legacy of duplicity, violence, and invasion.

The people of Groton, Connecticut, unveiled a monument to the controversial military leader of the Pequot War, Major John Mason, in 1889. The historical oration of the day weighed many sides of the conflict, including criticisms of the brutality of Mason and his militia, anticipated by Captain John Underhill (a participant) in his written account. This the orator coupled with his own accusations that Massachusetts was to be blamed as the instigator of the violence in the first place. In spite of nagging moral concerns, Mason's actions found justification in the ends. The orator urged the would-be critic to

THE MONUMENT TO THE MEMORY OF MILES STANDISH, NOW BUILDING ON
CAPTAIN'S ISLAND, DUXBURY.

Figure 8. *The Monument to the Memory of Miles Standish, Now Building on Captain's Island, Duxbury.* Etching of the monument to Miles Standish in progress at the time. Unknown engraver. From Shebnah Rich, *Truro—Cape Cod; or, Land Marks and Sea Marks* (Boston: D. Lothrop & Co., 1883), 63.

slowly broaden your view till the tired eye of your fancy rests upon the Pacific shores; gather in the vast intervening spaces reclaimed from savagery and waste for the occupation of sixty million people; turn the pages of history; note the growth and development of the nation, its beneficent influence in the march of human progress. . . . All this had not been, had John Mason been less prompt or less resolute.[37]

Even though Mason was of questionable moral character, the Pequot War secured the replacement of savagery with civilization in New England, and assured the nation of demographic and geographic reproduction across the continent. Mason's actions could be "justified by all the existing conditions" of the time, and "he has been abundantly vindicated by the process of time, the award of history, and the judgment of posterity."[38] These circumstances could be contrasted with the history of Mexico, where Spanish conquest resulted in "subjugation and slavery" for the conquered, whereas "the triumph of the English Puritan meant freedom and peace." Meanwhile, according to the orator, "the Pequot nation became extinct," the Pequot River was renamed the Thames, and the English settlement on the river was renamed New London.[39] Thus ended the first full-scale Indian war in New England, and thus was completed the replacement narrative for that people and place.

Monuments to other military conflicts also served to claim Indian lands. These included the "Bloody Brook" monument in South Deerfield, Massachusetts, dedicated in 1835. Here, a small marker over the burial place of Captain Thomas Lothrop's company (slain in King Philip's War, September 1675) that had been erected by "early settlers of Deerfield . . . had nearly disappeared, but the *spot* was known." On the strength of traditional accounts and guided by elderly gentlemen, a committee entrusted with the upcoming commemoration located the remains. They purchased land nearby, where the ambush reputedly began, and laid the cornerstone. The new monument would reinvigorate the memory of this bloody sacrifice, "and their children will know where their fathers bled and died to secure to them the rich boon they possess."[40] Also remembered with monuments were the first two settlers of Stow, Massachusetts, John Kettell and Matthew Boon, killed in King Philip's War. The site of King Philip's War captive Mary Rowlandson's return, Redemption Rock, was acquired in 1879 (though not placed into trust until 1953).[41] Haverhill, Massachusetts, matched Contoocook Island in New Hampshire in honoring the deeds of famed 1697 captive Hannah Duston (who slew twelve of her captors and made her escape) with a monument in 1879.[42] A monument in Fitchburg, Massachusetts, remembered John Fitch, captured with his family during the French and Indian War, though the precise date of the event—and the problem of whether the town's name came from him—were a matter of dispute.[43]

"Traditional accounts" about the "whats" and "wheres" of the past frequently infused the content of local histories. These oral accounts drove debates about the actual events and placement of the monuments in Deerfield and Stow. But one text calls such sources of information into question regarding the events monuments sought to cast in stone. A Dunstable, Massachusetts, history noted a monument erected in nearby Nashua, New Hampshire,

> to the memory of Rev. Thomas Weld, the first minister of old Dunstable [that] says he was killed by the Indians. Such was the tradition . . . but M. Hill has two letters from Mr. Farmer, in which he admits his error, and declares that Mr. Weld was not killed by the Indians. There was no Indian war in 1702, the year of his death. The inscription on the monument should be changed to conform to the fact.[44]

One might suppose that generalized ideas about Indian conflicts informed this error. Regardless of the precise factual basis of monuments, their presence inscribed meanings on the landscape by privileging particular peoples, events, histories, and interpretations.

By midcentury, a subscription drive had been mounted for the erection of a monument to missionary John Eliot, frequently erroneously scripted as the first missionary to Indians who certainly attained the status of the most famous (see Figure 9). The subscribers proposed removing his remains to Boston's Forest Hills Cemetery, where the commissioners had named an elevated site "Eliot Hills." The proposal for building a monument to Eliot there supposedly received support from surprising quarters: just prior to the publication of the sketch of Eliot's life prepared by the subscribers, the author tells us, the famed Ojibwe missionary George Copway (Kah-ge-ga-gah-bowh) dropped in on him. Copway announced that while visiting the east, "he came to Roxbury, for the express purpose of visiting the tomb of the Apostle." Displaying great familiarity with Eliot's work with Indians, Copway reportedly volunteered to advance the project and asked for an engraving of the proposed monument. In his purported response, Copway put himself down for twenty-five dollars toward the monument and wrote that "should I be successful, in securing a Home for my brethren in the North West, it has been my intention to erect two columns of granite to the sacred memory of two of the best friends, in years gone by, of the Indians—John Eliot and William Penn."[45]

By century's end, Eliot had been remembered with a monument in Natick, scene of his most famous success, near the gravesite of Daniel Takawampbait,

Figure 9. Reckoning of the proposed monument to missionary John Eliot. Note the feathered Indian gazing up at the massive column and pointing to the plaque that reads "Eliot, the Apostle to the Indians." J. H. Buford & Co., lithograph. Frontispiece for Henry A. S. Dearborn, *A Sketch of the Life of the Apostle Eliot, Prefatory to a Subscription for Erecting a Monument to his Memory* (Roxbury: Norfolk County Journal Press, 1850).

the seventeenth-century Indian pastor of the town. This constituted the only known memorial to any Natick Indians, in spite of the call for such a memorial in 1827 by a historian of neighboring Dedham.[46] This historian had even suggested an inscription for a monument that should be located in the Indian burial ground:

> Here are interred the Naticks, a tribe of native Indians, who were the first of that race to embrace Christianity. Soon after their conversion at Nonantum, in 1646, they were collected into a village at this place, by their great patron and missionary, the reverend John Eliot. Here the tribe lived and gradually declined, and became finally extinct before the year 1826.[47]

The alleged final extinction of Natick Indians, which would have come as quite a surprise to their descendants, paved the way for their replacement by New Englanders who might pay tribute to the noble missionary of the doomed Indians. Contiguously situated are key elements of the replacement narrative. While Natick Indians were "interred" on the spot, the missionary spirit of Eliot lived on. As if to punctuate the point, in 1875 and again in 1901, descendants of John Eliot mounted massive reunions at Natick "to celebrate the imperishable fame of our great ancestor and the undying renown of the ancient Eliot race."[48] At the 1901 reunion, orator William Sidney Elliott Jr. pointed out that "although but one son, Joseph Eliot, has male descendants living bearing the Apostle's name, yet through him have descended a countless progeny . . . in every part of this land." And should the orator have another son, he "would name him Eliot Elliott."[49]

Monuments to non-Indians, like the Myles Standish statue and the John Eliot memorials, participated in the replacement narrative in a different way. Actual or proposed monuments that honored New English claims to first peoples, places, and events argued for their preeminence and permanence, and they subtly seized indigeneity for themselves. Provincetown, evidently jealous of the claims to primacy mounted by Plymouth throughout the nineteenth century as Plymouth redefined itself as a tourist destination when the maritime economy faltered, reminded the public that it contained the place of "First Landing"—and they organized an association to build a monument to that claim. Provincetown could thus claim the Mayflower Compact, negotiated and signed in its harbor, whereby were agreed to "the first principles of self government and the foundation and root from which came the Constitution of the nation," not to mention the first birth and first death of the Pilgrims.[50] All of these claims implicitly argued that nothing Indians did could be part of a usable past. Descendants of Thomas Cushman gathered in 1858, "when the monument, which they had erected on Burying Hill, in memory of their venerated ancestry, was consecrated at a family gathering." This consecration proceeded "with exercises and ceremonies worthy of the occasion,—the first act of the kind ever attempted and performed by the united efforts of the descendants of any of the first comers of the Plymouth forefathers." They hoped to inspire other descendants of first families, who came among the "savage strangers" and founded a "great republic."[51] The people of Newton organized themselves to erect a monument to "the memory of its first settlers," which implicitly argued that Indians never "settled," just as their centuries-long reunions were dismissed as uneventful.[52] Even as all of these monuments elided any previous Indian history by completely ignoring it, they composed tangible, physical elements of the replacement narrative.

Agitation for the erection of a monument to Roger Williams began in 1859, spearheaded by one of his descendants.[53] The city of Providence finally unveiled its work in 1877, part of a massive public celebration with an estimated twenty thousand in attendance. The long-awaited monument was located

in the midst of fields which he received as a free gift from the great sachems Canonicus and Miantunnomi in grateful recognition of the many kind services he had continually done them, which for more than two centuries remained in the uninterrupted possession of his posterity. . . . What more fitting site could have been selected than a spot which thus recalls the estimate in which he was held by the original possessors of the soil?[54]

This passage encapsulates important elements of the Providence origin story, a peaceful coming together of local sachems and the father of Providence that legitimated New English possession of Indian homelands into the future. A discourse celebrating the 250th anniversary of Providence's origins recapitulated the story of Canonicus and Miantonomi's free gift, and suggested that a monument be erected to them as had been for Williams, its author evidently having missed the dedication of the Canonicus monument in Providence just four years before.[55]

As matters would have it, Roger Williams was not the first "settler" of Rhode Island. Of course, Indian peoples had possessed these lands for centuries, but Roger Williams was not even the first *non-Indian* in Rhode Island. A year before he arrived, the peculiar—and peculiarly forgotten—William Blackstone took up residence at a place that came to be called "Study Hill" (and eventually Cumberland).[56] That this amnesia had already transpired spurred the formation of the Blackstone Monument Association on July 4, 1855, at a playful gathering designed to rectify the fact that his successors in the

Blackstone River Valley had "too long remained in ignorance of the illustrious character and amiable oddities of him whose name it bears" (see Figure 10).[57]

Even a cursory glance at Blackstone's résumé suggests the oddity of this amnesia. For William Blackstone could boast a plethora of firsts any modern would envy (and his story is told in no fewer than fourteen local histories across southeastern New England): first inhabitant of Boston and Rehoboth in Massachusetts before heading to Rhode Island to become the first there.[58] In Boston, "he commenced his career of progress—planted his gardens and raised the first apples in Massachusetts," and he replicated the planting of orchards as he moved on.[59] But Blackstone parted company with his fellow Englishmen in significant ways: His status as the solitary inhabitant (apart from Indians, one supposes—and his wife, who is omitted in nearly every narrative) of Boston (then Shawmut) suited him fine: when hoards of other English people arrived with John Winthrop in 1630 Blackstone reputedly declared that he "left England because of his dislike of the Lords Bishops, but now he did not like the Lord-Brethren."[60] Squatting on Indian lands (rather

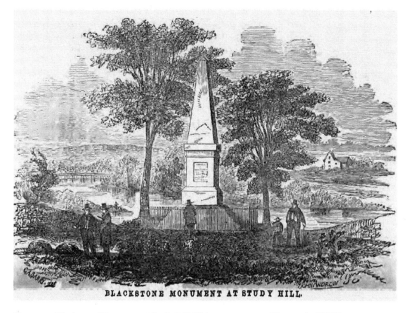

BLACKSTONE MONUMENT AT STUDY HILL.

Figure 10. *Blackstone Monument at Study Hill.* This monument to "first settler" William Blackstone is fittingly situated in a rural location, holding true to his legendary independence. Engraving signed by G. A. Barry and John Andrew. From William Blackstone, *An Address Delivered at the Formation of the Blackstone Monument Association, Together with the Preliminaries, and Proceedings at Study Hill, July 4, 1855* (Pawtucket: James L. Estey, 1855), 40.

than purchasing them), he traded with Indians and built a library of 185 books on "Study Hill."[61] The Indians "held him and his BOOKS in mysterious veneration."[62] The veneration attributed to Indians might be doubted, however, when one learns that his cottage and belongings were torched in King Philip's War just weeks after Blackstone's unrelated death.[63] Also, unlike most other first English people, "he left one son, but his race is extinct—no blood of Blackstone flows in any living veins."[64]

In 1880, the people of Groton, Massachusetts, gathered for the dedication of three monuments, whose juxtaposition is revealing. One noted the spot of the first meetinghouse, built in 1660 and burned by Indians in King Philip's War; another commemorated the Longley family, the parents and five children killed by Indians and three other children carried into captivity in 1694; the third celebrated Colonel William Prescott, commander of American forces at the Battle of Bunker Hill. These monuments honored "the pious memory of the founders of the town, who worshipped God in that rude and humble meetinghouse" later destroyed by Indians, the misfortunes of a family that symbolized the terror of the wilderness, and finally, a military officer who helped secure the break from Britain in the American Revolution.[65] Concord, Massachusetts, surpassed the efforts of Groton in laying seven commemorative tablets in 1885. Taken together, the seven tablets tell a replacement story in a multifaceted way. They are dedicated to the "Indian owners of Mesketaquid before the white man came"; the site of the meetinghouse, first dwellings, and first road; the house of the first minister where the Squaw Sachem sold the land that "gave them peaceful possession of the land"; the location of town founder Simon Willard's farm; the spot where the first town meeting was held; the field where the Minutemen mustered before the "fight at the bridge" (in the American Revolution); and the place where British troops retreated from the old north bridge.[66]

The sometimes decades-long campaigns to erect monuments attest to the commodification of memory, as Indian ways of memory making tied to place and shared storytelling gave way to static objects produced in market economies whose meaning frequently faded over time. Absent the regular recitation of history embedded in oral cultures that fueled history tied to place, the meaning of monuments threatened to become unmoored from memory. Commodified memory making divorced from storytelling threatened to produce landscapes punctuated with statues, plaques, and markers whose meaning dissipated across the years absent tangible connections made to them through storytelling.[67]

Historical Commemorations

Some monuments erected to enshrine the memory of departed Indians, first settlers, and other landmark peoples and events prompted elaborate dedication ceremonies that culminated in publications detailing the process. The commemoration of the monuments to Uncas, Miantonomi, and Roger Williams, for example, constituted one-time public events, but the publications that resulted conferred a sort of permanence on them that moved beyond the monuments themselves in that they were reproduced for consumption into the future regardless of the location of the reader. This ensured that these particular replacement narratives would continue to educate readers long after the actual events themselves had concluded. Other monuments received passing mention in publications dedicated to other purposes, and still more escaped the attention of published texts altogether, dotting the landscape of southern New England to be casually encountered into the future.[68]

Much has been rightly made of the centrality of historical commemorations, especially of the Fourth of July and other nationalistic moments, to the forging of political culture and nationalism in the early Republic and antebellum period. As David Waldstreicher has so forcefully argued, public festivals in the early Republic constituted crucial sites for engaging in celebration and mourning, working out tensions within politics, and articulating the relationship among local, regional, and national identities.[69] In addition to celebrations of the Fourth of July, Washington's and Jefferson's birthdays, special feasts and Thanksgivings, and the end of the slave trade, Waldstreicher also calls attention to the annual Forefathers' Day commemorations studied so exhaustively by John Seelye. These annual celebrations similarly engaged local, regional, and national issues, and argued for the centrality of New England in the forging of the nation.

In addition to commemorating the Fourth of July with public events, towns all over southern New England celebrated other historical events, and they frequently produced publications that detailed aspects of—and sometimes *virtually every aspect of*—their gatherings. Of the 447 texts I examined that contain material about Indians, no fewer than 145 publications appeared in connection with historical commemorations in southern New England. Of these, 39 were responses to the joint resolution of Congress that called on localities to celebrate the centennial in 1876,

> and that they cause to have delivered on such day an *Historical Sketch* of said county or town from its formation, and that a copy of said sketch may be filed, in print or manuscript, in the Clerk's office of said county, and an additional

copy, in print or manuscript, be filed in the office of the Librarian of Congress, to the intent that a complete record may thus be obtained of the progress of our institutions during the First Centennial of their existence.[70]

Towns throughout New England celebrated the centennial with public gatherings, historical orations, and publications to document the moment, and five items more appeared regarding events related to the American Revolution held prior to the centennial year.

What remained to celebrate in the remaining two-thirds of publications? Other events commemorated local experiences: church-related events, such as the gathering of the first church (fifteen), events of King Philip's War (five), the death of the first settler, death of the first pastor, the naming of the town, first exploration of the town, and the bicentennial of the arrival of John Winthrop in Charlestown (all one each). Two other sorts of (related) events dominated historical commemoration apart from nationalistic celebrations; both diverge in important ways from the latter, and their subject matter is telling. Forty-two publications related to the commemoration of the legal incorporation of particular towns, and thirty-five more paid tribute to the moment of "settlement."[71]

While these local celebrations have not received the same sort of attention from historians, their focus and content call our attention to the nineteenth-century New England obsession with claims to place. Not explicitly political or necessarily nationalistic in intent, they nonetheless frequently evidenced a fervent nationalism and made particular local and regional assertions about the construction of the nation and the content of national identity. But unlike the "newness" that David Waldstreicher observed as an important theme in nationalistic celebrations that balance the local, regional, and national, these nineteenth-century commemorations of settlement and/or incorporation instead declared the *antiquity* of particular places and were fundamentally *colonial* in purpose. In Norwich, Connecticut, an orator pointed out that "Pennsylvania claims the respect due to antiquity as well as to greatness; yet babes born in the good town of Norwich were men and women when Wm. Penn landed on the banks of the Delaware. This is the new world; and yet your town is older than the kingdom of Prussia, or the city of St. Petersburg."[72]

Local commemorations constitute crucial plotlines in the replacement narrative by audaciously claiming indigeneity for themselves and disseminating the message to the masses in vernacular form. By arguing that English people engaged in "first settlement," in particular, but also its proxy, "incorporation," local texts insist that Indian settlements and political organization failed to assert plausible claims to place. Such assertions are sometimes finely honed, as when Goshen picked "the first full day of being organized as proprietors" for their celebration, or when Barnstable, Massachusetts, settled on celebrating "the two hundredth anniversary of the legal organization of a civilized community on the peninsula of Cape Cod."[73] Celebrating proprietorship valorized English-style property ownership and thus trumpeted capitalism as the proper economic form, while arguments about the "legal" political organization of a "civilized" community buried previous Indian ways as illegitimate. In Weymouth, "the exact date of the first permanent settlement in Weymouth not having been fixed, it was agreed to hold the Celebration on the Fourth Day of July, A.D. 1874."[74]

Michel-Rolph Trouillot has observed that commemorations, as "rituals that package history for public consumption," play a "numbers game":

> The greater the number of participants in a celebration, the stronger the allusion to the multitude of witnesses for whom the mythicized event is supposed to have meant something from day one.
>
> By packaging events within temporal sequences, commemorations adorn the past with certainty: the proof of the happening is in the cycle of inevitability of its celebration.
>
> Cycles may vary, of course, but annual cycles provide a basic element of modern commemorations: an exact date. As a tool of historical production, the date anchors the event in the present. It does so through the simultaneous production of mentions and silences.[75]

Many of the texts chronicling historical commemorations remark on the enormous crowds that flocked to the celebrations (see Figures 11 and 12). These attendees participated in the ritual enactment of replacement narratives, and they ensured that audiences of historical narratives stretched well beyond the readers of local texts. They typically heard lengthy historical orations packaged in the form of public entertainment that naturalized a story of Indians being replaced by their non-Indian ancestors. The temporal story of Indian replacement became inevitable, a certainty that was anchored in explanations of contemporary racial formation.

While commemorations of "settlement" and incorporation might occur only infrequently (except at Plymouth, where Forefathers' Day was marked annually, though not just in Plymouth), celebrations of the Fourth of July were held annually and were wildly popular. Naturally, the main intent of Fourth of July centennial celebrations focused on the American Revolution and traced the origins and development of nationalism—particularly local contributions

Figure 11. *The Triumphal Arch with the Speakers Tent on Williams Park.* This etching depicts the massive audience drawn to the jubilee in Norwich, Connecticut, and suggests the diaspora of its population. Engraving from a photograph by William H. Jennings and a drawing by Henry V. Edmond. From John W. Stedman, *The Norwich Jubilee: A Report of the Celebration at Norwich, Connecticut, on the Two Hundredth Anniversary of the Settlement of the Town, September 7th and 8th, 1859* (Norwich: John W. Stedman, 1859), [40].

to the development of that nationalism. Even so, many publications stemming from the centennial paused to consider the Indian history of their localities even if only vaguely and briefly. While Lynn, Massachusetts, did not celebrate "with any pomp or pageantry, though the day did not pass unobserved," a local resident did publish a historical sketch in the centennial year.[76] Indians appeared briefly and anonymously as prior occupants of the place, and equally anonymously the author poised them for a final retreat:

> Every summer season we find encamped upon some of our outlying plains, or upon the beaches, a few individuals of the now almost extinct INDIAN TRIBES. . . . But they are poor and dispirited. And we can hardly doubt that before another Centennial Year arrives, the last remnant of those forlorn people will have forever passed away. A little more than two centuries ago the red race called this whole land their own. But where are they now? Receding down the dim vista of time, close on the steps of the mysterious people who preceded them in the occupation of the heritage.[77]

The orator for the centennial in nearby Billerica did more with the Indian history of his place. Instead of waxing eloquent about national affairs, he took

Figure 12. *The Dinner Tent in Front of the Free Academy.* This depiction of the bicentennial dinner in Norwich conveys the popularity of these celebrations and the enormous audiences for historical narratives that were the centerpiece of the programs. Engraving from a photograph by William H. Jennings and a drawing by Henry V. Edmond. From John W. Stedman, *The Norwich Jubilee: A Report of the Celebration at Norwich, Connecticut, on the Two Hundredth Anniversary of the Settlement of the Town, September 7th and 8th, 1859* (Norwich: John W. Stedman, 1859), [191].

seriously "the recommendation of the chief executive, that . . . I should rather turn your thought to some special points in our own local history."[78] These special points included discussion of the Wamesit people and their sachem Passaconaway, the missionary activities of John Eliot, local experiences in King Philip's War and other Indian conflicts, and the captivity of two Billerica children in 1695. Early on, he asserted that "the savage has no desire, nor method to perpetuate his memory. Indeed, why should it be perpetuated?"[79] And yet perpetuate it he did by his inclusion of Indians in his historical oration, as did most who reflected on the past in the context of the national centennial. Only a fraction of publications stemming from centennial Fourth of July commemorations failed to include Indians in some way (eight of a total of forty-seven publications).[80]

Like Fourth of July celebrations and other public events, historical commemorations dedicated to settlement, incorporation, and other local events were often festive occasions that might include parades, fireworks, orations, poetry, song, and dinners complete with elaborate toasting. By appealing mightily to the senses and disseminating particular versions of the past, present, and projected future, these commemorations participated in the production of replacement narratives in rich ways.

Included as part of the celebration of the 250th anniversary of the settlement of Boston, a procession of sixteen tableaux vivants brought this story to life as the final event of the festivities—"the first attempt to produce such a spectacle in Boston."[81] This ambitious undertaking began with a tableau dedicated to "History, Tradition, Allegory, and Time," and quickly moved on to the Norse, and then the landing of the Pilgrims. Tableaux four through seven encapsulated colonial history and dramatized Indian history to be left in the past, paving the way for the American Revolution in the next four tableaux (see Figures 13, 14, and 15). The procession finished with "allegory," with tableaux dedicated to commerce, Europe, Asia, Africa, America, and Boston, with a woman on a pedestal holding the city seal at the center, surrounded by personifications of "Peace, Prosperity, Justice, Education, Charity, and Industry."[82]

How did Bostonians script the replacement narrative? In the tableaux, the themes of colonial history that came to life were "Miles [*sic*] Standish's Fight with the Indians," "Chickataubut presenting Corn to Governor Winthrop," "Sam Adams demanding the Removal of the British Troops," and "Throwing overboard the Tea in Boston Harbor." In this drama, the martial masculinity of Standish is drawn from Longfellow's poem, and the actors portrayed the peaceful Hobomok standing over two slain Indians, along with Standish and two other armed Englishmen. That Boston thus linked its own local history to Plymouth is as intriguing as the depiction of English violence in the face of Indian friendship on this tableau. Chickataubut's gift of corn to Governor Winthrop tells a different story of friendship, and argues that Indians welcomed the English to Boston in amity and peace. The final historical depiction of Indians came in the famous incident of Indian impersonation during the Boston Tea Party, thus doubling the act of impersonation and completing the replacement narrative.[83] Indians later reappeared as allegorical figures on "America," the central figure being a woman riding a bison. Completing this tableau, "on one side stood the United States, directing the advance, and on the other stood Canada. Mexico was represented by a figure in Aztec dress, and South America by a half-breed Indian and Spaniard, habited in sombrero, poncho, and Indian girdle, carrying a horseman's carbine and lasso."[84]

Included among the festivities for Billerica's celebration of the two hundredth anniversary of town incorporation were multiple public events conducted with "manifest delight," culminating in a dinner for nearly one thousand people, complete with a full complement of toasts.[85] The recitation of

Figure 13. Tableaux I, II, and III, Boston 250th anniversary celebration. These tableaux for the 250th anniversary of the settlement of Boston depict the long history of exploration prior to the landing at Plymouth Rock, thus suggesting the heroic character of that landing. Tableau I grounds this story in "History, Tradition, Allegory, and Time." Unknown engraver. Boston, Massachusetts, *Celebration of the Two Hundred and Fiftieth Anniversary of the Settlement of Boston, September 17, 1880* (Boston: Rockwell and Churchill, 1880), 154.

Figure 14. Tableaux IV, V, and VI, Boston 250th anniversary celebration. These tableaux depict Myles Standish's murder of Pecksuot in response to a rumored Indian attack; Chickataubut giving corn to Governor Winthrop; and the signing of the Declaration of Independence, thus condensing all of colonial Indian history to two episodes. Unknown engraver. Boston, Massachusetts, *Celebration of the Two Hundred and Fiftieth Anniversary of the Settlement of Boston, September 17, 1880* (Boston: Rockwell and Churchill, 1880), 156.

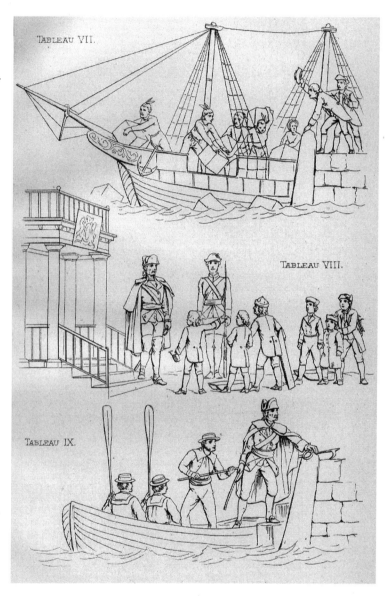

Figure 15. Tableaux VII, VIII, and IX, Boston 250th anniversary celebration. Tableau VII at the Boston celebration depicts the Boston Tea Party, one of the most famous instances of "playing Indian" in history. Tableaux VIII and IX continue the story of the American Revolution. Unknown engraver. Boston, Massachusetts, *Celebration of the Two Hundred and Fiftieth Anniversary of the Settlement of Boston, September 17, 1880* (Boston: Rockwell and Churchill, 1880), 158.

an epic poem composed by Daniel Parker, MD, of thirty stanzas that consumed twenty-seven pages in the published text preceded the dinner.[86] Here as elsewhere—such as the tableaux that meant to recapitulate Boston's history for visual consumption—historical commemorations gave play to imaginative renderings of history. Intended to engross and entertain, poetry and other literary genres placed a premium on romantic prose and imagery. In the process, poetic history entertained audiences and inculcated ideas about understanding history and racial formation in New England.

In the hands of Dr. Parker, the people of Billerica received a selective rendering of Indian history that clearly composed a replacement narrative. Unlike the precision of Boston's historical claims brought to life in the tableaux vivants, Parker's muse led him to cast his poem as a channeling of an anonymous Puritan and Indian, joined by Cotton Mather, who came to him in a dream, as narrators of Billerica's story—though Parker frequently fails to make clear just who is speaking when in the poem. Barely present in the first thirteen stanzas of the poem, Indians are vanished at the beginning of the fourteenth:

> By centuries now you count the years gone by,
> Since red men heard the pilgrim mother's sigh[.][87]

Sounding the themes of progress, the stanza declared an end to "heathenism"—seemingly issued by the anonymous Indian, who concluded the passage by asserting that "young science . . . she's made you what you are."[88] In this rendering, Billerica's Indian history has been long concluded, and the proper history of the town to be celebrated by the masses is an ancient Anglo-American one that stood in its place.

Stanza fifteen, cast as a dialogue between an Indian and a Puritan, offered a brief retrospective on King Philip's War that asserted the role of English wrongdoing in the conflict, but not in Billerica, where harmony governed Indian relations and no violence against Indians took place in the war. It closed with an admonishment by the Indian of those who offered friendship to "our race":

> Remembered should the Indians' trials be;—
> Your dwelling place was once his own.
> But Progress came and he must fight, and flee,
> And die, and be to fame unknown.
> Though sad the story, yet it told should be;—
> Though useless let him have his own.
> Now write my message down as this you hear!
> Tell all you wish to, what I say.

Two centuries ago I lived quite near
The spot you dwell upon to-day.[89]

And thus concluded the core story of the Indian history of Billerica, and also the perpetuation of the Indian race. Forged in the fire of colonial conflicts, still the people of Billerica could boast a peaceful Indian history and heed the warning of the spirit of Indians to remember that they once dwelled in the place they now claimed as their own. Parker's poem proceeded to a romantic and generic musing on Indians now past for the next five lengthy stanzas, the fourth of which paused to condemn the 1850 Fugitive Slave Act that the "wicked Congress" passed, requiring northerners to turn formerly Indian lands into "slave hunting grounds."[90]

Parker's commentary on the evils of slavery sought to distinguish New England's history from that of the slave-owning South, and it condemned the cowardice of Congress for forcing New Englanders to participate in its perpetuation.[91] Such political commentaries regarding slavery and race constituted one theme in asserting the special position of New England in historical commemorations and other texts. New English claims to exceptionalism extended beyond the narrowly national as well, as evidenced by Joseph White's response to the banquet toast "The first settlers of Billerica": "We are descended from men of no ordinary mould. The settlers of New England were a peculiar people. They were the 'seed wheat,' sifted by the winds of persecution from the chaff of the Old World, and wafted across the sea, to be sown, broad cast, in the virgin soil of the New." Here, White characterized colonialism as a winnowing process produced by the religious prosecution of the medieval world of Europe, and asserted New England as fertile for the reproduction of New Englanders in a vacant place.[92] Earlier on in the festivities, the historical orator had argued for New England's paternity of the nation as it replicated across the continent, quoting Bancroft's influential history to lend his assertion authority: "'I have dwelt,' adds this historian, 'the longer on the character of the early Puritans of New England, for they are the parents of one-third of the whole white population of the United States.'"[93]

A 1878 history of Westerly, Rhode Island, devoted chapter 5 to "the first whites," which took up a variation on the theme of "virgin land" available for the taking when the English arrived. Instead:

> Since the red men failed to fulfil the commission given to mankind to subdue and cultivate the earth, and make it a theatre of moral culture, Providence determined to supplant them, and give the vineyard to another people who should bring forth fruits thereof. Considering the greatness of the change, and

the established laws of human nature, the expulsion and replanting have been rapidly progressing and are nearly accomplished.[94]

A common theme in replacement narratives in New England, this passage made reference to the biblical passage invoked to justify colonialism. The asserted failure of Indians to use the land properly created the imperative for the English to assume stewardship over the land as a divine mandate. But the "virgin land" story by no means predominated in local texts, and the vanishing Indian did not prevail in every text either. In celebrating the two hundredth anniversary of the "settlement" of Norwich, Connecticut, a toast acknowledged "the friendship of the Mohegans" as "essential to the safety of our fathers, and the growth of the town." Rather than moving on to a story of extinction, this commentator instead asserted Mohegan dependence on New Englanders for "friendship and protection for their very existence, and for all the means of common and religious instruction," thus invoking colonialism as the mechanism for Indian survival and justifying the colonial regime.[95] This reversal, in which Mohegans depended upon New Englanders for "their very existence," got to the heart of colonialism.

Above all, historical commemorations constituted profound commentaries on the idea of place, and for that reason, local texts produced in this context frequently evidenced important tensions surrounding New English and Indian notions about place. In welcoming the throngs to the two hundredth anniversary of the settlement of Bristol, Rhode Island, the orator pointed out that "the dwellers upon this territory have always regarded it with a peculiar devotion. The Wampanoags of old returned to this spot with pride and pleasure, cherished it beyond all others, made it their kingly seat, clung to it until conquest and death, and we in the same spirit of devotion have met to-day."[96]

Given the persistent out-migration from New England that spanned the nineteenth century, a great many historical commemorations constituted massive reunions, since those who left New England wandered extensively— continuing the process of colonialism throughout the west and, in the case of the whaling and carrying trades, across the globe. In Norwich, it was noted:

The vagrant sons of this venerated parent, who have wandered far and wide to other states and other climes, retaining wherever they have gone affectionate memories of the old homestead, obey with willing steps the summons to this celebration. We gather, as was the wont of the buried race before us, around the council fires of the old wigwam. We meet to rear a monumental pillar on soil hallowed by departed virtue, patriotism and faith. We would live again the days of old. We transport ourselves back to the time when the white man's keel first glided through these waters, and the feller's axe first rung in the forest. We call up the images of the good and the brave who laid the foundation stones of this fair superstructure.[97]

This juxtaposition of Indian and New English mobility from a fixed place contains a profound irony, in that English notions about fixity and place figured centrally in dispossessing Indian peoples. While scheduled Indian mobility rooted in a seasonal economy offered a justification for English colonialism in the seventeenth and eighteenth centuries, in the nineteenth century New Englanders cast Anglo-Saxon mobility as normative. New Englanders could wander to the ends of the earth and still lay an uncontested claim to what were asserted as formerly Indian places.

In the end, what distinguished Indian from New English mobility was that New Englanders wandered farther and more permanently from "home" than Indians ever did, local histories notwithstanding. And the periodic New English reunions that punctuated the nineteenth century constituted a different sort of scheduled mobility than Indians engaged in. Historical commemorations in nineteenth-century New England operated as oral history, which included the ritual gathering of people, but in this case by a calendar that usually counted decades or centuries rather than an annual round or the season. In terms of place and compared to Indian ways, they occurred far less frequently and in effect attest to a New English *disconnection from* place.

Excavations

> These sons of nature held the right of soil
> On which, however, they disdained to toil;
> Void of invention, iron they had none—
> Their edge tools all were made of shell or stone.
> *Menunkatuck* was the Indian name,
> When to the English they transferred their claim,
> On contract fair their right they did assign,
> September, sixteen hundred, thirty-nine.
>
> Pleased with the site, they now enjoyed the purchase,
> Cleared up the ground, built fences, houses, churches,
> Soon did the savage howl and yelling cease,
> Succeeded by religion, love, and peace,
> And 'tis among their heirs and their assigns
> Now happiness resides and virtue shines.[98]

If descendants of the English could so confidently claim possession of particular locales, even from the great distances many of them had permanently relocated to, then what was the place of Indians? This "address" from a resident of Guilford, Connecticut, penned in 1812 and included in a later history, concisely and poetically summarized the principal themes of possession in the New England replacement narrative. New Englanders evidenced a strong propensity for locating Indians in the ground and on the landscape: Indian artifacts, graves, and place-names fueled the imagination of local historians. Local narratives mused over the material culture and skeletal remains they occasionally encountered, or over the Indian nomenclature that selectively continued to mark the New England landscape—and many pursued both themes.

A historian of Dunstable, Massachusetts, directly linked these potentially discrete topics, writing that "these old implements, together with the Indian names of 'Nashua,' 'Massapoag,' and 'Unquetynasset,' are almost the only memorials now remaining of the race of red men who, a little more than two hundred years ago, called the lakes and streams of Dunstable their own."[99] In taking up the pursuit of amateur archaeology and place making through naming, writers forged a starkly visible narrative that argued for the replacement of Indians with themselves. They literally buried Indians, their culture, and their history: no trace of their former presence remained except artifacts that from time to time were revealed. With the passing of Indian Polly Johns, in Leicester, Massachusetts, "the only memorials of the perished race are an arrowhead, a pipe, or a stone hatchet, occasionally turned up by the plough on the spots where they built their wigwams or planted their cornfields."[100]

In a centennial address in Barrington, Rhode Island, listeners heard about the development of "the best forms of civilization" there, to be contrasted with "the untutored Indian [who] had no skill in letters, possessed rude specimens of handicraft and a few implements." Farmers occasionally turned up "with [their] ploughshare[s], stone pestles and mortars, the hatchets, chisels and arrowheads" used in fishing, agriculture, and hunting. The orator relates that these periodic personal encounters with the Indian past prompted individuals who now claimed the land to muse about Indians. These artifacts of Indian industry are symbols, and "[farmers wonder] not that [Indians'] journeys are towards the setting sun, driven before the great tidal wave of civilization, whose intelligence, enterprise and courage know no bounds or barriers."[101] Such encounters with the Indian past are cast as casual and frequent, suggesting that virtually any farmer might be able to start up his own Indian museum in which to similarly muse about Indian pasts, and that the Indian presence on the land must have been exceptionally dense. Some who similarly reflected on artifacts and skeletal remains characterized Indians, finding both ingenuity and roughness, regarding them as "relics of a forgotten" rather than a remembered race.[102]

A Barrington, Rhode Island, history noted the chain of possession of "King Philip's iron kettle," seized by Benjamin Church during King Philip's War, sold at auction upon his death, and passed through several generations over 184 years. This prized relic symbolized the process of replacement in the colonial period, having been used by "the renowned warrior in his camp and wigwam."[103] Three histories of separate Massachusetts towns recorded a far more gruesome story of collection, telling readers that "in the cellar under . . . [the Leonard family's] house was deposited, for a considerable time, the head of King Philip."[104] This family supposedly gained Philip's friendship prior to the war, for which regard they were to be spared from harm, which renders the depositing of his skull puzzling indeed. Still more perplexing is the conflicting story of Philip's fate. Other narratives have Church receiving a bounty for the skull in 1676, after which it was placed on a stake in Plymouth, where it remained until 1718, when it was buried after Church's death.[105] The sword Church purportedly used to dispatch Philip could be found "in the historical rooms in Boston."[106]

In common with their present-day practitioners, some local experts fashioned historical interpretations by reading the material yield of the landscape as evidence of the Indian past, or offered extensive catalogs of Indian artifacts found locally.[107] In a discussion of the history of local "manufactures," a historian of East Greenwich, Rhode Island, began with pottery. This framing led him to assert that "the Narragansetts, or some other race, who inhabited this country previous to the Indians, manufactured articles of earthen ware from this same deposit of clay." Other evidence of Indian lives included quahog shells, evidently "carried to this spot by the former inhabitants of this continent." The pottery shards contained clay from "Gould's Mount, showing that the people who made this earthern [sic] ware, were not possessed of the conveniences of sifting and grinding the clay, as the moderns do when preparing it for use." This author owned some of these shards, and he once discovered an intact vessel "found in an Indian grave." Stone arrow and spear heads made of a particular flint not present locally but found in abundance in Maine suggested that "the race . . . which used them, must have had some traffic with those who inhabited these northern regions, or otherwise they must have traveled a great distance to procure them." This hobbyist archaeologist wondered how such implements could be constructed in the absence of steel hammers. The discussion of local manufactures begun with Indian ways read through artifacts, the historian proceeded on to tell the story of the non-Indian industries that replaced them, such as textiles, tanneries, and hat factories.[108]

Other texts, in pondering the ancient history of their places, wondered about the possibility that previous races predated the Indians encountered by their ancestors. Mississippian mounds especially fired the local imagination:

> All over the continent, but especially through its central regions, their works remain more skillful and imperishable than any the red men have left, bearing evidence of a higher degree of civilization. But when and whence they came, and who and what they were, and how they perished, what oracle will proclaim?[109]

This author completely distanced New England Indians from this landscape, settling on a narrative that did not allow for the "civilization" evidenced by Mississippians to be found locally. He even ventured that the presumed previous "Indian was but a modern compared with nations, the monuments of whose civilization and power excite our wonder and baffle our curiosity."[110] Looking locally, a minister in Southborough, Massachusetts, asserted that the "monuments" and "traces" of "a race of men, who once inhabited this continent . . . had made nearer approaches to civilization, and a greater progress in the arts of peace and war, than any of the numerous tribes of North American Indians."[111] Both of these narrators reflected the common nineteenth-century racist assumption that the grand earthworks of Mississippian peoples could not have been built by the Indians they encountered. Indeed, the obsession with amateur archaeology in New England may have reflected a desire to reveal a rich Indian landscape to compete with the Mississippian remains of the Midwest and Southeast.[112] But in any event, both of these accounts shared the midwestern analysis that disconnected New England Indians from remains. The latter claimed Indians knew nothing of their origins: "Their history does not exist.—Tradition is silent."[113]

In Newport, Rhode Island, local narrators took up the mystery of the "Old Stone Mill," participating in a centuries-old debate that continues into the present about the structure's origins. The mill had entered the local imaginary as a relic from the Norse, and a key nineteenth-century proponent of that theory assured his readers that "'no Indians ever did, or ever could build it,'" and "'it is certain that it has not been built by an Anglo-Saxon hand . . . [or] else some record must remain; and none does exist, or has existed, within the memory of man.'"[114] This commentary simultaneously dismissed the notion that Indians could have possessed the capacity for erecting such a structure, and asserted that had it been made by the English, documents would survive attesting to its origins—even if only as a memory of a document.

Occasionally, authors took note of Indian ways that marked the landscape, as Frances Manwaring Caulkins did in relating the story of the Indian memory pile that commemorated Miantonomi's murder.[115] In Woodbury, Connecticut, the street that led from the north to the south meetinghouses was laid out "nearly upon the old Indian trail leading from the *Nonnewaug* wigwams to Pootatuck village, passing the *grave* of Pomperaug by the rock, near the carriage house of N.B. Smith, Esq." An explanation of the dynamic Indian practice of history through the creation of memory piles for their leaders found its way into this text, and the author tells his readers that "a large pile of these pebbles had accumulated upon this consecrated spot previous to the settlement of the town, which remains till the present time."[116]

Other authors speculated on the locations of old Indian trails, and other evidence of Indian ways to be found on the landscape.[117] A historical address delivered at Topsfield, Massachusetts, spoke of the complex "unwritten geography of the aborigines."[118] The frontispiece of a history of Glastonbury, Connecticut, featured an "Indian Map of Glastenbury" that ironically mingled Indian with English place-names without comment (see Figure 16). The map located two Indian villages and no English towns—one was nestled between "Boiling Brook" and "Salmon Brook," and the other between "Sturgeon River" and "Salmon River."[119]

Some historians became preoccupied in a search for *English* relics and ruins. One fretted that "in groping back for something tangible of the olden times, relics of ancient Andover, we find scarcely a trace or thread of continuity, by which hand can clasp hand with the men and women of the former generations." Hardly any relics remained "except on paper" of the first generation "who cleared the forest, broke the ground, made their homes, reared their families, and found their graves during the first half century of Andover's incorporated existence."[120] No memorial "marked the spot where was laid the body of John Osgood, the first settler," and "no trace of Anne Bradstreet's grave is to be found."[121] These lamentations struggled to understand how the locations of these notable individuals—the first settler of Andover and the famed seventeenth-century poet—could be left unmarked and thus unremembered in the land. Other narratives shared this author's concern for the existence of material culture and ruins as precise evidence for their antiquity.

Memory making rooted to place in Andover contrasted markedly with the heavily demarcated Plymouth, which contained Forefathers' Rock and a plethora of place-names such as Captain's Hill to denote their precise claims to the place.[122] Bits of Forefathers' Rock, pilfered over the years, found their way out of Plymouth, only increasing its fame: "it is treasured by a great nation;

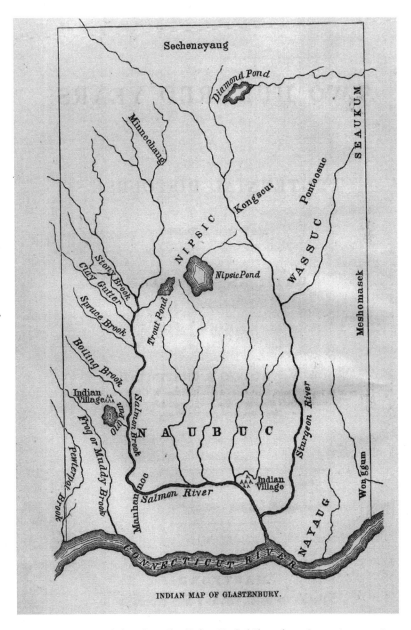

INDIAN MAP OF GLASTENBURY.

Figure 16. *Indian Map of Glastenbury.* This "Indian Map" of Glastonbury, Connecticut, contains a blending of Algonquian and English place-names. Unknown engraver. Frontispiece for Alonzo B. Chapin, *Glastenbury for Two Hundred Years: A Centennial Discourse, May 18th, A.D. 1853, with an Appendix, Containing Historical and Statistical Papers of Interest* (Hartford: Case, Tiffany, 1853).

its very dust is shared as a relic."[123] And while they were "unable to designate the exact spot" where many of its people were interred, they could locate its first burial ground. Cole's Hill partially washed away in 1735, displacing the remains of several of the fifty English people from the *Mayflower.* When human remains again were dislodged in 1855, town authorities called on Oliver Wendell Holmes Sr. to examine one of the skulls, and he "pronounced it a Caucasian skull, and thus, without doubt, the skull of one of the earliest settlers of Plymouth." Town authorities collected the exhumed remains and placed them "near the monument to Governor Bradford, where some appropriate structure is to be placed, designating the certain resting-place of some of the Pilgrim Fathers of New England."[124] Such place making that focused on English ruins is meant to signify their *antiquity,* whereas Indian ruins are made to narrate Indian *demise.*

Barkhamsted, Connecticut, heavily depleted by out-migration, contained plenty of English ruins that signified its claims to antiquity while narrating its abandonment in the nineteenth century. During the course of a two-hour historical address compiled and delivered by one who had joined the mass abandonment of the place thirty years prior at the age of twelve, the orator struggled to trace the history of Barkhamsted people who had "scattered far and wide. Probably more people have removed from the town since the beginning of this 19th century than are now living within its borders."[125] Barkhamsted people could now be found in "almost every state"; the celebration drew back an estimated five thousand to six thousand people, who were entertained by the fifty or sixty remaining families.[126] Of many who had left, though, "all trace of them and their descendants is lost."[127] The orator reconstructed Barkhamsted's history as best he could under the circumstances. He was certain he missed people in compiling a list of those who lived there prior to 1800, "for these old cellars, which can be seen along our roadsides, where the lilac, tansy and wormwood are growing around crumbling walls and falling chimneys, plainly prove that many, and, in some cases, large families have disappeared."[128] Taking as his theme the replication of population on the land, the orator instead found a seemingly wholesale diaspora that took place after 1840. "The resources of the town were exhausted as the forest disappeared," and the people began heading west even before Horace Greeley offered his advice to do so.[129] This fascinating set of observations turned upside down the typical argument, which had *Indians* disappearing *with the forests* rather than *non-Indians* disappearing *from the towns,* and called into question non-Indian notions of permanence. The town was rich in both Indian and English ruins, and one wonders who remained to sponsor the massive—and temporary—return.[130]

Naming

Naming is deeply implicated in the process of place making. A historian of Salisbury, Connecticut, offered an astute analysis of its significance:

> Our ancestors, here and elsewhere, had no respect for Indian character, and seemed to desire, with the extinction of the race, to extinguish all memorials of its existence. In nearly all instances, Indian names of prominent objects were discarded, and others adopted, frequently vulgar and without meaning. Indian names were always significant; but in almost every instance, their meaning is lost to us.[131]

This analysis, although perhaps excessively pessimistic about the loss of Indian names and meanings if the content of other local texts are taken into account, neatly summarized the process of claiming landscapes through naming. Another Connecticut historian agreed that the meaning—and undoubtedly the pronunciation—of Indian names was significant though lost to them. But for him, Indian geographical names were "almost the only enduring memorials of the aborigines . . . which survived their decay, and which still remain, constantly reminding us that our streams and hills were once the haunts of a different race of men."[132]

A historian of Dedham disagreed with him:

> I have no sympathy with those who are trying to revive what they call the beautiful Indian names, which are mostly uncouth and to us unpronounceable and meaningless. I am glad we are Dedham and not Chickatabut or Quinobequin; it shows that we belong to the great imperial race which subdued the wilderness . . . and having raised Massachusetts to her present perfection is leaving her . . . to spread her freedom and her principles over yet undeveloped lands.[133]

Yet another historian weighed in from a different angle: let the "dignified" Indian names remain, "and [do] not attempt to filch from the poor Indian, the right which God and nature gave him to imprint the seal of his own language upon those everlasting hills, lakes, ponds and streams!"[134] This appeal, delivered at the commemoration of "the first full day of being organized as proprietors," authorized the English claiming of Indian lands even while it argued against what is characterized as the theft of Indian place-names. Taken together, local texts engaged in a lively debate over the propriety and meaning of Indian place-names. Many weighed in on the issue, some painstakingly reported the meanings of the Indian place-names found within their locales, and sometimes they reported former Indian names and their English replacements.[135] All of them, even if they did not explicitly explain the stakes of renaming, engaged in a process of claiming Indian places as their own.

At the Concord, Massachusetts, commemoration, James Russell Lowell offered his own dubious interpretation of the Indian name for Concord, Musketaquid, "justified by my researches": ·

> The Indians were a brief and sententious people, and in a single word in their language you will find great length, and breadth, and depth of meaning. Mesketaquid . . . is the Indian name for a town of brave men, and fair women, and heroes and statesmen, and orators, and a people that never tires of talking about itself or hearing itself talked about for two hundred and fifty years.[136]

In his research Lowell clearly availed himself of the latitude that could be taken in the genre of a celebratory speech and offered a tongue-in-cheek linguistic analysis meant to pay tribute to the ancestors who replaced the "brief" Indian people. A Fairfield, Connecticut, history tells us in a footnote that "*Unquowa* is the Indian name of Fairfield, meaning 'go further,'" which may have been what the Indians told the English upon their arrival.[137]

The forces of replacement predominated in the place-name debate on the town level in southern New England, leaving only a little more than a dozen Indian designations on the map of towns: Acushnet, Agawam, Aquinnah, Chicopee, Cohasset, Mashpee, Mattapoisett, Nahant, Nantucket, Narragansett, Natick, Naugatuck, Pawtucket, Saugus, Seekonk, and Woonsocket. This massive replacement project must be understood in the context of the town system of southern New England whereby all of the land is encompassed by town boundaries. Rooted in the colonial period, the New England town system builds on the English surveying impulse that quickly held sway in the seventeenth century and that sought to measure and assert new systems of ownership over every inch of land.[138] In Connecticut and Massachusetts, themselves Algonquian place-names, a wealth of Indian names continued to dot the landscape within the imposed townscape, and geographical features blended the Indian (Connecticut River) with the English (Blackstone River). Also etched into the New England map were locations that employed a generic Indian imprint such as Indian Point, Wigwam Hill, Sachem's Head, and Sachem's Plain.[139] Red Mountain in Torrington, Connecticut, was reported to have derived its name from an episode in which a "white man reported that he shot an Indian."[140] Stories about other individual Indians encountered by the English lay beneath other localities such as Massasoit Spring, Will Hill, Canonicut Island, Mount Philip, Joe English Hill, Jackstraw Pasture, Jackstraw Hill, Captain Tom's Hill, Roger's Brook, Roger's Rock, Betty's Neck, and Squaw Betty.[141] At least two place-names referenced apocryphal stories about Indians and liquor that the authors classed as such: Jamaica Plain and

Rumstick.[142] In Andover, Pomp's Pond "is almost the only local reminder that negro slavery was one of our early institutions."[143] In Paxton, a historian fretted that the town retained the name of an odious colonial loyalist to England even after appointing a committee to petition the General Court to change it in the wake of the American Revolution.[144] The process of place making suggests an emergent nomenclature for a map that included Indian and English names, many of them springing from local stories steeped in relatively recent events.

A final story about naming offers a rich commentary on how it can operate as possession and a replacement narrative. A historian of Norwalk, Connecticut, took umbrage at a charge levied upon the town by the prominent historian John Warner Barber that "according to tradition, 'the [Norwalk] name is derived from the one-day's *North-walk*, that limited the northern extent of the purchase from the Indians.'"[145] This accusation, powerfully reminiscent of the "Walking Purchase" that Thomas Penn perpetrated on Delaware Indians in Pennsylvania in 1737, called into question the propriety of Norwalk's possession of Indian land, suggesting that its Indian deed involved trickery on behalf of the English. In countering this argument, the author provided evidence about the Indian deed, including some questionable procedures that he defended. He also provided some rather far-fetched linguistic evidence:

> (1.) The original deeds, in 1640, give the name Norwalke, as then designating the river, and there is the same evidence that that was the original Indian name, as that *Saukatuk* and *Rooton* were. (2.) All the settlements along the coast, and in the interior, were first called by their Indian names, and were changed only for specific reasons.

And finally, having located eleven different ways that Norwalk had been spelled in the colonial records, which apparently did not include "Northwalk,"[146] Bouton then rested his case that his ancestors had properly replaced Indian peoples through their land transactions, and rooted his explanation in an exceptionally dubious linguistic analysis.

Land

In narrating a story of Indian demise that associated local Indians with artifacts, relics, and burials, New Englanders paved the way for unambiguously establishing themselves in that place. Not that they did not evince an equally fervent fascination with relics and graves of their English ancestors. The allure of their own remains is readily apparent in the emergence and embellishment of the ancestor worship grounded most elaborately in the annual celebrations of Forefathers' Day in Plymouth and in other places New England descendants found themselves living in the nineteenth century. But the association of Indians with graves and artifacts remained largely a categorical one. While New English descendants could appreciate how the present and future connected to the past through the symbolism of their own ancestors' graves and artifacts, their invocation of Indian burials and relics argued that Indians could only be found in the past. This impulse formed a double act of colonialism, in that New Englanders appropriated and displayed Indian artifacts and bones as evidence of Indian demise, and constructed a story whereby Anglo Americans logically and rationally—legally, it is asserted—replaced Indian peoples and cultures with their own.

At the center of this story can be found pervasive and multilayered explanations about landownership that justified the colonial regime on which New England forged its modernity. Most local texts touched at least briefly on deeds or other "legal" means of land transmission, and some of these texts expended many pages in detailing the complex set of ideas that composed justification of the colonial state. While rarely fully articulated in single texts, the elements local narrators drew on included the doctrine of discovery, Crown grants, grants from colonial legislators and/or towns, and right of conquest following the Pequot War and King Philip's War. Sometimes, narrators recited colony policies that governed Indian land transactions to argue that their ancestors diligently attended to Indian rights.[147] Historians also frequently invoked the biblical injunction to "subdue the earth and multiply," and declared the land on which they built New English places "vacuum domicilium." A great many texts also detailed transactions from Indians for the very same land—sometimes by reprinting in their entirety every pertinent Indian deed—in order to eliminate any appearance of unscrupulous behavior on the part of their ancestors. Some texts explained that colony law and moral right dictated that their ancestors attend to both a grant of land from the governing body as well as the extinguishing of Indian claims.[148] These frequently elaborate treatises on landholding arrangements reveal a sensitivity that is explicitly acknowledged in many texts. At the centennial celebration of the incorporation of Westminster, Massachusetts, this query was posed: "The question is sometimes asked, by what title we hold our lands? Were they purchased, or how was the Indian title extinguished?"[149]

But, as the attendees at the celebration heard, it was not so easy to answer. Certainly in the case of Westminster, if "any wrong [had been] done to the native tribes, it was done by the body politic, and not by those who established themselves in this township," because at "the first settlement here, this region was destitute of inhabitants." But the orator did not let matters rest there. So as to assess "the justice and equity of the policy of our fathers toward the native tribes," he resorted to "first principles." These began with the Bible and the insistence on subduing and multiplying, which conferred a "better title," one that could support "a vastly greater population of civilized than of savage men." Providence dictated that "an uncivilized, pagan nation, fades away before a civilized, Christian nation." Even so, such first principles could never justify fraud, injustice, or oppression. Confining himself to local matters, the orator explained that "first settlement" had been preceded by a pestilence that nearly depopulated the place. No one could suggest that these few remaining "wild men of the woods" should retain possession of "this delightful country against the claims of a more civilized people, who were driven by oppression from their native land."[150]

Still, the argument continued, the region contained land enough for all, and the arduous crossing of the ocean represented an expenditure of labor that exceeded the labor Indians purportedly exerted on their soil. Where Indians actually planted and hunted, they should be left to enjoy their land, but their claims to land because they wandered over some part of it should not be elevated to the status of a right. In any event, when the several native leaders "put themselves under the Massachusetts Colony in 1644," their jurisdiction over "unsettled sections" was "virtually relinquished." And even more, because most Nashuas fought alongside Indians in King Philip's War, "they put all their country at the hazard of the conquest," which thus made it subject to the claim of right of conquest, even though the English waited half a century to exercise that claim, "when it had been for years abandoned by the Indians." All of these circumstances secured to the Massachusetts General Court title to the land at the time Westminster received its grant, and so it "would then, and now, be considered valid by the law of nations, as it is understood in the most enlightened and civilized countries."[151]

But what of the moral right, which could not be abandoned, even in the context of war? Here too the ancestors could be defended. "How then did our fathers treat the natives?" After the 1644 "voluntary submission" of Indians to the English, the English protected Indian possessions, and they even granted land to Indians in places such as Natick. Land grievances could be heard in the colonial courts, and in 1652 Massachusetts passed a law protecting Indian rights to lands they "'have by possession, or improvement, by subduing the same.'" Such rights continued to be defended in Grafton, Gay Head, Mashpee, and elsewhere. And in many other places, the General Court had granted

Indian land *to* Indians. The question of morality and justice, then, could be answered in favor of the English—at least the political body of Massachusetts, since unscrupulous individuals no doubt occasionally defrauded Indians. The uncivilized state of Indians in fact aggravated the crimes of these unprincipled people, since "an expiring nation, like expiring individuals, should be regarded with sympathy, and treated with kindness; and the individual, or the community, which violates this obvious principle, is guilty of a wrong, for which they must atone."[152]

Although many local historians devoted themselves to rather thorough justifications of their land tenure, such as the treatise offered to the people of Westminster, others gave more curtailed explanations. And while a great variety of explanatory narratives can be found, two recurrent references for discussions of landownership are striking in the local histories of New England. Interestingly, both refer to threats to New England in the seventeenth century, one of them standing in opposition to the colonial project, and the other representing an internal challenge. As for the external threat, local narrators regularly invoke the claim that "not one foot of land" in New England had been obtained prior to King Philip's War but through just land transactions. This phrase comes directly from the claim of Josiah Winslow, then governor of Plymouth Colony at the outbreak of King Philip's War, in response to Indian protests about land fraud as a prominent cause for their resistance movement. During the celebration of the second centennial of the settlement of Cape Cod, famed historian John Gorham Palfrey quoted Winslow with attribution (which is seldom the case in local texts): "Before the present troubles broke out, the English did not possess one foot of land in the colony, but what was fairly obtained by honest purchase of the Indian proprietors."[153] At a minimum, it should be noted, this claim forgets the massive dispossession based on the notion of right of conquest that occurred in the wake of the Pequot War. This point did not elude a historian of Wallingford, Connecticut, who merged these justifications: "Let any man demonstrate if he can, that in Connecticut a single rood of land was ever acquired of the Indians otherwise than by fair purchase, except what was conquered from the Pequots in a war as righteous as ever was waged."[154]

The threat internal to the colonial project came in the form of Sir Edmund Andros, shipped off to New England to reign in the independent-minded colonies after James II vacated their colonial charters. Andros challenged the legitimacy of land arrangement heretofore made between the colonies and Indians, and he characterized the deeds that colonists had hastily obtained from Indians to firm up their claims as worthless: "'the signatures of Indians to title deeds were of no more worth than the scratch of a bear's paw.'"[155] Local narrators frequently invoked this catchy phrase to argue just the opposite, and one ambitious chronicler of land arrangements coupled a comment on Andros's critique with the suggestion that "it would be interesting to consider the nature of this primitive proprietorship, for it has decided bearings upon the great modern question of the origin of property, and the significance of that 'institution,' in the history of civilization."[156] Later on in his history, he reflected that "of course the natives knew not that they were parting with their homes forever; neither did the new settlers know how swiftly their predecessors upon the soil would melt away before the glow and heat of a Christian civilization," thus suggesting that Andros might have been onto something after all even though he dismissed the concern as a moot point.[157] At least two other local historians, including the eminent Frances Manwaring Caulkins, crossed species in botching the reference, attributing the marks to cats rather than bears.[158]

Local narrators pressed the claim of rightful ownership even in the absence of precise documentation: "All Indian deeds were not recorded. Enough, however, have been found to justify the belief that they paid the Indian to his full satisfaction for every acre they took."[159] And some local historians took pains to establish chains of ownership stretching from Indian transactions into the present. For a historical discourse pronounced to celebrate the opening of the Wadsworth Atheneum in Hartford, the orator selected as his topic the many changes in ownership of the particular piece of land on which they constructed the building: "Here it is pertinent to state the curious and interesting fact, that the last individual proprietor of the land in question, is a *lineal descendant* of the first proprietor in severalty."[160] How could a claim to place be any more certain than by this dramatic narration of lineage *in place?*

The discourse commemorating the Wadsworth Atheneum constituted an extraordinary commentary on the issue of proper "chains of title" rooted ultimately in Indian transactions. The narrator summarized his mission toward the end of his oration:

> We have thus traced the title of the land we occupy, through all of its changes, from the sachem of Sukiauge to the corporation of Wadsworth Athenæum, with some notice of those through whose hands it has passed. In every instance, the title appears on the record, and that title is a perfectly legal one; so that if an exclusive and uninterrupted possession of those under whom we claim, for more than two hundred years, were of no avail, we could still vindicate our right to the soil, by authentic muniments, against all the world.[161]

This discourse on this particular parcel of land consumed thirty-three pages of the thirty-six-page tract. The narrator's tenacity in establishing this assertion is particularly evident when he confronted the uncomfortable absence of a deed for the transaction between William Goodwin and John Blackleach in 1659. Yet a "note" that recorded the price at the bounds of the land persuaded him that "we do not yet find a broken link or flaw in the chain of title."[162] Once he fully connected the links in the chain of title, he concluded his address by praising the efforts surrounding the still unfinished building, and declared, "It will be *permanent.*"[163]

A historian of Framingham, Massachusetts, similarly concerned himself with land title and assured his readers of the pains "first settlers" had taken to procure Indian land titles through legal means. Here he invoked a higher authority, relating, "We have somewhere met with a remark, attributed to the elder President Adams, that in all his practice at the bar, he never knew a contested title to land which was not traced back to the Indian grantors."[164] This argument would have been met with assent in Wenham, Massachusetts, where "the first settlers appear to have obtained their land by purchase, from the Indians, and one family at least, still hold their farm (now occupied by Mr. Daniel Perkins,) by a deed from its aboriginal possessor, and signed by him with an arrow, as his mark."[165]

Embedded in claims of proper landownership are notions of permanence, rarely made so explicit as in the recitation of the chain of title of the Wadsworth Atheneum. This persistently implicit foundational principle argues that Indians were *impermanent,* and thus not worthy of retaining possession of their land. Still, specific stories of land transfer found their place in the overwhelming majority of local narratives in order to deflect any possibility of critique. Few let it rest with the argument that "the red man laid no claim to lands in Townsend [Massachusetts]."[166] Even though many narrators concurred that "no Indian settlement existed, at the time of its discovery, within the limits" of the place they wrote about, still most described some mechanism by which Indian lands ran through legal channels to themselves.[167] Waterbury, Connecticut's historian, who made this assertion, proceeded to locate two possibly pertinent deeds (one in neighboring Farmington and another cited in a Litchfield, Connecticut, history). But he ultimately concluded that it was the 1686 grant from the colony that mattered most, and cited the colonial statute that regulated Indian land transactions to suggest that all must have proceeded legally.[168] Yet he later devoted an entire chapter to the details of land transactions, and made a claim that others from Connecticut echoed: "[T]he territory in question was all honestly purchased, most of it twice, and some of it three times. And it was bought not with baubles, but with hard cash. However it may have been in other cases, *our ancestors did not get possession of their lands by robbery, or finesse.*"[169] In East Hartford a historian paused to dismiss any frets over the failure to locate precise deeds, arguing that no doubt one was obtained, and in any event, none was necessary because the doctrine of discovery dismissed Indian rights and the colonial charter conferred indisputable title.[170]

In Newton, Massachusetts, Indians *did,* according to their local historian, possess the land by virtue of *"subduing the same,"* and even though there seemed to be no record of their forfeiture of title, "those lands were no doubt considered part and parcel of the common lands of the Cambridge proprietors."[171] Boston "does not appear to have been claimed by any Indians, until a long time after it was possessed by the English; nor do any indications of a prior settlement by the former come under the notice of those who early describe the place."[172] There and elsewhere, historians described the delayed appearance of claimants whose proper ownership is glossed as suspect, but whose quitclaims were obtained nonetheless.[173] Also in common with Boston, many of these quitclaims dated to the 1680s, which timing linked them to the challenges to legal title mounted by Edmund Andros and his critique of deeds and "bear's paws."[174] "Right of conquest" as a claim frequently appeared in Rhode Island, and occasionally Connecticut and Massachusetts, stemming from King Philip's War and the Pequot War.[175] In Bristol, Rhode Island, some Indians remained even after the English had obtained a deed from Massasoit, "until Philip's war, when being exterminated or driven away, their remaining rights to the territory were extinguished."[176] Following a dispute over the proper ownership of these lands, the government declared them "conquered," and ruled that they "should be sold to assist in defraying the expenses of the war," thus in effect compelling the Narragansett combatants to literally pay for their own conquest.[177] In Bridgewater, Massachusetts, Daniel Huntington informed his audience in 1821, the Pilgrims arrived in Plymouth and soon concluded "a friendly treaty with the natives, of whom they fairly purchased the land which they occupied," and, he claims, they remunerated the Indians for corn they "found" [stole] upon their arrival on Cape Cod.[178]

While many local narratives refuted the notion that Indian deeds had been obtained for "trinkets," others embraced this motif. An 1829 history of Lynn featured an etching of its foundational story on its frontispiece: "BLACK WILLIAM selling NAHANT to Thomas Dexter for a suit of Clothes."[179] (See Figure 1.) Even though the town of Lynn later rejected this 1629 bargain for

Nahant (part of Lynn's original bounds), as the text explains, the author selected the image as encapsulating the replacement of Indian people on the land. The image argues both that English people purchased the land and that Indians attached little value to the land, since they relinquished it for such meager considerations. And the argument about rights to Nahant reveals the logic behind English claims to Indian lands rather than serving as a critique of the terms of exchange. The depositions collected in 1657 about the dispute stemmed from a legal action filed by Dexter against the town for occupying the lands. At the heart of the argument stood the practice of enclosing the land by fencing, and just who "did first fence at nahant and by an act of generall court did apprehend by fencing that nahant was theires." A deposition from two local Indian leaders affirmed the story of Thomas Dexter, Black William, and the suit of clothes, thus reinforcing the "propriety" of the transaction, subtly arguing that just possession stemmed from the English cultural practice of fencing their fields.[180]

Variations on the Black William story found their place into histories of Nahant, Ipswich, and Swampscott. Nahant's historian related the Lynn account in encapsulated form.[181] In Ipswich, the story has Black William selling to William Witter for "two pestle stones."[182] The Swampscott text tells of William Witter's deposition testifying to the transaction from Black William to Thomas Dexter for "a suit of clothes, two stone pestles and a jewsharp," and continued:

> The parties occupied the entire day in making the trade, and it was not until Mr. Dexter had gone four miles through the woods, and played sixteen tunes on the jewsharp, before the assembled tribes, to convince them that the tongue was not leather, that he secured what he thought to be a good title to the land. The town afterwards treated the bargain as void, declaring that Black Will's deed was "of no more value than the scratch of a bear's paw."[183]

This fanciful story oddly positions Indians as discriminating consumers of trinkets in exchange for their lands, and offers a peculiar rendering of the notion of "good title" on the part of Mr. Dexter. This version moved on to close the books on Black William's story, when it explained that he was hanged in 1631 in Scarborough, Maine, "in revenge for the murder of William Bagnall, who was killed by the Indians in October, 1631."[184]

Simsbury, Connecticut, once subsumed the town of Canton, and thus they shared the story of a deed obtained in 1648 by John Griffin from Manahoose in compensation for a fire Manahoose set that "accidentally burned a large quantity of Griffin's combustible goods."[185] An apparent lone trespasser on

Indian lands who manufactured tar, pitch, and turpentine, Griffin continued his freelance land dealings with Indians by extracting additional deeds, which "were afterwards in some sort validated by a deed, given in 1680, in accordance with colony laws."[186] While this account allows for the shadow of doubt in the propriety of this transaction, a different observer of Simsbury's history places the story in broad daylight: "Some years afterwards, doubts arising as to the validity of this deed, as being contrary to a law of the General Court, in 1680, *for the same consideration*, viz: kindling a fire, and damage done thereby, 'and for many other good consideration and causes thereunto moving, they sold [the land].'"[187] Confronted by Indian protests over "the consideration of this deed," the narrator tells us with palpable consternation, the town sold a paltry one hundred and fifty acres "out of a tract ten miles square" to "extinguish the debt." He went on to dismiss the prevalent charge that since Indian land was of little or no value, the trifling sums paid to Indians were justifiable, pointing out that "it was to the Indian his sole means of subsistence. As to the white man, if of no value to him, why purchase it at all?" Even given the supposed degeneracy of the day, he asserted, "ninety-nine out of a hundred of these so-called purchases would be set aside for fraud or want of consideration."[188]

It is difficult to get to the bottom of stories such as those about Black William and the supposed arsonist Manahoose and separate grains of truth from blatant myth making. The 250th celebration of Taunton, Massachusetts, acted out the difficult tensions between mythology and fact in origin stories. The historical narrator of the day stood to proclaim that Elizabeth Poole was *not* numbered among the original purchasers of the town, and that "the popular tradition of her purchase of the place with a jackknife and a peck of beans must be ranked with the legend of Romulus and Remus as the founders of Rome, with that of William Tell as the Deliverer of Switzerland, or that of Pocahontas as the saviour of Captain Smith."[189] In her stead, he offered neither "an original deed" nor "any record" of the transaction, nor a date, but rather he figured "there is abundant reason to believe that it came from Massasoit," confirmed in 1663 by his son Philip. His claim rejected that of the "ladies of Taunton," who had erected a monument to Elizabeth Poole in the Mount Pleasant Cemetery more than fifty years earlier declaring her the "Foundress of the Town of Taunton." Additional support for the ladies of Taunton came in the town seal, which sported a rendering of the Elizabeth Poole transaction, and one of the tableaux vivants in the processions similarly disagreed with the orator.[190] (One wonders which claim would be more permanent.)

Stories about land and the events that transpired in particular places performed the cultural work of seizing Indian homelands. This passage, from an 1877 history of Guilford, Connecticut, offers a powerful example of the subtle ways in which this process operated:

> The places where most of the original settlers first located themselves are now known. The noted Stone house of Mr. Whitfield, said to have been built in 1639, erected both for the accommodation of his family and as a fortification for the protection of the inhabitants against the Indians, is supposed to be the oldest dwelling-house in the United States. . . . It is said that the first marriage was celebrated in it. . . . According to tradition the stone, of which this house was built, was brought by the Indians on hand-barrows, across the swamp, from Griswold's rock.[191]

This place, which was "originally inhabited by Indians," is claimed for the "settlers," suggesting that while Indians merely inhabited what came to be Guilford, the English people who came there made their own presence permanent. The places claimed by English people are "known." They built stone houses—including the alleged oldest one in the United States—assisted by Indians, to defend themselves against Indians, whose lands have been seized from them (see Figure 17). And they immediately established institutions

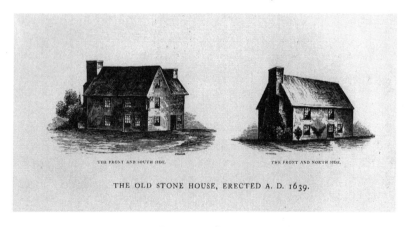

THE FRONT AND SOUTH SIDE.   THE FRONT AND NORTH SIDE.

THE OLD STONE HOUSE, ERECTED A. D. 1639.

Figure 17. *The Old Stone House, Erected A. D. 1639.* The page opposite this etching of the "Old Stone House" tells the reader: "The noted Stone house of Mr. Whitfield, said to have been built in 1639, erected both for the accommodation of his family and as a fortification for the protection of the inhabitants against the Indians, is supposed to be the oldest dwelling-house now standing in the United States." Unknown engraver. From Ralph D. Smith, *The History of Guilford, Connecticut, from Its First Settlement in 1639. From the Manuscripts* (Albany: J. Munsell, 1877), 15–16.

such as marriage that it is implied never occurred in this place before. Further on in the text can be found the details of the Indian transactions, including transcriptions of the multiple Indian deeds that initiated and authorized for this historian the replacement of Indian with English people in Indian places.[192]

In some texts, the replacement narrative is concisely stated, and the author proceeds to unfurl the tale of English origins. Tarrying briefly to discuss land title and King Philip's War, an orator in Suffield, Connecticut, related that "Pampunkshat and Mishnoasqus with their tawny associates, were destined by an overruling Providence, to give place to the white man;—the dark forest to the cultivated fields."[193] Rather than foregrounding divine providence and like many others, a historian of Barre, Massachusetts, rooted the town's origins in the Indian deed as initiating the process of transformation: "At this date, then, 1686, and by this instrument, the soil of our town passed from its Indian occupants and became the property of civilized men; and thus the initial step was taken for converting a 'waste, howling wilderness into a fruitful field.'"[194] An address delivered at Blanford, Massachusetts, acknowledged that Indians contested the process of "replacement" the English engaged in: "The Indians, being the original and rightful occupants of the soil, were unwilling to relinquish their titles and the graves of their ancestors. Hence the frequent Indian wars which proved such a scourge to the colonies."[195]

Local histories collapsed a complex and contested history of Indian and English interaction, and naturalized the notion of rightful English replacement of Indian peoples. Occasionally, as in an 1874 Brookline, Massachusetts, history, the narrative could be found condensed within a single paragraph:

> At this place was an Indian village, or settlement of "praying Indians," and an Indian burying-place was located on what John Ackers bought for his farm, on the west side of Brighton Street, including Ackers' Avenue, and all the ground now occupied by the Irish population. There was probably an Indian village here also, as many Indian relics have been ploughed out, on this ground, as well as Nonantum Hill. Many years after all the Indians were gone from this locality, some old Indians travelled a long distance from the west to visit these old graves of their fathers. . . . The cellar of the original Ackers' house was traceable within the memory of persons now living.[196]

Packed into this passage are multiple claims about the transformation of Brookline. In making reference to "praying Indians," the historian conjures up missionary outreach as central to the colonial history of the place. But the overwhelming message about Indian history suggests that it is in the past: the Indian burying place signifies the claimed Indian demise, and it is Indian relics that provide evidence of previous Indian presence, suggesting that there may have been an Indian village here. The author scripts Indians as gone in an intriguing and odd way: after they had been long gone from the place, elderly Indians traveled great distances to visit their fathers' graves. Is she suggesting that the Indians who had previously lived here had moved to the west? Or is she implying that these generic "graves of their fathers" evoked feelings of familiarity and reverence for any and all Indians? We cannot know. But the tone of the passage conveys a deep estrangement of Indians from this place and history. In their place are cast English farmers engaging in property transactions and building structures, who initiated the creation of a deeply rooted society. Though now occupied by Irish people, this place in Brookline is cast as categorically *not Indian,* and its lengthy history as a non-Indian place is asserted by the *English* ruins that are now nearly beyond the memory of the populace.

Chapter 3 Lasting

Texts Purify the Landscape of Indians by Denying Them a Place in Modernity

Temporalities of Race

Thomas Gray's poem "Change," which was read at the commemoration of the English arrival in Roxbury in 1830, provides a fascinating window on a crucial theme of nineteenth-century local narration in connection to what might be thought of as the temporalities of race.[1] Even though Indians are not the explicit focus of his poem, the implicit argument posed is that Indians reside in an ahistorical temporality in which they can only be the victims of change, not active subjects in the making of change. These ideas about Indian timelessness relegate Indians to the past by suggesting that they were passive and static by nature and that this foreclosed the possibility of their ongoing participation in the making of a future, which is categorically claimed by the English and their descendants. He argues that change made its debut appearance in what was to become the United States when the English found their way to the shores of Cape Cod. Those who arrived on the *Mayflower* encountered little but the "startled panther" and "the grim savage":

> But Change soon brightened o'er the forest glade—
> Light dawned on rills that long in darkness played.
> The good old Puritan in freedom trod
> The soil that owned no master, but its God
> With hymns of praise her slumbering echoes woke;
> Bade her free temples rise, her altars smoke—
> And freely gleaned, beneath no cloudless clime,
> The treasured spoils of unrecorded Time.[2]

In this passage Gray locates Indians in the misty past of unrecorded time, whereas the English introduce change—and thus history as a story of progress—as their own exclusive purview. Before the "good old Puritan" arrived to bring change, the poem asserts, the dark forests stood on lands owned by no one—the English freely took up the "spoils of unrecorded Time." Although Indians certainly would not consider themselves "masters" of the soil in the way implied, the claim that no one owned the land but God blatantly participates in the myth of virgin soil available for the taking.

Almost halfway into his poem, Gray turned to an extended and passionate consideration of the Cherokee—just then the target of Andrew Jackson's removal policy—that began with this passage:

> Lo! where thy power dread Change, we sorrowing see
> Sweep the fair portion of the Cherokee,
> Its chartered lord by nature, treaty, law—
> The savage once—the savage now no more.[3]

Here, the ability of Indians to change is symbolized by the Cherokee people, who are being targeted by removal policy: they are able to change, but once they have changed, they are no longer Indian. Indeed, the very changes Gray highlights are those *brought* by the English. Furthermore, for those coming to the poem after the Cherokees' story unfolded in the 1830s and they were forcibly moved to Indian Territory, their ability to change might be read as the pinnacle of futility. The Cherokee strategy of selectively embracing Euro-American ways and defending their homelands in the U.S. justice system was all in vain. This story starkly symbolized the impossibility of Indian futures, since their resistance to removal—rooted precisely in *change*—failed to protect them.

The setting for this commemoration being Roxbury practically compelled the poet to make at least passing reference to local hero John Eliot, which he did in a brief and vague stanza toward the end of his poem that pointed out the educational outreach of "the Apostle" to Indians and African Americans. And that closed the door on Indians.[4] Change had come to stay:

> Yes! on this native spot of native land
> Doth Change extend her all supreme command.
> Now, raises churches at each others door—
> Now, builds up streets where nothing stood before—
> Now, stirs the living, now walls up the dead—
> Now, moves an engine house, and builds a shed—
> Now, lays out princely roads with skill and pains[5]

And so forth. Where nothing but a timeless people in nature had existed before, New Englanders introduced Change into the Western Hemisphere and ushered the "native land" into modernity.[6] The assertion of modernity is made through the seemingly mundane erection of churches and roads, entirely eliding the dynamic world of Indian spirituality and elaborate network of trails and place-names rooted in history.

The temporalities of race suggested by Thomas Gray's poem gesture toward the racial thinking that fueled the myth of Indian extinction in nineteenth-century New England. Historical narration implicitly argued that Indians can never be modern because they cannot be the subjects of change, only its victims. This discourse locates Indians in an ahistorical temporality that relegates Indian history to a degeneracy narrative marred by racial mixing and cultural loss. Conversely, non-Indian New Englanders reserve to themselves the authorship of recorded time, which is subject to a progress narrative wherein racial mixing and cultural dynamism are asserted as the privilege of whiteness. African Americans, though not specifically my focus, can be seen to occupy a different position in this racial formation: whereas "mixture" results in degeneracy for Indians and progress for non-Indians, African Americans are narrated as polluted—their blackness can never be lost, washed away, or fully purified.[7] Even when emancipated, the stain of slavery remained, symbolized by the "one drop" rule that justified African American oppression in the racial formation of the United States. In this formulation, the possession of even "one drop" of African blood marked a person as black and thus subject to slavery and racial discrimination.

What are the underlying dynamics that fueled these temporalities of race? In this chapter I analyze the phenomenon of "lasting," a rhetorical strategy that asserts as a fact the claim that Indians can never be modern.[8] In juxtaposition to the many claims about "firsts" that local texts assert are an intriguing set of "lasts." The practice of what I call "lasting" in local narratives importantly participated in the production of a narrative of progress and historical time for non-Indians, mixture and degeneracy for Indians, and might be seen as juxtaposed with the notion of indelible pollution for African Americans. In these ways the very practice of historical writing participates in the creation of these temporalities of race. An essential location for "lasting" is to be found in the complex discourse surrounding "blood" in these narratives, most starkly in stories about the "last full-blooded" Indian. But local narratives found a multitude of other "lasts" to comment on that also perform important cultural and political work. Taken together, the practice of lasting bolstered non-Indians' claims about their own modernity even while they purport to purify the landscape of Indians.

Famous "Last" Indians and Their (Not So Famous) Descendants

Squanto was the first last Indian, but he was decidedly not the last.[9] Famously representing the peaceful embrace of the English in 1620, Squanto had returned to his homeland following years of slavery in Spain at the hands of Englishman Captain Thomas Hunt. He arrived only to find his village had vanished in the aftermath of the devastating epidemic of 1616–19 that "providentially" paved the way for English colonialism: "On the arrival of the Pilgrims at Plymouth, in 1620, they found their lot cast within the limits of a deserted Indian country. Of the name of the tribe which inhabited that section, its history or the cause of its departure, they knew absolutely nothing."[10] Squanto, "the sole remaining native of Patuxet," turned up shortly thereafter and embarked upon his career as one of the most famous go-betweens in the history of Indian America. Or so the story goes. Although dwarfed in importance by the welcoming diplomat Massasoit in nineteenth-century accounts, Squanto attained the status of icon in the twentieth century as a symbol of virgin land available for the taking and the imminent demise of Indian people who had once claimed this land as their home. The feminized Squanto gave historians permission to elide the complex history of Indian struggle and survival that followed in the wake of English colonialism.

Still, what might be thought of as the Squanto motif of "lasting" found fertile ground in the imaginations of nineteenth-century New Englanders, and authors frequently extrapolated its claims across the landscape. These claims about the end of the line for Indians flew in the face of the ongoing recognition of Indian survival in the commonwealth and state-level bureaucracies in the nineteenth century, and they depended on the degeneracy narrative of the temporalities of race. The assertion of "lastness" took many forms. Some modified their claims by including the locality or tribe of whom they are purported to be the last. Some "last" Indians, such as Charles Josias, signified the demise of Indians not long after the arrival of the English in the seventeenth century: he is claimed as the last Indian of Bridgewater (1840), Duxbury (1849), and Roxbury (1878).[11] Likewise, in an 1891 address delivered before the Massachusetts Society of Colonial Dames, a historian featured the seventeenth-century Pawtucket, Wannalancet as the "last of the Sachems of the Merrimac River Indians." While this assertion does not explicitly argue for extinction, it does suggest the demise of Indian autonomy in claiming the end of an Indian polity and a way of life. The Dames followed up on this subject in 1902 by placing a tablet on a large boulder to commemorate this purported last leader.[12] In Groton, Connecticut, in the wake of the Pequot War,

"Sassacus was soon afterwards killed by the Mohawks, and the Pequot nation became extinct."[13] King Philip was scripted as the last of his race in a lengthy poem prepared for the celebration of the 250th anniversary of the settlement of Bristol, Rhode Island. Stanza eighteen recounted the story of the Wampanoag who finally took Philip's life (and called into question King Philip's "lastness"):

> His recreant arm the death-shot sped,
> Brought to the dust that royal head,
>   The peerless Metacom,
>   The last and foremost of his race!
> Where erst *he* sought a resting-place,
>   Our fathers found a home.[14]

Fair Haven, Connecticut, claimed Charles, who perished in the eighteenth century, as "the last sachem of the Quinnipiacs."[15] He also appeared anonymously in a Bridgeport, Connecticut, history as "the last sachem who had exercised authority over all the branches of the [Quinnipiac] tribe" after whose death "the tribe was broken up . . . It seems probable that the race is now entirely extinct."[16] Nequitimaug and Bartholomew, signatories to an eighteenth-century deed in Sharon, Connecticut, were claimed as "the last of the tribe who had their head quarters at the Indian Pond."[17] Although the vagueness of these and other claims is striking, all of them gave their readers and listeners full permission to assume that no Indian futures were to be made in those quarters.

But many other accounts scripted their "last" Indians as solitary (and presumably lonely) survivors who somehow managed to maneuver the tricky shoals of English colonialism and find their way into the nineteenth century, only then to succumb to the inevitable process of replacement. At least one "last" Indian in New England preceded the exceedingly famous *Last of the Mohicans* conjured into extinction by James Fenimore Cooper in his 1826 novel. An 1821 history of Bradford, Massachusetts, concluded its account of what was possibly a "considerable settlement of Indians" by informing readers that "the last of these who resided here, was Papahana, who lived to a great age, in a hut near the mouth of Johnson's creek; the people of the last generation, knew him well."[18] The rich theme of "lasting" found its place on a broad canvas of cultural expression in the nineteenth century: the message echoed in historical writing, poetry, theatrical production, portraiture, and other venues.[19]

The romantic impulse behind isolating the "last of the race" in cultural production has been noted by scholars such as Brian Dippie, Jill Lepore, William

Simmons, and Jane Van Norman Turano. Dippie has pointed out that "Romantic poets, novelists, orators, and artists found the theme of a dying native race congenial, and added those sentimental touches to the concept that gave it wide appeal."[20] Lepore has richly analyzed the phenomenal popularity of John Augustus Stone's theatrical production *Metamora; or, The Last of the Wampanoags*, from 1829 "until at least 1887 . . . [it] was one of the most widely produced plays in the history of nineteenth-century theatre." Lepore also argued that Americans fashioned their national identity separately from Englishness through their appropriation of Indians and Indianness in artistic performance.[21] Simmons has traced the visual depiction of New England Indians from the seventeenth into the nineteenth century, including solitary Indian females scripted as last survivors.[22] Turano has written about how the "romantic idea of 'the last of the _____' took hold, especially in New England."[23] Among the etchings, paintings, and portraits she discusses are George Loring Brown's pre-1841 painting *The Last of the Wampanoags*, and depictions of Dorcas Honorable, Simon Johnson, Martha Simon, Eunice Mauwee, and Esther Kenyon, all claimed in one way or another to be "lasts" (see Figure 18). All of the depictions of Indians as "vanishing" contributed to the fame of individuals claimed to represent the end of Indian histories as well as to the much larger ideological project of "lasting."

Few "last" Indians reached the national audience that entertained the prospect of Esther Kenyon, "the last of the Royal Narragansetts." William Cullen Bryant and Sydney Howard Gay featured her visage and story in their five-volume *A Popular History of the United States* (see Figure 19).[24] They introduced their sketch by explaining that it is "worthy of passing notice, that in that part of this old town of Westerly, now called Charlestown, reside all that are left, in New England, of the tribe of Narragansett Indians, though there is not among them one of pure Narragansett blood."[25] The 120 people they enumerated as Narragansett worked as laborers and basket makers, and retained their tribal government. However,

> no scalps now hang in his wigwam; no squaw pounds his corn; no deer bounds through the forest to fall by his swift arrows; no enemy lurks in its recesses to be followed with stealthy tread and brought to sudden death . . . The blood of this royal race flows now only through the veins of one living person—Esther, an old woman in Westerly, living apart from her people, the only representative of the ancient Narragansett chiefs, and though not quite of the pure blood, the purest living of the Narragansett tribe.[26]

This portrayal of Esther Kenyon that acknowledges the perpetuation of "the tribe of Narragansett" nonetheless claims that the purity of its royal blood

EUNICE MAHWEE.

Figure 18. *Eunice Mahwee.* Eunice Mahwee, claimed to be "The Last of the Pequods." Unknown engraver. From "The Last of the Pequods," *Scribner's Monthly: An Illustrated Magazine for the People* 2, no. 6 (October 1871): 573.

Esther, the last of the Royal Narragansetts.

Figure 19. *Esther, the Last of the Royal Narragansetts.* Esther Kenyon is claimed to be the "Last of the Royal Narragansetts." Unknown engraver. From William Cullen Bryant and Sydney Howard Gay, *A Popular History of the United States* (New York: Charles Scribner's Sons, 1882), 3: 116.

ended even before Esther Kenyon. Melding notions of culture and blood, this sketch implies that the end of the race can be imminently expected.

Although not featured in a prominent history of the nation, Martha Simon became one of the most famous last Indians of New England. According to historian Daniel Ricketson, "During the middle and even to the latter part of the last century, a few of the lingering remnant of the once noble possessors of this soil remained, retaining to the last their ancient form of habitation, the wigwam or a hut." He claimed that only Martha Simon remained when he wrote his history in the 1850s, residing in Dartmouth, Massachusetts, as "one solitary specimen of a full-blooded native. . . . She is the last of her race."[27] Her fame attracted the luminary Henry David Thoreau to drop in on Martha Simon, the "last full blooded Indian" of New Bedford. He paid her a visit in 1856 and recorded this observation in his journals: "To judge from her physiognomy, she might have been King Philip's own daughter. Yet she could not speak Indian, and knew nothing of her race."[28] And Martha Simon's fame in the middle of the nineteenth century also inspired the well-known artist Albert Bierstadt to paint her portrait in 1857, which he titled *The Last of the Narragansetts* (see Figure 20).[29] Bierstadt's claim that Martha Simon represented the last Narragansett in the 1850s is undone in the 1879 Bryant and Gay history, which features the then still-living Esther Kenyon as the "last of the Royal Narragansetts."[30] But that Martha Simon received such attention underscores not just non-Indian fascination with the idea of Indian demise but also their obsession with the modern project of purification.

Perusal of other local histories reveals a New England thickly populated by "last" Indians throughout the nineteenth century, and occasionally into the twentieth. These histories tell us that among the "last Indians" of New England were "full-bloods" Alexander Quabish and Sarah David (of Dedham) who (in keeping with the genre), it is implicitly argued, left no progeny.[31] In Andover, Massachusetts, "some people now living remember Nancy Parker, who is said to have been the last Indian," although she warranted only a footnote in a six-hundred-twenty-six-page history of the town.[32] A 1924 history of nearby Lawrence rescued her from this relative invisibility, featuring her in a short paragraph in the main body of the text: "She was remembered by the very old settlers as a tall, wild-looking, but harmless and industrious Indian woman, making her rounds among the farmers of the region."[33] In Windsor, Connecticut,

> Tradition says that Coggery, the last male survivor of the Podunks, lived in a swamp not far from the site of the church in the First Society, and while intoxicated murdered his squaw, and then stabbed himself to death. Thus ignobly

Figure 20. Albert Bierstadt, *Martha Simon, the Last of the Narragansetts,* 1857. Martha Simon in a portrait by the famed painter Albert Bierstadt. From the collection of the Millicent Library, Fairhaven, Massachusetts.

perished the last of the Tontonimo's tribe, the most fearless and warlike of the clans of Ancient Windsor.[34]

Coggery's swampy home and murderous behavior secured him his status as Indian just long enough for him to be conjured up to represent Indian demise. In Natick, a historian claimed Solomon Dexter as "the only full blooded survivor of the tribe, unless we reckon a small number, who reside in or near Mendon, in the County of Worcester, who occasionally visit this place, as the land of their ancestors."[35] Here is yet another bit of vagueness, but the message of imminent disappearance would have been clear enough to non-Indian audiences. The author of an 1858 history of Branford, Connecticut, states, "I remember the last of them . . . Lydia, in her lone wigwam. . . . I have seen her once or twice at the week day lecture, sitting at the door, and listening to the preacher . . . She died at the age of 68."[36] An Oxford, Massachusetts, account remembered "Collicump. So far as known, the last wild Indian living within the limits of the town."[37] In Paxton, Aaron Occum "was the last remnant and representative of this race."[38]

An 1841 Farmington, Connecticut, narrative concerned itself with the fate of local Indians even beyond the supposed "last" Indian whose story it told, offering a splendid example of the degeneracy narrative in the temporalities of race. A hundred years before, "the Indian boys were so many and so strong, that they were esteemed more than a match for the whites of the same age." Game becoming scarce about that time, they moved on to Stockbridge, Massachusetts, and afterward they joined the Brothertown at Oneida in New York. Locally,

> a fragment of the tribe remained behind till they became extinct. The last male of unmixed blood, was buried December 21st, 1820, the day which completed the second century from the landing at Plymouth Rock, while the only surviving female stood trembling by the grave. . . . After the removal of the greater portion of the tribe to Oneida, they often visited their friends and sepulchres behind, and on such visits would hold dances at the old burying place, and evening powows, and give splendid exhibitions of their agility and strength.[39]

Here, the distinction between local "extinction" and Indian survival as migrants elsewhere similarly performs the function of "vanishing" Indian prospects for the future in Farmington. The claimed "extinction" signified by the burial of "the last male of unmixed blood" on what is claimed as the exact date of the bicentennial of Plymouth Rock was passionately mourned by the sole remaining female who "stood trembling by the grave." In effect this passage argues that while Indians might possibly perpetuate themselves elsewhere, remaining in Farmington could only lead to Indian extinction. The migrants might occasionally return to visit and celebrate with their friends (until they "became extinct"), but such reunions took place in the Indian burial ground, thus powerfully symbolizing Farmington Indian history as dead and buried. Further, apparently the act of departing from Farmington secured the ongoing strength and agility of Indians: they displayed this vigor during their periodic visits home, in marked contrast with the alleged fate of their relatives, left behind to face extinction.

Other places also featured "last" Indians who remained anonymous. One of Windsor's historians heard from an acquaintance that when he was a boy, he had seen "an Indian woman . . . the last of the tribe once occupying the ground, at Wilson station."[40] A Roxbury history reflected on its neighboring town, and explained that "the very last descendant of the Natick town has gone."[41] The minister of Dorchester who preached a sermon remembered the story told by Mr. Everett about a Indian man who turned up once or twice a year to, "with plaintive wailings, cut away the bushes from an ancient mound, which, as he thought, covered the ashes of his fathers; and then went back,— a silent melancholy man, the last of a perished tribe."[42] And in Wilbraham, a historian loaded his "last" story with rich detail. Abandoned by Indians in the wake of King Philip's War,

> one Indian squaw alone remained after the settlement commenced. Her wigwam was on a little brook . . . and gave the name to "Wigwam Hill," on which [Pliny Merrick's] . . . house stands, and where the first meeting-house and parsonage were erected. No one knows her origin or end. Alone, the last of that mysterious race who had chased the deer over these fields, trapped the beaver in these streams, speared the salmon in these rivers, enjoyed the freedom of these hills, kindled their evening fires by these springs, and, as they smoked their pipe, beheld the western sky lighting up when the sun went down, as if with the smile of the Great Spirit and of the heroes who had fallen in battle, and buried their kindred under these trees, she lived solitary, the curiosity of the early settlers, harmless, quiet, meditative, seldom entering any dwelling, and providing for her own wants. At last even she disappeared.[43]

This sole female survivor is scripted as eking out a living on the margins in the wake of King Philip's War. How she provided for herself is left as mysterious as her identity in the text. Her identity as Indian is indelibly linked to the cultural practices of her ancestors, rooted in a static and immutable past that could have no future.

Whether famous or anonymous, the notion of the solitary Indian survivor captured non-Indian imaginations throughout the nineteenth century, and practically categorically relegated Indian descendants to being not so famous by denying them a future. This motif found its way into the center of the celebration of the two hundredth anniversary of the incorporation of Westfield, Massachusetts, which consisted of a familiar blend of return, reminiscence, and renewal that brought "the wandering sons and daughters back again to the old homestead." In common with many others, this celebration featured a parade:

> At eight o'clock the "Invincible Phalanx of Ancient and Honorables," headed by the last of the aborigines, made their merry march through the streets,— some of their costumes faithful copies of those of "ye olden time," others of a nondescript and ridiculous nature, which brought forth peals of laughter from the spectators; their big drum and ear-splitting fife furnished a fitting accompaniment to their laughable ride.[44]

The people of Westfield apparently could think of no better way of ushering in a flamboyant display of their authorship of history and distinguishing it from the long gone past than by dramatizing the motif of "the last of the aborigines." This ebullient display of apparent masquerade constituted a very public display of Indian "lastness" that echoed throughout the literary and cultural production of nineteenth-century New England. It was displays such as this one that characterized most future public celebrations of Indianness in New England. Actual New England Indians instead tended to be relegated to anonymity rather than celebration and fame.

Race, Blood, and Culture

On one level, it is the extreme localism of nineteenth-century histories that fueled the "last of the _____ " genre that worked so powerfully in the service of the degeneracy narrative that argued for Indian extinction. Few observers followed the lead of the special commissioner to the Indians, John Milton Earle, who conducted a fascinating census of Indian people in the mid-nineteenth century. His method was to identify any Indian person no matter where they were located, and he assumed that kinship formed the fundamental link between present Indian peoples, their ancestors, and their status as Indians. By his count, no doubt incomplete, there remained well over one thousand Indians in Massachusetts in more than a dozen separate political groups when he published his findings in 1861.[45] Unlike observers such as Earle, most local narrators failed (or refused) to understand the complex regional kinship networks that remained at the core of Indian identity in New England, despite the nearly complete Indian dispossession that English colonists accomplished. Thus, their field of vision narrowed to the local, and they refused to understand the persistence of Indian kinship and mobility on the landscape, not to mention their ongoing measured separateness as political entities. It was easier for these historians to argue for extinction since they only looked locally when they looked to notice Indians at all, and because even then they saw Indian lives (and Indian history) only incompletely.

But even more, the narrow focus on the local exacerbated the powerful formula that enabled the degeneracy narrative, which involved as its central themes, first, ideas about Indian "blood" as a signifier for race, and the notion that Indian blood, when diluted, meant the diminishment or loss of "race": "the degenerate relics of a few of these tribes, here and there, still retain something of [the color] . . . of their ancestors from whom they trace a questionable descent."[46] And second, it involved particular ideas about Indian cultures and their presumptive diminishment, which disclosed their assumptions about Indians and history. Henry David Thoreau summarized this view concisely: "The fact is, the history of the white man is a history of improvement, and that of the red man a history of fixed habits of stagnation."[47]

Putting the formula together, the New England calculation dictated that Indians are only Indians when they possess "pure" Indian blood, and even then Indianness diminishes in proportion to the failure of Indians to display certain characteristics, notably among them: possession of unbroken homelands, defense of those homelands through diplomacy and warfare, speaking their own language, living in wigwams, engaging in hunting and fishing (and sometimes agriculture), displaying mastery of Native pharmacology, and producing Native material culture through craft work such as basket weaving. Euro-American insistence that Indians exist within this basic and unchanging cultural repertoire both argued that Indians were only Indians when they dwelled in a static and immutable past, and provided Euro-Americans with an ideological framework for the denial of Indian persistence. Indians, this construct tells us, could never be modern.[48] The best Indians could do to measure up to this formula was to be a people numerically diminished within a falsely restrictive category ("pure-blooded Indians") who pursued a diminished form of Indianness that at the core only continued to express itself in such pursuits as herbalism, craft manufacture, and "wandering." Taken together, this formula produced a regionally specific stereotype of the New England Indian: the solitary, itinerant maker and seller of baskets and brooms, or purveyor of Native medicine, who is often depicted as a woman.[49] As solitary survivors were disproportionately cast as females, the prospects for maintaining any "purity of blood" were scripted as bleak indeed. The final calculation could only signal the ultimate and inevitable extinction of New England Indians and their Indianness.

This formulation stood at the center of the double bind of settler colonialism. Since the earliest colonial moments, the English had insisted that for Indians to remain among the English they needed to adopt the trappings of Englishness and eschew all practices Indian. Most starkly revealed in missionary ideology, this imperative argued for the illegitimacy of Indian lifeways in everything from their political autonomy to their most fundamental means of being in the world: religion, language, social organization, economics, and material culture. In turn, as New England Indians transformed themselves in the aftermath of the devastating consequences of English colonialism and more in alignment with these imperatives, the English and their descendants denied that these transformed Indians were legitimately Indian.

A historian of Shrewsbury, Massachusetts, expressed this mind-set perfectly in his 1847 text:

> The race, humbled to be sure, is now what it was at the beginning, so far as it regards their nature and disposition. Once an Indian always an Indian. He cannot be civilized. The attempt has been repeatedly made and as often failed. He is sure to die in the operation. The white man can (the cases are numerous where he has) become an Indian, not only in habit and conduct, but even in nature. On the other hand, civilization is death to the Indian. If he could be civilized, he would, when it were done, be an Indian no longer, and when he ceases to be an Indian, he ceases to live.[50]

Hewing to the temporalities of race, this passage holds out change as the exclusive purview of non-Indians. Indians are categorically depicted as static and incapable of change. Even when concerted measures had been taken to "civilize" Indians, they cannot survive in this state. "Civilization" for Indians meant literal or figurative death—there is no other conceivable outcome. They must conform to the degeneracy narrative in the temporalities of race. Non-Indians, on the other hand, could and frequently did "go Native" in "habit and conduct" and "even in nature." Alternatively, writers depicted Indian change as anomalous, such as in this passage: "[The Indians'] teachers had committed the common mistake of trying to graft advanced English customs on undeveloped natures; and the result was comical incongruity, like the blanket and silk hat of the modern Indian of the West."[51]

But it is the coupling of the insistence of stasis for Indians with notions of blood that secured the mythology of Indian extinction. By invoking the insidiously specious scientific argument that equated purity of blood with race,

New Englanders and other intruders in Indian America loaded additional freight onto the burden of Indian survival. Even as Indians continued to reckon membership in their communities through the time-honored system of kinship, New Englanders invoked the myth of blood purity as identity in denying Indian persistence.[52]

How did New Englanders write the racial script for themselves? Numerous local narrators evidenced the thinking about Anglo-Saxon superiority so broadly in circulation by the mid-nineteenth century, whether in explicitly or implicitly invoking racial hierarchies, as in this statement about Stockbridge Indians found in an 1869 history: "[Indians] adopted the usages of civilized life with astonishing facility. They did not, however leap at once from the depths of barbarism to the plane which the Saxon race had reached only after ages and generations of painful climbing."[53] This claim referenced the notion that each race must proceed through each of the hypothesized "stages of civilization" rather than skipping quickly to the apex, epitomized by Anglo-Saxons. In Norwich, "the Providence of God had prepared the way for the peaceable settlement of the Saxon race," in allowing Indians to destroy one another.[54] In an 1845 history, a commentator invoked the climatic theory of racial diversity to account for deviation from the unitary "blood" of biblical creation, resulting in "the tall lithe form of the American Indian, and our own fair race before whom those Indians have melted away."[55]

Many texts invoked notions about the supposed blood purity of their own New England ancestors and asserted a mounting superiority of New England and the nation. An orator at the dedication of the John Mason monument, somewhat apologetically dismissing the commonly invoked foibles of "the founders," juxtaposed this purity with the history of miscegenation that was the Spanish and French legacy:

> And if, in the clearer light of to-day, the founders of New England seem to have been at times fanatical, bigoted, and intolerant, let us remember with profound gratitude that we are largely indebted to the rigor of discipline and severity of training which these qualities engendered for the pure stock and distinctive New-England character of which we are so proud. The half-breed races of Spanish America on one side, and French Canada on the other, are illustrations of the social conditions from which the rigid morality of the Puritan delivered us.[56]

Later in his speech the orator laid out a confusing comparison of the outcome of the Pequot War ("an end of the Pequot name and nation") with the outcome of the invasion of Mexico (which "extinguished the Aztec race"): "The triumph of the Spaniard [Hernán Cortés] meant for the conquered subjugation and slavery. The triumph of the English Puritan meant freedom and peace."[57] It is suggested that the Aztecs became "extinguished" but that they also survived to be subjugated, enslaved, and presumably sexually dominated, which it is claimed produced a heinous mixed-blood social order. On the other hand, New England's conquest of the Pequot, which it is claimed resulted in their complete extinction, laid the basis for a racially pure and triumphant social order characterized by "freedom and peace." Another author took a different look at the continent "planted [by] two races of Europeans, with different natures and aims. The Dutchman, with his feudal institutions . . . [and] [t]he Englishman, with his deep religious zeal, [and] his love for popular liberty."[58]

Yet many other local historians reflected instead on the *admixture* that is implied in the very term *Anglo-Saxon*, perhaps nowhere in such a revealing way as in Warren, Rhode Island. An 1845 oration delivered there during the dedication of the new Baptist church contained a fascinating account of Welsh Baptists. Beginning with the premise that "the Welsh race, from which the ancestors of this church sprung, are the only pure descendants of the ancient Britons. . . . They were a wild aboriginal race, probably the descendants of Gomer, the eldest son of Japeth, who was the youngest son of Noah."[59] The orator provided rich elaboration on this theme:

> Wave after wave of foreign population poured in upon the native race, and became intermixed with the British stock. The most numerous and successful of these invading hordes, were the *Angles*, a valiant race of Germanic origin from the vallies [sic] of the Elbe. . . . By this juncture of the Angles with the Saxons, and both together being grafted on what remained of the original British in England, was laid the foundation of modern English institutions, and the basis of the Anglo-Saxon character.
>
> The unconquered remnants of the ancient British were crowded step by step, by each successive wave of foreign immigration that swept over from the Continent, till they were entirely driven out of England, and took a final refuge in the sequestered vallies and mountain fastnesses of Wales . . . Here these relics of the original Cambrian race, the only pure descendants of the British stock, known by the more modern name of Welsh, have lived for 1400 years, an unmixed and homogeneous people, leaving behind them among the Anglo-Saxon conquerors of their former territory, but a small portion of their blood, and but few distinct traces of their national character.[60]

The orator continued to echo the language of blood, mixing, purity, and race in following the subsequent fate of the "race." Following the "disappearance of the British" from England came "an almost entire extinction of Christianity among the compound relics, which formed the Anglo-Saxon race." Ferocious conflicts ensued between those devoted to "the barbarous religion of these heathen invaders" and the remaining "British Christians."[61] In the end, "the remnants of the old British race" found refuge in secluded areas of Wales, and almost all the Anglo-Saxons "became nominally Christians."[62] And "from that period onward till the death of Llewellyn, the last prince of the British blood, in 1724" the history of the "Cambro-British people is involved in much obscurity."[63] This whole reflection on race could be rewritten to narrate many of the experiences of Indians, but with one crucial difference: even though Llewellyn is claimed as the "last prince of the British blood" and unlike countless "last" Indians, his race did *not* become extinct, but rather it was perpetuated and transplanted to Warren, Rhode Island, where now resided the only pure descendants of the ancient Welsh Baptists. How could this be? Powered by the narrative of progress, mixture and change ensure an ever better future for this race.

Three and a half decades later, an orator in Lynn, Massachusetts, testified about mixture as well. He pondered the fact that New Englanders boasted of the "Saxon blood" they had in their veins, and wondered whether it had been "changed or diluted." He declared that "here in New England, reasoning only from a climatic standpoint, one might conclude that it is retained in a rather improved condition." Centuries before, the "Saxon race," though rude and barbarous, had formed a sturdy character on the "frigid Shores of the Baltic," steeped in an stalwart devotion to "wild freedom and manly aspiration, with ambition running, perhaps, into tribal insolence." Then followed the barbarous Roman invasion of the British Isles and "the Saxons came, fraternized with the Britons," and ultimately dominated:

> The blood of the two races intermingled, and the controlling power of the Saxon was presently manifest, the benign influences of Christianity intervening to temper and elevate. Then down through generations, not essentially changed by the Norman intermingling, rectifying and warming, flowed this heroic northern blood to the New England settlers; and from them, have we ourselves received what is perhaps our richest possession—a possession which has done so much to make England and America what they are.

This narrator's articulation of the racial mixture inherent in the concept of "Anglo-Saxon" exposes the central contradiction of racial purity.[64] Rather than the stark separation of pure races, he surveys a long history of mixture. And for the New English and American descendants of the Anglo-Saxons, this is a mixture of blood that *improves* the stock.

Here and elsewhere, authors drew upon a discourse of blood, purity, mixing, and race in broad circulation that created a stark double standard in the contest for modernity and endurance. With regard to the temporalities of race, the requirements of blood purity and change as criteria of Indianness narrate Indian degeneracy, whereas for non-Indians, mixture invigorates the race and change is inextricable from the progress narrative that signals their difference and superiority. Rather than reconstructing a lengthy history of mixing, Charles Francis Adams declared that "for two centuries New England was remarkable for its preservation of the race of original settlers comparatively free from admixture with any other. This has now ceased in a measure. A very large portion of the laboring population is now of Celtic and not of Saxon origin." This mixture, destined only to increase in the future, did not trouble Adams, because public education might serve to fuse society and stave off fissures potentially produced by "the mere fact of diversity."[65] Although Adams is not explicit on this point, his formulation suggests that the "admixture" he has in mind does not involve actual couplings across "racial" lines, but rather the fact of other ethnic minorities immigrating to New England localities. Others acknowledged "mixture." A narrator in Barre, Massachusetts, drew upon John Gorham Palfrey's *History of New England* in reflecting on the remarkable homogeneity of the population. And even though in Barre, "the blood got a little mixed" with that of the Scots-Irish who arrived in the eighteenth century, "it is by no means certain that the Scotch-Irish infusion did not invigorate it."[66]

Concerns over the implications of immigration, such as those expressed here, intensified over the course of the nineteenth century along with the surge in numbers. Even so, many narrators reconciled such demographic changes, as did a historian of Worcester in 1884. Some, he tells the audience, have viewed surging immigration with "alarm," but he believes the wave of foreigners, especially those of "the Irish race . . . which began about 1830, has enriched Worcester with its abundant tide."[67] How else would the railroads have been built so speedily?[68] The arrival of the Irish among the English benefited both, and on a basis of equality, according to this narrator.[69] More broadly speaking, he speculated:

> Supposing the entire mass to be fused, the Celtic and Teutonic blood, the Latin and the Norman, would be mingled in much the same proportions as they were in the veins of the original English settlers. The American of the future, supposing present forces to continue, and all white elements to fuse equally, would be almost as much an Anglo-Saxon as the America of 1820.[70]

At the two hundred and fiftieth anniversary of the incorporation of Dedham, Massachusetts, a toast to *"Our Naturalized Fellow-Citizens!* [emphasis in the original]" prompted a musing on immigration. The respondent reflected on the foreign origins of the founders of the Republic, then proclaimed they had the foresight "to perceive that its destiny and mission was to be the home of a more comprehensive nationality than any that the world had yet seen, in which all *civilized* races should merge to form the mightiest people of all time."[71]

The discourse of "mixture" employed by some writers did not necessarily suggest that people of diverse backgrounds actually made unions and reproduced. Many, like the Worcester orator who pondered the implications of Irish immigration, can be taken to comment on a shift away from New English homogeneity that did not necessarily entail "mixing" of the demographic sort. Instead, some authors pondered the emergence of an ethnically diverse nation. Tracking changes in the population of Westerly, Rhode Island, in 1878, one observer noted that the past three decades had witnessed tremendous shifts because manufactures had lured Europeans to fill jobs when New Englanders could not meet the demand. This "new and strange population" transformed Westerly: "We have really become a polyglot people. Here we have Indians, Yankees, Negroes, English, Irish, Scotch, Germans, French, and some from other countries."[72] This method of categorization that (unusually) included Indians among those present and accounted for also asserts native-born New Englanders (Yankees) alongside other racial and ethnic groups. In effect, this argues for their stark separateness as well as the impossibility for Indians, African Americans, or the equivalent of foreign nationals to be included in the category "New Englander." One could hardly suppose that marriages and reproduction could ensue across these seemingly rigid boundaries. At a reunion in Rochester, Massachusetts, the President of the Day welcomed the massive crowd by asserting "irrespective of nationality and of descent—. . . irrespective of political preferences or denominational difference, we come as Americans." To punctuate the point, he embedded a little rhyme in the middle of this sentiment:

> For Saxon, or Dane, or Norman, we,
> Teuton or Celt, whatever we be[73]

Conspicuously absent here are Indians and African Americans, but he did invite the Irish to the banquet. More to the point, even while he claimed such categories did not matter, his thinking about them still prompted him to break into verse in contemplating the nation. And next to the stage came the orator of the day, who began by noting that "before me are scores through whose veins Pilgrim blood is coursing."[74]

Not everyone offered such assessments. During the celebration of the national centennial, people gathered in Sheffield, Massachusetts, heard a lengthy set of reflections on race and the nation. The orator of the day declared himself "zealous in the defence of the rights of every man, of whatever race or color," yet he did not go so far as to "believe that the races of men are equal in all those qualities which the highest type of manhood shows." Whether or not it be fair, he explained that the races themselves made such distinction, "and, so long as they remain distinct and separate, they will continue with the lines plainly and sharply drawn between them." History has demonstrated, he continued, that "the Anglo-Saxon leads all in the progressive march of nations."[75] And these Anglo-Saxons "became the founders of a nation, destined at the outset to amaze and startle the world," drawing "refugees from nearly every nation in Europe." Fleeing Europe from the eighteenth century onward, "here came Germans, Netherlanders, Irish, Scots, Huguenots, Swedes, and Moravians, losing their nationalities in the formation of a new one."[76] He continued to mount his case for the superiority of the nation as New Englanders replaced barbarism with civilization throughout his oration, but toward the end he took a confusing turn (considering his earlier remarks): "This nation is cosmopolitan. No other nation in the world, in this respect, resembles it. The crossing of the higher types of mankind has been found to increase the vigor of its physical and intellectual growth. The result of such commingling of the races and nationalities is not within the ken of human vision."[77]

Remarkable overall in the many and varied reflections that connected race, region, and nation is the strain of argument that held that mixture "invigorated" or "improved" or "enriched" the dominant race, an argument we would do well to juxtapose with the notion of "mixed" Indian blood (about which, more later in this chapter). Frequently such mixture is overlooked in favor of claims about the racial purity (and superiority) of Anglo-Saxons, which elides their actual impurity, and the speciousness of blood arguments in general. (After all, even if one were to accept the *idea* of purity, how can one ever be sure, lacking precise documentation commencing with the beginning of time?)[78] Even though texts exhibit tensions over the notion of mixture in the dominant race, many writers are able to elevate mixture—whether in the inclusion of ethnic groups supposedly kept homogeneous within themselves, or even through their "miscegenation"—as *improving* the white race. For Indians, in contrast, it is argued that "mixture" resulted in *degeneration* rather than improvement.

Still, the New England obsession with blood trumped other possible considerations, and its legacy is etched deeply. The preoccupation with New England "blood" and genealogy (read: kinship) is richly evident in the very existence of the Mayflower Society and the Daughters of the American Revolution, which carefully track claims to membership in these exclusive "originary" groups. It is even more interestingly revealed in the massive genealogical craze in New England, possibly nowhere more so than in the concerted efforts of Bradford family descendants to locate ancestors everywhere and anywhere—powered more recently by their own Web site that embraces Y-DNA testing to extend their reach.[79] These imperatives have deep roots in the nineteenth century, where genealogical considerations permeate local accounts. In Southampton, Massachusetts, even though the towns' residents had no famous people or events to relate in their history, "the Puritan blood flows in our veins. We claim a common descent with the Winthrops, the Hookers and the Stoddards of more favored towns. *Our* ancestors helped to plant inestimable civil and religious institutions."[80] Among those gathered in Barnstable, Massachusetts, in 1839 to celebrate the second centennial of the English arrival at Cape Cod, famed historian John Gorham Palfrey asked who "has not blood in his veins from this our copious Barnstable fountain . . . here we are . . . a band of brothers and sisters,—of cousins at the furthest,—seated, a widely-gathered family meeting, on the broad and hospitable ancestral hearthstone."[81] At a reunion of the Cushman family in 1855, many of them strangers to one another, those who had assembled heard that there was a time "when the blood which flows in our veins was centered in a single household near the spot where we are now gathered."[82] The descendants scattered and here, "strangers looking upon each other for the first time, yet one family!"[83] Here, it is claimed, the blood that flows in the veins of these Americans from far and wide was the *first* to be found in this very spot, which might be fruitfully juxtaposed with stories about Indians and blood: the whole enterprise of the "last of the ____" is concerned with locating the very spot where could be claimed the *last* Indian. For non-Indians, this claimed first spot is made to initiate a narrative of origins and progress that fanned out across the continent, but for Indians that spot signified the end.

As these passages suggest, the rhetoric of blood conveyed deep meaning about the identity of New Englanders and the claims they could make, and a lengthy response to a toast to Rose Standish made by Rev. E. E. Hale at the "consecration" of the Myles Standish monument richly—and humorously—exposes the symbolism inherent in this construct:

> I am in the midst, say, in round numbers, of 562 descendants of the Pilgrims, myself being the only one among them in whose veins there runs not a drop of

Pilgrim blood. (Laughter.) In the last Pilgrim celebration that I attended . . . I chanced to be in the society of a venerable matron who had well informed herself in the history [of the landing] . . . and I ventured to say that my only plea for Pilgrim ancestry was based on my hope that it would prove that my venerated ancestor, Madam Pepper, belonged to a Pilgrim family. . . . I said I knew she was not in the Mayflower, but I hoped it might yet prove she was in the Fortune, or in the Ann. But I found jesting on this subject dangerous. With a look of perfect iciness she asserted that could not be; that no Pepper ever came over in the Ann, the Fortune, or the Mayflower. It is dangerous joking on such subjects here, sir. They all have their genealogy,—not in the first pages of their Bibles; no,—they have it in their heads.[84]

Thus did the Reverend Hale poke fun at the deadly seriousness with which New Englanders traced their blood and imbued it with meaning. His story both amused his Pilgrim-blooded audience and encapsulated a symbolic construct of priority and purity rooted in ideas about New England families and descent. The bulk of his response expounded on his claim that "the truth is, the women who came out in the Mayflower solved the problem of emigration," for all prior attempts at "settlement" in North America (north of Mexico) by the English, French, and Spanish he declared failures. Until after the Puritan ascendancy,

even Jamestown was a failure . . . [because] the men came over alone. . . . They returned to England because they had not brought their homes with them; because their Rose Standishes stayed at home. . . . It was the women of Plymouth who made the colony of Plymouth the first permanent colony. . . . It is in the transfer of homes that emigration and colonization have succeeded in America.[85]

Such a scenario made possible claims of blood purity so central to the New England narrative of firsting and lasting. Women possess procreative bodies, and their presence forestalled the heinous racial intermixture that horrified New Englanders about other places. The racial formation of New English colonialism secured the region as a white place free from "miscegenation," where subsequent "mixture" improved rather than degenerated the race.

An anecdote found in a Milford, Connecticut, Thanksgiving sermon offers additional testimony about the stakes in stories about blood purity in New England. It noted that Roger Sherman, a signer of the Declaration of Independence, descended from a local minister. He had been apprenticed to a shoemaker in his youth. According to the story, during a heated debate in the First Continental Congress,

John Randolph of Virginia in whose veins was Indian blood, cried out, in his shrill piping voice for the purpose of insulting him, that he "should like to know what the gentleman from Connecticut, when he left the cobbler's bench for that Hall, did with his leather apron;"—received for answer:—"Sir, I cut it up to make moccasins for the descendants of Pocahontas!"[86]

Sherman could apparently think of no better way to defend the purity and honor of himself—and Connecticut—than by retorting with an insult steeped in charges of miscegenation. Sherman's purported accusation that Randolph descended from Pocahontas's people aimed to plot the deep differences between New England and the South rooted in racial formations. Although the Milford narrative failed to point it out, the Randolph family—and other older families in Virginia—proudly proclaimed their descent from Indians, which might readily disarm Sherman's furious assault.[87]

For white New Englanders, the project of tracing their blood back to the Puritan beginning and establishing its purity stood in contrast to their depictions of Indians. Instead of origins and purity, they scripted Indian peoples as impure and dwindling rapidly toward extinction:

From the report of a committee on Indian affairs in Rhode Island, made to the General Assembly in 1833, "it appears that the whole number of all grades and conditions of the once numerous and warlike tribes of Narragansetts (the only tribe now existing in the State), was one hundred and fifty-eight. Of this number, only seven were of genuine Narragansett blood, and several of these have since died; fourteen were half-blood, and one hundred and fifty-eight of different grades, less than half-blood, with twenty foreigners, who have no connection with the tribe, except by marriage and other promiscuous intercourse."[88]

The strict blood accounting performed by such governmental officials cast suspicion on Indians by insisting that only "full-blooded" Indians "were of genuine" blood—in this case, Narragansett. Once "numerous and warlike," they are scripted as diminishing and dubious. Intermarriage with "foreigners" is characterized as "promiscuous intercourse" rather than "improvement" or "invigoration" or "enrichment." Presumably citing the same report (although it provided different numbers), another Rhode Island account from twenty-five years later continued that

[n]ot a pure-blooded Indian now remains among them. Modified by civilization, the tribe has at times put on a little of the hope and vigor of true life. Indeed, the aboriginal life has almost wholly disappeared. A subtle decay seemed to be in the Indian nature, and it is only too evident that this remnant of the hordes of the forest must soon follow their fathers to the land of forgetfulness.[89]

Such language, in common circulation, sought to plot two vastly different trajectories for the Indian and non-Indian populations of New England according to the temporalities of race. The construct relied upon the application of completely opposite criteria for establishing race: In the case of white New Englanders, the possession of any drop of "Puritan blood" enabled one to claim membership in that special category, and the problem of "purity of blood" was elided. In the case of Indians, any "admixture" of other "blood" *diminished* their Indianness in the New England imaginary, and "mixing" invalidated Indian claims to their identity: "There are none of unmixed blood remaining in my native town to-day. Half-breed and quarter-breeds gain a precarious living by fishing, or picking cranberries in the bogs around Ponkipog Pond; but the aborigines of two centuries ago have departed, and forever."[90]

Compare these constructs not just to claims about drops of Puritan blood but also to the embrace of all who could draw any connection to the town of Hadley, Massachusetts, during its two hundredth anniversary celebration: "The large hospitalities of the occasion rightly embrace and welcome all who, by descent or intermarriage, by blood or by residence, from far or near, are related not merely to the geographic but the human Hadley of two hundred years ago."[91] New England Indians could never expect such expansive definitions of inclusiveness of their own communities to pass muster with non-Indian New Englanders.

In effect, what such claims about New Englishness assert is an implicit "one drop" rule for themselves. Any claim to a "drop" of New English or Puritan blood, any vague connection one could make to the "Puritan fathers" entitled the claimant to membership in the New English race—a race that is asserted as pure even while it is acknowledged by many to be forged in mixture. The vagueness of these claims might be fruitfully put alongside the vagueness of "lasting" claims made about Indians, as they move in completely opposite directions. And this fascinating parallel to the "one-drop" rule for African Americans—which relegated them to a pollution narrative that subjected them to slavery and racial discrimination should a claim of even a single drop of African blood be asserted—must also be contrasted to New English requirements for Indianness. In that construct, *any* "mixture" of Indian "blood" with any other "blood" renders the individual *less* Indian, until the possibility of acknowledging the Indianness of New England Indians vanishes in the New English imaginary. What we have here, then, is a theory of racial purity built on the fact of impurity that is used to call into question the Indianness of Indian people in the present, and their likelihood to survive as a people into the future.

Descent

An 1855 history of Medford, Massachusetts, offers a revealing illustration of how the idea of "purity of blood" governed New English interpretations of Indian prospects for the future: "The last Indian here was 'Hannah Shiner,' a full blood, who lived with 'Old Toney,' a noble-souled mulatto man . . . Hannah was kind-hearted, a faithful friend, a sharp enemy, a judge of herbs, a weaver of baskets, and a lover of rum."[92] Hannah's assumed "blood quantum" qualified her for Indianness (as did her pharmacological knowledge and basket-making skills, and, perhaps, her purported fondness for rum, which also fit within stereotypical ideas about Indians). But even though she had a mate, and may even have had children, those children could not be counted as "Indian" because the mixed ancestry of their father would have diluted their blood.

The problem of descent found perhaps its boldest statement in an 1877 history of Block Island. Near the end of a chapter on Indians appears a sketch of the Church family. It begins with a discussion of Peter Church, "a full blood Indian, [who] fought for the English, in the old French War . . . [whose] grave is in the colored burial ground." Next came his daughter Mary, who "worked in different families," and who bore six children all but one now deceased. Mary's children also reproduced, although they were "now widely scattered." Two of these children, "very respectable half-breeds, females, from Stonington, visited the Island in the summer of 1876."[93] Isaac Church, Peter Church's grandson and Mary Church's son,

> is still living, at the age of eighty-eight, as he informs the writer. He can give but little information of his ancestry—he does not know who was his father, but remembers well his mother who was more easily identified. If his father were not an Indian his mother was surely a full-breed, and *vice versa*, for his hair and features are thoroughly Manissean. . . . It is easy to predict that many will be at his [funeral], and that many a tender recollection of "Uncle Isaac" will be cherished by the children now living, who in maturer years will speak of him as the last and worthy representative of the ancient Manissean lords of the soil, who will soon be known only in history.
>
> The descendants of Isaac Church are too far removed from aboriginal blood to be classed with Indians.[94]

This sketch of the Church family provides a literary smoking gun—Isaac Church's descendants are "too far removed from aboriginal blood" to be counted as Indian. This flatly proclaims the mechanisms behind the ideology of disappearance through blood mythology. Leaving aside whether Isaac Church did not know about his ancestry or merely declared not to know in the face of probing questions from outsiders, this depiction argues that his descendants could not be counted as Indians because of an asserted distance from "aboriginal blood." Even though Isaac himself "looked" Indian because of the appearance of his hair and eyes, this construct suggested that his descendants failed the test of blood purity—a construct invented by non-Indians whose interests it served. Few such blatant statements appear in the historical literature, but their proxies are abundantly distributed in the cultural production of nineteenth-century New England.

The blood distance that purportedly disqualified Isaac Church's descendants from their Indianness did not, however, according to this historian, affect Isaac's nephew Aaron, the son of Isaac's brother Titus. Aaron's Indianness can be detected in his *actions:* "*Aaron Church* . . . has left a reputation that indicates his descent from the murderers of Capt. Oldham."[95] The mysterious murder of the shady fur trader John Oldham served as the pretext for the military excursions of the Pequot War. In 1830, Aaron allegedly participated in a conspiracy to capture a ship that he had signed onto, with the coconspirators killing two crew members. In his attempt to flee with his booty, Church encountered rough seas, and "the pirate . . . went down with his ill-gotten gain."[96] We cannot know whether this historian made the Oldham connection in flight of rhetorical fancy, but if he meant his assertion literally, he argued for the biological transmission of the behavioral practice of piracy. And he suggested that such purported propensities could be biologically transmitted across nearly two centuries, in contrast to the insistence that the Indianness of Isaac Church's descendants terminated in a stark break at a particular genealogical juncture.

Such stories about descent appeared even in places such as Mashpee, Massachusetts, whose continuing Indian presence is frequently acknowledged in nineteenth-century historical accounts. In an 1860 history, the author lamented, "alas! The day has passed when . . . 'the conversion of the poor heathen Indians'—can be reached. They are almost extinct. . . . If *any* drop of their blood still lingers in the veins of any, let them be kindly dealt with at least." According to this historian, "the last of the race, of purely Indian blood, was ISAAC SIMON. . . . The Indian language, and the pure Indian blood, extinct, a promiscuous race of colored people, in diminishing numbers, now constitute the population of Mashpee."[97] Here the mixture of blood is reputed to be the result or the cause of promiscuity, and perhaps, it is implied, that mixture itself is a factor in Indian diminishment. The members of this "promiscuous race of colored people, in diminishing numbers" did not speak an Indian language (at least not to the historian), and could barely be counted as

Indians because of the strict requirements of cultural stasis and blood purity. Similarly in Dudley, Massachusetts, there remained "a small tract of land near the great pond, which is still occupied by a few degraded descendants of the original proprietors,"[98] and in Newburyport there could be found "a few poor and degenerate Indians, the last of their race, wasted by the pestilence, and destroyed by the hand of savage enmity," where long ago they "sought the protection of the coming sovereigns of the land."[99] In contrast, a historian of Worcester observed, "Fortunately, none of the posterity of the Indian *here* remain, to contrast their degradation with the lofty and in some points noble character of the ancient tribes."[100]

These discussions of Indian descent are intended to bring under suspicion the legitimacy of Indianness by calling into question the possibility of its purity. In Mashpee, the concept of "promiscuity" is evoked without exploration. Elsewhere can be found the concept of "questionable descent," as in the Leicester, Massachusetts, passage quoted earlier in which the author referred to the "degenerate relics" of some tribes that "still retain something of the color, and much of the habits of thriftlessness of the ancestors from whom they trace a questionable descent." This historian dispatched local Indians as long since gone: Polly Johns had died there five decades before, this author claimed, "the last person in town having Indian blood in her veins."[101] An 1853 address delivered in Dudley made reference to "a small tract of land near the great pond, which is still occupied by a few degraded descendants of the original proprietors of these fruitful hills and valleys."[102] Promiscuous, questionable, degenerate, degraded—all of these concepts cast suspicion on Indian survivors whom local observers attempted to narrate out of existence as Indians.

New Englanders invoked the notion of descent for themselves as well as for Indians with a completely different analytical outcome, one that advanced their own claims of progress. As articulated at the Rochester, Massachusetts, bicentennial celebration, what better reason for Americans to gather than "to the contemplation of the people . . . which, in the same short period of time, subdued a continent of barbarism, revealed the majestic resources of our country and advanced our free republic abreast of those grand old nations of Europe from whom it is our privilege to trace an *honorable* descent."[103]

An address delivered at the celebration of the two hundred and fiftieth year of the incorporation of Topsfield, Massachusetts, in 1851 offers a pithy commentary on matters of descent that is worth quoting at length:

> It may, perhaps, be expected that I shall touch upon the question of progress and degeneracy,—and revive, if not rashly attempt, to settle that long-agitated

dispute—the contest for superiority between the ancients and the moderns. In the great elements of mind and character, has Topsfield advanced or declined as it has grown older? . . . But the same intellectual and moral elements are here still. The blood which warmed those rural sages and heroes, yet flows, it is to be hoped, undebased, in your veins. . . . I love to cherish an undoubting faith in humanity, and in progress. I look not at individual cases of degeneracy and degradation—such have always existed. I make no reference to whole families, once prosperous and respectable, now ignoble or extinct. So it has ever been. We must look at man, as he appears in the great mass, and in the long run,— and then we find his career to be ever onward and upward.[104]

Here, the orator lays out for the people of Topsfield the connection between the superiority of progress and modernity on the one hand, versus implicit inferiority and degeneracy of the ancients on the other. While Indians are nowhere directly implicated in this passage (and we can be fairly certain that the author did not include Indians or other people of color under the rubric of "man"), the language of intellectual and moral traits transmitted through blood can be extrapolated to Indians. Topsfield people could be afforded the blood that produced "rural sages and heroes," and could hope that this blood remained "undebased, in your veins." Further, Topsfield people might witness individual instances of "degeneracy and degradation," or even families "once prosperous and respectable, now ignoble or extinct," as has always been the case. In spite of such individual cases, for non-Indians, the grand trajectory of "onward and upward" would not be affected. Such degeneracy is scripted as routinely exceptional for non-Indians, while it is asserted as normative for Indians. Importantly, this historian links "degeneracy" not just with the "ignoble" but also with extinction.

The same history that declared an end to the Indianness of Isaac Church's progeny offered up a different and equally intriguing commentary on descent in a story about a local pond:

For fifteen years it [Fort Island Pond] has been the home of a resident whose age is not known, but his race is notorious. He is evidently a descendant of ancestors living here while King Philip and his warriors were scalping the white people of the main-land. He is seen only once or twice a year, and when seen a few years ago by a sturdy young man, the latter hastened to the house faint and trembling and tried to describe the "old settler." During the summer of 1876, he was seen again, and from the description given of him, his appropriate name seems to be, the *Fort Island Pond Serpent*. The above facts are easily authenticated. The serpent is evidently a large, old, black water-snake, entirely harmless, and as shy as the Indians who possibly worshiped his forefathers.[105]

The dramatic tension developed in this passage leads the reader to believe that at any moment a skulking Indian is about to spring from the landscape of Fort Island Pond. But no. This historian used Indians as a metaphorical device in informing his readers that a black water snake might occasionally be encountered near the pond, and his use of this device is richly evocative of nineteenth-century thinking. Like Indians, snakes are regarded as a "race," and a "notorious" race at that. Like Indians, snakes are found lurking in the wilderness and are to be feared as dangerous and violent. Like Indians, these snakes are portrayed as descendants stretching back to the time of King Philip's War. And like Indians, this narrative suggests that a single remaining representative of the snake's race could be sighted in 1876, the bicentennial year of King Philip's War. Still, in the end this narrative tells the reader that both snakes and Indians are "harmless" and "shy," perhaps suggesting that even if they are harmless, Indians could be sneaky. For Indians, the snake's ancestors might even have held a venerated place in their religion.

Lasting

> To a citizen of this modern town, it will not seem improbable when we suggest that the last deer of Rhode Island was shot on the margin of Wallum Lake. . . . The prowess of our factory boys now manifests itself in a terrible slaughter of chipmunks and pigeon woodpeckers, it may be with the same old iron bound smooth bore that their ancestors used, to shoot Nipmucs and black bears.[106]

Stories about "last" Indians shared the stage with other "lasts" in nineteenth-century local accounts, as in this little snippet that appears toward the end of an 1856 Burrillville, Rhode Island, account. Here, the author unambiguously links modernity with the extinction of animal species such as deer—and imminently, one supposes, chipmunks and pigeon woodpeckers as well. He also draws a parallel between the talented young marksmen of the factory and their ancestors. Perhaps these boys are engaging in the apparently senseless slaughter of birds and small animals with the same weapons their forefathers used to shoot Indians and bears, which is not specifically analyzed as a terrible slaughter in this passage but rather as a distant and entirely expected—even noble and necessary—outcome in the origins of modernity. Underlying this passage are assumptions about the incongruity of the denizens of the wilderness—Indians and wildlife—coexisting in the modern order. On the previous page the author had straightforwardly explained that "the Indians have disappeared, and the whirr of the spindle and the din of the factory bells tell us the Anglo Saxons rule here."[107] Also mentioned in the concluding passages are other vanishing or vanished creatures, such as wolves and herring, though Burrillville retained the now incongruous place-names "Herring Pond" and "Wolf Hill." This history of slaughter culminated in the rich landscape of factories and a set of puzzling place-names. "Nothing remains of the old, save the rocky hill, whose thunder splintered battlements seem to fortify the village, and the name the Indians gave to the river and the valley."[108]

In the broadest sense, such stories about "lasts" participate in the degeneracy narrative implied in the temporalities of race. The extinction of species that Indians relied on for their livelihood fueled the historical rupture of purification on the landscape. Like the Burrillville history, an 1878 history of Ridgefield, Connecticut, links stories about change with the retention of Algonquian names for a mountain and several ponds, such as "Mammenusquah, Nisopack, Aokeets, and Umperqauge. There are no Indians at present living in the town, except one who has learned the mason trade and has married a white woman."[109] Several pages of thick description of the landscape follow this observation, and the author informs the reader that "there were formerly deer, bears, wolves, panthers, and wild-cats in our woods, and beaver in our ponds, but they are now extinct."[110] Observations about the depletion of species can be found in other local accounts. In Topsfield, "by the bounty occasionally offered for the destruction of wolves, we perceive that it was long before the wilderness, here, ceased to be a *howling* one."[111] In Salisbury, Connecticut, readers were informed that "the last of Bruin's race, ever found upon our soil, was killed by Richard P. Stanton . . . in the winter of 1821."[112]

These outcomes helped set modernity in motion for New Englanders and were not to be lamented. In contrast, local narrators periodically used a now obsolete sense of "extinction," one that referred to institutions or cultural practices, to delineate less salubrious changes that had transpired: "The Topsfield fisheries gradually declined, and are now, alas! extinct."[113] The environmental onslaught thus brought both favorable and unfavorable transformations. Such changes contributed to economic decline in Falmouth, Massachusetts, which

> was once famous for its whaling fleet and shipping interest. . . . Among the more notable [ships constructed here] are the Uncas, Awashonk, Pocahontas, Hobomuk, William Penn, Bartholomew Gosnold, Pomonett, George Washington, Brunette, and Enterprise. With the decline of whaling, the building of vessels also became extinct.[114]

Some of the intriguing set of names attached to ships built in Falmouth pay tribute to (mostly) New England Indians, perhaps subtly acknowledging the importance of Indians in transmitting knowledge about whaling to New

Englanders as well as to their presence on whaling ships throughout the duration of the industry.[115] This linkage also unwittingly attached Indians to a different process of "extinction" than the larger project of "vanishing" Indians.

Local narrators found the metaphor of lasting useful in thinking about the histories of their places, and in doing so, they participated in the construction of a narrative of modernity for New England in subtle ways. Writers variously took note of institutions, cultural practices, events, and individuals that signified modernity. In a Lowell, Massachusetts, history, it was asserted that "ere long the natives wholly disappeared . . . and in 1726 their right to the land east of that river [the Concord] became extinct," which purported event stood for the securing of "modern" property relations.[116] A Bridgewater, Connecticut, history took note of "the last trial in the State of Connecticut for the crime of witchcraft,"[117] and in Newton, Massachusetts, "the last remnant of slavery was Tillo (Othello), a life-long encumbrance of the estate of General William Hull."[118] In Truro, a historian paused to remember "Hector the last slave."[119] These narrators took pains to point out the ending of institutions and cultural practices that stood in opposition to modernity, thus purifying their histories and landscapes. Witchcraft gradually fell into disuse in the colonial period, and the gradual abolition of slavery was accomplished beginning in the early nineteenth century throughout New England. While all sorts of practices, peoples, and creatures had become extinct, New England as a cultural symbol of modernity pressed on. Indeed, ending prosecution of witchcraft and the institution of slavery helped secure that very modernity, and in the case of slavery, in stark contrast to the South.

The use of the extinction construct also extended to non-Indian people. Perhaps most telling is its use in an 1857 history of Greenwich, Connecticut. Following a discussion of the strong local Tory sentiment during the Revolution is a passage that plots the fate of Tory descendants. Of the thirty-four families identified as Tory, only twelve remained. "The immediate descendants of the others are but few, and in many instances the race is quite extinct. There seems to have been a doom upon them and their descendants."[120] Like Indians, Tories were incongruent with modernity; their descendants were doomed to extinction, and their extinction helped the process of purification implicit in the narration of modernity. Tories stood in for the degenerate practice of monarchy in the imaginary, thus signifying ancient practices left behind with the stark break of the American Revolution. This can also be seen in Southampton, Massachusetts, where the orator pointed to the date on which "the last warrant for a town meeting . . . was issued in 'his Majesty's name,'" thus placing the Crown in the past in favor of the republic of the future.[121] In Cohasset, Massachusetts, the town's forefathers "left behind the rural homes which are not yet extinct," architectural wonders "standing there as a type of New England institution . . . which have lasted until this day."[122] Here, the rural New England homes stood as a metaphor for the modernity they helped usher into the Western Hemisphere.

Other "lasts" that took their place alongside the last deer of Rhode Island, "last of the Bruin's race," the last slave, the last Tory, and the last prosecution for witchcraft argued for the beginnings of modernity, as they left behind the superstitions surrounding witchcraft. An 1855 Plymouth history precisely indicated that "the last survivors of the Mayflower, who signed the [*Mayflower*] compact, were John Howland . . . and John Alden . . . Mary, daughter of Isaac Allerton . . . died in 1699, aged ninety, and was the last of the one hundred passengers who arrived at Cape Cod harbor."[123] A history of Harwinton, Connecticut, contained a chapter subsection titled the "Last-Surviving Children of the First Settlers."[124] These individuals precisely marked the passage of particularly momentous times in the origins of modernity. Other histories took notice of the participation of particular places in grander projects in discussing lasts: "Nathan Lock, [was] the last survivor of these patriots a century ago . . . but the spirit of the fathers descended to the children's children."[125] Also noted was the last survivor of the Gaspee incident in Providence, the last woman alive "whose cradle was rocked in the commotion of [the Revolutionary] war" in Braintree, and even the "last *colored* [emphasis in the original] survivor of the Revolution, who dwelt in Windsor," as well as the last survivor of the War of 1812 in Watertown.[126] Importantly, these "lasts" either explicitly or implicitly made arguments about the perpetuation of New England institutions of modernity ("spirit of the fathers descended to the children's children").

But, pace Topsfield's historian previously cited, the notion of "lasting" also found expression in individual instances. Invoking a sense of "extinction" no longer in common usage, local narrators periodically reflected on the fate of particular families in forging their histories, sometimes linking "race" and "extinction" in the process. A lengthy poem read in Mendon, Massachusetts, celebrating incorporation reflected on the progeny of "settlers," and one stanza on the Taft family explained that the Taft "race is yet not *quite* extinct."[127] Edward Everett's son William reported in his response to the toast "*The Sons and Daughters of Dedham, and their Descendants wherever dispersed!* [emphasis in the original]" that "the last of my own race born in this town was my grandfather Oliver."[128] Embedded in a record of births in Dunstable is this annotation: "The reader will notice the large number of children in the families, and will naturally inquire why it is not so at present. Is the blood of the Pilgrims to become extinct?"[129] A genealogical appendix in a Haddam, Connecticut, history noted that "the families of one half of the first settlers are extinct, or gone from these towns."[130]

Such constructions suggest that New English families—even Pilgrim-descendèd New Englanders writ large—might share the fate they claimed awaited New England Indians. A final example, confusing on the face of things, may offer a clue to untangling this problem: "If a proprietor removed [from town], he, as a general rule, took all his near kindred with him; or if any were left, they did not stay long. Thus the names of Hancox, Jones, Newell, Stanley, and Gaylord, became extinct, *temporarily or permanently.*"[131] This author invoked a sense of "extinct" in wide circulation, defined by the *Oxford English Dictionary* as "of things comparable to a fire or light (*e.g.* life, hope, passion, disease, etc.): Quenched; that has ceased to burn or shine." Fires, hope, passion, and disease (although not people, of course) might "cease to burn or shine," but such outcomes might indeed be reversed. Thus we can account for the possibility of *temporary* extinction for New England families: having become "extinct" by departing, they might be rekindled by returning. The reversal of extinction for Indians did not similarly find play in the imaginations of New Englanders. Instead, merging the multiple usages of "extinction" still in circulation in the nineteenth century, New Englanders reserved the malleability of the fate for themselves. For Indians, the now widely deployed sense of the end of the line for species and races took an unshakable hold. In the non-Indian imaginary, once "extinguished," the Indian "race" was not to be rekindled.

Indeed, the extinction theme proved so resonant that it found rich expression in multiple ways. Plenty of other local texts drew attention not to particular "last Indians," but instead to specific events claimed as the end of aspects of Indian history. The featured events are frequently associated with Indians and violence. Thus ended, for example, "the last hope of the Pequod" in the wake of the Pequot War, the life of the "last survivor" of the Pigwacket Fight, the individual "remembrance" of "the last French war," the "last great struggle" (King Philip's War), "last battle of red Philip's race," the "last [Indian] alarm" in their town, "the last of Indian warfare and depredations within our borders," and "the last mischief which was done by the savages in Brook-field."[132] Featured elsewhere were "the last man killed by an Indian within the bounds of Groton," "the last of the race who here died by the hand of a white man," "last [Indian] attack," and "the last person killed, [who] was an

Indian boy at work with Nathaniel and Oliver Wilder," which paralleled an account of Lancaster, Massachusetts, where, poetically, "it may be considered, as worthy of remark, that the last person killed by the Indians, in this place, was himself an Indian."[133] A historian of Hadley, Massachusetts, noted "the last fortified residence of our Indians in the land of their fathers . . . This high plain, formerly called Fort Plain, is now crossed by the rail-road many feet below the surface."[134]

Varieties of Vanishing

Although plenty of "last" Indians received notice in local texts, other narrative constructions chimed into the chorus that declared the myth of New England Indian extinction. Included among these varieties of vanishing Indians are local texts that make no mention whatsoever of Indians, thus implicitly arguing for the disappearance of Natives who have been replaced by themselves. A rich variety of other forms of vanishing Indians, both implicit and explicit in their formulations, found their way into local texts. Taken together, they composed a deafening anthem that persuaded New Englanders and others of its dubious veracity. Local texts, then, form a composite extinction narrative that resonated everywhere and whose message was unmistakable: New England Indians had either ceased to exist, or their prospects for the future had dimmed to the vanishing point. The relentlessness of this message of extinction figured crucially in the large project of "lasting" in which local histories participated.

Local texts are littered with phrases that convey the message of vanishing Indians. Noting, for example, the Indian Hill Burial place that contained the skeletal remains "of the aborigines who lived here before the white people," implies that Indian history consisted of a preface to the real history that came next, and, leaving nothing to the imagination, this historian continued that there was no Indian left "to speak of, since the French war," and only a few "Indian tools" to be occasionally found "telling us of their haunts."[135] Even more aggressively dismissing Indian history, local narrators frequently dispatched Indians by suggesting that there was likely never a "permanent settlement within our borders," or that Indians only occasionally turned up to hunt or fish, thus demoting their possession of their homelands to mere chance encounters.[136] And still more common than these constructions are the great many narratives that incorporated Indian history, sometimes in great detail, and then dropped the narrative thread, and thus they implicitly argued for Indian extinction. Texts sometimes inform their readers that their localities were "once a favorite residence of the Indians," or that the town once "had its full quota of aboriginal inhabitants," and move on to the non-Indian history they are most concerned with in any event.[137] Annals-style local accounts are particularly prone to dropping Indians from their texts, since by definition, they are reproducing year-by-year narratives in which Indians are less and less likely to register as significant to their story. Sometimes local Indians only appear to transfer title of the land itself.[138] By dropping Indians out of the narrative of localities after using Indian history to establish non-Indians' own modernity, such accounts suggest to the reader that Indians have vanished from the possibilities of the future, thus completing the project of modernity.

And in nearly every instance, Indian history is narrated in the past tense, which places an additional burden on the possibility of Indian futures. While use of the past tense is a natural choice in historical narration, no one is prone to conclude that the non-Indian peoples whose history is being related have vanished into thin air. Absent explicit acknowledgment of Indian survival, on the other hand, an average reader might be inclined to follow their assumptions about Indian extinction when encountered by the past tense.

More tangible claims for vanishing Indians found expression in texts, as in statements such as "the Quinnipiacks have long since been extinct." In common with other historians, he failed to tell his reader how or when this outcome had been secured, continued by relating various events involving Indians, and then dropped them from the story. They are more generalized yet somehow certain claims that found expression in constructions such as, "The race has gone to the 'happy hunting ground' and no one mourns their departure," and "a few desperate ones hung about the settlements seeking revenge [after the Pequot War]; but they soon melted away, and their few descendants had none of their fathers' ambition. Now none are to be seen."[139]

Even more explicit explanations for Indian extinction participated in the construction of the vanishing Indian. Disease that thinned Indian ranks is sometimes offered as the departure point for local Indians, and even when (as in the case of Squanto's people) epidemics are not invoked as an explanation for sudden disappearance of Indians, they do compose a narrative thread that suggests the implausibility of Indian survival. One text asserts that "this portion of the continent was very thinly peopled" in the first place, and then "the population, not crowded at best, had been greatly reduced by a pestilence of few years before the commencement of the plantation at Plymouth . . . reducing large clans almost to the point of extinction." While this claim is puzzling given the theme of this text (commemorating the Battle of Bloody Brook from King Philip's War), its message is that Indian survival stood as a dubious prospect at best even before the full-time arrival of the English.[140]

As precise benchmarks for asserting the extinction of New England Indians, the Pequot War and King Philip's War became popular explanations in local texts. After the Pequot War, "that brave and fierce tribe was entirely extinguished";[141] the results were "the entire discomfiture and final extinction of this once powerful Indian tribe," or "the small army under Captain Mason exterminated or scattered these savages on that memorable day which delivered the colonists of Western Massachusetts and Connecticut from their fear of evil." As for King Philip's War, "it is probable, that the Indians left Andover, at the commencement of Philip's war, and that few, if any, families have resided there since. The residence of an Indian family in Andover is not now recollected by the oldest inhabitants."[142] Elsewhere, "the Nonotuck Indians were enticed to espouse the cause of King Philip in the war of 1676, and on his death they abandoned this fair valley and left it to the undisputed possession of the whites. . . . Not a descendant remains amongst us; nor do we know where a descendant is to be found."[143] Other places joined in the claim that local Indians devoted themselves to the resistance, which doomed them: "They resided at this place till Phillip's war, as it was called, in 1675 and 76, when they joined the hostile Indians, and never returned . . . [they are] utterly extinct here."[144] These narrative constructions resonated with the larger imaginative literature, such as locally produced poetry and nationally consumed theatrical productions that celebrated King Philip as the end of the line. And for a great many texts that do not precisely explain how these conflicts purportedly signaled the vanishing of Indians, again, their failure to take up any aspect of Indian history in the aftermath of the conflicts makes the implicit argument of the vanishing Indian.

The two last examples signal an additional theme in vanishing Indians. Some texts, rather than declaring the precise end of Indian peoples locally, suggest that Indian survivors moved elsewhere. They cleansed the local landscape by declaring an imaginary in which "the feeble remnants" (who had somehow survived smallpox and "moral contagion") had been "driven beyond the Mississippi, [and] are crossing the flanks of the Rocky Mountains. They have but one more remove to make, that is to the burial-place of their race."[145] One text made a direct reference to removal policy then being implemented: following Indian diminishment from "war and pestilence[,] . . . [o]nly a few remnants of scattered and fast wasting tribes remain on this side of the Mississippi. . . . They may find a temporary resting place in the territory provided for them on the other side of the 'father of waters.'"[146] Another text engaged in an equally sweeping claim of disappearance and removal that distanced human agency from claimed historical outcomes: "Forces which your fathers could not control have driven the Massachusetts Indian into his grave, and the tribes that survive him beyond the Missouri."[147] Even though creating such distance from causation, the author went on to point out that "the Indian question is still an unsolved problem. There is no part of our national history on which we can dwell with less satisfaction, unless it be our treatment of the negro."[148] The theme of migration elsewhere also found a factual basis in the local histories that traced the actual movement of Stockbridge people to the Oneida Nation in New York, and onward to Green Bay, Wisconsin, with some moving onward west of the Missouri.[149]

Other Indians from southern New England resisted by relocating elsewhere, either through individual or group migration. Dispossessed after the Revolution in spite of siding with the Americans, Mahicans from Stockbridge, Massachusetts, found their way to the Oneida Nation in New York before moving on to Wisconsin in 1828.[150] A composite group of Indian converts under the leadership of Mohegans Joseph Johnson and Samson Occom arrived in Wisconsin not long afterward, having also found refuge for a time among the Oneida.[151] These migrations represented a different sort of resistance to colonialism that also translated into New England Indian survival as the Stockbridge-Munsee and Brothertown communities in Wisconsin even while contributing in particular ways to the notion of New England Indian disappearance.

Overall, the "lasting" that local histories engaged in regarding New England Indians blended the precise with the imprecise, the erroneous assertion of finality along with the vaguely claimed story of the end of the line that echoed resoundingly in the emergent national literature and other cultural productions of the nineteenth century that "vanished" Indians on a much grander imaginary scale. Some writers craved the precision that drove them to make claims about the exact last physical location at which one could find an Indian: "the last place in town which they occupied, was in the limits of Pascommuck, where they had a village and a fort, probably on what is now known as Fort Plain, in the rear of the East District school-house."[152] In Boston one could find Powwow Hill, which is where "till within a few years, [they] . . . were in the habit of holding an annual feast."[153] Others needed the comfort of an exact date: "The number of the [Natick] tribe, in 1749, was one hundred and sixty-six; in 1763, was thirty-seven; in 1797, was twenty; in 1826, was extinct."[154] Others contented themselves with the less clear-cut explanation: "'Long did the Indians hang on the borders of civilization, and watch for opportunities to annoy, to carry away, or to kill their enemies.'"[155] And still others satisfied themselves with brief encapsulations of Indian history, especially symbolized by burial places that had "been piously guarded by all owners and every generation out of respect to the dead of a nearly extinct race."[156]

Such narratives performed the cultural and political work of purifying the landscape of Indians, using a degeneracy narrative that foreclosed Indian futures. Through the multilayered process of "lasting," non-Indians argued for a rupture that enabled their own modernity and demonstrated their progress. Yet the narratives themselves contained multiple ruptures. Inconsistencies, confusion, and accounts of Indian survival can also be detected in local texts, suggesting a larger—and different—truth regarding New England Indians.

Chapter 4 Resisting

Claims in Texts about Indian Extinction Fail Even As They Are Being Made

Struggle and Survival

The temporalities of race that insisted Indians remain mired in a static past blinded New Englanders to an important fact: Indians resisted their effacement from New England in the nineteenth century by embracing change in order to make their way in a changing world, as they had done for centuries. Their ongoing resistance to settler colonialism took multiple forms and translated into their survival as Indian peoples. Driven to understand Indianness through a degeneration narrative about race that insisted on blood purity and coupled with an understanding of Indians reckoned within the temporalities of race, non-Indians failed to accord Indian peoples a legitimate place in modernity. They failed to recognize New England Indians as modern peoples who looked to the future and instead constructed a pervasive myth of Indian extinction.

Evidence to the contrary was certainly available. In fact, through much of the nineteenth century Connecticut, Massachusetts, and Rhode Island all extended official recognition of Indians through complex guardianship systems, a fact that apparently eluded local historians, not to mention the general public. Through these official structures, Connecticut recognized the Mohegan, Pequot, Niantic, Schaghticoke, Tunxis, and Paugussett peoples who remained in their homelands.[1] In Massachusetts, John Milton Earle identified the Chappequiddick, Christiantown, Gay Head, Mashpee, Herring Pond, Natick, Punkapoag, Troy (Fall River), Hassanamisco, and Dudley as "distinct bands, communities, or tribes having funds or reservations, or which have them and are recognized as wards of the State." He added the Dartmouth and Yarmouth as groups without the same relationship to the state. Others had left their communities and "lost their original rights," and still others resided "either in neighborhoods, or scattered abroad in the community," something that was certainly true in Connecticut and Rhode Island as well.[2] He remarked that their descent might not be "precisely known, but of whose identity as Indians, there is no doubt."[3] Rhode Island continued to recognize the Narragansett and in 1840 created a commissioner to oversee that relationship.[4]

As Amy E. Den Ouden has argued, the Mohegan, Pequot, and Niantic reservations, created in the seventeenth century, "were the locus of community life for Native peoples, as well as sites of ancestral and ongoing struggle. In a very real sense, then, they were homelands."[5] Although Den Ouden's focus is on the eighteenth century, her observations could readily be extended to the nineteenth century and beyond to those three reservations and other Indian places. New England Indians remained in their homelands and continually remade their lives in dialogue with their non-Indian neighbors. They refused the notion that Indians could never be modern by selectively incorporating elements of the non-Indian material, spiritual, and intellectual world even while continuing to identify as Wampanoag, Pequot, Mohegan, and more. In places such as Aquinnah (Gay Head), Mashpee, and Narragansett, Indians retained relatively intact land bases and continually remade their lives there. Other communities, such as the Eastern Pequot, Mashantucket, Paugussett, Schaghticoke, and Dudley Nipmuc, held smaller parcels of land where fewer people could rely on the land for a living, and others migrated to villages and towns in the area to find work. Still others, such as the Tunxis and Hassanamisco Nipmuc, had been made largely landless and many migrated to villages and cities in the region to find work.[6] A dense network of kinship connected Indian people across the landscape of southern New England that both influenced and responded to Indian movement throughout the region.

Indians continued to work the land they still owned and to keep livestock, and they continued to hunt and fish in getting a living. They also participated in the market economy as consumers of manufactured goods, household items, and food.[7] They entered the wage labor economy in gendered ways. A great many Indian men participated in the whaling industry, and in places such as Christiantown, they did so as young men in order to accumulate capital to build a house and get a start in life.[8] They also produced manufactures such as cane-bottomed chairs, and they earned wages as laborers in cities and villages as barbers, shoemakers, cooks, and the like.[9] Indian women participated in wage labor as well, and they also continued to produce baskets, brooms, and to rely on their knowledge of pharmacology to earn a living as healers. Indentured servitude affected men, women, and children alike, as Indians— especially those made entirely landless and bound by relations of debt— struggled to get by.[10]

Some Indians converted to Christianity and either formed their own congregations complete with Indian deacons and ministers or attended non-Indian congregations. In places such as Martha's Vineyard, Indians used the institution of Christianity to remake their communities in dialogue with English colonialism by embracing elements of the new religion even while holding strong to their own traditions and their Wampanoag identity.[11] At Schaghticoke, Moravian missionaries arrived in the nineteenth century and gained some adherents without displacing Indian ways.[12] Indians also erected their own schools, although, like churches and ministers, they sometimes struggled to maintain them. By the 1830s state governments established educational systems that embraced Indians, replacing the educational outreach of the Society for the Propagation of the Gospel.[13]

To say that Indians survived settler colonialism and remade their lives is not to suggest that all of this happened without mammoth struggles. Relegated to the least productive lands where they did retain them, enmeshed in abusive servitude arrangements that fractured families, drawn away from home for long periods of time earning wages as laborers or in the dangerous whaling industry, Indians suffered racial discrimination and scorn from non-Indians. They also endured corrupt overseers or guardians, whose actions they protested through the only real means available to them: petitioning the government for redress of their grievances, a mode of resistance rooted deeply in the seventeenth century that attests to the long history of fraudulent non-Indian behavior and Indian resistance.[14] Abusive guardians mishandled Indian funds at places such as Hassanamisco, and they arrogantly appropriated Indian resources such as timber that they had been entrusted to protect in Mashpee, Mashantucket, Aquinnah, and other places.[15]

Not surprisingly, conflict characterized internal matters as well, particularly around issues of community membership and access to resources. David Silverman has shown the ways that race fueled rancorous debates about belonging and resources at Aquinnah. Controversies became especially heated over the rights of African American men who married Indian women as well as those of their offspring, framed in terms of race but importantly rooted in concerns about whether and how the tribes would integrate outsiders or "foreigners," a dynamic also found elsewhere.[16] As John Wood Sweet has argued about the late eighteenth century, it is not surprising to see in these disputes that some Indians absorbed ideas about race in circulation in the broader society that spurred campaigns to exclude African Americans who had married into the group in places such as Mohegan.[17]

Stories of Indian struggle and survival in southern New England deserve our notice. Just remaining in their homelands to be counted—however erroneously—represented an astonishing story of resistance given the determination of non-Indians to make them disappear. Indians steadfastly defended their land, identity, and place as modern people in New England against tremendous odds. In this chapter, I look at ruptures in the narrative of Indian extinction and the ways in which Indian peoples refused to be replaced on the landscape. Local narrators frequently demonstrated uncertainty in their conclusions about Indian fates, presenting conflicting evidence about Indian extinction even within a single text. Others stand at odds with other data, such as governmental censuses that establish a vibrant Indian presence where historians have argued otherwise. And some texts acknowledge the ongoing presence of Indian peoples, allowing for the reconstruction of an incomplete Indian geography from texts produced for other purposes.

No one personified Indian resistance in New England better than the Pequot minister, activist, and public intellectual William Apess. While I briefly survey his life history, which tells us so much about the experiences of New England Indians in the nineteenth century, in this chapter I focus primarily on Apess's articulation of a political stance for New England Indians in modernity in his works that gained publication between 1831 and 1836. I take up his activism in connection with the Mashpee Revolt in 1833, a resistance movement against the oppressive and corrupt guardianship system in Massachusetts. I then analyze his *Eulogy on King Philip,* a remarkable political tract that proposes to undo the replacement narrative and that I argue advances a revolutionary idea: that Indians could both exercise self-determination as Indian peoples and become citizens, that is, the notion of dual citizenship. William Apess very visibly and vocally ruptured the extinction narrative and articulated a political position that imagined Indian peoples as both citizens of the United States and as entitled to their political autonomy as separate Indian peoples.

Why did New Englanders have such trouble recognizing New England Indians as such? On one level, their assumptions about Indianness that were shaped by the temporalities of race preconditioned them to understand Indians through the degeneration narrative. But on another level, they refused to recognize them because it was useful not to. Recognizing Indians entailed fulfilling obligations to them with regard to protecting their lands and other resources and attending to their needs under the system of guardianship that had organically developed over more than two hundred years of colonialism. It also stood in the way of the modernizing project of purification that was so preoccupied with completion. New Englanders' refusal to recognize Indians as Indians took a devastating turn in the latter half of the nineteenth century. This chapter ends with a discussion of the disastrous policy of "termination," or "detribalization," taken up to one degree or another in Connecticut, Massachusetts, and Rhode Island. Articulated in connection with debates about the abolition of slavery and conferring citizenship on African Americans, this policy terminated state recognition of the political status of many New England tribes. Resisted by most Indians, this policy sought to complete the process of purification implicit in the making of modernity. But as was so frequently the case, "termination" became yet another instance of wishful thinking. Just because state governments purported to "terminate" their recognition of tribes, that did not mean they were not there. Indians continued to engage with modernity in ways that preserved their Indianness in New England.

Uncertainty

In a sermon delivered in Avon, Connecticut, in 1851, Rev. Joel Grant asserted that an Indian man named Manasseth, then incarcerated on a life sentence in the state prison after his conviction for murder, quite possibly represented the one remaining "descendant" of the Tunxis race. Immediately following this declaration, Grant added:

> This whole matter of "last descendants" is believed to be very uncertain.— "Indians" who came from the vicinity of Stockbridge, Ms., lived recently in Guilford, Ct. By one of their company, a half-breed, a man "towards seventy" years old in 1856, intelligent, surnamed Madison, the statement was made that his father, whom some public business had brought into Western Massachusetts "in the revolutionary war," was a brother of James Madison, President of the United States. As well ludicrous as lugubrious has become the once tender wail: "Who is there left to mourn for Logan?"—each "Logan" being "*e pluribus unum.*"[18]

The minister's observations were quoted at the tail end of a two-page footnote titled "Indians in Harwinton" in a history of that Connecticut town. His densely packed summation of the state of Indian affairs covered extensive ground. Leaving aside the question of the "last" Tunxis for a moment, the minister's anecdote about James Madison's brother's purported relative provided him a platform on which to declare his claim absurd and mournful.

The minister then referenced a story in wide circulation in the nineteenth century—the massacre of the entire extended family of John Logan, a Mingo, by Colonel Michael Cresap, amidst the violence of Lord Dunmore's War in 1774.[19] Logan purportedly delivered a speech in the wake of the massacre and Thomas Jefferson made Logan's speech famous by including it in his *Notes on the State of Virginia*. Logan lamented that his lifetime pursuit of peaceful relations ended with the massacre that prompted him to take revenge. His speech included the widely cited lines, "There runs not a drop of my blood in the veins of any living creature. . . . Who is there to mourn for Logan? Not one."[20] The minister's tweak of the speech adds additional power to his claim about uncertainty over "last descendants" by borrowing the nationalistic phrase "out of many [states] one [nation]"—suggesting that there were many Logans, and presumably, many left to mourn the proverbial Logan.

But more to the point, by calling into question the "whole matter of 'last descendants,'" the minister revealed a degree of doubt that most nineteenth-century narrators seemed unwilling to entertain. And he had good reason. After all, while he claimed the incarcerated Manasseth to be quite possibly the last of the Tunxis, the Tunxis themselves had been honored with a monument to their passing nineteen years before.[21] While he did not elaborate on his rationale in doubting the "last descendants," in making this statement he inflicted a crack on the façade of the extinction story. Yet other observers unintentionally provided material that might be regarded as confusing at best. An 1835 Grafton, Massachusetts, history offered this retrospective of that place:

> In reviewing the past, nothing strikes us so forcibly as the change which has taken place since this town was first known to the English. We have seen that Eliot, nearly two hundred years ago, came here, and first preached the gospel to the Indians. That race, then free and conscious of their rightful possession of the soil, had no suspicion that the day of their extinction was so near at hand;— that their council fires would so soon cease to burn;—that the forests through which they roamed would disappear, and that their hunting and fishing places would be occupied by the habitations and improvements of the white man. . . . Two centuries have passed—and they have vanished.[22]

This passage seamlessly argued for the complete and certain extinction of Indians who greeted the English two hundred years before in freedom and in uncontested possession of their homelands. How could they know that the fate that awaited them, extinction, soon would come to pass? The passage constitutes a concise and unambiguous replacement narrative. A brief appendix, however, reported "it was not till about ten years ago [c. 1825] that the 'last of the Nipmucks' ceased to exist," and that "in 1830 there were fourteen of a mixed Indian and negro race, which still hold some of the Indian lands, and receive the benefit of the small remaining fund."[23] This latter claim, published in 1835 and on the face of matters indeed uncertain and confusing in light of the "last" assertion of circa 1825, suggests that this historian employed the temporalities of race in insinuating that "blood mixture" disqualified these Indians from "genuine" Indianness.

A different historian of Grafton who published his work in 1879 reproduced these observations practically verbatim (and without attribution), but included additional material that made Grafton's Indian history (in the hands of non-Indians) equally confusing.[24] This text asserted that "Mary Printer *alias* Thomas, the last of the full blooded Indians of this tribe, and the last blood descendant of the Hassanamesits, died in Worcester, February 10, 1879." How, one might wonder, could Mary Printer Thomas qualify as the "last full blooded" Indian when the "last of the Nipmucks" had purportedly "ceased to exist" in 1825? Or was it 1835? Adding even more cause for uncertainty, the historian noted further that "there are indeed, several farms in the possession of the heirs of the Indians, married to negroes; but it is said there is not one male in the town at this day, who is all of Indian extract or blood."[25] Here again is deployed the iron fist of racial purity. But the author even undid this suggestion of disqualified Indianness when, more than two hundred pages later, he drew attention to the Indian burial ground, "where the last remnants of the race were interred." He claimed that "many aged persons can remember when the last degraded remnants of the race, once inhabiting the soil we occupy, inclosed in rude coffins of rough boards, hastily put together, and without any religious ceremony, were conveyed to this repository of the dead."[26] So which was it? Such a confident declaration of extinction flew in the face of the acknowledgment of surviving Indians, however this author sought to discredit their authenticity.

The confusion over the status and fate of Indians evident in—and between—these two Grafton histories echoed elsewhere. In three late-nineteenth-century Nantucket histories, a template for mapping the extinction story emerged and was reinforced. An 1871 tourist guide informed the reader that in 1822 "the last Indian died," and that in 1855 "Abram Quary (last man with Indian blood in him) died."[27] An 1875 *Handbook of Nantucket* had the "last of the race, of full blood" dying in 1821 instead of 1822, and "Abraham Quary, the last representative of the Nantucket tribe of Indians" passing in 1854 instead of 1855: thus "the whole race of Indians that our ancestors found here having done precisely as their neighbors on the main land did" in spite of avoiding the warfare that devastated tribes on the mainland.[28] An

1882 account noted the "last Indian" who died in 1822, and sided with the *Handbook* in dating Abraham Quary's death in 1854: "in this man's veins ran the last drop of blood of a once happy and prosperous people. In the Athenæum Library hangs a fine oil painting of this half-breed, and the mournful and thoughtful expression of his face tells the whole story."[29] Of course he looked mournful, given that this representation purported to bring the fate of his people to a neat and complete end. But a 1914 history of Nantucket revised what had seemed a well-inscribed fact (see Figure 21). It also noted the death of Abraham Quary (on November 25, 1854), but closed its "'last roll-call' of the Nantucket Indians (Copied from a private Indian Register hitherto unpublished)" with "Darkis Onerable (Dorcas Honorable), [who] died Friday night, January 12, 1855 . . . aged seventy-nine years. Buried from Baptist Church.— The last of her race!" (see Figure 22).[30] Dorcas Honorable was the subject of a photograph, reproduced in this volume with the caption "The last pure-blooded Nantucket Indian" inscribed under her name.

Sometimes authors even changed their minds in a single text, simultaneously revealing their own confusion and, presumably, confusing their readers as well. A Norton, Massachusetts, text noted that "Charles Josias, the son of Jeremy and great-grandson of Chickataubut, 'is said to have been the last of his race,'" but six pages later it identified "an Indian by the name of Quock; probably the last of that noble and vigorous yet much abused race who had a habitation within our borders."[31] A Scituate, Massachusetts, history pointed to "the last of all the Matakeesetts in this town," Comsitt, "a bright and enterprising man, who enlisted into the Revolutionary army and lost his life."[32] That the author followed this claim with the observation that "his family received some assistance from the Town as late as 1786" was confusing enough, but a footnote on the following page echoed the Norton history in asserting that the seventeenth-century leader "Charles Josias (son of Jeremy) was the last of the race."[33] A poem read during the bicentennial celebration at Dartmouth, Massachusetts, lamented Philip as "the last of MASSASOIT'S race," and asked, "But where is Philip's son?" The next stanza answered the question, pointing out that his wife and son had been sold into slavery in Bermuda. A footnote to this stanza reinforced the melancholic truth of the matter, but confusingly added that "John Hopper, son-in-law of Philip, and Betty Hopper, Philip's grand-daughter, were residents of Rochester and died there. Betty was proud of her descent and refused all intercourse with the common people of her race."[34]

Recall also the observations of Daniel Ricketson, Henry David Thoreau, and Albert Bierstadt about the famous last Indian Martha Simon. When they

Figure 21. *Abram Quary, the Last Nantucket Indian Half-Breed.* Abram Quary is claimed as "the Last Nantucket half-breed" in a 1914 history of Nantucket. Photograph by Henry S. Wyer. From R. A. Douglas-Lithgow, *Nantucket: A History* (New York: G. P. Putnam's Sons, 1914), 56.

Figure 22. *Dorcas Honorable.* Dorcas Honorable is claimed to be the "last pure-blooded Nantucket Indian." Photograph by Henry S. Wyer. Courtesy of the Nantucket Historical Association, GPN4321.

trained their eyes on her they variously identified her as Wampanoag, Narragansett, and Nemasket, and they located her in both New Bedford and Dartmouth, which should lead us to question their powers of observation.[35] But there is even more evidence that bumped up against the narrow constraints each of them sought to impose on Martha Simon and other nineteenth-century New England Indians. One year after Daniel Ricketson published his history of New Bedford that included Martha Simon, Massachusetts Commissioner for Indian Affairs John Milton Earle identified one hundred and eleven Indians of Dartmouth, "whose descent is not precisely known, but, of whose identity as Indians there is no doubt."[36] And seventy-three years later, a historian updated Dartmouth's "last" story, though not his assumptions about the performance of Indianness: "Charlotte Mitchell, the last descendant of Massasoit . . . rehearsed Indian tradition and Indian lore to her visitors, and appears at historical and other functions in Middleboro to show adults and children how Indian women appeared when her ancestors roamed the forests, paddled their canoes on Assawampsett pond and owned the town."[37]

So too did the Jaha family and nearly all persisting Indian peoples in New England live an Indianness that historians and other local observers failed to recognize as such. Memorialized as the last Nipmuc of Oxford, Massachusetts, who had passed on by 1894, Julia Jaha was asserted to have been an active and devout convert to Christianity who could read and who "recalled the family [in which she was put to service] with great respect."[38] Most of this memorial elaborated on this basic theme, thus trivializing and domesticating both her life and a powerful critique acknowledging that Indians might have legitimate complaints to file that surprisingly closed the brief sketch and remained uncommented on by its recorder: "Julia ever testified that her tribe were conscious of great injustice done to them in all their transactions with the English, and then added with much feeling of grief, 'They would destroy the graves of our dead as of no account and make a field of grain of our Indian sepulchre.'"[39] Julia Jaha Dayley (then resident in Oxford) was among the ninety-four Dudley Indians listed in the aforementioned census of Indians published thirty-four years before this history came out, along with five more relatives in her generation plus nine more in the next, whose immediate kinship network connected Oxford to Webster, Spencer, Worcester, and Uxbridge.[40]

And so the "whole matter of 'last descendants'" of New England Indians was indeed rather uncertain. Whether the ambiguity can be detected within a single text, or by comparing the claiming of "lastness" across multiple texts concerning a single locality, authors and readers alike frequently failed the test of consistency. Vague declarations such as "the Pequots as a nation were soon nearly extinct," contained in a New London, Connecticut, history written by well-known author Frances Manwaring Caulkins, opened the door to various interpretations.[41] Did she mean to narrow the focus on the autonomous status of the tribe by qualifying her observation with "as a nation"? Furthermore, in suggesting that extinction appeared to be on the horizon—in this case in the wake of the Pequot War—did Caulkins mean for her readers to assume that that outcome eventually came to pass even though she could not precisely add a date to the supposed conclusion of the story?

Such ambiguities permeated her narrative: thirteen pages after her claim about impending extinction she wrote that the land that was to become New London "was a conquered country. No Indian titles were to be obtained, no Indian claims settled. It was emphatically, as it was then called, *Pequot;* the land left by an extinguished tribe; or if not extinguished in fact, legally held to be so, and doomed to extinction."[42] Here Caulkins makes reference to the Treaty of Hartford of 1638, which declared the Pequot dissolved as a nation, banished them from the colony, and divided the people between the English allies in the war, the Mohegan and the Narragansett.[43] On this basis, Caulkins could argue that even if Pequot people survived the conflict, their corporate existence had been "legally" terminated by the colony of Connecticut and their fate as doomed to extinction could be assumed. The Pequot, of course, had other ideas. Stories about Indians can be found woven throughout Caulkins's nearly seven-hundred-page volume, including the observation that "Mashantucket, the last retreat of the Pequot Indians, is in Ledyard."[44] After a brief description of the reservation, Caulkins continued:

> Only sixteen of the tribe, in 1850, were regarded as *regular Pequots,* that is, inheriting by the mother, which is the Indian law of succession, and on that side of full blood. . . . . In 1766, the whole number of the tribe was 164, of whom only thirty were men. Of the forty-six females over sixteen years of age, thirteen were widows. . . . The last full-blooded Pequot of this tribe, pure by father and mother, was Frederick Toby, who died in 1848.[45]

She also acknowledged three families on a reservation in North Stonington and noted that some families from these two reservations had "removed to the west."[46] Finally, she pointed to a Niantic reservation in East Lyme where there lived "scarcely a dozen individuals."[47] But what stands out in her discussion is the notion of being a *regular Pequot*—explicitly a claim that Pequots themselves enforced matrilineal descent from a "full-blooded" Pequot as the criterion for being "regular." Although firm conclusions will not likely be forthcoming given the devastation of early contact experiences and their impact on social relations, certainly by the mid-nineteenth century the Pequots reckoned—and the state courts recognized—bilateral descent in membership rules for the Pequot, in contradiction of Caulkins's restrictive and erroneous claim.[48]

Two final examples of local texts and their perplexity on the matter of Indian extinction versus Indian survival shed light on some of the dynamics at work in the nineteenth-century Indian landscape of New England. A history of Duxbury, Massachusetts, mentions several Indians who appeared in the vital records in the eighteenth century, which effectively let the matter rest. But a footnote pointed out the oft-cited Charles Josiah as "the last of the race," and further complicating matters, the next footnote observed that "recently, an interesting report has been presented to the Legislature of Massachusetts . . . from which it appears there are remains of twelve tribes within the bounds of the State, numbering in all 847, including people of color connected with them; but of these only six or eight are of pure blood."[49] This referenced a report commissioned by the governor of Massachusetts to inquire after Indians in 1849 that enumerated 847 individuals encompassed in eleven tribes in 1849: Chappequiddick, Christiantown, Gay Head, Fall River or Troy, Marshpee [Mashpee], Herring Pond, Grafton or Hassanamiso, Dudley, Punkapoag, Natick, and Yarmouth.[50] Although the author got the number of tribes and the date of the document wrong, clearly he was referring to the report of F. W. Bird, commissioned by the Massachusetts legislature to look into the condition of Indians in the Commonwealth, which had somehow come to his attention. A Dorchester, Massachusetts, history claimed that the Punkapoag occupied a land grant there in 1656, "and there the lapse of years has nearly extinguished their lamp." This text also referred to the 1849 "Report of the Commissioners relating to the Condition of Indians," and similarly relegated this fact of Indian survival in a footnote.[51] All of these instances of acknowledging Indian survival in New England allow us to see Indian resistance to the extinction myth.

Indians in Attendance

When the town of Natick celebrated the gift of a John Eliot–translated Algonquian Bible on the bicentennial of the first visit Eliot made to the Nonantum Indians on October 28, 1846, inhabitants packed the town hall to join in the festivities. According to one account of the gathering, included in the crowd was "the only lineal descendant of the Natick tribe, a girl about sixteen years of age, [who] occupied a central seat at the table, and was the chief object of attention during the evening."[52] One can only imagine the spectacle and wonder what passed through the mind of the supposed last lineal descendant as she listened to an oration that defended the expenditure for a volume of "a barbarous dialect of a tongue that is never to be spoken again; of a people which has already ceased to exist, except this one poor Indian girl, the orphan daughter of a departed race."[53] Who was she? What was her name? Why did she participate in this objectifying ritual?

While the account is mute on these questions, the motivations of the organizers of the Eliot first visit anniversary seem closer to the surface. Although the text does not explicitly say so, this spectacle participated in the familiar ritual of "lasting" that served the project of extinction ideology. Yet the very presence of the Natick teenager at center stage simultaneously calls into question the disappearance story and can instead be read as resistance. After all, local texts had predicted the inevitable extinction of the Natick people for decades.[54] Three histories of neighboring towns had indeed declared them "extinct" in 1826.[55] And yet there she was, more than two decades later, living evidence of the falsity of earlier extinction claims.

Other Indians in attendance at historical commemorations included "a score or two" of Mohegans whose ancestors had been involved in land transactions to Norwich, Connecticut, in 1659, who attended the celebration of the bicentennial of the town.[56] The orator of the day even paused to personally address the Mohegan contingent, who "were seated near the speaker":

> Descendants of Uncas, whose fathers bade our fathers welcome to their wigwams and their hunting grounds, we welcome you to this jubilee. Yet our joy is not without its sorrow when we see that you have lost what we have gained, that your numbers are few, and your sachems are gone. Be assured that it is the Great Spirit himself who has ordered that every race, like every man, should act his part and die. But grateful remembrance shall live, and until yonder memorial shaft of granite shall have crumbled to the dust, until our race shall be no more, succeeding generations shall be taught that Uncas was the white man's friend.[57]

Like the Natick teenager, these Mohegans remained mute while on display (or at least that is what the text suggests to the reader) when confronted with this account of their history and prospects for the future. The organizers of the event and the orator on the stage mounted a performance intended to symbolize the tried-and-true motif of the helper Indian (Uncas), memorialized by the nearby monument to him (dedicated seventeen years before), and to insist on the imminent departure of the race. What did the Mohegans think when they were informed, point blank, that their own Great Spirit had dictated the race "should act his part and die"? One might suppose this prediction was met with skepticism and scorn. Buried in a footnote in the appendix at the end of this text are the basic findings of a Connecticut legislature's report that enumerated 102 Mohegans ("though all of them are not of pure Indian blood") living on reservation lands held in common.[58] This acknowledgment of Mohegan survival, relegated to the margins of a text that argued against that possibility, helps us think about Indian resistance to the directive to depart and offers testimony to New English perplexity regarding the racial order. And the attendance of "the living adult males of the Mohegan" at the dedication of the John Winthrop monument during the 250th anniversary of the founding of New London in 1896 ("accepted by Lemuel Fielding 'on behalf of his tribe'") brought predictions of Mohegan demise into question once again.[59]

At least two Narragansetts participated in the ceremonies surrounding the Canonicus monument in 1883. In fact, like the Mohegans in Norwich, they took center stage, although it does not appear that they were afforded an actual voice in the proceedings either. Instead, former governor Elisha Dyer spoke for one of them: he "introduced Moses B. Prophet, of the Narragansett Tribe, who, he said, 'unites with us in behalf of his people in this tribute of love and honor to the memory of this noble old chieftain.'"[60] Surely this is a plausible act of ventriloquism, although it remains unclear why Prophet was not allowed to speak for himself. The organizers did not, however, relegate him to complete passivity, because "the memorial was then unveiled by Mr. Prophet, revealing an oblong boulder of granite, five feet in height, and about two feet square, on which had been cut the name 'Canonicus,' in large letters, and, beneath it, a rude bow and arrow."[61] Appearances by Narragansetts on stage served as bookends for the day's festivities. After the conclusion of a lengthy historical address that testified to the stellar qualities of Canonicus and the English alike, "Annie A. Thomas, a little Narragansett Indian girl, stepped upon the platform and in behalf of the tribe, presented [Prophet] with a bouquet of flowers."[62]

What prompted the erection of the Canonicus memorial a couple of centuries in the wake of his life? Although many had long advocated the monument, the townspeople finally took action because of "the interest in Indian affairs, growing out of the late formal dissolution of the Narragansett tribe of Indians."[63] By legislative action (discussed later in this chapter), in 1880 Rhode Island declared that the separate existence of the Narragansett Tribe had been "terminated." And according to the orator of the day, on the occasion of the "formal termination" at Fort Ninigret, "some of the members of its feeble remnant *there* bore public testimony to the justice and equity that marked the dealings of the state."[64] Apparently, an occasion so grave as "finis" being "written on the chronicles of the Narragansetts" did call forth the necessity of hearing directly from the people.[65]

In spite of their "dissolution," Narragansetts refused to disappear in the aftermath of the legislative action that sought to make that happen. Not only did they survive as a people apart, they also continued to attend public displays about Indian history. In 1906, twenty-three years after the dedication of the Canonicus monument, "three lineal descendants of the noble but now almost vanished Narragansett Tribe" unveiled a monument to the Great Swamp Fight of King Philip's War. The "rugged granite shaft, frostriven from the native hills, untouched by tool of man" shared the symbolic power of the Canonicus monument, but this time "as a fitting emblem of the rugged and unadorned Pilgrim and Puritan of sixteen hundred and seventy-five."[66] It also resembled the Canonicus monument in intending to pay tribute to both parties in the cultural encounter, "both victor and vanquished, to all that was highest and truest in their lives."[67] They consciously foregrounded Puritan religious ideals over their "religious intolerance and their unjust treatment of the natives of the land," on the one hand, and the "brave Sachem of the Narragansetts, who here fought valiantly for his rights, his people and their homes" over their participation in a war of destruction on the other.[68] "The weaker race gave way to the stronger," and the descendants could "afford to be generous" to Indians who had vanished.[69] And in 1939, following a decades-long saga of excavation and historical revisionism, "an honor guard comprising a delegation of Narragansett Indians and four men in colonial military uniform stood by and watched" as the supposed remains of Roger Williams finally received a ceremonious reburial in Roger Williams Park overlooking Providence.[70]

What motivated the organizers of such festivities to invite Indians to attend and even participate in public displays of history and memory? One non-Indian speaker at the Rochester, Massachusetts, bicentennial celebration explicitly took on this question:

> Though doing what I have never known to have been done before on an occasion of this kind, your committee have nevertheless done well to invite to this entertainment, this feast of reason and flow of soul, living representatives of the nationality and people that possessed this goodly land before our Pilgrim fathers came hither. And we are thus enabled to see, to look upon, question and hold converse with the lineal descendants of those for who for thousands of years, for aught we know, here lived, moved and had a being, swaying unquestioned and unobstructed the sceptre of power, true representatives of pre-historical centuries and pre-historic men.[71]

Although he erroneously claimed originality for Rochester in inviting Indian attendance, the speaker did lay bare plausible motivations for the practice. Celebrants treated Indians in attendance as living relics, symbols of what they constructed as a "prehistory" of their localities. They made them into objects of curiosity and informants—presumably, then, not so mute as the published accounts of such events would lead the reader to believe.

In the case of Rochester, the organizers landed a prominent Indian woman and her two daughters for the event, whom they featured in elaborate etchings on the frontispiece of the published volume documenting the celebration (see Figures 23 and 24). Interestingly, they listed the women without distinguishing them as Indians among the invited guests. Even more interestingly, in this passage they employed the Algonquian names for Zerviah Gould Mitchell's daughters Charlotte (Wootonekamuske) and Melinda (Tewelema), although their etchings bore both names.[72] Among other things, the women sat through a prayer that asked, "Father of the spirits of all flesh, we most meekly beseech Thee to remember for good the few relicts here to-day of those primal lords of these ancient forests. O pour upon them, and all the aborigines of our land, the riches of Thy grace and the bounties of Thy providence!"[73]

Like all the other Indians in attendance who are acknowledged in published accounts of local festivities, Zerviah Gould Mitchell and her daughters apparently remained silent while others purported to speak on their behalf. The tenth toast made toward the end of the celebration no doubt caught their attention, dedicated as it was to "the Aborigines,—once the rightful owners of the soil; we should cherish the few who remain with us in a careful and Christian spirit."[74] The respondent, General Ebenezer W. Peirce, was a genealogist whom Zerviah had hired to write a book about her ancestors, and "'also make record of the wrongs which during all these generations have been endured by my race.'"[75] Although we do not know if Peirce aired these "wrongs" during the celebration, we do know he treated the audience to an overview of that history from Massasoit to the present. Indeed, saving his punch line for the end, he concluded this sketch with a genealogical account that connected the Indians in attendance, "living representatives of the nationality and people that possessed this goodly land before our Pilgrim fathers came hither," to their ancestor, Massasoit.[76] Zerviah Gould had married Thomas C. Mitchell, "who was of mixed blood, part English and part Cherokee Indian. . . . Her two daughters, here upon the stage, are of a family of eleven children, three sons and eight daughters, of whom one son and five daughters survive."[77] So interestingly, in the case of these descendants of the iconic Massasoit, an exception was made to the blood purity rule. A note in the appendix to the volume

WOOTONEKAMUSKE.
CHARLOTTE L. MITCHELL.

Figure 23. *Wootonekamuske—Charlotte L. Mitchell.* Engraving of Wootonekamuske, or Charlotte L. Mitchell, in Native dress, posing before what is presumably Assawampsett Pond. Along with her sister and mother, she was an honored guest at the Rochester, Massachusetts, bicentennial celebration. Russell & Richardson lithograph, Boston. Frontispiece for Rochester, Massachusetts, *Rochester's Official Bi-Centennial Records, Tuesday, July 22, 1879, Containing the Historical Address of Rev. N. W. Everett; The Responses by Lieut.-Gov. Long, Hon. W. W. Crapo, M.C., Judge Thos. Russell, and Others* (New Bedford: Mercury Publishing Co., 1879).

TEWELEMA.
MELINDA MITCHELL.

Figure 24. *Tewelema—Melinda Mitchell.* Etching of Tewelema (Melinda Mitchell),
honored guest with her sister and mother at the Rochester, Massachusetts,
bicentennial celebration. Russell & Richardson lithograph, Boston. Frontispiece for
Rochester, Massachusetts, *Rochester's Official Bi-Centennial Records, Tuesday, July 22,
1879, Containing the Historical Address of Rev. N. W. Everett; The Responses by
Lieut.-Gov. Long, Hon. W. W. Crapo, M.C., Judge Thos. Russell, and Others* (New Bedford:
Mercury Publishing Co., 1879).

informs the reader that the women used to live in North Abington, but now they reside at Betty's Neck in Lakeville. "The daughters were richly dressed in Indian costumes, in the style of their ancestors two hundred years ago. . . . The old lady appeared in her usual European costume of black."[78]

When members of the Massasoit Monument Association gathered in Warren, Rhode Island, fourteen years later to drum up financing for their project, they also invited the Mitchell daughters to attend (though apparently not their eighty-five-year-old mother, mistakenly identified as "Terviah" in the text dedicated to the event).[79] Although they apparently declined, the historical narrator noted that he knew "this family of Massasoit well, and they are people whose character is worthy of their great ancestor. This family ought to come and live here in Warren."[80] If they had attended, they might have viewed three tableaux "representing Massasoit's childhood, Massasoit and Roger Williams, and the end of the Wampanoag nation."[81] And they might have done so having been escorted to their seats by "a number of young gentlemen who were dressed in Indian costumes" who assisted the ushers for the day.[82]

And so the townspeople of Warren somehow concluded they had to settle for impersonators in order to have Indians in attendance. So too did attendees at the reunion of John Eliot descendants in 1875. Among those welcoming them to the gathering were a group of non-Indians billed as "the South Natick 'Indians' . . . [who] comprised the guard of honor and escorted the guests to the auditorium," a move made necessary, one might guess, because "the last Natick Indian died in 1875" (the very year of the gathering), in spite of the fact that an orator proclaimed that "they are to-day *almost* extinct."[83] In Rowley, Massachusetts, among a procession of women and men in historical costume could be seen a man "in full Indian costume, carrying the pipe and armour of the late *Black Hawk,* an Indian chief," in apparent commemoration of the recent epic resistance of the Sac and Fox leader.[84] In these examples, it is also not clear whether the "Indians" in attendance had a voice in their performance.

Likewise, the people of Bridgewater, Massachusetts, settled for an impersonator in their remarkable bicentennial festivities that celebrated the legal incorporation of the town. According to the published program of the day, on June 3, 1856, the Bridgewater people sat through historical addresses, recited poetry, and hymns on this theme so thorough and rich that the program itself filled 140 pages when published. The Indian impersonator who closed the festivities wrapped up a dazzling display of historical memory punctuated with periodic nuggets of Indian history.[85]

In the principal historical address, the speaker relates that the Bridgewater people engaged in two legal land transactions with Indian possessors of the soil: one from the sachem Ousamequin, and a second (conducted by that gentle friend of the Indians, Myles Standish) from Massasoit. (The narrator failed to point out that Ousamequin and Massasoit were one and the same person. One can only guess that he did not know.) In a passage that may be familiar, because it opens this book, he connected these events to a particular place:

> Tradition points out the spot where this act of purchase was completed, which once bore the name of "Sachem's Rock."[86] But it is sad to think, that, of all that race who then peopled this region, nothing but tradition now remains. It is sad to recall in how short a time not a drop of the blood of the Sachem of Pokanoket, whose hand of friendship welcomed our fathers to these shores, was to be found in the veins of any living being.[87]

In this passage, a physical landmark is invoked in order to evoke a virtuous Bridgewater history of just property transactions, to replace one set of traditions with another, and to collapse a complex history of interaction and conflict into a "short" time that culminated in a lamentable and entirely unexplained story of Indian disappearance. Bridgewater people are told that their ancestors bought the land from the friendly Indians who, sadly, have exited stage left. "Not a drop of [their] blood" remained in any survivor.

Following the program for the day, after hearing the lengthy historical address, the attendees endured 111 four-line stanzas of a poem by James Reed of Boston, who, appropriately, is not remembered in the annals of great poetry. Let me edit out 109 of these stanzas, and note only 2:

> So scenes will often pass from mind
> Which never should have been forgot
> Thus, not so long ago, we find
> The town of Bridgewater was not.
>
> The town of Bridgewater was not:
> How comes it that the town has been?
> 'Twas purchased in a single lot
> Of famous old Ousamequin.[88]

The poet's admonishment to the people to remember that once "Bridgewater was not!" underscored his larger point; namely, the virtues of Bridgewater people were displayed in the town's very foundational act: Bridgewater came to "be" only through legal purchase from a famous Indian. (Apparently Mr. Reed had nodded off earlier when the historian told us there were *two* purchases.)[89] Little else about Indians made the final draft of Mr. Reed's epic poem: three brief mentions underscored that Indians lived in the woods, were "more fearful than bears," and were "bloody-red bowmen."[90]

Following the singing of a four-verse hymn that also stressed the legal purchase from the Indians, a commentator informed the audience of the exact terms of the Massasoit purchase (and laid out the going rate for Indian land): seven coats, nine hatchets, eight hoes, twenty knives, four moose skins, and ten and a half yards of cotton cloth, all costing about twenty-five dollars (thus establishing that Bridgewater was worth a dollar more than Manhattan). In his words,

> Such was the town valued at by the possessors, after a long period of occupation by savage tribes, and . . . was not destined to be increased in value by their mode of life, had they possessed it until the present time. Peopled by a civilized, Christian people, in the short space of two hundred years, the value of this same territory is more than five millions current money.[91]

Thus have the Bridgewater people put Indian land to higher uses (the almighty market), and they've even far outstripped neighboring Duxbury (which, we are told, has superior advantages), thus rendering "the superiority of Bridgewater the more to her credit."[92] John Locke would have been proud.

And for the final speech of the day, the Bridgewater people were in for a special treat, for the final speaker was none other than "a representative of the Pokanoket tribe [who] made the following response":

> BROTHERS,—I have come a long way to meet you. [Indeed: all the way from extinction to Bridgewater, Massachusetts.] I am glad that our good old father Massasoit still lives in your memory. The fields were once the hunting-grounds of the red men; but they were sold to the white men of Bridgewater. The red men have been driven towards the great water at the West, and have disappeared like the dew; while the white men have become like the leaves on the trees, and the sands on the sea-shore.
>
> Brothers, our hunting-grounds grow narrow; the chase grows short; the sun grows low; and, before another Centennial Celebration of the Incorporation of Bridgewater, our bones will be mingled with the dust.[93]

At last, an "Indian" stands on the stage and speaks for himself, supposedly to celebrate the Bridgewater people who have allegedly replaced his own, and to RSVP in advance for the next centennial. He stands, anonymously, and at the very end of the celebration, to proclaim that Bridgewater people had legally purchased his ancestors' homelands and to predict his own people's extinction. What are we to make of the fact that the Pokanoket speech came last? That the Bridgewater people have been absolved *by a Pokanoket person* of the messier details of English colonialism? That the inevitable culmination of the collision between "savagery" and "civilization" *is* Indian extinction? (Actually, the real reason the speech came last was because three short hymns that were to close the celebration were "omitted for lack of time.")[94]

But more to the point, why did the people of Bridgewater settle for what was likely an anonymous Indian impersonator when they could have turned to any number of actual Indian people in the vicinity? The short answer to this question is that they preferred the story their commemoration told. But we would be remiss not to note that John Milton Earle's report on Massachusetts Indians, finished just three years after the Bridgewater celebration, enumerated hundreds of Indians living in the vicinity. Traveling no more than ten or so miles, they could have learned about Indian families in Stoughton, Abington, Pembroke, Middleborough, and Plymouth, totaling 43 people in 1859. Going a little farther away, they might have found Indian families in more sizable clusters: in Canton (31), in Dartmouth (27), in Fall River (31), in Herring Pond (42), in New Bedford (81), in Wareham (19), and in Westport (50). Venturing onto Cape Cod at that time, they might have encountered Indians in Orleans (4), Sandwich (18), Barnstable (40), Yarmouth (63), and Mashpee (309).[95]

In fact, if they had gone to Abington, they might have encountered none other than noted Massasoit descendant Zerviah Gould Mitchell (aged fifty-two) and her family, which in 1859 included Alonzo (eight), Ann (twelve), Lydia (fifteen), John (eighteen), and Doloris (twenty-four), as well as the daughters who took the stage at the Rochester bicentennial twenty years later. Charlotte (ten) and Melinda (twenty-three) rounded out the family at the time. How could those responsible for mounting the elaborate festivities in Bridgewater fail to take note of the descendants of Massasoit whom later commemorators displayed so proudly and prominently?

Incomplete Indian Geographies

Disruptions in the narrative of Indian extinction took the form of uncertainty in and between local texts, and the fact of Indian attendance at public events that insisted on the inevitability of Indian extinction. Still other texts explicitly identified surviving Indian communities in New England, acknowledging the resiliency of Indian resistance to the ongoing legacy of English colonialism. Further compelling evidence of Indian survival in New England can be found in the state-level bureaucracies that Connecticut, Massachusetts, and Rhode Island maintained, even though each of them took steps to curtail their official acknowledgment of Indian nations in the seventeenth through the nineteenth centuries. All of this evidence helps flesh out a geography of Indian survival that undermines the extinction story and instead narrates Indian resistance to their effacement from New England.

To be sure, this evidence bears the considerable weight of nineteenth-century racial ideology, and must be read with these considerations in mind. Reconstructing a nineteenth-century Indian geography of southern New England that would satisfy the ideological requirements of racial purity could only narrate the story New Englanders found most satisfying—extinction, either imminent or already accomplished. A more nuanced approach that resists artificial and politically expedient arguments about blood purity and Indianness narrates the opposite: the ongoing vibrancy of Indian peoples throughout the region.

Recognition of the continuing existence of the Mohegan in Connecticut found expression in several local histories published between 1820 and 1880, although those that relegated this story to footnotes or appendixes required vigilance on the part of the reader. The terse sentences that acknowledge Indians reveal much. A Lebanon historical address sketched the separation of the Mohegan from the Pequot, explaining the dynamics that led Uncas to depart Stonington and cross the Thames, "where he established himself on lands which have since been held by the remnant of Indians, in the present town of Montville."[96] End of story, but at least we know from this that the Mohegan live on in Montville. Whether or not your average nineteenth-century reader embraced this bit of nuance is another matter. The participants in the bicentennial celebration of the settlement of Norwich heard more: "The Mohegans, from whom our fathers bought this 'nine miles square,' several score of whose descendants are our neighbors to this day, were originally a part of the Pequot tribe, and were of the same race with the Mohicans of the Hudson, the last of whose warriors has been so fitly commemorated by the great novelist of America." In this rendering, Mohegans are embraced as contemporary neighbors (although this mention is coupled with a reference to James Fenimore Cooper's fictional *Last of the Mohicans*—a subtle gesture that reveals a larger mind-set). As noted earlier, some of those neighbors silently shared the stage with those who assured them the Great Spirit had deemed that they become extinct.[97]

But the explanatory footnotes appended to the published volume of proceedings pointed to a more complex reality that is worth quoting at length:

> At the last session of the Connecticut legislature, (May, 1859,) a committee . . . was appointed to inquire into the condition of the Mohegans, and report to the legislature whether a sale of their reserved lands would be expedient.

From the facts then elicited, it appears that there are now in the tribe one hundred and two persons, though all of them are not of pure Indian blood. A considerable portion of the reservation made in 1790 to the tribe, by the State, and distributed among the families then living, has reverted to the tribe in common. It was proposed that this common land should be sold for the benefit of the tribe, but the legislature refused to grant the power, and a committee consisting of Gov. Buckingham, Senator Foster and Hon. J. A. Hovey, was appointed to inquire what course should be pursued, and report to the next legislature.

Divine service is regularly maintained in the chapel at Mohegan, and a Sabbath School is kept up chiefly by the efforts of Gen. Wm. Williams.[98]

This explicit acknowledgment of the ongoing political existence of the Mohegan tribe by the state of Connecticut did not find its way into the formal proceedings of the day, and so the oral culture of non-Indian commemoration carried the message of imminent disappearance. But in spite of its problematic rendering of Moheganness, this passage nonetheless constitutes a significant and profound rupture in the extinction narrative in the printed word.

William Leete Stone, who delivered a historical oration at the Uncas monument commemoration, found his subject matter so rich that he prepared a book on the lives of Uncas and Miantonomi. His pocket volume contained the lengthiest and most detailed accounting of Mohegan survival in all of these narratives, even though he proved himself just as confusing as anyone else on the matter of Mohegan survival. Toward the end of the body of the text, he declared Indians extinct.[99] But in the appendix we find that "in regard to the Mohegans, although never engaged in war against the Anglo-Saxons, they, too, in obedience to what seems to be the design of an inscrutable Providence, dooming the entire race to annihilation, have dwindled away to a mere handful of souls, the wreck of what they must once have been."[100] And still later:

I was informed by one of them [Mohegans] on the 5th of July, 1842, that their present number is between seventy and eighty; but a recent publication in Norwich states that the number of families now remaining is only thirteen numbering between sixty and seventy individuals. Their social condition, moreover, has been greatly improved within the last thirty years. They all reside in comfortable dwellings, and some of the families appear to be in a good condition for small farmers. The oldest person now living in the tribe is John Uncas, a Revolutionary pensioner, supposed to be between eighty and ninety. Their secular affairs are managed by an agent appointed by the county court, to whom he is accountable for a just distribution of the avails of their lands. The royal blood is not extinct, and they have yet among them a female of the ancient *regéime [sic]*, whom they call their Queen.[101]

Stone's narrative of the Mohegan community includes a not uncommon resort to accounting and the suggestion of a diminution in Mohegan numbers. But it is fundamentally a recognition of the survival of the people that stands in contrast with the breezy and romantic declaration of extinction lodged only pages before. And in describing Mohegan "secular affairs" Stone makes an allusion to the existence of the ongoing political relationship of the tribe with the state, described in more detail in the 1859 bicentennial celebration.[102] Moreover, if we choose to accept the lead of these commentators in resorting to demographic accounting, the Mohegans had increased from "between seventy and eighty" or the more modest assessment of "between sixty and seventy individuals" in 1842 to "one hundred and two persons" in 1859—a dramatic demographic increase of between 30 and 40 percent in seventeen years (if such accounting practices can be given credence).

Not surprisingly, in taking up the story of the venerable Uncas, Stone found occasion to touch upon the Pequot as well. His narrative shared the approach of many in pointing to the actions of the colony of Connecticut in the aftermath of the Pequot War:

> Their nation was extinguished, or directed to be extinguished, by law; even the name of their beautiful river, it was decided by the council of the pale-faces, should be changed from Pequod to Thames; and the town of Pequod, where Sassacus held his dusky court, was called New-London,—the new name being conferred as a testimony of the love the colonists bore their parent country.[103]

This expansive sentence seemed to say it all: the Pequot had been legislated out of existence in the seventeenth century and their places claimed in the process of renaming, all stock set pieces in the replacement narrative. And so the tone of the second-to-last page of the appendix of the book made sense: "It is a remarkable fact, that notwithstanding the pains taken by the early colonists to extirpate the Pequods, or to extinguish their name, a remnant of the race, and the name also, were preserved in their ancient country for more than a century after the enactments directed to that end." What's more:

> In a letter to the Publishing Committee of the Massachusetts Historical Society, by William T. Williams, Esq. of Lebanon, dated July, 1832, he says:—"There is a remnant of the Pequods still existing. They live in the town of Groton, and amount to about forty souls, in all, or perhaps a few more, or less, but they have about eleven hundred acres of poor land reserved to them in Groton, on which they live. They are more mixed than the Mohegans with negro and white blood, yet are a distinct tribe, and still retain a hatred to the Mohegans. . . . This, however, may be owing to their being more mixed with other blood. It is very rare

that there are any intermarriages with either of the tribes to each other;—they still, so far as circumstances admit, retaining the ancient grudge. The most common family name among them is Meazen. Nearly half of the survivors call themselves by that name."[104]

In this passage, Stone grapples with what must have been a conundrum for him. Pequot survival had to be "remarkable" to non-Indians who had been indoctrinated to believe that they had been "extinguished." And, given the history of colonialism in New England, Pequot (and other Indian) survival was *indeed* remarkable. Like many other acknowledgments of the persistence of New England Indians into the modern world, Stone lodged this commentary in the appendix. Others resorted to footnotes as the proper place for information that struggled against the master narrative of New Englanders replacing extinct Indians.

Frances Manwaring Caulkins located her comparatively expansive account on pages 604 and 605 of her 679-page history of New London—in chapter 35, which promised to probe the recent history of towns that were offshoots of the original New London. In three beefy paragraphs, Caulkins tells her readers that

> Mashantucket, the last retreat of the Pequot Indians, is in Ledyard. The reservation consists of about 900 acres. . . . That portion of the reservation which has been cleared, is leased to white tenants. . . . These sixteen [regular Pequots, as discussed earlier] belong to five families; eight more, (the *George* family,) are of mixed origin; two families of the Stonington tribe are residents on the land, making in all seven families, and about thirty persons.[105]

Having located the Mashantucket Pequot in Ledyard, Caulkins turned to the Eastern Pequot:

> In North Stonington only three families are left, comprising from fifteen to twenty persons, on a reservation of 240 acres, which is leased out to white tenants. Several families from these two reservations have at different times removed to the west and settled among other tribes. In 1850, certain Indians dwelling in Wisconsin, and bearing the surnames of *Charles*, *George*, *Poqumup* and *Skesooch*, applied to the Connecticut legislature for a share of the rental of the Groton lands; but they were not able to prove the purity of their descent.[106]

Cloaked in the language of blood and purity, these passages nonetheless help establish a nineteenth-century Indian geography of survival that the overwhelming bulk of historical material argues against. Caulkins also acknowledged another persisting community: "The Niantic Indians have here [Black

Point] a reservation of 240 acres, to which an ancient gateway and a green lane leads from the side of the public road. Here we still find ancient names of the tribe, Nonesuch, Sobuck and Wawqueet, although the whole community now comprises scarcely a dozen individuals."[107] But remarkably, her sketch of Montville entirely elided the contemporary Mohegan community, noting only the numbers of Indian church members in the middle of the eighteenth century, and then dropping them from consideration. Such elisions help plot the selective and distorted vision of even those who expressed some sort of provisional interest in Indian survival.

Another local history that brought Indians into the contemporary setting located two more communities in Connecticut:

> The day of the Indian is passed, and that of the railroad and telegraph has come; yet we do not need to ride or walk far from our daily haunts to find a few mixed descendants of the aborigines. These are mainly offshoots from the Pequots. They have lived for a long time in a narrow valley where a small stream and a large one unite, a spot which they have named, as Mr. Lossing tells us, *Pish-gach-ti-gock*—"the meeting of the waters." The name on white lips was changed to Scatacook, and the Indians became known as the Scatacook Indians. During a former generation these wards of civilization used to frequent the villages, peddling baskets and small wares to gain a livelihood.
>
> At the beginning of the present century a remnant of the Paugussetts were still living in Woodbridge, bearing the name of Mack, and within a few years some, who were supposed to be their descendants, have frequently been seen in our streets offering for sale the baskets they had made.[108]

This passage revealed the author's mind-set in its mixing of present and past tense. Even so, he acknowledges the ongoing existence of the Schaghticoke and Paugussett people in his densely packed, incomplete, and distorted rendering of a continuing Indian presence. A historian of Ridgefield only managed a fleeting and anonymous statement that: "There are no Indians at present living in the town, except one who has learned the mason trade and has married a white woman."[109]

Several Rhode Island texts made at least fleeting mention of Indian survival, including the New Shoreham history that noted in passing the "widely scattered" family of Mary Church (discussed in chapter 3), some of whom could be found in Stonington, Connecticut.[110] A history of Warwick observed, "In 1832 they remained [in Charlestown] the same in number [as in 1766: 315], but only seven of them were of pure Indian blood. In 1861 their number was found to be reduced to two of three-fourths blood, ten of half blood, and sixty-eight of less than quarter blood."[111]

A Rhode Island history noted the contents of a report by an 1833 committee on Indian affairs, which included yet another accounting of New England Indian survival: "'it appears that the whole number of all grades and conditions of the once numerous and warlike tribes of Narragansetts (the only tribe now existing in the State), was one hundred and fifty-eight.'" This oft-cited report invoked the language of blood in counting just seven "'of genuine Narragansett blood,'" several of whom it is said have since died. "'Three thousand acres of land in Charlestown, now in their possession, is all that is left to them of their ancient domain.'"[112]

As suggested in several of the Rhode Island texts that acknowledged Indian survival, one would be hard pressed to deny the continuing presence of the Narragansett if one turned one's attention to Charlestown. An eighty-eight-page historical sketch of that town is laced through with material on Indian history, and nearly every one of the numerous documents that are reprinted in the text involve Indians in one way or another. Toward the end of the text in a section about the Narragansett Indian school, it is noted:

> As early as 1815, the old school building was superseded by the present one, and named the Narragansett Indian School-house, in honor of the famous tribe of Indians, whose descendants still hold a small portion of the land by reservation. It may seem strange that the Indians owned the first school-house; but it is nevertheless true. . . . In this house the few surviving members of the Narragansett Indians hold their annual council, and it is here that they also have their school.[113]

This author found it jarring that Narragansett could somehow be thought of as participating in modernity by owning "the first school-house." But more to the point, this sparse passage tells us the Narragansett continue their political existence on retained homelands, where their councils continue to meet annually and, one might guess, they do a whole lot more than that. Twenty pages before, he declared that Canonchet was the "last sachem of the race" whose death signaled "the nation was extinguished forever," which constitutes an excellent example of textual uncertainty.[114]

Rather than focusing on the Indian schoolhouse as a locus of Indian survival, Westerly's historian looked to the Indian church in neighboring Charlestown, attributing to the church a major role in the preservation of the people: "But for the existence and influence of this Christian church, doubtless the remnant of the Niantic monarchy, like the most of the other tribes in our land, would long since have passed away. Like salt it has preserved them from utter decay."[115] A new stone church had been built in 1860, which the author suggested might end up being "the last monument of civilization left by the once mighty Niantics."[116] The author declared that the Niantics had never been maltreated: "Both under the English and American rule, as wards of the colony and of the State, they have been protected, nourished, and aided with generous and Christian care," even though individual non-Indians might not have always been similarly inclined. Reprinted in the book is an account of the history and present circumstances of the tribe published in the *Providence Journal* of October 17, 1866. It is a remarkable acknowledgment of the continuing political existence of the tribe, who "elect their own officers, and are governed by their own laws," and who were at present embroiled in a struggle with the state of Rhode Island over the continued official acknowledgment of their existence (about which, more later in this chapter).[117]

Local narrators acknowledged Nipmuc survival in Dudley, Massachusetts, where there was "a small tract of land near the great pond, which is still occupied by a few degraded descendants of the original proprietors,"[118] and in Grafton, where "in 1830 there were fourteen of a mixed Indian and negro race, which still hold some of the Indian lands, and receive the benefit of the small remaining fund."[119] Farther to the west in Springfield, an orator asserted that "seldom have any of the remnants of the Indians been seen here by any now living, unless when transiently passing through the town, from the west; and those that have been here were, probably, of the Mohegan, or Grafton tribes."[120] And in Gay Head, a historian observed, "the Indian blood has been mixed and confounded, and the native language, once used in Scripture study and in psalms, has utterly died away. The visitor, however, may yet see Indian features, cabins, gardens, schools and occupations. The present preacher amongst them is Charles H. Kent, a white man."[121] In the former Praying Town of Natick a minister asserted, "[the] number [of Indians] is now reduced to two or three."[122] A historian updated this story in 1835 by claiming that "[Hannah Dexter's] grandson, Solomon Dexter, is now the only full blooded survivor of the tribe, unless we reckon a small number, who reside in or near Mendon, in the County of Worcester, who occasionally visit this place, as the land of their ancestors."[123]

Such fleeting notices of Indian survival left the impression that the story was nearly over for Indian peoples in Massachusetts and in southern New England more generally. They frequently contained the standard brew of racial thinking that invoked the temporalities of race that underwrote the degeneracy narrative. As elsewhere, they also occasionally gesture toward something more that is going on. One might read the snippet from the Grafton history (which is buried in a footnote in the appendix to the text) and wonder, what "small remaining fund"? Although the author never explicitly says so, the fund he likely had in mind stemmed from the sale of the land of the former Praying Town in 1727, the proceeds of which were reserved to the descendants of the original Indian proprietary families.[124] If so, this mundane clause buried in a footnote referred to the unique guardianship relationship that acknowledged the ongoing separate existence of the Nipmuc people in Grafton, though it seems unlikely that an average reader would be equipped to decode this.

A comparison of two Westborough texts, one published in 1889 and the other only two years later, demonstrates the ways in which authorial perspectives and visions could deviate quite dramatically. The 1891 volume noted conflicts over land belonging to the Indians in the Praying Town of Okommokamesit that they lost, then declared that "they faded away."[125] It went on to acknowledge two stories about Indians from the eighteenth and nineteenth centuries, but dismissed them as evidence of local Indian survival on the grounds that "these were not Okommokamesit Indians, but stragglers from the Hassanemesits."[126] Rather than offering this dismissive treatment of Indians, Harriette Merrifield Forbes's 1889 text is steeped in Indian history. It weaves Indians into the narrative, and attends to Indian legends as part of the local history even though its bottom line is declension of the Indian presence like other local literature. Tellingly, the frontispiece of the volume is a photograph of an Indian woman, Deb Brown, with her hair pulled back, wearing a fancy floral dress with a ruffled collar. Toward the end of her history, Forbes noted, "some remnants of the tribe have remained in their old home, still praying for the money which is their just due. In 1841, when a new trustee was appointed, it was found there were no funds. In a report made in 1861 to the Governor and Council by John Milton Earle, special commissioner, he says: 'The State in its sovereign capacity took their property into its keeping, and has suffered it to be squandered or lost.'"[127] Later still she asserted that no Hassanamiscoes remained in Westborough, but that one family lived in Grafton. In the very same paragraph, Forbes tells of the two and a half acres of land belonging to Sarah Maria Cisco, who received money annually from the state, and whose "is the only land in the town, if not in the State, which has never passed out of the hands of the Hassanamiscoes. She is now seventy years old, is partially of colored blood. Her husband is partly colored and partly of the Narragansett tribe. They have several children."[128]

A similarly mysterious and incomplete acknowledgment of the ongoing existence of Indian peoples in New England could be found embedded in a lengthy disputation on the justice of English colonialism: "And to show that this faith [regarding Indian land rights] has been kept, we can point to the grants that are made to this day to the Indians at Grafton, Gay Head, Marshpee, and other places."[129] The author let this observation dangle, refusing to flesh out anything more about these extant tribes.

Dorchester's historian added a footnote to his assertion that the Praying Town of Punkapoag drew Indians there after the grant of land in 1656, until "the lapse of years has nearly extinguished their lamp." It was composed of a passage quoted from the "Bird Report":

> "The names of the different tribes in the State are as follows:—Chappequiddic, Christiantown, Gay Head, Fall River or Troy, Marshpee, Herring Pond, Grafton or Hapanamisco, Dudley, Punkapog, Natick, and Yarmouth. The whole number of Indians, and people of color connected with them, not including the Natick, is 847. There are but six or eight Indians of pure blood in the State; one or two at Gay Head, one at Punkapog, and three, perhaps four, at Marshpee. All the rest are of mixed blood; most of Indian and African."—*Report of the Commissioners relating to the Condition of the Indians—1849.*[130]

In the tens of thousands of pages that composed the collective published historical record of localities in Massachusetts, this completely unanalyzed footnote contained the most geographically comprehensive recognition of Indian survival in the Commonwealth. Presumably one could not rely on the casual reader to distill from this footnote the complex Indian reality that was still only incompletely communicated in the language and sheer existence of this report. A commission appointed by the Commonwealth to investigate the present-day situation of Indians in Massachusetts, in spite of the racial ideology of the day that would condition them toward nonrecognition of Indian peoples, still managed to identify eleven tribes numbering by their (no doubt incomplete) count of 847 Indians.

Of the more than three hundred Massachusetts local accounts published between 1820 and 1880 that contain Indian material, only a handful acknowledged the ongoing existence of Indian peoples in the Commonwealth, and three of these failed to identify the Indians they did recognize with tribal labels. Two more histories made reference to annual visits by Indians from northern New England.[131] In this curious collective account of Indian survival, the Indian town of Mashpee occupied an analogous position to the Narragansett in Charlestown, Rhode Island. How could one *not* recognize the Mashpee, whom John Milton Earle enumerated at 403 individuals who continued to possess 16,132 acres of their homelands in 1859? Indeed, two histories made fascinating reference to the still-present Mashpee. Plymouth's historian noted in passing that "its Indian name was Umpame, written Apaum, in the Colony

Records, and still so called by the natives of Massapee," which indicated that still-present Mashpee people continued to employ Algonquian places-names, even for the place non-Indians claimed as their "first."[132] And a historical commemoration celebrating incorporation in Kingston as part of the "Old Colony" of Plymouth ought to include all of the towns of the Cape "(including the new Indian town of Mashpee)," according to one of its number.[133] That Mashpee could be deemed "new" spoke not to Indian ways of being on the land but on Massachusetts's bureaucratic procedures. Nonetheless.

But Medfield's commemoration of the bicentennial of its burning during King Philip's War contained the most extensive and interesting notice of Mashpee or any other single tribe. Why would Mashpee, located some seventy miles away, occupy the attention of the people of Medfield? The respondent to a toast, John B. D. Cogswell, chairman of the judiciary in the Massachusetts legislature, had particular reasons for choosing to reflect on Indians, "and to present them, or some of them, in a different light from that in which we naturally would regard them, upon this day."[134] He stood to provide an encapsulated history of Indians from "First Encounter" to the present, including his own boyhood memories and present-day relationship with them. His father had taken him

> to see the last survivor of all the great numbers of Indians who once lived in the lower towns of the Cape. . . . all passed away, by the inexorable law which decreed death to the Indians in the presence of the white man, except in the town of Mashpee, which still remains occupied by the descendants of the Indians, now few in number, who are the first of their race who have ever been enfranchised, relieved from tutelage, and declared to be citizens,—Mashpee having been created a town in 1870. And in the following year I had, as candidate for Representative to the General Court, the honor of receiving the first Indian votes ever thrown anywhere in this country.[135]

Cogswell told the audience he had attended religious services at the Mashpee church just two summers previously, and that he felt

> justified . . . in the name of these late constituents of mine, who, though of Indian origin, are nevertheless peaceful and obedient and worthy citizens of the Commonwealth, to tender from them, the descendants of the peaceful Indians of the Cape, to you, the descendants of those whom their kinsmen ravaged and spoiled two hundred years ago, to-day the olive-branch of peace.[136]

The president of the day then stood to read a response to the response, written by a former commissioner of Indian affairs, who could not attend: "The remaining tribes of Indians in our land,—we will harbor towards them no feeling of revenge for the deeds of their fathers, but pity them for the wrong they are made to endure, and seek their welfare by the cultivation of mutual peace and mutual helpfulness."[137]

Interestingly, a two-volume *county* history that constructed a narrative about Cape Cod contained the most extensive accounting of Indians in Massachusetts extending richly into the seventh decade of the nineteenth century when it was published.[138] Indeed, the author announced in the title that Indians would be part of this story: *The History of Cape Cod: The Annals of Barnstable County, Including the District of Mashpee* (though one would need to know that Mashpee was an Indian place). True to his word, Frederick Freeman provided extensive accounts of Indian history on the Cape, and a detailed narrative of nineteenth-century Indian affairs in Mashpee. Uniquely, this text devoted nearly thirty pages to a detailed post-Revolutionary War history of Indian affairs that both acknowledged the status of Mashpee as an officially recognized Indian place within a colonial bureaucracy of oversight, and gave voice to the vehement Indian protests over the management of their affairs. This long-festering situation culminated in what came to be called the "Mashpee Revolt," in which Indians successfully challenged the paternalistic oversight of the Commonwealth, which had defrauded them of property and their rights for so long, and gained incorporation as a district in which they regained essential elements of self-government.[139] They continued to be recognized as a tribal entity within the bureaucratic structure devoted to Indian affairs. In acknowledging the events that culminated in the Mashpee Revolt, which Lisa Brooks has recently interpreted as a dramatic recovery of Native space, this history stands apart from every local history from southeastern New England between 1820 and 1880.[140] It is also a remarkable exception in another respect: This volume comments on the participation of "WILLIAM APES, a regularly ordained preacher of the Pequot tribe, [who] came to Mashpee, 'was adopted by the tribe, and invited to preach to them and assist them in gaining their liberty'" (see Figure 25).[141] No history devoted to a particular town anywhere in New England acknowledges even the existence of the remarkable minister, activist, and public intellectual William Apess, who became briefly famous—even notorious—in the 1830s for his bold actions in defense of Indian peoples and their rights.

Apess gave voice to a powerful counternarrative of Indian history that briefly gained a hearing, and then faded away, only to be reasserted in the late twentieth century. In this he has much in common with African American public intellectuals Maria Stewart and David Walker, who in this same modern

MR. WILLIAM APES,

A NATIVE MISSIONARY OF THE PEQUOT TRIBE

OF INDIANS.

Figure 25. *Mr. William Apes[s], a Native Missionary of the Pequot Tribe of Indians.* Portrait of published author, activist, and minister William Apess, a Pequot, that hangs in the American Antiquarian Society. Courtesy of the American Antiquarian Society.

moment stood before the public to make radical calls for racial justice.[142] All three penned important works in southern New England in the late 1820s and 1830s decrying racial injustice and became widely known and even feared public figures who receded from public memory until recently.[143] Whereas Stewart and Walker boldly challenged slavery and the back-to-Africa movement spearheaded by the American Colonization Society (1816), Apess emerged at this time as a public intellectual who articulated Native demands and argued for the recognition of the social, cultural, political, and legal place of New England Indians in modernity.[144]

Writing and Talking Back: William Apess as Political Theorist

William Apess was born into poverty in western Massachusetts. His early life must have paralleled that of many Indians in southern New England in the many decades following the catastrophic King Philip's War of 1675–76. This pan-Indian resistance movement led by the Wampanoag leader Metacom (called King Philip by the English) ripped through New England and for a time seemed like it might succeed in turning out the English. Instead, King Philip's War represented the final military resistance of Indians in southern New England. New Englanders seized even more Indian land in the wake of this conflict by "right of conquest," and Indians there became less and less visible to non-Indians. They suffered further dispossession of their homelands into the nineteenth century, and throughout this time, they endured dramatic demographic change through the combined impact of epidemic disease, military conquest, ill health, and more. Made marginal in their own homelands, Indians reshaped their lives in all sorts of ways, including by finding employment in wage labor, the whaling industry, military service, peddling Native crafts (especially baskets and brooms), and suffering indentured servitude when relations of debt threatened families. The challenges of sheer survival under these conditions made a tremendous impact on William Apess and other New England Indians. His family splintered, and as a young boy, Apess found himself living with a grandmother who was cruel to him and eventually beat him so severely it took him nearly a year to recover. In his later years, Apess would come to understand that the liquor introduced to Indian communities, and the experience of dispossession, contributed to his grandmother's rage of which he became the victim.[145] Removed from his family, he was indentured to Anglo families from whom he frequently fled. Somehow along the way, Apess managed six winters of schooling that would empower him to find a clear and effective voice of public protest against the oppression New England Indians suffered.[146]

Much of what we know about William Apess's life comes from his autobiography, published in 1831, and from the amazing detective work of Barry
O'Connell, who published an annotated edition of Apess's collected writings
along with an indispensable introduction that narrates his life in 1992. *A Son
of the Forest: The Experience of William Apes, a Native of the Forest* passionately
plots Apess's life story, his peripatetic journey from household to household
in servitude, his service as a soldier in the War of 1812, and, significantly, his
spiritual quest that brought him to the Methodist religion as a convert at age
fifteen and then later as a minister. Apess was thirty-three years old when he
published *Son of the Forest*. He followed this volume with four more publications, two of which are devoted to religion (although they also rippled with
political commentary), and two more that are more overtly political in nature
(although also infused with concerns about religion). For reasons that remain unclear, Apess moved to New York City, perhaps, as Robert Warrior has
argued, to carve out a career for himself as a writer.[147] He died in New York
under equally mysterious circumstances in 1837 at the age of thirty-nine.

In 1833, William Apess arrived as a preacher in the Indian town of Mashpee, Massachusetts, a place where Indian peoples had managed to retain a
viable land base as a communal resource. He soon found himself at the center
of a long-standing dispute between the Mashpee people and their non-Indian
"overseers"—officials appointed by the Commonwealth of Massachusetts to
manage Indian affairs according to the bureaucracy that had organically
developed there. The Mashpee had long bristled under the corrupt actions of
the overseers, who unilaterally and defiantly abused their power over everything from leasing out Indian lands and woodlots to non-Indians, indentur-
ing Indian children out of their families, binding out adults and children for
employment to non-Indians, and regulating entry into the community. Also
at issue was the religious establishment: The Mashpee had thrust upon them
a minister by the unfortunate name of Phineas Fish who was not of their
choosing and not at all to their liking, and who was supported by a trust
administered by Harvard College for the benefit of Indians. The Indians re-
acted to his lackluster abilities by attending their own services conducted by
their own preacher, Blind Joe Amos and, after his arrival, William Apess, leaving Fish to minister to a congregation composed almost entirely of non-Indians.

Apess galvanized the people, who adopted him into the tribe, and over the
course of the next year he became the public face in what has been called the
"Mashpee Revolt." This protest movement is the subject Apess's fourth book,
*Indian Nullification of the Unconstitutional Laws of Massachusetts Relative to the
Marshpee Tribe; or, The Pretended Riot Explained* (1835). It consists of the reams

of collected documents and newspaper reports of the movement along with Apess's commentary on the epic struggle for Mashpee self-determination. The newcomer Apess provided fresh energy for the long-festering dispute, and the political leadership of the Mashpee embraced him in this role.

To his readers, Apess's allusion to the then raging battle over states' rights in the guise of the Nullification Crisis would have been readily apparent. He references the position of the southern states and in particular South Carolina regarding the tariffs that extended trade protection for northern industries by taxing foreign manufacturing imports. Southerners such as John C. Calhoun articulated a position that states could effectively nullify a federal statute, and armed hostilities threatened to break out. But for his own purposes, Apess could only have been suggesting that Indians have the right to nullify the unjust laws of the state of Massachusetts. In effect, he is asserting a parallel between governmental entities in order to assert the political status of New England tribes vis-à-vis the state.

The Nullification Crisis invoked in his title was not his only recourse to political theories and battles of the moment. In protesting their condition, the tribe also drew a parallel between their own circumstances and those of the Cherokee Nation, just then embroiled in its own resistance to the state of Georgia and to Andrew Jackson's odious removal policy that sought to cleanse the east of Indian nations by forcing them across the Mississippi River to Indian Territory, succinctly conveyed in this excerpt from the Mashpee petition of protest:

> Perhaps you have heard of the oppression of the Cherokees and lamented over them much, and thought the Georgians were hard and cruel creatures; but did you ever hear of the poor, oppressed and degraded Marshpee Indians in Massachusetts, and lament over them? If not, you hear now, and we have made choice of the Rev. Wm. Apes to relieve us, and we hope that you will assist him. And if the above complaints and reasons, and the following resolutions, will be satisfactory, we shall be glad, and rejoice that you comply with our request.
>
> *Resolved,* That we will rule our own tribe and make choice of whom we please for our preacher.
>
> *Resolved,* That we will have our own meeting house, and place in the pulpit whom we please to preach to us.
>
> *Resolved,* That we will publish this to the world; if the above reasons and resolutions are not adhered to, and the Rev. Mr. Fish discharged.
>
> The foregoing addresses and resolutions were adopted by a vote of the tribe, almost unanimously. Done at the Council House at Marshpee, May the 21st, 1833.[148]

Removal policy as a touchstone held deep symbolic value for New England-ers—Indians and non-Indians alike—because of the vehement protests lodged by New England's politicians in opposition to the policy. For Indians, nothing served their political agenda of self-determination more effectively and they repeatedly invoked the Cherokee, the efforts of the state of Georgia to obliterate their political existence, and the policy itself to rebuke politicians and prompt them to recognize the survival and sovereignty of New England Indian tribes. As a result of these staunch efforts, the Mashpee succeeded in winning back substantial powers of self-determination and they eventually rid themselves of the unpopular Reverend Fish as well.

William Apess's final publication followed in 1836, two years after the Mashpees' triumph over their overseers. This powerful oration, titled *Eulogy on King Philip, as Pronounced at the Odeon, in Federal Street*, took up the New England tradition of commemoration and turned it on its head, as this passage makes abundantly clear:

> Let the day be dark, the 22nd day of December 1622, let it be forgotten in your celebration, in your speeches, and by the burying of the rock that your fathers first put their foot upon. For be it remembered, although the Gospel is said to be glad tidings to all people, yet we poor Indians never have found those who brought it as messengers of mercy, but contrawise. We say, therefore, let every man of color wrap himself in mourning, for the 22nd of December and the 4th of July are days of mourning and not of joy. . . . Let them rather fast and pray to the great Spirit, the Indian's God, who deals out mercy to his red children, and not destruction.[149]

William Apess's bold statement on behalf of New England Indians proposed to undo the replacement narrative that argued for a glorious and honorable New England history entailing the rightful replacement of Indian peoples and cultures with Anglo-American peoples, institutions, and ideals. The basic contours of this story had been well entrenched by this time. Persecuted English people landed at Plymouth Rock, bringing with them religious and political freedom that would become the bedrock of the nation. Lamentably (for some), Indian peoples failed or refused to accept the blessings of European religion and culture that were extended to them, and consequently they tottered on the verge of extinction in New England as they would presumably elsewhere as the nation expanded to its natural boundaries.

William Apess had a rather different take on this slice of history, as even a cursory glance at his *Eulogy* reveals. He delivered the *Eulogy* twice in January of 1836, first at the Odeon Theatre and then upon request at the Boylston

Theatre, both in Boston. He rose to pay tribute, not to the supposedly originary dates of the nation and New England's special role in that project, but
rather to the death of the heroic Metacom, Native resistance leader of the devastating 1675–76 war labeled after his "English" name: King Philip's War.[150]
As Barry O'Connell has pointed out and Maureen Konkle has elaborated on,
in his choice of format—a historical oration—Apess took up a standard New
England means of commemorating the past.[151] But in his revisionary oration,
"Forefathers' Day" (which he mistakenly dated to 1622) and the Fourth of July
represented not days of celebration of origins but rather of forgetting and of
mourning "for every man of color." And Plymouth Rock, so richly symbolic
of "national origins," ought to be buried. Furthermore, Apess argues that
those same men of color should look to the Great Spirit rather than the Gospel
for lasting mercy that would not sanction the destruction the nation sought
to achieve for Indians—an interesting suggestion given the Christian cast of
Apess's life and most of his publications. Apess's message in the *Eulogy* is one
of Indian resistance, not destruction and eclipse, which is how memorials,
commemorations, and monuments scripted the post–King Philip's War history on which non-Indians insisted.

Indeed, *Eulogy on King Philip* offers an unparalleled commentary on the
problem of memory in nineteenth-century New England. Apess took up his
pen and then took to the stage to argue against non-Indian claims to shaping
the public memory of Indians. More than offering simply a counternarrative,
Apess challenged the very mode of memory and commemoration by mocking
the uses non-Indians made of this genre. He challenged the ways non-Indians
used the mode of commemoration to erase Indian perspectives on the past
and prospects for the future. His oration instead pointed out the pretense of
claiming to remember history in ways that negated Indians and their own
versions of the past, present, and future, calling attention to the selective and
distorted memory of such commemorative practices.

In his caustic and clever oration, Apess boldly recast this story by arguing
for the fame of the seventeenth-century Wampanoag resistance leader Philip,
who ought rightfully to take his place alongside Philip of Macedon, Alexander
the Great, and George Washington in memory. Along the way, he entered into
a fascinating dialogue with the tropes of memory and commemoration in making the case for the honorable and enduring presence of Indian peoples into
the present and future. As has been noted, some non-Indian writers shared
Apess's sympathetic perspective on New England Indian history, but he
departed from these authors by (in the words of Barry O'Connell) "giving this
history a contemporary resonance, connecting the past treatment of Indians

to present policy and calling for change."[152] What's more, even while employing the contemporary grammar of blood and degradation, Apess insisted on the centrality and the dignity of Indian peoples and their perspectives on history.

Apess's larger aims become apparent at the outset of his oration. Even though the *Eulogy* is ostensibly devoted to Philip's memory, he immediately complicates and raises the stakes: he stands to speak *not* about "the fame of a noted warrior" (which he proclaims in his title) but *instead* "to bring before you beings made by the God of Nature, and in whose hearts and heads he has planted sympathies that shall live forever in the memory of the world." His oration is not just about Philip, then, but about "justice and humanity for the remaining few," concepts that inspired him "to vindicate the character of him who yet lives in their hearts and, if possible, [to] melt the prejudice that exists in the hearts of those who are in the possession of his soil, and only by the right of conquest." Embracing the language of memory and commemoration, Apess draws attention to "those few remaining descendants who now remain as the monument of the cruelty of those who came to improve our race and correct our errors . . . [E]ven such is the immortal Philip honored, as held in memory by the degraded but yet grateful descendants who appreciate his character."[153] In reminding listeners and readers about the importance of oral history to Indians, and suggesting Indian people as monuments, Apess argued for the enlivening of memory and for its reproduction into the future. The proper context for memory making regarding Philip is the contemporary and enduring Indian community.

After framing his oration in relationship to the still-present Indian peoples whose historical narratives differed fundamentally in purpose and perspective, Apess told about the history of colonialism in New England. His account constituted an examination of the deep historical context of the war that reached back to the 1614 enslavement of Indians from Cape Cod, an "inhumane act of the whites [that] caused the Indians to be jealous forever afterward, which the white man acknowledges upon the first pages of the history of his country."[154] Apess's account ranged widely across New England history as well as detailing the events of the war itself in order to "lay those deeds and depredations committed by whites upon Indians before the civilized world, and they can judge for themselves."[155] A long train of heinous acts, from the enslavement that preceded actual English invasion, through theft, broken treaties, and unjust land dealings, laid the groundwork for the conflict. There could be no mistaking what conclusions Apess drew about New Englanders: "I do not hesitate to say that through the prayers, preaching, and examples of those pretended pious has been the foundation of all the slavery and degradation in the American colonies toward colored people."[156] Here, Apess calls attention not just to the selective and distorted practices of commemoration but also to how these practices themselves are a mode of violence against Indian people.

Apess asks, "Where shall we place this hero of the wilderness?"[157] He places him in the context of the enduring communities who cherish Philip's memory and their *own* versions of history, and as human beings equal to whites yet rightfully separate from them. I would like to point out that even more, Apess is struggling to make the argument for Indian peoples as entitled to their measured separatism as Indian peoples with rights of self-determination, *and* as entitled to citizenship in the United States—in other words, something like the present-day situation of dual citizenship for federally recognized tribal nations.[158] His arguments move beyond claiming equality and justice for Indians and other people of color.[159] He roots these claims in history and in critiques of present-day Indian policies. That he struggles to express these ideas is not surprising, given that the concept of dual citizenship for Indian people awaited formulation in the law—I am arguing that he is working through a set of ideas that form a concept long before its time. Dual citizenship for Indians did not gain full expression in the law until the *United States v. Nice* decision from 1916 that ruled that Indian individuals did not lose their status in their own nations even when they gained U.S. citizenship through the various haphazard methods that were available to them at the time. The guarantee of citizenship status for Indians awaited the Indian Citizenship (or Snyder Act) of 1924.[160]

Without an incipient theory of dual citizenship, Apess's oration might seem at odds with itself. One cannot read this remarkable text without being struck by the boldness of Apess's voice, and his steadfast commitment to telling an Indian story of autonomy—of the political sovereignty of Indian nations that confronted the unjust invasion of their homelands by people who hypocritically cloaked their actions in religion. What, then, to do with Apess's closing thoughts: "And while you ask yourselves, 'What do they, the Indians, want?' you have only to look at the unjust laws made for them and say, 'They want what I want,' in order to make men of them, good and wholesome citizens."[161] How could it be that Apess ends his oration by arguing for citizenship for Indians in spite of his relentless assault on the injustice of non-Indians in virtually every respect, and in view of his own role in the securing of a measured autonomy for Mashpee people in the three years previous to the *Eulogy*? It seems to me that the most convincing way of reading this tension—the idea that the solution for Indian peoples is citizenship bumping up against Apess's strident defense of Indian self-determination evident in the *Eulogy* and elsewhere (especially *Indian Nullification*)—lies in the then still inchoate idea of dual citizenship.

In this sense, we can see Apess struggling to come to a political stance regarding the present and future of Indian peoples within the colonial regime that moves even beyond his important claim about the endurance of New England Indian peoples and their securing of justice. Apess's call for citizenship is arresting: in proposing an innovation in unprecedented ways of thinking about Indian sovereignty he announces himself as a modern. In passionately pointing to what Indians are demanding, he is boldly refusing to be static. Indians want to be citizens and they want justice. Justice, in my reading of Apess's more secular writings, involves securing both the self-determination of tribal nations and the extension of the rights of U.S. citizenship as an acknowledgment of Indian humanity and equality.

A strong undercurrent runs through the *Eulogy* regarding Indian rights and autonomy and their relationship to the practices of Indian sovereignty. In common with non-Indian sources he drew upon, Apess foregrounds a history of treaty making that began with Massasoit in the 1620s, although in his version, it is New Englanders who compiled a hefty record of treaty violations. He carried through with this history of Indian sovereignty and diplomacy in narrating the story of Philip's refusal to capitulate to the audacious demands of the Pilgrims that he be summoned to account for the murder of John Sassamon in 1675, the event that served as the immediate trigger of King Philip's War: "The king answered them thus: 'Your governor is but a subject of King Charles of England; I shall not treat with a subject; I shall treat of peace only with a king; when he comes, I am ready.'"[162]

Toward the end of the *Eulogy*, Apess links New England Indian history to contemporary sovereignty struggles, implicitly invoking the Cherokee crisis over removal in a richly evocative passage:

> How deep, then, was the thought of Philip, when he could look from Maine to Georgia . . . and how true his prophecy, that the white people would not only cut down their groves but would enslave them. . . . Our groves and hunting grounds are gone, our dead are dug up, our council fires are put out, and a foundation was laid in the first Legislature to enslave our people, by taking from them all rights, which has been strictly adhered to ever since. Look at the disgraceful laws, disfranchising us as citizens. Look at the treaties made by Congress, all broken. Look at the deep-rooted plans laid, when a territory becomes a state, that after so many years the laws shall be extended over the Indians that live within their

boundaries. . . . this is the course that has been pursued for nearly two hundred years. . . . What, then, shall we do? Shall we cease crying and say it is all wrong, or shall we bury the hatchet and those unjust laws and Plymouth Rock together and become friends?[163]

It is significant, I think, that Apess's geographical frame for this overview of U.S. federal Indian policy begins with northern New England and directly moves the listener's (and reader's) attention to the hotbed of present-day sovereignty struggles, Georgia. Why not, for example, South Carolina, a place he had invoked during the Mashpee revolt, or even Florida, the southernmost place in contrast to the northernmost that the United States claimed, and the location of a different sort of resistance to removal? Because, I would argue, nothing would more clearly evoke the image of unjust assaults on Indian sovereignty than Georgia's attempt to obliterate the Cherokee Nation, as well as the Supreme Court cases that came to define the concept of "domestic dependent nationhood" in U.S. case law. This juxtaposition aligns New England Indian nations with other tribal nations of the contemporary and the future. That sovereignty is Apess's focus is underlined by his reference to U.S.–Indian diplomacy using the international convention of treaty relations, even though his proximate intent is to point out the United States' propensity for violating them. Here too in this passage does Apess set up what might seem like a paradox unless one takes into consideration the still unarticulated concept of dual citizenship: he alludes to the presumptuousness of the Northwest Ordinance of 1787, with its intent to incorporate future states into the United States through the territorial system, which would theoretically extend state and U.S. laws over Indian people as an assault on Indian sovereignty in the same breath that he laments the disfranchisement of Indians. Apess further links New England tribes to these struggles by extending the chronology of this critique to the prehistory of the United States. The colonialism of the United States is two hundred years old and not just confined to the present. And it did not end with U.S. independence from Great Britain following the American Revolution.

In this passage and elsewhere, Apess grapples with the clash of polities that lay at the heart of the colonial relationship, and takes umbrage at the denial of citizenship for Indians as an issue of rights and justice. He is arguing for the fundamental equality of Indian people that should entitle Indians to citizenship in the nation at the same time he insists on the disgracefulness of depriving Indian nations of their autonomous existence. Here and elsewhere in his writings, Apess insists on the rights of Indian people as equal citizens *and* the right of Indian nations to exist as sovereign entities in a diplomatic relationship with the federal government. With this frame in mind, Apess's rhetorical questions, "What, then, shall we do? Shall we cease crying and say it is all wrong, or shall we bury the hatchet and those unjust laws and Plymouth Rock together and become friends?" take on a different cast. In burying the unjust laws that intended to obliterate Indian sovereignty (and Plymouth Rock for good measure), Indian sovereignty would be acknowledged, as would the Indian right to citizenship. So too might we revisit Apess's puzzling parting shot: "What do they, the Indians, want? you have only to look at the unjust laws made for them and say, 'they want what I want,' in order to make men of them, good and wholesome citizens." The unjust laws he had in mind, I'd like to suggest, include those that denied the sovereign status of Indian nations. "Good and wholesome" Indian citizens enjoyed the rights of self-determination in their own nations (the central theme of the Mashpee struggle) as well as citizenship in the United States, rather than suffering the emasculating and dehumanizing denial of these rights.

Taken together, Apess's vision obliterates ideas that lay at the center of the New England project of nationalism, which argued for the primacy of a new modern social order non-Indians claimed as their hallmark to the exclusion of the ongoing existence of Indian nations. Their accounts of the past, present, and future entailed a process of replacing Indians physically and imaginatively on the landscape of New England. That is, they formulated a history that negated previous Indian history as a "dead end" (literally) and substituted Indian history with a glorious New England history of just relations and property transactions rooted in American diplomacy that legitimated their claims to Indian homelands, and to the institutions they grounded there. Apess rejects this construct by insisting on the equality and integrity of Indian peoples—natives of the land—and the fact of Indian survival and endurance into the future. He reclaims indigeneity from non-Indians who attempted to seize it through the construct of modernity. New England history *is* Indian history, and Indian people continue to resist the audacious colonialism inaugurated by those who stumbled onto Plymouth Rock (not to mention the filiopietistic ceremonies New Englanders performed there in mining the historical oration as commemoration). Along the way, he exposes the racism honed in the colonial encounter that New England Indians were forced to live with in the present. He told of personal experiences with prejudice in Connecticut "where they are so pious that they kill the cats for killing rats, and whip the beer barrels for working upon the Sabbath."[164] Such false piety could be found at the center of the colonial project—the ideological framework for the replacement narrative, succinctly stated by Apess himself: "And as the seed of iniquity and prejudice was sown in that day, so it still remains; and there is a deep-rooted popular opinion in the hearts of many that Indians were made, etc., on purpose for destruction, to be driven out by white Christians, and they to take their place."[165]

William Apess took the stage to reclaim New England as an Indian place, and in this sense and many others he is a remarkable figure. That he is unique in the history of Indian writing in New England is on one level undeniable. No other Indian intellectual managed to compile a public life and record of publication in any way comparable to that of William Apess in its sheer complexity and volume. Yet Indian writing has a long history in New England, beginning in the seventeenth century and extending into the present, and Apess represents only one especially significant point in this arc.[166] Furthermore, Indian intellectuals and intellectual life long antedated the presence of non-Indians in New England, and continued to fashion and refashion Indian ways of being into the future.[167] Even in spite of their relative obscurity in the written record, New England Indians continued to shape and reshape their lives as Indian people into the future whether or not non-Indians chose to recognize them as such.

This text and Apess's public appearances are in and of themselves stunning acts of resistance. The story he tells challenges the notion of a natural break with ancient superstitions that clears the way for modernity, and points out the violence of the claim. Rather, he emphasizes the habits of superstition and myth making *non-Indians* engaged in through their peculiar mode of commemoration. Instead, the supposed "ancients" are the "moderns," and it is the ancients who theorize what it will mean to have a nation-state with more than one sovereign. The impassioned appeal he makes in *Eulogy* to the ongoing existence of Indian peoples as separate entities and as entitled to just treatment as citizens—couched in the language of commemoration—argued for the modernity of Indian people.

Apess's other writings speak to the ongoing vibrancy of Indian peoples in New England even as they struggled within a colonial regime that wished Indians would simply disappear. Indians appear as modern peoples forging their own dignified lives into the future in spite of the horrors that accompanied their treatment as racial others. One can only imagine what might have happened if other Indian people had somehow been empowered to leave the paper trail Apess produced, and that detailed Indian stories written from Indian perspectives could be replicated across the landscape. His autobiography tells a profound story of Indian survival and resistance that resonates with a longer narrative of dispossession and colonialism in New England. We can draw larger implications about Indian history and survival from the writings of William Apess that undo the project of purification in the service of modernity, and indeed Apess incorporates the stories of Indian peoples more broadly throughout his writings. His writings allow us to read the "official" record in a far more nuanced way and to recognize more fully the ways that New England Indian peoples have always claimed New England as theirs.

"Termination"

New Englanders had other ideas, William Apess's eloquent testimonials about Indian survival and integrity notwithstanding. In the last half of the nineteenth century, the state legislatures of Connecticut, Massachusetts, and Rhode Island took measures that purported officially to "terminate" the ongoing legal recognition of Indian peoples still present in their own homelands, echoing the gesture Connecticut had made to legislate the Pequot out of existence in the wake of the Pequot War in 1637.[168] These actions and others paralleled a mythology that New Englanders had been haphazardly forging in cultural production throughout the nineteenth century, namely, that Indian peoples as Indians had ceased to exist as such. Indeed, these forces interacted, with notions about racial purity and blood importantly influencing debates about the status of Indian communities.[169] In that sense, the multiple projects of "termination" sought to complete the project of purification that lay at the center of non-Indians' assertions of their modernity. This self-serving process of purification amounted to an abandonment of the trust and responsibility implicit in the notion of guardianship as it had organically developed in New England, and it carried grave consequences for Indian people.

Although the processes transpired in various ways throughout New England—and were linked to the national struggle over race, slavery, citizenship, and equality—all of the movements toward "terminating" New England tribes were rooted in the failure of non-Indian New Englanders to recognize Indian peoples as Indian because of their constructs of modernity and purification. The best evidence that this project was deeply flawed can be found in the still-unfinished process of *rerecognizing* New England Indian peoples through federal processes that began in the 1970s.[170] Thus, long before the U.S. Indian policy of the 1950s of "terminating" the federal relationship with tribes turned out to be a colossal case of wishful thinking, New Englanders embarked on official state-level actions to legislate Indian peoples out of existence that were doomed to failure.[171] Indeed, predictions of the vanishing Indian that can be dated at least as early as the now-iconic Squanto, "last of the

Patuxet," are among the oldest and most stubborn tropes in Indian America that continue to be revealed as mythological.

Even while non-Indians failed to understand the Indianness of still-present Indian peoples—which translated into their failure to *recognize* Indians as such—the states of Connecticut, Massachusetts, and Rhode Island did indeed extend official recognition to tribes.[172] While the relationship between each state and tribe varied in particular details, parallels can be drawn among them and between these relationships and those that operated on the federal level. The situation in New England (and generally speaking in other former English colonies) differed from that in other areas of the United States in that federal Indian policy as developed in the new nation did not specifically govern Indian affairs.[173] Nonetheless, state bureaucracies did exist that gave shape to Indian affairs in nineteenth-century New England. These bureaucracies grew organically from colonial policies, and so straightforward and comprehensive blueprints for these relationships do not exist.[174] Instead, the general shape of Indian policy and its bureaucracy can only be understood by taking into account the actual state of affairs and the periodic legislation that took up Indian relations from time to time. Indian affairs in this context often seem tremendously haphazard, as officials involved with tribes rarely concerned themselves much with those tribes under their oversight on the one hand, and Indian peoples frequently sought to avoid their oversight on the other.[175] Rhode Island created an office of commissioner of the Narragansett Indians in 1840, but neither Connecticut nor Massachusetts developed even this modicum of regularized bureaucracy regarding Indian affairs.[176]

The 1859 report filed by John Milton Earle, appointed to investigate the condition of Indian peoples in Massachusetts, offers an excellent snapshot of Indian affairs that can be extrapolated across nineteenth-century southern New England:

> There has been neither order, system, nor uniformity of purpose, in our legislation concerning the Indians. The subject has not been studied, nor the facts ascertained, or the relations correctly understood, by successive legislatures, and consequently much of the legislation has been special in its character, and too often dictated by mere expediency for the occasion, to get over a present difficulty . . . and the whole matter has become so complicated, that he must be a patient man who will trace out the legislation, and digest it, and a wise one, if he can tell, when he has done it, precisely what the legal relations of the Indians are, and what their various rights, in relation to property, whether held in severalty or in common, having reference as well to the Indian traditional law as to the statutes of the Commonwealth.[177]

Although writing specifically about Massachusetts, Earle could equally have included Connecticut and Rhode Island in his assessment. Among his recommendations for rectifying the situation was the appointment of a single commissioner for Indian affairs in the Commonwealth so that some more comprehensive vision and understanding of the state of affairs might be achieved, a recommendation that was not implemented.[178]

So what were the constituent elements of official state recognition? Although exceptions can be found to nearly every generalization one might wish to draw, some fundamental points can be made. The relationship between the states and the tribes, developed organically beginning in the seventeenth century, can be characterized as that of a guardian to a ward—a concept famously summarized in Chief Justice John Marshall's majority opinion in the landmark decision *Worcester v. Georgia* in 1832 that gave shape to the *federal* definition of Indian affairs. Based on colonial and then state statutes—sometimes general and other times specific to tribes and even individual Indians—the state acted as a guardian over Indian peoples and their property. The state held reservation lands and other resources that remained in Indian hands in trust—with a theoretical system of oversight that prohibited the sale of Indian lands and resources without the approval of official guardians or overseers appointed by the legislature. Indian lands and other resources held in common remained exempt from taxation. Furthermore, and specifically related to their tax-exempt status as wards of the state, Indians were not guaranteed citizenship in their localities, the state, or the United States. Although, as Earle found in his rather extensive investigations, some Indians in Massachusetts did indeed pay taxes and exercise the franchise, such arrangements were highly individualized.[179] In the case of the Deep Bottom Indians on Martha's Vineyard, he noted that "they have never been under guardianship, *and* are not considered as entitled to the rights of citizenship."[180] No New England state guaranteed Indians citizenship prior to the 1869 passage, after more than two decades of agitation, of the Massachusetts Indian Enfranchisement Act. Indeed, the state of Connecticut did not extend citizenship to any tribes except the Mohegan and Niantic until 1973.[181]

Throughout southern New England, abolitionism and the mounting crisis of the Civil War precipitated debates over the status of Indian peoples, although these debates varied in their particulars from place to place. As Deborah A. Rosen has argued, debates over extending citizenship to Indians took up the issue of Indian civil rights, but also were concerned with economics and gender: specifically, calls by non-Indians for privatization of Indian property to absorb it into the market economy, and agitation over female control of property in the tribes that diminished the status of their non-Indian husbands.[182] Earlier, in connection with the events that collectively composed the "Mashpee Revolt" and the activism of William Apess, media attention had

> forced Massachusetts to acknowledge that Christiantown, Chappaquiddick, Gay Head, Mashpee, and Herring Pond were "five communities within the state, but not of it, subject to its laws, but having no part in their enactment; within the limits of local municipalities, yet not subject to their jurisdiction; and holding real estate in their own right, yet not suffered to dispose of it except to each other."[183]

In Massachusetts, agitation over the status of Indian peoples began in earnest in 1849 and continued until the passage of the Massachusetts Indian Enfranchisement in 1869.[184] Within this twenty-year span, the legislature commissioned three investigations, headed by men committed to abolition and the Radical Republican agenda, on the status and situation of Indians in Massachusetts, all of which "were explicitly charged with determining when and how the Indians could be made full citizens of the Commonwealth."[185] After the passage of the Civil Rights Act of 1866, legislators voiced concerns over being in violation of federal statutes if they did not extend citizenship to Indians.[186] This decades-long debate is the context for the John Milton Earle report, which constitutes one of the most comprehensive sources for understanding New England Indians in the nineteenth century. The report itself offered specific recommendations on the pace of enfranchisement, suggesting gradual actions in keeping with the particular situations in different communities rather than so incorporating all Indians immediately.[187]

As noted by Ann Marie Plane and Gregory Button, enfranchisement in Massachusetts bore remarkable similarities to the General Allotment Act of 1887, sponsored by Massachusetts senator Henry Dawes, in removing Indian lands from trust protection and rendering them a taxable resource as well as in its citizenship objectives.[188] It echoes equally, I would argue, with the termination policy initiated in 1953 in its language of liberation that cloaked the real intent: that of ending the trust relationship embedded in Indian nationhood in a definitive legislative action, which went further than policy as it unfolded after the Dawes Act. This language from the 1849 Bird Report could have been entered into the congressional record in 1953: "'The progress of civil and ecclesiastical liberality has released all but the Indian from these disabilities [disenfranchisement]. The African, the Turk, the Japanese, may enjoy, in Massachusetts, all the privileges of American Citizenship. The Indian alone, the descendant of monarchs, is a vassal in the land of his fathers.'" What is left unsaid here is that enfranchisement in Massachusetts entailed the ending of the guardianship relationship that recognized the separate nationhood of Indian peoples in southern New England. It would have been possible, as subsequent history tells us, for Massachusetts and other states to extend citizenship to Indians without ending guardianship, which is precisely what happened with the passage of the Indian Citizenship Act of 1924, which finally guaranteed citizenship to Indians without obliterating the trust status and the nation-to-nation relationship that characterizes tribal nations within the United States.[189] It is also vital to note here that there is a distinction between the exterior *recognition* of Indian separateness and its actual *existence*. Recognition in this context refers to the diplomatic relationship between separate nations.

Responding to the Earle Report, in 1862 the Massachusetts legislature passed "An Act concerning the Indians of the Commonwealth." The first provision addressed the legal status of Indians:

> All Indians and descendants of Indians in this State are hereby placed on the same legal footing as the other inhabitants of the Commonwealth, except such as are or have been supported, in whole or in part, by the State, and except also those residing on the Indian plantations of the Chappequiddick, Christiantown, Gay Head, Marshpee, Herring Pond, Fall River, and Dudley tribes, or those whose homes are on some one of said Plantations and who are only temporarily absent.[190]

By this act, Massachusetts extended citizenship to nearly four hundred Indians while continuing the guardianship relationship with the seven enumerated tribes whose membership totaled 1,241 by Earle's accounting procedures. In effect, this terminated the official recognition by the Commonwealth of these Indian people. An additional provision made citizenship a possibility for any other Indian "or person of color" upon application to the town clerk where they resided and the paying of a poll tax, which would terminate their recognition as Indian.[191] Additional alterations followed this legislation, such as the

> imposition of district status on Gay Head [which] augured profound changes for the community. By increasing the power of elected officials and denying women the right to vote, it disrupted the egalatarian [sic] traditions of the Indians. It also established the groundwork for terminating their communal system of land tenure by hastening the development of a system of codified laws and recorded deeds.[192]

Agitation for terminating the official recognition of Indians categorically excluded from the enfranchisement continued after the passage of the act in

1862. The House of Representatives appointed additional committees to "study the feasibility 'of removing the civil and political disabilities under which they are placed, and of merging them in the general community as citizens.'"[193] Finally, the legislature passed the Massachusetts Indian Enfranchisement Act in 1869, which purported to eliminate what then governor William Clafin declared a "'political anomaly.'"[194] He continued:

> These persons are not Indians in any sense of the word. It is doubtful there is a full-blooded Indian in the State. . . . A majority have more or less the marked characteristics of the aboriginal race, but there are many without a drop of Indian blood in their veins. The marriage of a foreigner with a member of a tribe transforms the foreigner into an Indian. The result of this singular system has been a heterogeneous population, in which the characteristics of the white and negro races have already nearly obliterated all traces of the Indian.[195]

Steeped in the nineteenth-century language of blood, this declaration brought together the mythology of blood with the political project of termination, neatly encapsulating the process of purification.

Not surprisingly, enfranchisement and the "duties and liabilities" that accompanied that change in legal status engendered controversy and rancorous dispute within Indian communities. Earle reported opposition to the change in every community where he reported inquiring (Chappequiddick, Christiantown, Gay Head, and Mashpee), and he himself opposed changes in those communities as well as in Herring Pond. At Chappaquiddick, the "older members of the tribe, thoughtful, considerate, and prudent persons . . . believed . . . it would operate disastrously on the tribe; that most of them would soon become the prey of the shrewder and sharper men outside, that the little property they possess would be wrested from them."[196] At Gay Head, wrangling over land and the status of the community had begun early in the century and continued through the enfranchisement struggles.[197] At Chappequiddick and Christiantown, the land loss that followed the ending of legal protections fractured the communities and they moved to Gay Head or elsewhere.[198]

The administration of Indian affairs in Connecticut unfolded equally organically,[199] and discussions about citizenship may have also been precipitated by events of the Civil War.[200] Connecticut terminated its guardianship of the Mohegan in 1872, apparently at the request of the tribe, and they extended them citizenship and removed restrictions on land allotments that had been made to individuals in 1861.[201] According to tribal historian Melissa Jayne Fawcett, Mohegans requested this alteration in response to the corruption of their overseers, who allowed "desecrations and theft of tribal land" to undermine the people.[202] Connecticut later acted similarly to terminate the Niantic. No other Connecticut tribes were terminated in the nineteenth century, and state recognition of the tribes has extended continuously into the present.[203] But interestingly, the issue of "termination" resurfaced in 1953, when a bill was introduced into Congress "'to end the second class citizenship of Connecticut's few remaining Indians,'" specifically the Eastern Pequot.[204] The bill's language "was identical to the language in the 1872 Mohegan bill."[205] The effort failed. Debate over the status of Connecticut Indians continued until the 1973 legislation that created the Connecticut Indian Affairs Council, which "'granted all the rights and privileges afforded by law, that all of Connecticut's citizens enjoy. It is further recognized that said Indians have certain special rights to tribal lands as may have been granted to them in the past by treaty or other agreement.'"[206]

Reconciling the "rights" issue also provided the pretext for addressing the situation of the Narragansett in Rhode Island in the Civil War era—although "termination" received a public hearing as early as 1832.[207] There, in 1866, the legislature appointed a committee to look into the possibility of terminating the guardianship relationship of the state to the tribe and liquidating tribal lands on the premise that the state was not "bound to extend to the members of the tribe any peculiar or special privileges not enjoyed by all the inhabitants of the State," in spite of the long history of treaty relations inaugurated in the colonial period that protected tribal jurisdiction over their lands that they acknowledged.[208] The committee met with the tribe and "sundry citizens of Charlestown" during which it informed the assembled group that equality before the law "without regard to race or color" had culminated in the civil rights amendments. This prompted a "concern" on the part of the legislature and citizens of the state that "this tribe, to whose ancestors our ancestors were under so many obligations, should still claim to owe allegiance to their tribe, rather than to the State, and to maintain even a semblance of another jurisdiction amongst us."[209] Furthermore, they opined, no one should be part of a "privileged class in the State." But the committee had approached the tribe in order to "hear the views of others," including the "officers and members of the tribe."

The Narragansetts obliged. According to the newspaper account of the gathering, they delivered their reply "with dignity and propriety of manner," informing the committee that they had not initiated the meeting, and as far as they knew, were living in peace and prosperity, thus calling into question the purpose of the whole affair. They continued by taking up the idea of citizenship, informing the committee that they had traveled the country, and "heard much said about the rights of the negro; of negro citizenship and negro equality; but we have not found the place where this equality and these rights exist, or the negroes who enjoy them."[210] Astutely pointing out the failure of the law to guarantee African American equality, the Narragansetts rejected the possibility that the law could similarly ensure their rights. They stated further:

> We are not negroes: we are the heirs of Ninigret, and of the great chiefs and warriors of the Narragansetts. Because, when your ancestors stole the negro from Africa, and brought him amongst us, and made a slave of him, we extended to him the hand of friendship, and permitted his blood to be mingled with ours, are we to be called negroes, and to be told that we may be made negro citizens? We claim that while one drop of Indian blood remains in our veins, we are entitled to the rights and privileges guaranteed by your ancestors to ours by solemn treaty, which, without a breach of faith, you cannot violate. We did not go to the white man, but the white men came to us. When we were powerful and he was weak, he claimed our protection and we extended it. We are now weak, and our grasping neighbors, of a grasping race, are seeking the remaining remnant of our inheritance, and will not give over while an inch of our territory remains to us, and until the members of our tribe are beneath the soil, or are scattered to the winds of heaven. . . . We deny your right to take from us that which never came from you.[211]

The Narragansetts asserted their sovereignty as an *inherent* right not subject to termination by the state. They continued on to predict that if terminated, their lands, held mainly by the women, would be steadily eroded through taxes, and they would be left impoverished. Furthermore, "your imperious draft cannot touch us now; we may volunteer to fight your battles, but now you cannot force us into the ranks of your army to be shot down without our consent." The right to vote amounted to nothing. The effort to terminate the Narragansett similarly came to nothing at that time.

Thirteen years later, in 1879, Rhode Island renewed its efforts to abolish the tribe. During hearings on the issues, all five Narragansett tribal council members lodged their disapproval, even though they agreed to have their school closed. Later that year at an undocumented meeting, and for reasons that are not clear, the council agree to sell tribal lands. This action, perhaps based on a misunderstanding of what was at stake, did not involve the full membership of the tribe. Indeed, tribal members protested the action in 1881, and a close reading of the documentary record reveals opposition during the hearings on the matter.[212] The year before, the state of Rhode Island passed legislation that "purported to abolish tribal authority and tribal relations, declared tribal members citizens, ended the state's relationship with the tribe, and which authorized the sale of all land held in common."[213] With this act of "detribalization," Rhode Island legislated the Narragansett out of existence. Virtually all of the remaining 927 acres belonging to the tribe fell into non-Indian hands, leaving only two acres that surrounded the Narragansett Church that retained special status and have done so into the present.[214]

In effect, New England pursued termination to eliminate the claims that can be made by Indians by virtue of being nations, such as the protection of Indian homelands. Individual Indians and even delegations to commemorations could remain and be recognized as individuals, even if incompletely. But such actions removed Indian survivors, usually cast as "colored" or "mixed" or "black," from an Indian nationhood recognized by the state, and subjected them to a degeneration narrative.

This brief synopsis of Indian affairs as the nineteenth century drew to a close cannot possibly do justice to the extraordinary complexity of the situation: this is a story that is still being reconstructed, and each tribal history contains its own crucially unique elements. But for the purposes of the New England project of purification, this much can be said: the collective actions of the state governments in the era surrounding the Civil War, steeped in the mythological temporalities of race, sought to terminate the separate existence of the astonishingly resilient Indian peoples of southern New England. As the eloquent statements by the Narragansetts made clear, as long as they retained even one drop of metaphorical "Indian blood," they would defend their nationhood. So, as for "termination" and so much more, Indians, then and now, had other ideas.

Conclusion The Continuing Struggle over Recognition

In 2000 the U.S. Census Bureau implemented a dramatic change in enumerating "race" and especially in how it counted American Indians. Rather than insisting upon a unitary classification of race and employing the monolithic category "American Indian or Native Pacific Islander," this census permitted respondents to designate more than one race, and it elicited precise tribal information. These new guidelines yielded fascinating and complex grids of information for Indian America. For southern New England, the Census Bureau reported a total of 16,333 respondents residing there in 2000 who, alone or in any combination of races, proclaimed their Indianness. The census draws our attention to the Golden Hill Paugussett, Mohegan, Narragansett, and Schaghticoke, to the Hassanamisco, Chaubunagungameg, and Nipmuc, to the Mashantucket, Pequot, and Paucatuck Eastern Pequot; and to the Gay Head (Aquinnah), Mashpee, Wampanoag, Seaconeke, and Pocassett. Even using the most restrictive classification that indicated only one race and tribe, the census reported 7,932 New England Indians.[1]

These new enumeration guidelines make comparisons with previous censuses perilous, because the way "race" has been defined has varied from census to census, and because of the methods of data collection. Sometimes census collectors have recorded their own judgments about race, and at other times respondents have been allowed to self-identify, so that consistency is lacking. Self-identification is also potentially problematic in that some non-Indians might falsely claim Indianness as well. These observations substantiate longstanding problems relating to "counting" Indians over the years and could be customized to fit other demographic sources relating to New England (and other) Indians.

In spite of potential problems, the numbers yielded in the 2000 census are worthy of notice, composing as they do elements of an essential and enduring Indian presence in New England. In fact, in a very real sense these census figures constitute the only demographic information for southern New England that can be considered remotely comprehensive. While it is true that from time to time listings of Indian peoples in various places and circumstances were produced from the seventeenth century onward, frequently because Indians attempted to assert and secure their rights within the colonial relationship, never before had Indians had the freedom to identify themselves as Indians in a manner that could come close to reflecting the realities of their own self-identified Indian geographies. Leaving aside federal censuses, with their considerable issues surrounding data collection and ideas about race and identity, other demographic sources suffer from their own flaws. Besides the problematic slippage of categories from "Indian" to "Negro," "Black," or "Person of color," vital and other sorts of records that could substantiate Indian demography increasingly failed to take note of Indian peoples as they steadily lost land and other property in the ongoing workings of colonialism.[2] And given the oppressive experience of living within the racial formation of nineteenth-century New England, Indian peoples usually had little incentive to identify themselves in the first place.[3] In addition, gendered patterns of Indian mobility that responded to processes of dispossession further undermined the possibility of producing accurate and complete demographic data on Indians. Under these circumstances, and coupled with prevailing attitudes about blood purity and cultural stasis, New Englanders convinced themselves that Indians were on the verge of extinction.

Local texts in the nineteenth century produced a collective narrative that cannot account for the 2000 census results, let alone the realities of Indian New England in the twenty-first century. These texts coalesced into a master narrative that insisted on Indian extinction and that argued that Indians can never be modern. This narrative was pervasive and persuasive to non-Indians: it argued that racial mixture and culture "loss" diluted the Indianness of New England Indians to the vanishing point.

Yet something even more fundamental is potentially lost in this story by focusing exclusively on "race." What sets American Indians apart from other peoples in the racial formation of the United States is Indian nationhood. In the words of Lumbee political scientist David E. Wilkins, "Indian peoples are nations, not minorities."[4] Tribes themselves possess the inherent power to determine tribal citizenship, which historically has been determined by ancestry and belonging, typically defined with reference to social, cultural, territorial, and other criteria.[5] Fundamental to this distinction is the indigeneity of Indian nations that can be distinguished from other so-called minorities in the United States because of the long history of diplomacy and treaty making with European intruders, which is at the center of their political status as inherent sovereigns.[6] By the late nineteenth century, the federal government began to use dubious notions of "blood quantum" rooted in erroneous ideas about the science of race in order to reduce federal responsibility for tribes. In this formulation, Indians must meet blood quantum requirements in order to be recognized by the federal government. Tribes themselves frequently, but not always, use blood quantum for determining tribal citizenship as well.[7]

"Recognition" further muddies the water in the case of New England. The United States came into existence long after English colonialism largely dispossessed New England Indians, and tribes there lack a treaty relationship *with the United States.* In 1978 the federal government created the Branch of Acknowledgment and Research within the Bureau of Indian Affairs in order to extend recognition, or acknowledgment, to tribes who, for a variety of reasons, lacked this status. Congress also possesses the power to recognize tribal nations. Some states also acknowledge tribes as political entities within their bounds, including Connecticut and Massachusetts.

Ironically, a number of the most complete listings of Indian peoples from the nineteenth century were produced precisely in connection with actions associated with efforts to terminate the ongoing official recognition of the separate status of Indian peoples.[8] Two of these purported to detail the numbers and circumstances of Indians in Massachusetts. In the first, the commissioners appointed to inquire after Indians enumerated 847 individuals encompassed in eleven tribes in 1849: Chappequiddick, Christiantown, Gay Head, Fall River or Troy, Marshpee (Mashpee), Herring Pond, Grafton or Hassanamiso, Dudley, Punkapoag, Natick, and Yarmouth. Twelve years later, the Earle Report enumerated 1,610 individuals in the eleven tribes identified in 1849 as well as five more: Dartmouth, Mamattakeeset, Tumpum, Deep Bottom, and Middleborough (plus "miscellaneous" Indians).[9] Comparing these two enumerations would suggest that rather than tottering on the verge of extinction, Massachusetts Indians were either in the midst of a population explosion, or something was seriously amiss in nineteenth-century data collection for Massachusetts Indians.

Two other listings of Indians—one each for Connecticut and Rhode Island—offer an additional irony. A list of Mohegans was prepared in 1861 in connection with the division of most of their remaining homelands into individual holdings. Present-day Mohegans use this document and other lists prepared before this time to determine their citizenship, requiring that individual be descended from someone on the lists.[10] An 1880 listing of Narragansetts was used by Rhode Island when the tribal lands were divided, done in connection with the state's "detribalization" of the people. Today, that roll also serves as the basis for citizenship in the tribe.[11] Thus, in both cases, efforts by the state to dismantle their corporate existence compose one crucial element in securing their official status as federally recognized tribes today. In addition, although these documents had been produced in order to eliminate the collective existence of tribal entities, both of them became critical pieces of evidence in the legal process of reestablishing their status as tribal nations recognized by the federal government in the twentieth century.

These ironies and many others offer windows into understanding the disconnect between ideas non-Indian New Englanders came to hold about Indian peoples and their futures and the actual persistence of Indian peoples who continued to resist colonialism in complex and ever-changing ways. Indian resistance in New England has taken many forms over the centuries, and has translated into their endurance in their homelands as peoples with a measured separatism.[12] Even while struggling to maintain themselves within colonial relationships that sought to dispossess and then "disappear" them, Indian peoples forged their own modernity and destiny. Nowhere is Indian resistance and survival more remarkable than in their still incompletely successful efforts to persuade non-Indians to officially recognize their survival as Indian peoples. This form of recognition involves an almost impossibly rigorous bureaucratic process that must be achieved using a deeply flawed and incomplete documentary record that frequently was forged in processes that were meant to bureaucratically make Indians disappear.[13]

Among many other things, the contemporary process of recognition reflects a retraction of the nineteenth-century notion that Indians can never be modern. This passage, from the 1983 decision to extend federal acknowledgment to the Narragansett Nation, draws our attention to an entirely different narrative than the one collectively composed in nineteenth-century local texts:

> The Narragansett Indian Tribe is the modern successor of the Narragansett and Niantic tribes which, in aboriginal times, inhabited the area which is today the state of Rhode Island. Members of the tribe are lineal descendants of the aboriginal Niantic and Narragansett Indians. . . . Evidence indicates that the Narragansett community and its predecessors have existed autonomously since first contact, despite undergoing many modifications.[14]

Here, the Narragansett Nation is recognized as indigenous, autonomous, continuous, and modern. This modern formation is predicated on rejecting erroneous nineteenth-century temporalities of race that insisted upon a degeneration narrative for Indians in favor of recognizing Indian ways of belonging rooted in lineage and kinship. Likewise, the capacity for and normality of change is acknowledged as the rightful purview of the Narragansett. Following "first contact," the Narragansett Nation maintained its measured separatism from non-Indians by continuously remaking itself as a self-determined people.

The acknowledgment decision recapitulated the history of colonialism experienced by the Narragansett after "first contact." It pointed out the development of the guardianship system in Rhode Island, which began in 1709 and "continued until 1880, when the state legislature of Rhode Island enacted a so-called 'detribalization' act." The decision acknowledged the fact that the Narragansett continued their measured separatism as a social, cultural, and political community in spite of their "detribalization," and the fact that "essentially all of the current membership are believed to be able to trace to at least one ancestor on the membership lists of the Narragansett community prepared after the 1880 Rhode Island 'detribalization' act."[15] Thus the historical record that aimed to bring into alignment the degeneration narrative of Indian demise with non-Indian political expectations served instead as crucial evidence of Indian resistance and survival.

The federal acknowledgment of the Narragansett and other Indian nations dramatically demonstrates the futility of policy based on wishful thinking. Tribes that have achieved federal acknowledgment have overcome the colonial archive that is the collective record of local history production in the nineteenth century. They have asserted their measured separatism in keeping with the broader situation of tribal peoples in the United States.

The process of recognition in New England is highly contested terrain and will in all likelihood remain so into the future.[16] Following the Narragansett decision four more tribal nations gained acknowledgment. The Mashantucket Pequot achieved congressional recognition in 1983, whereas the Aquinnah (1987), Mohegan (1994), and Mashpee Wampanoag (2007) successfully navigated the federal acknowledgment process. In the case of the Mashpee, their recognition reversed the controversial and highly visible rejection of their nationhood in federal district court in 1977. Their triumph thirty years later attests to their resilience and determination to remain an Indian people apart.

Other New England tribal nations have different stories to tell. The Hassanamisco Nipmuc, Golden Hill Paugussett, Eastern Pequot, and Schaghticoke all have been denied federal recognition in highly politicized and fiercely contested battles that have not ended. In the case of the Nipmuc, delays in issuing an anticipated positive finding under the Clinton administration allowed the new Bush administration to deny them. The Eastern Pequot and Schaghticoke

Tribal Nation both gained federal recognition in 2004 only to have it rescinded in October 2005 following the determined opposition of grassroots organizations and the lobbying efforts of Connecticut's attorney general, Richard Blumenthal. They suffered this denial in spite of the continuous recognition of their status by the state of Connecticut into the present, which the Bureau of Indian Affairs rejected as insufficient evidence of their continuous existence. Both groups are fighting the ruling in the courts. So in ironic juxtaposition to the "terminated" Narragansett and Mohegan, their ongoing relationship to the state failed to secure federal recognition for the Eastern Pequot and the Schaghticoke.

The highly charged issue of Indian gaming casts a long shadow over the recognition process in southern New England and elsewhere. But the stubborn persistence of the mythology of Indian extinction in New England, rooted in ideas about the purification process of modernity, plays a powerful role as well. Operating according to erroneous notions of Indian authenticity calculated according to the degeneracy narrative and the temporalities of race, and equipped with the colonial archive that narrated Indian extinction, those who refuse to recognize New England Indians as such find materials to support their position. In their fight against this discourse, New England Indians are forced to rely on a record that sought to make them disappear in order to prove their survival. Whether they have (yet) succeeded or not, they continue to remake themselves as Indian peoples in their homelands and in modernity. More than five hundred years of Indian resistance to colonialism suggests that the struggle will not end.

Acknowledgments

This book has been a labor of love for more than a decade, and along the way I have accumulated enormous debts that I am grateful to have the opportunity to acknowledge here. So many smart and generous people offered their carefully composed thoughts on elements of this project that I am sure to miss some of them, and for that I apologize.

Its first iteration came in the context of a McKnight–Land Grant Professorship at the University of Minnesota that I was awarded in the early 1990s. Several colleagues offered indispensable advice as I tried to articulate my central idea, but the great readings by Ann Waltner especially helped me sort out what I wanted to do at that early stage.

My reading group (Anne Carter, Anna Clark, Lisa Disch, Kirsten Fischer, Jennifer Pierce, and Gabriella Tsurutani) read every chapter, sometimes more than once, and offered incredible insights that shaped this book in important ways. Lisa and Jennifer read my first fitful pages when I was trying to collect my thoughts and gave me amazing guidance as I tried to structure my arguments and the book as a whole, especially in turning my attention to Bruno Latour. Jennifer turned around an invaluable read of chapter 4 very late in the game that helped me enormously. Colin Calloway provided a fabulously helpful reading of the entire manuscript. Jim Merrell generously read nearly every chapter—and, in the case of the Introduction, three versions; the final one is infinitely better because of his advice.

The first fleeting attempt at developing my argument came at an American Anthropological Association session that paid tribute to Raymond Fogelson. I benefited greatly from the comments by the late William Sturtevant and audience feedback as well as the editorial assistance of Sergei Kan and Polly Strong, who edited the terrific volume that grew out of a series of Fogelson tribute sessions from the AAA and the American Society for Ethnohistory in 1996. Maureen Konkle, David Noble, Barry O'Connell, David Roediger, Nancy

Shoemaker, and Alfred Young gave me encouraging feedback on the first extended writing of this project, central features of which appear in chapters 3 and 4. David Wilkins provided incredibly helpful advice as I worked through my argument about citizenship in chapter 4, and participants in the American Indian Studies Workshop and Early American History Workshop at the University of Minnesota offered sage advice over the years on virtually every chapter. Members of the American Indian Studies Workshop include Joseph Bauerkemper, Christina Berndt, Lisa Blee, David Chang, Kelly Condit-Shrethsa, Boyd Cothran, Demetri Debe, Jill Doerfler, Robert Gilmer, Margot Iverson, Sheryl Lightfoot, Chantal Norrgard, Laurie Richmond, Keith Richotte, Andrea Robertson, Heidi Stark, Jenny Tone-Pah-Hote, Rachel Walker, and Kate Williams; members of the Early American History Workshop include Sarah Chambers, Boyd Cothran, Demetri Debe, Kirsten Fischer, Katie Goetz, Ed Griffin, John Howe, Gina Martino, Rus Menard, Lisa Norling, Andrea Robertson, J. B. Shank, Kathleen Vandevoorde, and Serena Zabin. I feel lucky to have such engaged colleagues who graciously and cheerfully offer sound advice. For friendship and support I also thank my colleagues Patricia Albers, Brenda Child, Tracey Deutsch, Rod Ferguson, Colleen Hennen, Erika Lee, Malinda Linquist, Mary Jo Maynes, Pat McNamara, Kevin Murphy, and John Nichols. I have greatly benefited from conversations about this project with Phil Deloria, Thomas Doughton, LeAnne Howe, Kehaulani Kauanui, Tsianina Lomawaima, Barry O'Connell, and Michael Witgen.

I had the good fortune of extended periods of research at the incredible American Antiquarian Society and the Newberry Library with the generous support of NEH Fellowships. As always, I benefited enormously by the fabulous staff of the AAS, especially Georgia Barnhill, John Hench, Lucia Knoles, Tom Knoles, Marie Lamoureux, Carolyn Sloat, and Laura Wasowicz, as well as the amazing team of pages and volunteers during my nine months in Worcester. Of the terrific fellows in residence at the time, I especially note the good cheer and intellectual support of Scott Casper, Helen Deese, Paul Erickson, Rene Gentilles, and Brett Mizelle. At the Newberry, John Aubrey, Jim Grossman, John Powell, LaVonne Brown Ruoff, and Helen Hornbeck Tanner helped me renew my ties to that incredible place. A boisterous group of fellows and resident researchers made those four months especially productive and fun, including Terry Bouton, Pat Crain, Ann Cruz, Fran Dolan, Greg Dowd, Kathleen DuVal, Laura Edwards, Martha Few, Amy Froide, Elliott Gorn, Janine Lanza, Kate Rousmaniere, and Michael Willrich. Finally, Harvey Markovitz gifted me a plaster Indian statue that adorned my carrel during my stay and became a reliable source of joking and pranks. At the University of Minnesota, in addition to the McKnight–Land Grant Fellowship, I received travel support from the McMillan Travel Award Fund for a final research trip.

I acknowledge the hospitality of those who invited me to present my research at their institutions and the abundantly useful feedback I received in the process. I presented a version of chapter 2 at the Library Company of Philadelphia, sponsored by the McNeil Center for Early American Studies, where Dan Richter and a large and engaged group gave me incredible advice. Several months later I went on what came to be called "my northeastern speaking tour" by my gracious hosts at Cornell, Yale, and Harvard. Angela Gonzalez was a fine host in Ithaca, and Audra Simpson asked great questions. Alyssa Mt. Pleasant drove me from Ithaca to New Haven and took me under her wing, and Paul Costa, Alan Trachtenberg, and Laurie Weinstein offered especially helpful feedback. In Cambridge, Lisa Brooks cared for my every need, and I enjoyed valuable conversations with Judy Kertesz, Malinda Maynor, and Laurel Thatcher Ulrich.

I presented material from chapter 3 at the University of New Hampshire, where Barry O'Connell set me straight on some important matters. At UCLA, Steve Aron and the late Melissa Meyer were great hosts, and Kevin Terraciano offered welcome encouragement. Matt Garcia graciously hosted me at Brown University, and Karl Jacoby, Shep Krech, Patricia Rubertone, and William Simmons shared their insights. At Michigan State University, Susan Applegate Krouse and Susan Sleeper-Smith generously extended their encouragement. Material from this chapter was also the focus of lively seminars at the AAS and the Newberry Library.

I presented elements of chapter 4 at the American Society for Ethnohistory meeting in Williamsburg, Virginia, and at the Native American and Indigenous Studies meeting at the University of Oklahoma, and I received helpful suggestions from the audiences there. Evan Haefli hosted me at Columbia University, and Karen Kupperman invited me to present at the Seminar in Early American History at New York University. I had terrific conversations with that group and received especially helpful input from Barbara Krauthamer. Fred Hoxie hosted me at the University of Illinois, where a great discussion during and following my seminar included input from him as well as Antoinette Burton, Jody Byrd, LeAnne Howe, and David Roediger.

I have been working on this project so long that my first research assistant, Anne Enke, is now a tenured associate professor at the University of Wisconsin. Anne sleuthed her way through the University of Minnesota collections to gather the first harvest of local texts that gave me a place to start; that local sample was the basis for a working paper that went through many versions until I finally broke it up and included parts of it in chapters 3 and 4. More recently, Boyd Cothran has been an incredible research assistant, tracking down and putting into press-ready form the illustrations for this book in heroic fashion and helping immensely with the final stages of manuscript preparation.

My heartfelt thanks to the Indigenous Americas series editors, Robert Warrior and Jace Weaver, who have been unstintingly helpful from start to finish. At the University of Minnesota Press, I thank Doug Armato, Danielle Kasprzak, Richard Morrison, and especially Jason Weidemann for all of their great support: it has been a wonderful experience to work with all of them.

This book is for Timothy J. Kehoe. He too has been subjected to at least one draft of every chapter of this book, and he offered suggestions that improved them. I could not be more fortunate than to have him as a life partner.

Notes

Author's Note on Sources

1. *Connecticut: A Bibliography of Its History*, ed. Roger Parks (Hanover, N.H.: University Press of New England, 1986); *Massachusetts: A Bibliography of Its History*, ed. Roger Parks (Boston: G. K. Hall, 1976); and *Rhode Island: A Bibliography of Its History*, ed. Roger Parks (Hanover, N.H.: University Press of New England, 1983).

Introduction

1. On Washburn's political and legal career, see Robert M. Spector, "Emory Washburn: Conservator of the New England Legal Heritage," *American Journal of Legal History* 22 (1978): 118–36. Washburn was governor in 1854–55.

2. Bridgewater, Massachusetts, *Celebration of the Two-Hundredth Anniversary of the Incorporation of Bridgewater, Massachusetts, at West Bridgewater, June 3, 1856; Including the Address by Hon. Emory Washburn, of Worcester; Poem by James Reed, A.B. of Boston; and the Other Exercises of the Occasion* (Boston: John Wilson and Son, 1856), 20.

3. Ibid., 46.

4. Ibid.

5. John Milton Earle, *Report to the Governor and Council concerning the Indians of the Commonwealth, Under the Acts of April 16, 1859* (Boston: William White, Printer to the State, 1861). Earle's report constitutes essential evidence about Indians, but it is also problematic emanating as it does out of nineteenth-century racial thinking that limited his field of vision. For a nice discussion of problems with this text and their bearing on contemporary recognition struggles, see Christopher J. Thee, "Massachusetts Nipmucs and the Long Shadow of John Milton Earle," *New England Quarterly* 79 (2006): 636–54.

6. See, e.g., David L. Ghere, "The 'Disappearance' of the Abenaki in Western Maine: Political Organization and Ethnocentric Assumptions," in *After King Philip's War: Presence and Persistence in Indian New England*, ed. Colin G. Calloway, 72–89 (Hanover, N.H.: University Press of New England, 1997).

7. On California see David Glassberg, "Making Places in California," in *Sense of History: The Place of the Past in American Life* (Amherst: University of Massachusetts

Press, 2001), 165–202, and on Washington see Coll Thrush, *Native Seattle: Histories from the Crossing-Over Place* (Seattle: University of Washington Press, 2007), 88, 96.

8. See also Mohegan tribal historian Melissa Jayne Fawcett, *The Lasting of the Mohegans: The Story of the Wolf People* (Uncasville, Conn.: The Mohegan Tribe, 1995).

9. As Amy E. Den Ouden has pointed out, "Seventeenth-century makers of Indian policy probably understood little of local Native experiences of and responses to the ongoing processes of conquest, or of the nature of the political relationships that were sustained and created between Native communities in Connecticut after English military supremacy had been established in 1637." Den Ouden, *Beyond Conquest: Native Peoples and the Struggle for History in New England* (Lincoln: University of Nebraska Press, 2005), 22.

10. See, e.g., Kathleen J. Bragdon, *Native People of Southern New England, 1500–1650* (Norman: University of Oklahoma Press, 1996); Lisa Brooks, *The Common Pot: Recovering Native Spaces in the Northeast* (Minneapolis: University of Minnesota Press, 2008); Daniel R. Mandell, *Tribe, Race, History: Native Americans in Southern New England, 1780–1880* (Baltimore: The Johns Hopkins University Press, 2008); Colin G. Calloway, ed., *After King Philip's War: Presence and Persistence in Indian New England* (Amherst: University of Massachusetts Press, 1993); Colin G. Calloway and Neal Salisbury, eds., *Reinterpreting New England Indians and the Colonial Experience* (Boston: Colonial Society of Massachusetts, 2003); Jack Campisi, *The Mashpee Indians: Tribe on Trial* (Syracuse, N.Y.: Syracuse University Press, 1991); Fawcett, *The Lasting of the Mohegans;* Laurence M. Hauptman and James D. Wherry, eds., *The Pequots in Southern New England: The Fall and Rise of an American Indian Nation* (Norman: University of Oklahoma Press, 1990); Ann McMullen and Russell G. Handsman, eds., *A Key into the Language of Woodsplint Baskets* (Washington, Conn.: American Indian Archaeological Institute, 1987); Russell M. Peters, *The Wampanoags of Mashpee: An Indian Perspective on American History* (Jamaica Plain, Mass.: R. M. Peters, 1987); Patricia E. Rubertone, *Grave Undertakings: An Archaeology of Roger Williams and the Narragansett Indians* (Washington, D.C.: Smithsonian Institution Press, 2001); Neal Salisbury, *Manitou and Providence: Indians, Europeans, and the Making of New England* (New York: Oxford University Press, 1982); David J. Silverman, *Faith and Boundaries: Colonists, Christianity, and Community among the Wampanoag Indians of Martha's Vineyard, 1600–1871* (Cambridge: Cambridge University Press, 2005); William S. Simmons, *Spirit of the New England Tribes: Indian History and Folklore, 1620–1984* (Hanover, N.H.: University Press of New England, 1986); and Laurie Weinstein, ed., *Enduring Traditions: The Native Peoples of New England* (Westport, Conn.: Bergin & Garvey, 1994).

11. Ruth Wallis Herndon and Ella Wilcox Sekatau, "The Right to a Name: The Narragansett People and Rhode Island Officials in the Revolutionary Era," in Calloway, *After King Philip's War,* 114–43, 118. For an overview of race and the shifting use of categories in the Americas see Jack D. Forbes, *Africans and Native Americans: The Language of Race and the Evolution of Red-Black Peoples* (Urbana: University of Illinois Press, 1993).

12. Thomas L. Doughton, "Unseen Neighbors: Native Americans of Central Massachusetts, a People Who Had Vanished," in Calloway, *After King Philip's War,* 207–30.

13. Den Ouden, *Beyond Conquest,* 28–29.

14. Ibid., 30–33. On the census, map, and museum as colonial projects see Benedict Anderson, *Imagined Communities,* 2nd ed. (New York: Verso, 1991), 163–85. A useful recent discussion of race and the U.S. census is Martha Hodes, "Fractions and Fictions in the United States Census of 1890," in *Haunted by Empire: Geographies of Intimacy in North American History,* ed. Ann Laura Stoler, 240–70 (Durham: University of North Carolina Press, 2006). All Indians, regardless of circumstances, were at least technically enumerated in the U.S. census as of 1890 (248–49).

15. For an extremely useful overview of local history writing in New England from its origins through the late twentieth century, see David D. Hall and Alan Taylor, "Reassessing the Local History of New England," in *New England: A Bibliography of Its History,* ed. Roger Parks (Hanover, N.H.: University Press of New England, 1989), xix–xlvii. (Hall wrote part 1, Taylor part 2.) Other helpful treatments include Lawrence Buell, *New England Literary Culture: From Revolution through Renaissance* (Cambridge: Cambridge University Press, 1986), especially chapters 8 and 9; Carol Kammen, ed., *The Pursuit of Local History: Readings on Theory and Practice* (Walnut Creek, Calif.: Altamira Press, 1996); and Carol Kammen, *On Doing Local History: Reflections on What Local Historians Do, Why, and What It Means* (Walnut Creek, Calif.: Altamira Press, 1995). On local historians and Connecticut see Bruce Daniels, "Antiquarians and Professionals," *Connecticut History* 23 (1977): 91–97, and Dorothy Ann Lipson, "The Historian and Nineteenth-Century Connecticut, 1800–1865," *Connecticut History* 23 (1982): 123–40. For a treatment of local history keeping in one place over time see Michael C. Batinski, *Pastkeepers in a Small Place: Five Centuries in Deerfield, Massachusetts* (Amherst: University of Massachusetts Press, 2004).

16. Michel-Rolph Trouillot, *Silencing the Past: Power and the Production of History* (Boston: Beacon Press, 1995), 25.

17. Hall and Taylor, "Reassessing the Local History," xxix–xxi. On the demographic characteristics of antebellum New England writers more generally, see Buell, *New England Literary Culture,* 375–97.

18. Hall and Taylor, "Reassessing the Local History," xxvi.

19. The classic study is Buell, *New England Literary Culture.* Other helpful studies of New England's claims to regional and national influence in the context of decline include Joseph A. Conforti, *Imagining New England: Explorations of Regional Identity from the Pilgrims to the Mid-Twentieth Century* (Chapel Hill: University of North Carolina Press, 2001), and John D. Seelye, *Memory's Nation: The Place of Plymouth Rock* (Chapel Hill: University of North Carolina Press, 1998).

20. Lucy Maddox, *Removals: Nineteenth-Century American Literature and the Politics of Indian Affairs* (New York: Oxford University Press, 1991), esp. 15–28. She notes that debates over removal were not at all resolved by midcentury but that they became "muted" or "subsumed" under debates about slavery and sectionalism (35). Simply put, the "Indian problem" asserts that the American nation can and should geographically

expand to spread the institutions of republican virtue across the continent. How to accomplish "westward expansion" as a moral project with a continent possessed by its indigenous inhabitants?

21. See the Author's Note on Sources for an explanation of my selection principles and methodology.

22. Hall and Taylor, "Reassessing the Local History," xx. Hall dates the first local history to 1816, a brief account of Billerica, Massachusetts. He notes that "local history arose suddenly about 1820, and made rapid progress thereafter . . . the enterprise was sustained throughout the century . . . [and] decay . . . is increasingly apparent after 1880."

23. Robert Warrior, *The People and the Word: Reading Native Nonfiction* (Minneapolis: University of Minnesota Press, 2005), 39.

24. Hall asserts that local history waned after 1880 due to a "changing relationship between authors, publishers, and the local community." Hall and Taylor, "Reassessing the Local History," xx. On the commercialization of the genre, see xxx.

25. Trouillot, *Silencing the Past*, 55. For an interesting volume on encounters with archives see Antoinette Burton, ed., *Archive Stories: Facts, Fictions, and the Writing of History* (Durham, N.C.: Duke University Press, 2005).

26. Trouillot, *Silencing the Past*, 52.

27. Ibid., 29, 119, and throughout.

28. For a related argument about the denial of Indian survival in local histories see Den Ouden, chapter 6, "'Race' and the Denial of Local Histories," in *Beyond Conquest*. See Hall and Taylor, "Reassessing the Local History," for an excellent assessment of the strengths and weaknesses of the genre from its origins through the late twentieth century, xxxi–xlvii, but esp. xxxi–xxxiii.

29. Bruno Latour, *We Have Never Been Modern*, trans. Catherine Porter (Cambridge, Mass.: Harvard University Press, 1991). Hall and Taylor make the point that nineteenth-century New England local histories express a sense of distance, loss, and rupture from the past in their overview of the genre. "Reassessing the Local History," xxv–xxvi. Recent insightful studies that take up the problem of Indians and modernity include Philip J. Deloria, *Indians in Unexpected Places* (Lawrence: University Press of Kansas, 2004); Paige Raibmon, *Authentic Indians: Episodes of Encounter from the Late-Nineteenth-Century Northwest Coast* (Durham, N.C.: Duke University Press, 2005); Thrush, *Native Seattle*; and Robert A. Williams, Jr., *Like a Loaded Weapon: The Rehnquist Court, Indian Rights, and the Legal History of Racism* (Minneapolis: University of Minnesota Press, 2005).

30. Reginald Horsman, *Race and Manifest Destiny: The Origins of American Racial Anglo-Saxonism* (Cambridge, Mass.: Harvard University Press, 1981).

31. Paige Raibmon makes the observation that "real Indians could never be modern," in her excellent study of the problem of "authenticity" and Indianness, *Authentic Indians*, 7.

32. Alonzo Lewis, *The History of Lynn* (Boston: J. H. Eastburn, 1829).

1. Firsting

1. Enoch Sanford, *History of Raynham, Massachusetts, from the First Settlement to the Present Time* (Providence: Hammon, Angell & Co., 1870).

2. Myron O. Allen, *The History of Wenham, Civil and Ecclesiastical, from Its Settlement in 1639, to 1860* (Boston: Bazin & Chandler, 1860); Abiel Abbott, *History of Andover, from Its Settlement to 1829* (Andover: Flagg and Gould, 1829); Elias Nason, *A History of the Town of Dunstable, Massachusetts, from Its Earliest Settlement to the Year of Our Lord 1873* (Boston: Alfred Mudge & Son, 1877); and Sidney Perley, *The History of Boxford, Essex County, Massachusetts, from the Earliest Settlement Known to the Present Time, a Period of about Two Hundred and Thirty Years* (Boxford: by the author, 1880).

3. John Murdock Stowe, *History of the Town of Hubbardston, Worcester County, Massachusetts, from the Time Its Territory Was Purchased of the Indians in 1686, to the Present* (Hubbardston, Mass.: publishing committee, 1881), and David Wilder, *The History of Leominster, or the Northern Half of the Lancaster New or Additional Grant, from June 26, 1701, the Date of the Deed from George Tahanto, Indian Sagamore, to July 4, 1852* (Fitchburg: Reveille Office, 1853).

4. Samuel Orcutt and Ambrose Beardsley, *The History of the Old Town of Derby, Connecticut, 1642–1880, with Biographies and Genealogies* (Springfield, Mass.: Springfield Printing Co., 1880). In fact, and in common with many other local texts, the authors failed to contain Indian history in their preface alone—Indians appear in the body of their text as well.

5. Josiah Howard Temple and George Sheldon, *A History of the Town of Northfield, Massachusetts for 150 Years, with an Account of the Prior Occupation of the Territory by the Squakheags: and with Family Genealogies* (Albany: Joel Munsell, 1875).

6. On the ethnography of early New England see especially Bragdon, *Native People of Southern New England.* Also immensely useful is Howard S. Russell, *Indian New England Before the Mayflower* (Hanover, N.H.: University Press of New England, 1980).

7. Bragdon, *Native People of Southern New England,* and William Cronon, *Changes in the Land: Indians, Colonists, and the Ecology of New England* (New York: Hill and Wang, 1983).

8. Latour, *We Have Never Been Modern,* 10.

9. Rev. J. W. Alvord, *Historical Address, Delivered in the First Congregational Church in Stamford, CT., at the Celebration of the Second Centennial Anniversary of the First Settlement of the Town* (New York: S. Davenport, 1842), 3.

10. William Cothren, *History of Ancient Woodbury, Connecticut, from the First Indian Deed in 1659 to 1854, Including the Present Towns of Washington, Southbury, Bethlehem, Roxbury, and a Part of Oxford and Middlebury* (Waterbury: Bronson Brothers, 1854), [9].

11. Latour, *We Have Never Been Modern,* 10–11. See also David W. Noble, *Death of a Nation: American Culture and the End of Exceptionalism* (Minneapolis: University of Minnesota Press, 2002), for a brilliant discussion of how such ideas have structured historiography, American studies, and American culture more broadly, and Avery F. Gordon, *Ghostly Matters: Haunting and the Sociological Imagination* (Minneapolis: University of

Minnesota Press, 2004), for a provocative discussion of the "seething presence" of silenced violence that haunts the present.

12. Some of the most interesting work in American Indian studies of late takes up the idea of Indian authenticity with regard to "race" and culture. For excellent studies that pursue similar themes see Deloria, *Indians in Unexpected Places;* Maureen Konkle, *Writing Indian Nations: Native Intellectuals and the Politics of Historiography, 1827–1863* (Chapel Hill: University of North Carolina Press, 2004); Raibmon, *Authentic Indians;* Circe Sturm, *Blood Politics: Race, Culture, and Identity in the Cherokee Nation of Oklahoma* (Berkeley and Los Angeles: University of California Press, 2002); and Williams, *Like a Loaded Weapon.* Robert Warrior figures this notion as "the tyranny of expectations and the rhetoric of ancientness and novelty" in analyzing the intellectual work of Pequot William Apess and Kiowa writer N. Scott Momaday. Warrior, *The People and the Word,* esp. 34–26 and 153.

13. Noble, *Death of a Nation,* xlii.

14. Ibid., especially xxxvii–xliii. The quotation is from xliii.

15. For an illuminating analysis of this process in nineteenth-century American literature, see Timothy B. Powell, *Ruthless Democracy: A Multicultural Interpretation of the American Renaissance* (Princeton, N.J.: Princeton University Press, 2000), esp. 30–48. Powell's multicultural analysis of nineteenth-century literature argues that "the country's will to monoculturalism and the historical forces of cultural diversity are almost equally powerful" and continuously contentious (63). Taking up the presence and absence of Indians in Nathaniel Hawthorne's *The House of the Seven Gables,* Powell argues in his first chapter, "Writing in the service of nation building, Hawthorne's romance preserves the myth of monocultural unity by perpetuating the 'historical error' that 'the original occupant of the soil' was white" (47). His third chapter focuses on Henry David Thoreau's *Walden* and other works, and points out the ways in which Thoreau removes Indians "from the discursive landscape in order to . . . imaginatively construct himself as a 'native' American" (85).

16. Rev. Solomon Clark, *Antiquities, Historicals and Graduates of Northampton* (Northampton, Mass.: Steam Press of Gazette Printing Co., 1882), 46–48.

17. Haverhill, Massachusetts, *Foundation Facts concerning Its Settlement, Growth, Industries, and Societies* (Haverhill: Bridgman & Gay, 1879), 3–6.

18. On the ancient origins of the annals tradition, see Hall and Taylor, "Reassessing the Local History of New England," xxii.

19. James Thatcher, *History of the Town of Plymouth, from Its First Settlement in 1620, to the Present Time: With a Concise History of the Aborigines of New England, and Their Wars with the English, &c,* 2nd ed. (Boston: Marsh, Capen & Lyon, 1835).

20. Ibid., 30, and William Shaw Russell, *Pilgrim Memorials, and Guide to Plymouth, with a Lithographic Map, and Eight Copperplate Engravings* (Boston: Crosby, Nichols and Company, 1855), 22–30, which includes "statements and remarks, prepared after a very thorough reexamination of existing records, which are fully confirmed by traditionary information obtained from many aged persons, in frequent conversations, within the last fifty years" (25).

21. Thatcher, *History of the Town of Plymouth*, 24. On the contest between Plymouth and Jamestown in claiming the origins of the nation, see Ann Uhry Abrams, *The Pilgrims and Pocahontas: Rival Myths of American Origin* (Boulder, Colo.: Westview, 1999), and Seelye, *Memory's Nation*. On the actual "firstness" of Jamestown, see Karen Ordahl Kupperman, *The Jamestown Project* (Cambridge, Mass.: Harvard University Press, 2007).

22. Thatcher, *History of the Town of Plymouth*, 330.

23. Charles W. Jenkins, *Three Lectures on the Early History of the Town of Falmouth Covering the Time from Its Settlement to 1812* (Falmouth: L. F. Clarke, 1889), [4] (emphasis added).

24. Thatcher, *History of the Town of Plymouth*, 23. Famous in the sense that he is cited in many local texts, whether they had to do with Plymouth directly or not. "Formerly famous" in the sense that few people today know who he was.

25. Ibid., 33.

26. Ibid., 323.

27. Ibid., 17 and 19.

28. Ibid., Sabbath, 28; town, 28; offense, 37; prison, 83; marriage, 91; horses, 110; lands, 163; bell, 217; church, 259; pastor, 266; and wharf, 319.

29. Shebnah Rich, *Truro—Cape Cod; or, Land Marks and Sea Marks* (Boston: D. Lothrop & Co., 1883), [57].

30. Rich, *Truro—Cape Cod*, 177.

31. E. Richardson, *History of Woonsocket* (Woonsocket, R.I.: S. S. Foss, 1876), [5].

32. For an account of Concord's claims, see Lemuel Shattuck, *A History of the Town of Concord; Middlesex County, Massachusetts, from Its Earliest Settlement to 1832; and of the Adjoining Towns, Bedford, Acton, Lincoln, and Carlisle; Containing Various Notices of County and State History not before Published* (Boston: Russell, Odiorne, 1835), 340–60.

33. Rev. Myron S. Dudley, *History of Cromwell: A Sketch* (Middletown: Constitution Office, 1880), [1].

34. Joseph White, *Charlemont as a Plantation: An Historical Discourse at the Centennial Anniversary of the Death of Moses Rice, the First Settler of the Town, Delivered at Charlemont, Massachusetts, June 11, 1855* (Boston: T. R. Marvin & Sons, 1858), 6–7.

35. Ibid., 8 (hardships/fear).

36. Ibid., 11.

37. Ibid., 22–24.

38. Ibid., 38.

39. North Providence, *A Report of the North Providence Celebration at Pawtucket, North Providence, of the One Hundredth Anniversary of the Incorporation of the Town, June 24, 1865* (Pawtucket: Robert Sherman, Printer, 1865), 13.

40. Charles Brooks, *History of the Town of Medford, Middlesex County Massachusetts, from Its First Settlement, in 1630, to the Present Time, 1855* (Boston: James M. Usher, 1855), [v]–vi.

41. See, e.g., Lyman H. Atwater, *The Completion of Two Centuries: A Discourse Preached*

in Fairfield on Thanksgiving Day, November 28, 1839 (Bridgeport: Standard Office, 1839), 5. On the iconography and contest over Plymouth Rock and its meaning, see Seelye, *Memory's Nation.*

42. Seelye, *Memory's Nation,* 3–35.

43. Udo J. Hebel, "Forefathers' Day Orations, 1769–1865: An Introduction and Checklist," *Proceedings of the American Antiquarian Society* 110, pt. 2 (2000): 377–416.

44. Russell, *Pilgrim Memorials, and Guide for Visitors to Plymouth Village: With a Lithographic Map, and Seven Copperplate Engravings* (Boston: C. C. P. Moody, 1851), 6–7. Russell refers to the fracturing of the mythic rock during the 1770s, when some enterprising "patriots" decided to move it to the courthouse and place it near a liberty pole. Seelye, *Memory's Nation,* 23.

45. Isaac H. Folger, *Handbook of Nantucket, Containing a Brief Historical Sketch of the Island, with Notes of Interest to Summer Visitors* (Nantucket: Island Review Office, 1875), 21.

46. Samuel Gardner Drake, *The History and Antiquities of Boston, the Capital of Massachusetts and Metropolis of New England, from Its Settlement in 1630, to the Year 1770. Also an Introductory History of the Discovery and Settlement of New England, with Notes, Critical and Illustrative* (Boston: Luther Stevens, 1856), 12.

47. Ibid., 13, and John J. Babson, *History of the Town of Gloucester, Cape Ann, Including the Town of Rockport* (Gloucester: Procter Brothers, 1860), 14.

48. Drake, *History and Antiquities of Boston,* 20.

49. Babson, *History of the Town of Gloucester,* 20.

50. Edward Everett, *An Address Delivered on the 28th of June, 1830, the Anniversary of the Arrival of Governor Winthrop at Charlestown* (Charlestown: William W. Wheildon, 1830), 12–13.

51. Rev. Grant Powers, *An Address, Delivered to the People of Goshen, Connecticut, at Their First Centennial Celebration, September 38, 1838* (Hartford: Elihu Geer, 1839), 5–6.

52. Kathleen J. Bragdon, *The Columbia Guide to American Indians of the Northeast* (New York: Columbia University Press, 2001), 40–41.

53. Charles Henry Stanley Davis, *History of Wallingford, Conn., from Its Settlement in 1670 to the Present Time, Including Meriden, Which Was One of Its Parishes until 1806, and Cheshire, Which Was Incorporated in 1780* (Meriden: Mount Tom Printing House, 1870), 92.

54. Joseph Story, *A Discourse Pronounced at the Request of the Essex Historical Society, on the 18th of September, 1828, in Commemoration of the First Settlement of Salem, in the State of Massachusetts* (Boston: Hilliard, Gray, Little, and Wilkins, 1828), 16.

55. James Dimon Green, *An Oration Delivered at Malden, on the Two Hundredth Anniversary of the Incorporation of the Town, May 23, 1849* (Boston: George C. Rand, 1850), 5.

56. Rev. Darius Francis Lamson, *History of the Town of Manchester, Essex County, Massachusetts, 1645–1895* (Manchester: The Town, 1895), 5–6.

57. Lynn, Massachusetts, *Proceedings in Lynn, Massachusetts, June 17, 1879, Being*

the Two Hundred and Fiftieth Anniversary of the Settlement, Embracing the Oration, by Cyrus M. Tracy, and the Addresses, Correspondence, Etc., with an Introductory Chapter and a Second Part, by James R. Newhall (Lynn: 1880), 8–9.

58. Salisbury, *Manitou and Providence*, 115–19.

59. Rubertone, *Grave Undertakings*, 13, and Paul A. Robinson, "Lost Opportunities: Miantonomi and the English in Seventeenth-Century Narragansett Country," in *Northeastern Indian Lives, 1632–1816*, ed. Robert S. Grumet, 13–28 (Amherst: University of Massachusetts Press, 1996).

60. Michael Leroy Oberg, *Uncas: First of the Mohegans* (Ithaca, N.Y.: Cornell University Press, 2003).

61. Rich, *Truro—Cape Cod*, 32.

62. Bragdon, *Columbia Guide to Indians of the Northeast*, 154, and Neal Salisbury, "Squanto: Last of the Patuxet," in *Struggle and Survival in Colonial America*, ed. David G. Sweet and Gary B. Nash, 228–46 (Berkeley and Los Angeles: University of California Press, 1981).

63. Thatcher, *History of the Town of Plymouth*, 32.

64. Ibid., 33.

65. Ibid., 34–35.

66. Ibid., 36.

67. J. Lewis Dimon, "The Settlement of Mount Hope: An Address at the Two Hundredth Anniversary of the Settlement of the Town of Bristol, R.I. Delivered September 24, 1880," in *Orations and Essays* (Boston: Houghton, Mifflin, 1882), 147–48.

68. William Shaw Russell, *Guide to Plymouth, and Recollections of the Pilgrims* (Boston: G. Coolidge, 1846), xvii.

69. Ibid., [v].

70. Ibid., x–xi. This poem was carved into individual pieces in subsequent, much expanded editions of Russell's guide, which served more precisely as introductions to chapters. These included: "Samoset, the Indian Sagamore," with the subtitle "His Interview with the Pilgrims," and "Watson's Hill," with the subtitle "Massasoit."

71. Russell, *Pilgrim Memorials* (1855), 121 and 123.

72. Thomas Durfee, *A Historical Discourse Delivered on the Two Hundred and Fiftieth Anniversary of the Planting of Providence* (Providence: Sidney S. Rider, 1887), 16.

73. William R. Staples, *Annals of the Town of Providence from Its First Settlement, to the Organization of City Government, in June, 1832* (Providence: Knowles and Vose, 1843), 21.

74. John Pitman, *A Discourse Delivered at Providence, August 5, 1836, in Commemoration of the First Settlement of Rhode-Island and Providence Plantations. Being the Second Centennial Anniversary of the Settlement of Providence* (Providence: B. Cranston & Co., 1836), 18 (banishment) and 20–21 (quotation). The complexities of these land claims will be addressed in chapter 3.

75. Canonicus Memorial, *Services of Dedication, Under the Auspices of the Rhode Island Historical Society, September 21, 1883* (Providence: Providence Press Company, 1883), 13.

76. Staples, *Annals of Providence*, 10–11.

77. Canonicus Memorial, *Services of Dedication*, 26.

78. Orlo D. Hine, *Early Lebanon: An Historical Address Delivered in Lebanon, Conn., By Request, the National Centennial, July 4, 1876, by Rev. Orlo D. Hine with an Appendix of Historical Notes, by Nathaniel H. Morgan of Hartford, Conn.* (Hartford: Case, Lockwood & Brainard, 1880), 9.

79. Frances Manwaring Caulkins, *History of New London, Connecticut, from the First Survey of the Coast in 1612, to 1860* (New London: H. D. Utley, 1895), 54.

80. William L. Stone, *Uncas and Miantonomoh: A Historical Discourse, Delivered at Norwich, (Conn.) on the Fourth Day of July, 1842, on the Occasion of the Erection of a Monument to the Memory of Uncas, the White Man's Friend, and First Chief of the Mohegans* (New York: Dayton & Newman, 1842), ix. For a recent biography of Uncas see Oberg, *Uncas*.

81. Thomas S. Collier, comp., *A History of the Statue Erected to Commemorate the Heroic Achievement of Maj. John Mason and his Comrades, with an Account of the Unveiling Ceremonies* (Published by the Commission, 1889), 39.

82. Matthew Henry, "Commentary on Isaiah 35," blueletterbible.org. Henry was a seventeenth- and early-eighteenth-century minister in Chester, England. According to his commentary on this verse, it prophesied that "whatever is valuable in any institution is brought into the gospel. All the beauty of the Jewish church was admitted into the Christian church, and appeared in its perfection, as the apostle shows at large in his epistle to the Hebrews. Whatever was excellent and desirable in the Mosaic economy is translated into the evangelical institutes."

83. I created these categories in order to get a sense of the different ways Indian history is included in local narratives. The categories are, of course, somewhat arbitrary, and I could have included others, such as Indian culture, a category that would have attended to ethnographic information. I rejected that category because such information is too difficult to filter out of others. The broader category "other Indian conflict" includes major wars involving Indians from elsewhere. I chose not to separate out particular "French and Indian " wars, because the combatants were principally from outside New England. To be included in any of the categories, narratives had to go beyond merely mentioning something like the Pequot War, but even if a history included only a sentence or so, I did count it.

84. Two excellent surveys of this history are Francis Jennings, *The Invasion of America: Indians, Colonialism, and the Cant of Conquest* (New York: Norton, 1975), and Salisbury, *Manitou and Providence*.

85. William Biglow, *History of the Town of Natick, Mass., from the Days of the Apostolic Eliot, 1650, to the Present Time, 1830* (Boston: Marsh, Capen, & Lyon, 1830), 80 (1759); Oliver N. Bacon, *A History of Natick, from Its First Settlement in 1651 to the Present Time; with Notices of the First White Families, and also an Account of the Centennial Celebration, Oct. 16, 1851, Rev. Mr. Hunt's Address at the Consecration of Dell Park Cemetery* (Boston: Damrell & Moore, Printers, 1856), 21; and Obed Macy, *The History of Nantucket, Being a Compendious Account of the First Settlement of the Island by the English, Together*

with the *Rise and Progress of the Whale Fishery; and Other Historical Facts Relative to Said Island and Its Inhabitants,* 2nd ed. (Mansfield: Macy & Pratt, 1880), 57. A previous epidemic (1745–46) escaped the notice of Natick's nineteenth-century historians. Jean M. O'Brien, *Dispossession by Degrees: Indian Land and Identity in Natick, Massachusetts, 1650–1790* (Cambridge: Cambridge University Press, 1997), 189.

86. Thatcher, *History of Plymouth,* 17.

87. O'Brien, *Dispossession by Degrees,* and Silverman, *Faith and Boundaries.*

88. Trudie Lamb Richmond and Amy E. Den Ouden, "Recovering Gendered Political Histories: Local Struggles and Native Women's Resistance in Colonial Southern New England," in Calloway and Salisbury, *Reinterpreting New England Indians and the Colonial Experience,* 190–91.

89. Wolfgang Hochbruck and Beatrix Dudensing-Reichel, "'Honoratissimi Benefactores': Native American Students and Two Seventeenth-Century Texts in the University Tradition," in *Early Native American Writing: New Critical Essays,* ed. Helen Jaskoski, 1–14 (Cambridge: Cambridge University Press, 1996).

90. Bernd C. Peyer, *The Tutor'd Mind: Indian Missionary-Writers in Antebellum America* (Amherst: University of Massachusetts Press, 1997), and Hilary E. Wyss, *Writing Indians: Literacy, Christianity, and Native Community in Early America* (Amherst: University of Massachusetts Press, 2000). On the tradition of Indian nonfiction writing see Konkle, *Writing Indian Nations,* and Warrior, *The People and the Word.*

91. Peyer, *The Tutor'd Mind,* especially 76–84, and Dana D. Nelson, "'(I Speak like a Fool but I Am Constrained)': Samson Occom's *Short Narrative* and the Economies of the Racial Self,'" in Jaskoski, *Early Native American Writing,* 42–65.

92. Sarah Loring Bailey, *Historical Sketches of Andover, (Comprising the Present Towns of North Andover and Andover), Massachusetts* (Boston: Houghton, Mifflin, 1880), 165.

93. Alonzo O. Chapin, *Glastenbury for Two Hundred Years. A Facsimile of the 1853 edition with the Addition of Topical and Personal Name Indexes by Ruth How Hale. Also Additions and Corrections to Text Made by Goslee (c. 1880) and Whittles (c. 1960)* (Hartford: Findlay Bros., 1976), 49.

94. Ashbel Woodward, *A Historical Address Delivered in Franklin, Connecticut, October, 14th, 1868, on the Two Hundredth Anniversary of the Settlement of the Town, and the One Hundred and Fiftieth Anniversary of Its Ecclesiastical Organizations* (New Haven: Tuttle, Morehouse & Taylor, 1870), 88. On Occom see, e.g., Peyer, *The Tutor'd Mind,* 54–116; Wyss, *Writing Indians,* 123–53; Joanna Brooks, *American Lazarus: Religion and the Rise of African-American and Native American Literatures* (New York: Oxford University Press, 2003), 51–86; and Brooks, *The Common Pot,* 51–105.

95. On the history of the formation of Brothertown see Brad Devin Edward Jarvis, "Preserving the Brothertown Nation of Indians: Exploring Relationships amongst Land, Sovereignty, and Identity, 1740–1840" (PhD dissertation, University of Minnesota, 2006).

96. Columbia, Connecticut, *The 150th Anniversary of the Organization of the Congregational Church in Columbia, Conn., October 24th, 1866. Historical Papers, Addresses,*

with Appendix (Hartford: Case, Lockwood, 1867), 58. This notice comes in a rather full discussion of Wheelock's Moor's Charity School and other missionaries are discussed as well (7, 58–69). Hine, *Early Lebanon*, 54–63; *The Uncas Monument: Published Once in Three Hundred and Fifty Years, 1491–1842* (Norwich: John G. Cooley, 1842), 3; John W. Stedman, *The Norwich Jubilee: A Report of the Celebration at Norwich, Connecticut, on the Two Hundredth Anniversary of the Settlement of the Town, September 7th and 8th, 1859* (Norwich: John W. Stedman, 1859), 135; Daniel Coit Gilman, *A Historical Discourse, Delivered in Norwich, Connecticut, September 7, 1859, at the Bi-Centennial Celebration of the Settlement of the Town* (Boston: Geo. C. Rand and Avery, 1859), 40; and Frances Manwaring Caulkins, *History of Norwich, Connecticut, from Its Possession by the Indians, to the Year 1866* (Hartford: Case, Lockwood, 1866), 269.

97. A. Dunning, *A Historical Discourse, Preached in Thompson, CT., February, 1855* (Worcester: Henry J. Howland, n.d.), 5; Henry Bronson, *The History of Waterbury, Connecticut: The Original Township Embracing Present Watertown and Plymouth, and Parts of Oxford, Wolcott, Middlebury, Prospect and Naugatuck* (Waterbury: Bronson Brothers, 1858), 268 (in a section on miscellaneous items); and Henry R. Stiles, *The History of Ancient Windsor, Connecticut, including East Windsor, South Windsor, and Ellington, Prior to 1768, the Date of their Separation from the Old Town; and Windsor, Bloomfield and Windsor Locks, to the Present Time. Also the Genealogies and Genealogical Notes of those Families Which Settled within the Limits of Ancient Windsor, Connecticut, prior to 1800* (New York: Charles B. Norton, 1859), 100. On Stockbridge see Patrick Frazier, *The Mohegans of Stockbridge* (Lincoln: University of Nebraska Press, 1992).

98. See Barry O'Connell, ed., *On Our Own Ground: The Complete Writings of William Apess, a Pequot* (Amherst: University of Massachusetts Press, 1992), introduction, for his relationship to Methodism. See Warrior, *The People and the Word*, on Apess's career as a writer.

99. See chapter 4.

100. Cronon's *Changes in the Land* remains indispensable for understanding this history. On the impact of animals on relations, see Virginia DeJohn Anderson, *Creatures of Empire: How Domestic Animals Transformed Early America* (New York: Oxford University Press, 2004).

101. On the Pequot War see Alfred A. Cave, *The Pequot War* (Amherst: University of Massachusetts Press, 1996). Details of the Treaty of Hartford are on 161.

102. Den Ouden, *Beyond Conquest*, 15–16.

103. The most recent full-scale account is Cave, *The Pequot War.*

104. Stedman, *Norwich Jubilee*, 163.

105. Ibid., 160. On the historiography of the war see Cave, *The Pequot War,* 1–12 and 168–78. On the Pequot War as part of a larger process of asserting a masculine political and cultural hegemony in New England, see Andrea Cremer, "Enemies Incarnate: Religion, Sex, Violence, and Contests for Power in New England, 1636–1638" (PhD dissertation, University of Minnesota, 2007).

106. Collier, *History of the Statue*, oration, 22–50. The quotation is from 45.

107. Jill Lepore, *The Name of War: King Philip's War and the Origins of American Identity* (New York: Alfred A. Knopf, 1997), xi–xii.

108. On shifting practices of Indian slavery and servitude see Margaret Ellen Newell, "The Changing Nature of Indian Slavery in New England, 1670–1720," in *Reinterpreting New England Indians and the Colonial Experience*, 106–36.

109. Lepore, *The Name of War*, 173–74.

110. Ibid., 49–52 and 125.

111. Only three contemporary accounts of the Pequot War were published: those of combatants John Underhill and John Mason, plus one by minister Philip Vincent. Lieutenant Lion Gardener's manuscript was not published until 1833.

112. Lepore, *The Name of War*, 50–51.

113. Braintree, Massachusetts, *Centennial Celebration at Braintree, Mass., July 4, 1876* (Boston: Alfred Mudge & Son, 1877), 30, and John Gorham Palfrey, *A Discourse Pronounced at Barnstable on the Third of September, 1839, at the Celebration of the Second Centennial Anniversary of the Settlement of Cape Cod* (Boston: Ferdinand Andrews, 1840), 17.

114. Sylvester Judd, *History of Hadley, Including the Early History of Hatfield, South Hadley, Amherst, and Granby, Massachusetts, by Sylvester Judd, with Family Genealogies, by Lucius M. Boltwood* (Northampton: Metcalf, 1863), 135–92.

115. Lucius I. Barber, *The Burning of Simsbury: A Bi-Centennial Address, in Commemoration of That Event, Delivered in the Congregational Church in Simsbury, Conn., on Sabbath Evening, March 26, 1876* (Hartford: Case, Lockwood & Brainard Co., 1876); Luther B. Lincoln, *An Address at South Deerfield, August 31, 1838, on the Completion of the Bloody Brook Monument, Erected in Memory of Capt. Lothrop and His Associates, Who Fell at the Spot, September 18 (O.S.) 1675* (Greenfield: Kneeland & Eastman, 1838); and Collier, *A History of the Statue.*

116. Evan Haefeli and Kevin Sweeney, *Captors and Captives: The 1704 French and Indian Raid on Deerfield* (Amherst: University of Massachusetts Press, 2003); Richard R. Johnson, "The Search for a Usable Indian: An Aspect of the Defense of Colonial New England," *Journal of American History* 64 (1977): 623–51; and Colin G. Calloway, *The American Revolution in Indian Country: Crisis and Diversity in Native American Communities* (Cambridge: Cambridge University Press, 1995).

117. John Crowell, *The Colonial and Revolutionary History of Haverhill: A Centennial Oration* (Haverhill, Mass.: Gazette Print, 1877), 14.

118. O'Brien, *Dispossession by Degrees*, chapter 3.

119. See, e.g., Doughton, "Unseen Neighbors," in Calloway, *After King Philip's War;* O'Brien, *Dispossession by Degrees;* and Donna Keith Baron, J. Edward Hood, and Holly V. Izard, "They Were Here All Along: The Native American Presence in Lower-Central New England in the Eighteenth and Nineteenth Centuries," *William and Mary Quarterly,* 3rd ser. 53 (1996): 561–86.

120. Daniel Vickers, "The First Whalemen of Nantucket," in Calloway, *After King Philip's War,* 90–113; McMullen and Handsman, *A Key into the Language of Woodsplint Baskets;* Jean M. O'Brien, "'Divorced' from the Land: Resistance and Survival of Indian

Women in Eighteenth-Century New England," in Calloway, *After King Philip's War*, 144–61; and Nan Wolverton, "'A Precarious Living': Basket Making and Related Crafts Among New England Indians," in *Reinterpreting New England Indians and the Colonial Experience*, 341–68.

121. John A. Sainsbury, "Indian Labor in Early Rhode Island," *New England Quarterly* 48 (1975): 378–93. The percentage is from 379.

122. Ruth Wallis Herndon and Ella Wilcox Sekatau, "Colonizing the Children: Indian Youngsters in Servitude in Early Rhode Island," in *Reinterpreting New England Indians and the Colonial Experience*, 137–73.

123. Luther Wright, *Historical Sketch of Easthampton, Mass., Delivered before the Young Men's Association, of Easthampton, Oct. 7, 1851* (Northampton: Gazette Office, 1852), 4–5.

124. Ibid., 4.

125. Brooks, *History of the Town of Medford*, 80.

126. James M. Usher, *History of the Town of Medford, Middlesex County, from Its First Settlement in 1630 to 1855, Revised, Enlarged, and Brought Down to 1885* (Boston: Rand, Avery, 1886), 98.

127. Charles Brooks, "Indian Necropolis in West Medford, Mass.; Discovered Oct. 21, 1862," *Massachusetts Historical Proceedings* (1862–63), 363.

128. Davis, *History of Wallingford, Conn.*, [7]–35.

129. Mason A. Green, *Springfield, 1636–1886, History of Town and City Including an Account of the Quarter-Millennial Celebration at Springfield, Mass., May 25 and 26, 1886* (Springfield: C. A. Nichols, 1888), 13, and Stiles, *History of Ancient Windsor*, 102–3.

130. Charles Francis Adams, *An Address on the Occasion of Opening the New Town Hall, in Braintree, July 29, 1858* (Boston: William White, 1858), 37–38.

131. Gilman, *A Historical Discourse, Delivered in Norwich*, 11.

132. Josiah P. Tustin, *A Discourse Delivered at the Dedication of the New Church Edifice of the Baptist Church and Society, in Warren, R.I., May 8, 1845* (Providence: H. H. Brown, 1845), 96–97. The quote is the final sentence of Irving's sketch. Washington Irving, "Philip of Pokanoket: An Indian Memoir," *The Sketch Book* (New York: Macmillan, 1929), 365.

133. Lepore, *The Name of War*.

134. Sudbury, Massachusetts, *Bi-Centennial Celebration, 1676–1876 at Sudbury, Mass., April 18, 1876, Including the Oration by Prof. Edward J. Young, of Harvard College* (Lowell: Marden and Rowell, 1876), 26.

135. "It has been the lot of the unfortunate aborigines of America, in the early periods of colonization, to be doubly wronged by the white men: they have been dispossessed of their hereditary possessions by mercenary and frequently wanton warfare, and their characters have been traduced by bigoted and interested writers. The colonist often treated them like beasts of the forest, and the author has endeavored to justify him in his outrages. The former found it easier to exterminate than to civilize, the latter to vilify than to discriminate." Washington Irving, "Traits of Indian Character," in *The*

Sketch Book, 331. See also Jean M. O'Brien, "'Vanishing' Indians in Nineteenth-Century New England: Local Historians' Erasure of Still-Present Indian Peoples," in *New Perspectives on Native North America: Cultures, Histories, and Representations,* ed. Sergei Kan and Pauline Strong Turner, 414–32 (Lincoln: University of Nebraska Press, 2006).

136. Leonard Bacon, *Thirteen Historical Discourses, on the Completion of Two Hundred Years, from the Beginning of the First Church in New Haven, with an Appendix* (New Haven: Durrie & Peck, 1839), 330.

137. See also Stiles, *Ancient Windsor,* 82.

138. Barber, *The Burning of Simsbury,* 13–14.

139. Ibid., 23.

140. Ibid., 27.

141. Ibid., 27–28.

142. Ibid., 26–27.

143. Ibid., 28.

144. Stedman, *The Norwich Jubilee,* 124. See also Reading, Massachusetts, *Historical Address and Poem, Delivered at the Bi-Centennial Celebration of the Incorporation of the Old Town of Reading, May 29, A.D. 1844* (Boston: Samuel N. Dickinson, 1844), 8.

145. Edward Everett, *An Address Delivered at Bloody Brook, in South Deerfield, September 30, 1835, in Commemoration of the Fall of the "Flower of Essex," at that Spot, in King Philip's War, September 19 (o.s.) 1675* (Boston: Russell, Shattuck, & Williams, 1835), 6.

146. Ibid.

147. Canonicus Memorial, *Services of Dedication,* 23.

148. Ibid.

149. Stedman, *Norwich Jubilee,* 132. See also Story, *A Discourse,* 73–74.

150. Everett, *An Address Delivered on the 28th of June, 1830,* 39.

151. Braintree, Massachusetts, *Centennial Celebration at Braintree,* 13. Hobart's casting of Wampatuck as the first tribal sachem in the region constitutes an interesting case of firsting: Is he asserting that tribal leadership awaited the arrival of the English to come into being?

152. Charles Hudson, *History of the Town of Marlborough, Middlesex County, Massachusetts, from Its First Settlement in 1657 to 1861; with a Brief Sketch of the Town of Northborough, A Genealogy of the Families in Marlborough to 1800, and an Account of the Celebration of the Two Hundredth Anniversary of the Incorporation of the Town* (Boston: T. R. Marvin & Son, 1862), 97–98. The quotation is from 98.

153. Roxbury, Massachusetts, *Roxbury Centennial: An Account of the Celebration in Roxbury, November 22, 1876, with the Oration of Gen. Horace Binney Sargeant, Speeches at the Dinner and Other Matters* (Boston: Rockwell and Churchill, 1877), 29.

154. Falmouth, Massachusetts, *The Celebration of the Two Hundredth Anniversary of the Incorporation of the Town of Falmouth, Massachusetts, June 15, 1886* (Falmouth: L. F. Clarke, 1887), 46–47. The quotation is from 47.

155. See Bacon, *Thirteen Historical Discourses,* 95 ("How often and how justly, has Penn been lauded for the fact that, under his administration his colony had no collision

with the Indians. And is not the same praise due to the civil and religious leaders of the New Haven colony . . . ?"), and Barber, *Burning of Simsbury,* 16.

156. Judd, *History of Hadley,* 113. A footnote says Grahame, in his *History of the United States,* vol. 2, 346, has corrected the error of these writers. Other references to William Penn include James L. Kingsley, *A Historical Discourse, Delivered by Request before the Citizens of New Haven, April 25, 1838, the Two Hundredth Anniversary of the First Settlement of the Town and Colony* (New Haven: B. W. Noyes, 1838), 22; Lincoln, *An Address Delivered at South Deerfield,* 13; Green, *An Oration Delivered at Malden,* 14–15; and David Willard, *Willard's History of Greenfield* (Greenfield: Kneeland & Eastman, 1838), 13–15.

157. Middleborough, Massachusetts, *Celebration of the Two-Hundredth Anniversary of the Incorporation of Middleborough, Massachusetts, October 13, 1869, Including the Oration of Hon. Thomas Russell, Address by his Honor, Mayor Shurtleff, of Boston, and the Other Exercises of the Occasion* (Middleborough: Gazette Office, 1870), 24.

158. Ibid., 24–25.

159. Charles Ellis, *The History of Roxbury Town* (Boston: Samuel G. Drake, 1847), 116–17.

160. Story, *A Discourse,* 67–68.

161. Ibid., 70–72.

162. Ibid., 72–74.

163. Ibid., 74.

164. Ibid., 77.

165. For explicit claims about this see William J. Miller, comp., *Celebration of the Two-Hundredth Anniversary of the Settlement of the Town of Bristol, Rhode Island, September 24th, A.D. 1880* (Providence: Printed by the Providence Press Co., 1881), 36, and reprinted separately as Dimon, "The Settlement of Mount Hope," 146.

166. Mason Noble, *Centennial Discourse, Delivered in Williamstown, Mass., November 19, 1865* (North Adams, Mass.: James T. Robinson, 1865), 18.

167. Rich, *Truro—Cape Cod,* 75.

168. [Edward H. Spalding, comp.], *Bi-Centennial of Old Dunstable, Address by Hon. S. T. Worcester, October 27, 1873. Also Colonel Bancroft's Personal Narrative of the Battle of Bunker Hill, and Some Notices of Persons and Families of the Early Times of Dunstable, Including Welds, Tyngs, Lovewells, Farwells, Fletchers, Bancrofts, Joneses and Cutlers, by John B. Hill* (Nashua, N.H.: E. H. Spalding, 1878), 13–14.

169. Harriet F. Woods, *Historical Sketches of Brookline, Mass.* (Boston: Robert S. David, 1874), 308.

170. Russell, *Pilgrim Memorials* (1851), [v]. Clearly Russell has something wrong here, as White would have been fifty-six rather than eighty-four if he had been born and died as reported.

171. Suffield, Connecticut, *Proceedings at Suffield, September 16, 1858, on the Occasion of the One Hundred and Fiftieth Anniversary of the Decease of the Rev. Benjamin Ruggles, at Suffield, Conn.* (Springfield, Mass.: Samuel Bowles and Co., 1859), 57–58.

172. Cf. Joanne Pope Melish, *Disowning Slavery: Gradual Emancipation and "Race" in New England, 1780–1860* (Ithaca, N.Y.: Cornell University Press, 1998).

173. Joel Hawes, *An Address Delivered at the Request of the Citizens of Hartford, on the 9th of November, 1835. The Close of the Second Century, from the First Settlement of the City* (Hartford: Belknap & Hamersley, 1835), 19.

174. Billerica, Massachusetts, *Celebration of the Two Hundredth Anniversary of the Incorporation of Billerica, Massachusetts, May 29th, 1855* (Lowell: S. J. Varney, 1855), 40.

175. Princeton, Massachusetts, *Celebration of the One Hundredth Anniversary of the Incorporation of the Town of Princeton, Mass., October 20th, 1859, Including the Address of Hon. Charles Theodore Russell, the Poem of Prof. Erastus Everett, and other Exercises of the Occasion* (Worcester: William R. Hooper, 1860), 84.

2. Replacing

1. Jonathan Brace, *A Leaf of Milford History: A Thanksgiving Sermon, Preached in the First Church, Milford, Conn., November 25, 1858* (New Haven, Conn.: E. Hayes, 1858), 5.

2. On the memory and commemoration of King Philip's War in historiography, literary production, and material culture, see Lepore, *The Name of War.* For a fascinating study of how "place stories" operated to dispossess and expropriate Indians see Thrush, *Native Seattle.*

3. Trouillot, *Silencing the Past,* 116.

4. Ibid., 118.

5. Keith Basso, *Wisdom Sits in Places: Landscape and Language among the Western Apache* (Albuquerque: University of New Mexico Press, 1996), 76–77.

6. Caulkins, *History of Norwich,* 33–36. Quotations are from 37 and 36. Spellings of his name vary. Most contemporary scholars use "Miantonomi," and I follow that practice here.

7. Ibid., 37.

8. Ibid.

9. Simmons, *Spirit of the New England Tribes,* 251–56.

10. Caulkins, *History of Norwich,* 38, and *The Uncas Monument,* 4, no. 2. See also Rubertone, *Grave Undertakings,* 177–78.

11. Robert S. Nelson and Margaret Olin, eds., *Monuments and Memory, Made and Unmade* (Chicago: University of Chicago Press, 2003), 6.

12. Oberg, *Uncas,* 100–107. Oberg argues that Uncas merely complied with the terms of the Treaty of Hartford of 1638 in his complicity with the English, and that it was subsequent historians who cast Uncas as villainous in his actions.

13. Stone, *Uncas and Miantonomoh,* ix, and Oberg, *Uncas,* 3–7.

14. Stone, *Uncas and Miantonomoh,* ix; Oberg, *Uncas,* 3–7; and *Uncas Memorial.*

15. Stone, *Uncas and Miantonomoh,* [vii].

16. William Lester Jr., *A Sketch of Norwich: Including Notes of a Survey of the Town* (Norwich: J. Dunham, 1833), 4.

17. Thomas Day, *A Historical Discourse, Delivered before the Connecticut Historical*

Society, and the Citizens of Hartford, on the Evening of the 26th Day of December, 1843 (Hartford: Case, Tiffany and Burnham, 1844), 6 and 11–12.

18. Noah Porter Jr., *A Historical Discourse, Delivered by Request, before the Citizens of Farmington, November 4, 1840, in Commemoration of the Original Settlement of the Ancient Town, in 1640* (Hartford: L. Skinner, Printer, 1841), 62.

19. Ibid.

20. Ibid., 26.

21. Orcutt and Beardsley, *The History of the Old Town of Derby, Connecticut*, lvi.

22. Lamson, *History of the Town of Manchester*, 9 (Masconomo: a boulder "as a memento of the chief who first welcomed the white man to these shores, and of a once numerous but now vanishing race"); Canoncicus Memorial, *Services of Dedication* (Canonicus: a boulder. "Long after *thy* posterity shall have disappeared from among men, the descendants of the white man, and his associates, whom thou befriended, will hand down thy name to *their* posterity with the same reverence they received it from their ancestors"; p. 18); and Martha Norkunas, *Monuments and Memory: History and Representation in Lowell, Massachusetts* (Washington, D.C.: Smithsonian Institution Press, 2002), 163–64 (Passaconaway: a statue). On the Canonicus Memorial, see also Rubertone, *Grave Undertakings*, 180–81.

23. Usher, *History of the Town of Medford*, 509.

24. Middleborough, Massachusetts, *Celebration of the Two-Hundredth Anniversary of the Incorporation of Middleborough*, 49. (The text reports that "this stone was erected by Mr. Levi Reed, of Lakeville.")

25. Seelye, *Memory's Nation*.

26. Massasoit Monument Association, *Exercises under the Auspices of the Thalia Club, Warren, R.I., February 8th, 1893, for the Benefit of the Massasoit Monument Fund, with Addresses, Poems, Etc.* (Providence: E. A. Johnson, 1893), 4, and personal communication, e-mail from Pat Read, president of the Massasoit Historical Association, May 18, 2004.

27. Massasoit Monument Association, *Exercises under the Auspices of the Thalia Club*, 40.

28. Ibid., 5.

29. Seelye, *Memory's Nation*, 447.

30. Ibid., 636.

31. Ibid., 534–38.

32. Salisbury, *Manitou and Providence*, 112–24 and 129–30.

33. Seelye, *Memory's Nation*, 536.

34. Stephen M. Allen, *Myles Standish, with an Account of the Exercises of Consecration of the Monument Ground on Captain's Hill, Duxbury, Aug. 17, 1871* (Boston: Alfred Mudge & Son, 1871), 17.

35. Ibid., 16.

36. Ibid., 3.

37. Collier, *History of the Statue*, 42–47. The quotation is from 45. In 1994, after

eleven months of contentious meetings, a committee in Mystic, Connecticut, voted to move the Mason statue out of the town. Spurred to action by Eastern Pequot Lone Wolf Jackson, who was a member of the committee, and other Native activists, they debated interpretations of the Pequot War without coming to conclusions, but unanimously decided that moving the statue was the right thing to do because of Indian sensitivity. Two years later the statue was rededicated in Windsor, Connecticut, with a different plaque that shifts the focus on Mason away from the Pequot War and toward his role as a founder of Windsor. In 2006, a Web site devoted to moving the statue back to Mystic went live. See the *Hartford Courant* article at archnet.asu.edu/archives/ethno/Cournat/day5.htm on the decision; the *New York Times*, 7 July 1996, on the removal to Windsor; and thepequotwar.com for the drive to move the statue back (all accessed 27 October 2008).

38. Collier, *History of the Statue*, 45.

39. Ibid., 48–49.

40. Everett, *An Address Delivered at Bloody Brook*, [38]–41. The first quotation is from 38, and the second quotation, by General E. Hoyt, is from 41. The monument was completed three years later. Lincoln, *An Address Delivered at South Deerfield*.

41. Stow, Massachusetts, *Bi-Centennial Celebration of the Town of Stow, Mass., May 16, 1883* (Marlboro, Mass.: Pratt Brothers, 1883). On monuments dedicated to the memory of King Philip's War more generally, see Eric B. Schultz and Michael J. Tougias, *King Philip's War: The History and Legacy of America's Forgotten Conflict* (Woodstock, Vt.: Countryman Press, 1999).

42. Haverhill, Massachusetts, *Foundation Facts concerning Its Settlement*, 25.

43. William A. Emerson, *Fitchburg, Massachusetts: Past and Present* (Fitchburg: Blanchard & Brown, 1887), 27.

44. [Spalding], *Bi-Centennial of Old Dunstable*, 41.

45. Henry A. S. Dearborn, *A Sketch of the Life of the Apostle Eliot, Prefatory to a Subscription for Erecting a Monument to his Memory* (Roxbury: Norfolk County Journal Press, 1850), 28–32. The quotation is from 31–32.

46. Amos P. Cheney, *Natick, Massachusetts, Its Advantages for Residence, and as a Place of Business, Prepared under the Direction of the Board of Selectmen* (Natick: Bulletin Steam Print, 1889), 11–12.

47. Erastus Worthington, *The History of Dedham, from the Beginning of Its Settlement in September, 1635 . . . to May, 1827* (Boston: Dutton and Wentworth, 1827), 30. There is also a stained glass window of Eliot preaching to the Indians in the First Congregational Church in Woodstock, Connecticut, labeled "John Eliot Preaching the Gospel to the Wabquassets at Pulpit Rock, 1690." I'm indebted to Flo Waldron for this information.

48. Historical, Natural History, and Library Society of South Natick, Mass., *Proceedings at the Reunion of the Descendants of John Eliot "The Apostle to the Indians" at Guilford, Conn., September 15th, 1875* (n.p., 1901), 13.

49. Ibid., 27.

50. Herman A. Jennings, *Checquocket; or, Provincetown*, 2nd ed. (Provincetown: Advocate Office, 1893), 13–14. It was dedicated in 1910. Seelye, *Memory's Nation*, 561–64.

51. Nathaniel B. Shurtleff and Henry W. Cushman, *Proceedings at the Consecration of the Cushman Monument at Plymouth, September 16, 1858: Including the Discourse and Poem Delivered on that Occasion, Together with a List of Contributors to the Monument* (Boston: Little, Brown, 1859), [iii].

52. Newton, Massachusetts, *A Brief Notice of the Settlement of the Town of Newton, Prepared by a Committee Who Were Charged with the Duty of Erecting a Monument to the Memory of Its First Settlers, September, 1852* (Boston: C. C. P. Moody, 1852).

53. For a fascinating discussion of the details of commemorating Roger Williams see Rubertone, *Grave Undertakings*, especially 22–36. On John Winthrop, see Francis J. Bremer, "Remembering—and Forgetting—John Winthrop and the Puritan Founders," *Massachusetts Historical Review* 6 (2004): 39–70.

54. J. Lewis Dimon, *Ceremonies at the Unveiling of the Monument to Roger Williams, Erected by the City of Providence* (Providence: Angell, Hammet, 1877), 9 and 26.

55. Durfee, *A Historical Discourse*, 18.

56. Blackstone is the subject of a recent hagiography: Louise Lind, *William Blackstone: Sage of the Wilderness* (Bowie, Md.: Heritage Books, 1993).

57. William Blackstone, *An Address Delivered at the Formation of the Blackstone Monument Association, Together with the Preliminaries, and Proceedings at Study Hill, July 4, 1855* (Pawtucket: James L. Estey, 1855), 4.

58. Sylvanus Chace Newman, *Rehoboth in the Past. An Historical Oration Delivered on the Fourth of July, 1860. Also an Account of the Proceedings in Seekonk, [the Ancient Rehoboth,] at the Celebration of the Day, Completing Two Hundred and Sixteen Years of Its History* (Pawucket: Robert Sherman, 1860), 37.

59. Blackstone, *Blackstone Monument*, 3. This claim about first apples challenged William Shaw Russell's assertion that Peregrine White planted the first apple trees in Plymouth. Russell, *Pilgrim Memorials* (1851), v.

60. Drake, *History and Antiquities of Boston*, 96.

61. Blackstone, *Blackstone Monument*, 18. The author cites Blackstone's inventory.

62. Ibid., 17.

63. Ibid., 18.

64. Ibid., 4. The connection between the author of this text, William Blackstone, and his subject is not made clear but is certainly intriguing given this claim of extinction.

65. Samuel Abbott Green, *An Historical Address Delivered at Groton, Massachusetts, February 20, 1880, by Request of the Citizens, at the Dedication of Three Monuments Erected by the Town* (Cambridge: John Wilson & Son, 1880). The quotation is from 7.

66. Concord, Massachusetts, *Celebration of the Two Hundred and Fiftieth Anniversary of the Incorporation of Concord, September 12, 1885* (Concord: The Concord Transcript, 1885), 12–13.

67. Norkunas, *Monuments and Memory.*

68. Ibid.

69. David Waldstreicher, *In the Midst of Perpetual Fetes: The Making of American Nationalism, 1776–1820* (Chapel Hill: University of North Carolina Press, 1997). See also Susan G. Davis, *Parades and Power: Street Theatre in Nineteenth-Century Philadelphia* (Berkeley and Los Angeles: University of California Press, 1986); Simon P. Newman, *Parades and the Politics of the Street: Festive Culture in the Early American Republic* (Philadelphia: University of Pennsylvania Press, 1997); and Len Travers, *Celebrating the Fourth: Independence Day and the Rites of Nationalism in the Early Republic* (Amherst: University of Massachusetts Press, 1997).

70. Reproduced in Lynn, Massachusetts, *Centennial Memorial of Lynn, Essex County, Massachusetts, Embracing an Historical Sketch, 1629–1876, by James R. Newhall, and Notices of the Mayors, with Portraits* (Lynn: Thomas B. Breare, 1876), [iii].

71. In one case, it is unclear what they are commemorating.

72. Stedman, *Norwich Jubilee,* 118–19.

73. Powers, *An Address, Delivered to the People of Goshen,* 14–15, and Palfrey, *A Discourse Pronounced at Barnstable,* 3.

74. Weymouth, Massachusetts, *Proceedings on the Two Hundred and Fiftieth Anniversary of the Permanent Settlement of Weymouth, with an Historical Address by Charles Francis Adams, Jr., July 4th, 1874* (Boston: Wright and Potter, 1874), 76.

75. Trouillot, *Silencing the Past,* 116–17.

76. Lynn, Massachusetts, *Centennial Memorial,* 73.

77. Ibid., 91–92.

78. Elias Nason, *Billerica: A Centennial Oration* (Lowell: Marden and Rowell, 1876), [5].

79. Ibid., [7].

80. A scattered few other texts were published for the centennial year, and some orations found their way into periodical literature. The numbers I use here do not include commemorations of particular events of the revolution, such as the Battle of Bunker Hill.

81. Boston, Massachusetts, *Celebration of the Two Hundred and Fiftieth Anniversary of the Settlement of Boston, September 17, 1880* (Boston: Rockwell and Churchill, 1880), [153].

82. Ibid., 155–62.

83. On the impersonation of Indians in the Boston Tea Party and throughout American history, see Philip J. Deloria, *Playing Indian* (New Haven, Conn.: Yale University Press, 1998).

84. Boston, Massachusetts, *Celebration,* 155–62.

85. Billerica, Massachusetts, *Celebration of the Two Hundredth Anniversary,* 10 and 75–86.

86. Ibid., 49–75.

87. Ibid., 59.

88. Ibid., 60.

89. Ibid., 60–61.

90. Ibid., 65.

91. On the process of creating the "Free White Republic as New England," see Melish, *Disowning Slavery.*

92. Billerica, *Celebration of the Two Hundredth Anniversary,* 85.

93. Ibid., 40.

94. Frederic Denison, *Westerly (Rhode Island) and Its Witnesses, for Two Hundred and Fifty Years, 1626–1876, Including Charlestown, Hopkinton, and Richmond, Until their Separate Organization, with the Principal Points of their Subsequent History* (Providence: J. A. & R. A. Reid, 1878), 37.

95. Stedman, *Norwich Jubilee,* 213–14.

96. Miller, *Celebration of the Two-Hundredth Anniversary,* 27.

97. Stedman, *Norwich Jubilee,* 117.

98. Ralph D. Smith, *The History of Guilford, Connecticut, from Its First Settlement in 1639. From the Manuscripts* (Albany: J. Munsell, 1877), 124–25.

99. Elias Nason, *A History of the Town of Dunstable, Massachusetts, from Its Earliest Settlement to the Year of Our Lord 1873* (Boston: Alfred Mudge & Son, 1877), 67. This rhetorical construction is pervasive in local texts.

100. Emory Washburn, *Historical Sketches of the Town of Leicester, Massachusetts, during the First Century from Its Settlement* (Boston: John Wilson and Son, 1860), 48.

101. Thomas W. Bicknell, ed., *An Historical Address and Poem, Delivered at the Centennial Celebration of the Incorporation of the Town of Barrington, June 17, 1870, with an Historical Appendix* (Providence: Printed by Providence Press Co., 1870), 127–28.

102. Salisbury, Connecticut, *Historical Addresses Delivered by Hon. Samuel Church, October 19, 1841, and Ex-Gov. A. H. Holley, July 4, 1876, Together with a Record of Proceedings at the Centennial Celebration in Salisbury, Conn.* (Pittsfield, Mass.: Chickering & Axtell, 1876), 4 in Church's address.

103. Bicknell, *An Historical Address and Poem,* 155.

104. Thomas Gage, *The History of Rowley, Anciently Including Bradford, Boxford, and Georgetown, from the Year 1639 to the Present Time, with an Address, Delivered September 5, 1839, at the Celebration of the Second Centennial Anniversary of Its Settlement* (Boston: Ferdinand Andrews, 1840), 192. See also H. E. Miller, *History of the Town of Savoy* (West Cummington, Mass., 1879), 15 (a tiny book in which this is the only Indian content), and Sanford, *History of Raynham,* 36. The latter reprints the Rowley story verbatim, and attributes it to a 1793 history of Raynham. It also tells us that the friendship of the Leonards ensured that Raynham and Taunton escaped damage during the war.

105. Lepore, *The Name of War,* 174–78. For a Narragansett account of the fate of Philip's skull, see Lepore, 190.

106. Gage, *History of Rowley,* 191.

107. Denison, *Westerly (Rhode Island),* 33–36, and 29–30 (includes a discussion of the "royal burying ground"—a large mound).

108. Daniel H. Greene, *History of the Town of East Greenwich, and Adjacent Territory, from 1677 to 1877* (Providence: J. A. & R. A. Reid, Printers and Publishers, 1877), 51–52. Other texts that suggest the possibility of some race existing here previous to Indians include Salisbury, Connecticut, *Historical Address*, p. 7 in Church's address, and Jeroboam Parker, *A Sermon Delivered at Southborough, July 17, 1827, the Day Which Completed a Century from the Incorporation of the Town* (Boston: John Marsh, 1827), 6.

109. West Springfield, Massachusetts, *Account of the Centennial Celebration of the Town of West Springfield, Mass., Wednesday, March 25th, 1874, with the Historical Address of Thomas E. Vermilye, the Poem of Mrs. Ellen P. Champion, and Other Facts and Speeches* (Springfield: Clark W. Bryan, 1874), 49.

110. Ibid.

111. Parker, *A Sermon Delivered at Southborough*, 6.

112. This was suggested to me by Susan Sleeper-Smith, whose work with nineteenth-century local histories in the Midwest reveals their obsession with Mississippian mound builders.

113. Parker, *Sermon Delivered at Southborough*, 6.

114. John Ross Dix, *A Hand-book of Newport, and Rhode Island* (Newport: C. E. Hammet Jr., 1852), 28–37. The quote is from 33. Numerous Web sites are devoted to the ongoing mystery of the Old Stone Mill, which retains its mystique. See, e.g., the Web site of the Redwood Library and Athenaeum in Newport.

115. Caulkins, *History of Norwich*, 38. On memory piles—also called "sacrifice rocks, wishing rocks, or 'taverns'"—see Simmons, *Spirit of the New England Tribes*, 251–56.

116. Cothren, *History of Ancient Woodbury, Connecticut*, vol. 1, 38.

117. See, e.g., Nason, *A History of the Town of Dunstable*, 28.

118. Nehemiah Cleaveland, *An Address, Delivered at Topsfield in Massachusetts, August 28, 1850: The Two Hundredth Anniversary of the Incorporation of the Town* (New York: Pudney & Russell, 1851), 5.

119. Chapin, *Glastenbury for Two Hundred Years*, frontispiece.

120. Bailey, *Historical Sketches of Andover*, 1–2.

121. Ibid., 23 and 130.

122. Russell, *Pilgrim Memorials* (1855), 18 (Forefathers' Rock) and 100 (Captain's Hill).

123. Ibid., 24.

124. Ibid., 65 (exact spot), 78 and 83–84 (Cole's Hill), 78 (remains).

125. William Wallace Lee, *Barkhamsted, Conn., and Its Centennial, 1879, to Which Is Added a Historical Appendix* (Meriden, Conn.: Republican Steam Print, 1881), 8–9.

126. Ibid., 8.

127. Ibid., 19.

128. Ibid., 35.

129. Ibid., 67.

130. Ibid., 44.

131. Salisbury, Connecticut, *Historical Addresses Delivered by Hon. Samuel Church*, 51. This passage is from Church's address.

132. Ashbel Woodward, *A Historical Address Delivered in Franklin, Connecticut, October, 14th, 1868, on the Two Hundredth Anniversary of the Settlement of the Town, and the One Hundred and Fiftieth Anniversary of Its Ecclesiastical Organizations* (New Haven: Tuttle, Morehouse & Taylor, 1870), 46.

133. Dedham, Massachusetts, *Proceedings at the Celebration of the Two Hundred and Fiftieth Anniversary of the Incorporation of the Town of Dedham, Massachusetts, September 21, 1886* (Cambridge: John Wilson and Son, 1887), 130–31.

134. Powers, *Address Delivered to the People of Goshen*, 18.

135. See, e.g., Nason, *History of the Town of Dunstable*, 11, 57, 58, 61, and 63.

136. Concord, Massachusetts, *Celebration of the Two Hundred and Fiftieth Anniversary of the Incorporation of Concord, September 12, 1885* (Concord, Mass.: The Concord Transcript, 1885), 76–77.

137. Fairfield, Connecticut, *Centennial Commemoration of the Burning of Fairfield, Connecticut, by the British Troops under Governor Tryon, July 8th, 1779* (New York: A. S. Barnes, 1879), 47.

138. On the town system of New England see John Frederick Martin, *Profits in the Wilderness: Entrepreneurship and the Founding of New England Towns in the Seventeenth Century* (Chapel Hill: University of North Carolina Press, 1991).

139. J. E. A. Smith, *The History of Pittsfield, (Berkshire County,) Massachusetts, from the Year 1734 to the Year 1800, Compiled and Written, under the General Direction of a Committee* (Boston: Lee and Shepard, 1869), 45 (Indian Point); Joseph B. Felt, *History of Ipswich, Essex, and Hamilton* (Cambridge: Charles Folsom, 1834), 6 (Wigwam Hill); Smith, *History of Guilford*, 46–47 (Sachem's Head); and Caulkins, *History of Norwich*, 36 (Sachem's Plain). The latter two contained stories about the origins of the name, both derived from the murder of Miantonomi. Sachem's head, the text relates, is the location where the head of the (in this narrative unnamed) sachem was staked "in the fork of a large oak tree . . . where the skull remained for many years."

140. Samuel Orcutt, *History of Torrington, Connecticut, from Its First Settlement in 1737, with Biographies and Genealogies* (Albany: J. Munsell, 1878), 169.

141. Massasoit Monument Association, *Exercises under the Auspices of the Thalia Club*, 4 (Massasoit Spring); Felt, *History of Ipswich*, 4 (Will Hill—likely referring to "Black William"; see below); W. E. Simonds, *Celebration at Collinsville, by the Inhabitants of the Town of Canton, Conn., of the One Hundredth Anniversary of the Independence of the United States of America, July 4th, 1876* (Hartford: Fowler, Miller, 1876), 10 (Mount Philip); [Spalding], *Bi-Centennial of Old Dunstable*, 89 (Joe English Hill); Herman Packard DeForest and Edward Craig Bates, *The History of Westborough, Massachusetts* (Westborough: The Town, 1891), 6 (Jackstraw Pasture); Harriette Merrifield Forbes, *The Hundredth Town: Glimpses of Life in Westborough, 1717–1817* (Boston: Rockwell and Churchill, 1889), 27–28 (Jackstraw Hill); William Barry, *A History of Framingham, Massachusetts, Including*

the Plantation, from 1640 to the Present Time, with an Appendix, Containing a Notice of Sudbury and Its First Proprietors . . . (Boston: James Munroe and Co., 1847), 141 (Captain Tom's Hill); Dix, *A Hand-book of Newport,* 138 (Canonicut); Bailey, *Historical Sketches of Andover,* 27 (Roger's Brook and Roger's Rock); Middleborough, Massachusetts, *Two-Hundredth Anniversary* (Betty's Neck); and Taunton, Massachusetts, *Quarter Millennial Celebration of the City of Taunton, Massachusetts, Tuesday and Wednesday, June 4 and 5, 1889* (Taunton: The City Government, 1889), [233] (Squaw Betty). On Indian place-names see R. A. Douglas-Lithgow, *Dictionary of American-Indian Place and Proper Names in New England* (Salem: Salem Press, 1909).

142. Ellis, *The History of Roxbury Town,* 86, and Bicknell, *Town of Barrington,* 24.

143. Bailey, *History of Andover,* 39. This text is rich in place-name analysis, including material on sites such as "Bear Hill, Bruin Hill, Wolfe-pit Meadow, Wild-catt Swamp . . . [that] suggest the denizens of the woods and meadows, most of which have long ago disappeared." Bailey argues for the retention of local names over the "trite and flavorless commonplaces" found everywhere (38–39).

144. Charles Paxton was marshal of the Admiralty Court when the town was incorporated in 1765. Paxton, Massachusetts, *Centenary Memorial of Paxton: or the Exercises of the Hundredth Anniversary of the Incorporation of the Town; Including a Historical Address, by George W. Livermore . . . of Cambridge . . .* (Worcester: Edward R. Riske, 1868), 27 and 31.

145. Nathaniel Bouton, *An Historical Discourse in Commemoration of the Two-Hundredth Anniversary of the Settlement of Norwalk, CT., in 1651* (New York: S. W. Benedict, 1851), 15.

146. Ibid., 14–16.

147. William Cothren, ed., *Second Centennial Celebration of the Exploration of Ancient Woodbury, and the Reception of the First Indian Deed, Held at Woodbury, Conn., July 4 and 5, 1859* (Woodbury: Published by the General Committee, 1859), 34.

148. Worthington, *History of Dedham,* 19. Worthington fretted that he could not find such deeds as he insisted must have been gotten (22).

149. Westminster, Massachusetts, *Celebration of the One Hundredth Anniversary of the Incorporation of Westminster, Mass., Containing an Address, by Hon. Charles Hudson, of Lexington* (Boston: T. R. Marvin, 1859), 60. For examples of texts that invoke multilayered justifications for dispossessing Indians, see William Chauncey Fowler, *History of Durham, Connecticut, from the First Grant of Land in 1662 to 1866* (Hartford: Wiley, Waterman & Eaton, 1866), 11; Cothren, *Ancient Woodbury,* [21]–31; Alfred Sereno Hudson, *The History of Sudbury, Massachusetts, 1638–1889* (Sudbury: R. H. Blodgett, 1889), 57–69; and Abner Morse, *Genealogical Register of the Inhabitants and History of the Towns of Sherborn and Holliston* (Boston: Damrell & Moore, 1856), 267–72.

150. Westminster, *Celebration,* 60–61.

151. Ibid., 61–62.

152. Ibid., 62–63. For a strikingly similar sentiment see Charles Hudson, *History of the Town of Marlborough, Middlesex County, Massachusetts, from Its First Settlement in*

1657 to 1861; with a Brief Sketch of the Town of Northborough, a Genealogy of the Families in Marlborough to 1800, and an Account of the Celebration of the Two Hundredth Anniversary of the Incorporation of the Town (Boston: T. R. Marvin and Son, 1862), 62.

153. Palfrey, *Discourse Pronounced at Barnstable*, 13. See also Virginia Baker, *Sowams, the Home of Massasoit: Where Was It?* (Boston: David Clapp & Son, 1899), [3]; Drake, *History and Antiquities of Boston*, 456; Sudbury, Massachusetts, *Bi-Centennial Celebration*, 29; and Cothren, *Second Centennial Celebration of the Exploration of Ancient Woodbury*, 32. One text used the phrase as a launching pad for a searching counterargument to this claim: Barber, *The Burning of Simsbury*, 14. Another quoted Winslow in full: "'I think I can clearly say, that before these present troubles [King Philip's War] broke out, the English did not possess one foot of land in this colony but what was fairly obtained by honest purchase of the Indian proprietors; nay, because some of our people are of a covetous disposition, and the Indians, in their straits, are easily prevailed with to part with their lands, we first made a law that none should purchase or receive by gift any land of the Indians, without the knowledge and allowance of our court,'" citing Hubbard's narrative. Orin Fowler, *History of Fall River, with Notices of Freetown and Tiverton, as Published in 1841* (Fall River: Almy and Milnes, 1862), 15.

154. Davis, *History of Wallingford, Conn.*, 11.

155. Francis Samuel Drake, *The Town of Roxbury: Its Memorable Persons and Places, Its History and Antiquities, with Numerous Illustrations of Its Old Landmarks and Noted Personages* (Roxbury: The author, 1878), 48. The phrase is attributed to Joseph Lynde of Sagadahoc in Maine, who recalled uttering a version of the phrase in an encounter with Andros when he presented his own deeds for inspection. Emerson Baker, "A Scratch with a Bear's Paw: Anglo-Indian Land Deeds in Maine," *Ethnohistory* 36, no. 3 (1989): 235. Baker argues that the deeds represented legitimate transactions between well-informed parties.

156. Orcutt and Beardsley, *The History of the Old Town of Derby, Connecticut*, xxxviii.

157. Ibid., [lvii], and William C. Seymour, *History of Seymour, Connecticut, with Biographies and Genealogies* (Seymour, Conn.: Record Print., 1879), 32. For other references to the "bear's paw" quote see Drake, *History and Antiquities of Boston*, 456.

158. Caulkins, *History of Norwich*, 260. Interestingly, the frontispiece to this volume features an illustration of Connecticut governor Samuel Huntington rather than an etching of the author, as is often the case. For "cat's paw" see also Hine, *Early Lebanon*.

159. Morse, *Genealogical Register*, 267.

160. Day, *Historical Discourse*, 31.

161. Ibid., 35.

162. Ibid., 16.

163. Ibid., 36.

164. Barry, *History of Framingham*, 12.

165. Allen, *History of Wenham*, 48.

166. Ithamar Sawtelle, *History of the Town of Townsend, Middlesex County, Massachusetts, from the Grant of Hathorn's Farm, 1676–1878* (Fitchburg: Blanchard & Brown, 1878), 33.

167. Bronson, *History of Waterbury, Connecticut*, 2.

168. Ibid., 3–4.

169. Ibid., 64. Others that claimed multiple purchases include G. W. Perkins, *Historical Sketches of Meriden* (West Meriden: Franklin E. Hinman, 1849), 10, and Davis, *History of Wallingford, Conn.*, 11.

170. Joseph O. Goodwin, *East Hartford, Connecticut: Its History and Traditions* (Hartford: Case, Lockwood & Brainard, 1879), 40.

171. Francis Jackson, *History of the Early Settlement of Newton, County of Middlesex, Massachusetts, from 1639 to 1800, with a Genealogical Register of Its Inhabitants, Prior to 1800* (Boston: Stacy and Richardson, 1854), 84.

172. Drake, *History and Antiquities of Boston*, 119.

173. Ibid., 456.

174. O'Brien, *Dispossession by Degrees*, 74–78.

175. Bicknell, *Historical Address*, 22 (King Philip's War, and prior deed from Massasoit), and Pitman, *A Discourse Delivered at Providence*, 28 (Pequot War, and prior deed to Roger Williams, 21); Caulkins, *History of New London*, 51 ("The whole extent of the new settlement was a conquered country. No Indian titles were to be obtained, no Indian claims settled"); Sanford, *History of the Town of Berkley, Massachusetts*, 59 (King Philip's War).

176. Tustin, *A Discourse Delivered at the Dedication of the New Church Edifice*, 165.

177. Ibid., 166.

178. Daniel Huntington, *A Discourse, Delivered in the North Meeting-House in Bridgewater, on Friday, Dec. 22, 1820, Being the Second Centurial Anniversary of the Landing of the Pilgrims at Plymouth* (Boston: Ezra Lincoln, 1821), 10.

179. Lewis, *The History of Lynn*.

180. Ibid., 106–7 and 32.

181. Alonzo Lewis, *The Picture of Nahant* (Lynn: Thomas Herbert and Co., 1855).

182. Felt, *History of Ipswich*, 3.

183. Waldo Thompson, *Swampscott: Historical Sketches of the Town* (Lynn: Thomas P. Nichols, 1885), 9.

184. Ibid. Lewis also relates this story of Black William's demise, and it includes the William Witter deposition testifying on behalf of Thomas Dexter. Lewis, *History of Lynn*, 43 and 32. It is not clear where the embellishment about sealing the "good title" comes from.

185. W. E. Simonds, *Celebration at Collinsville, by the Inhabitants of the Town of Canton, Conn., of the One Hundredth Anniversary of the Independence of the United States of America, July 4th, 1876* (Hartford: Fowler, Miller, 1876), 10, and Noah A. Phelps, *History of Simsbury, Granby, and Canton, from 1642 to 1845* (Hartford: Case, Tiffany, and Burnham, 1845), 11.

186. Simonds, *Celebration at Collinsville*, 10.

187. Barber, *Burning of Simsbury*, 15.

188. Ibid.

189. Taunton, Massachusetts, *Quarter Millennial Celebration,* 33–34.

190. Ibid., 280 and 33.

191. Smith, *History of Guilford,* 16–17.

192. Ibid., 62–76.

193. Suffield, Connecticut, *Proceedings on the Occasion,* 32.

194. Barre, Massachusetts, *A Memorial of the One Hundredth Anniversary of the Incorporation of the Town of Barre, June 17, 1874* (Cambridge: John Wilson and Son, 1875), 38. No citation is offered for the quote.

195. William H. Gibbs, *Address Delivered before the Literary Association, Blanford, Mass., September 21, 1850, upon the History of That Town* (Springfield: G. W. Wilson, 1851), 19.

196. Woods, *Historical Sketches of Brookline, Mass.,* 308–9.

3. Lasting

1. For this phrasing and interpretive insight I am indebted to a wonderfully useful reading by Lisa Disch.

2. Thomas Gray, *Change: A Poem Pronounced at Roxbury, October 8, 1830, in Commemoration of the First Settlement of that Town* (Roxbury: Charles P. Emmons, 1830), 6–7.

3. Ibid., 12.

4. Ibid., 24.

5. Ibid., 21.

6. See William Cronon's masterful study of the transformation of New England's ecology under colonialism, *Changes in the Land.*

7. See Michael Omi and Howard Winant, *Racial Formation in the United States: From the 1960s to the 1990s,* 2nd ed. (New York: Routledge, 1994). For an important examination of blood thinking, colonialism, and indigeneity in Hawaii, see J. Kehaulani Kauanui, *Hawaiian Blood: Colonialism and the Politics of Sovereignty and Indigeneity* (Durham, N.C.: Duke University Press, 2008).

8. Scott Lyons has called for the practice of "rhetorical sovereignty" as "the inherent right and ability of *peoples* to determine their own communicative needs and desires in this pursuit, to decide for themselves the goals, modes, styles, and languages of public discourse." Lyons, "Rhetorical Sovereignty: What Do Indians Want from Writing?" *CCC* 51 (2000): 447–68.

9. See Sally L. Jones, "The First but Not the Last of the 'Vanishing Indians': Edwin Forrest and Mythic Re-creations of the Native Population," in *Dressing in Feathers: The Construction of the Indian in American Popular Culture,* ed. S. Elizabeth Bird, 13–28 (Boulder, Colo.: Westview, 1996). On the "nineteenth-century discourse of the disappearance of Native Americans [that] projects the extinction, dissolution, and vanishing of the Indian peoples of central Massachusetts," see Doughton, "Unseen Neighbors." For a discussion of the role of local history writing in creating the myth of the vanishing Indian in Maine see Ghere, "The 'Disappearance' of the Abenaki in Western Maine," and for Seattle see Thrush, *Native Seattle,* generally and for last Indians see 88 and 96.

10. Bicknell, *An Historical Address and Poem*, 18.

11. See "last of the race," Naham Mitchell, *History of the Early Settlement of Bridgewater in Plymouth County, Massachusetts, Including an Extensive Family Register* (Boston: Printed for the author, 1840), 17; "The father of Chickatabut was Josias Wampatuck; and his grandson, Jeremy, was father of Charles Josiah, the last of the race . . . —*Drake.*" Justin Winsor, *History of the Town of Duxbury, Massachusetts, with Genealogical Registers* (Boston: Crosby & Nichols, 1849), 75; and Drake, *The Town of Roxbury*, 7. Just prior to this claim, the author writes that "no distinct traces of aboriginal occupation have ever been observed in Roxbury, not even an Indian name."

12. Charles Cowley, "The Last of the Sachems of the Merrimac River Indians," *Contributions to the Old Residents' Historical Association, Lowell, Mass.* 6, no. 4 (1904): 377–427. The information on placing the tablet comes from 402 and 409.

13. Collier, *A History of the Statue Erected to Commemorate the Heroic Achievement of Maj. John Mason*, 49.

14. Miller, *Celebration of the Two-Hundredth Anniversary of the Settlement of the Town of Bristol*, 59.

15. Horace C. Hovey, *Fair Haven: Centennial Discourse Delivered in the Second Congregational Church, Fair Haven, Connecticut, Sunday, July 9th, 1876* (New Haven: Tuttle, Morehouse & Taylor, 1876), 7. For the same story, see also John Warner Barber, *History and Antiquities of New Haven, (Conn.,) from Its Earliest Settlement to the Present Time* (New Haven: J. W. Barber, 1831), 25. He is also referred to without naming him in Davis, *History of Wallingford, Conn.*, 32, and with some embellishment in Charles H. Levermore, *The Republic of New Haven: A History of Municipal Evolution* (Baltimore: N. Murray, Publication Agent, The Johns Hopkins University, 1886), 173.

16. William B. Hincks, *Historical Notes Respecting the Parish of Stratfield and Newfield, Now Bridgeport, Conn.* (Bridgeport, 1871), 32.

17. Charles F. Sedgwick, *A History of the Town of Sharon, Litchfield County, Conn., from Its First Settlement* (Hartford: Case, Tiffany, 1842), 12.

18. Gardner B. Perry, *A Discourse, Delivered in the East Parish in Bradford, December 22, 1820; Two Hundred Years after the First Settlement in New-England, Containing a History of the Town* (Haverhill: Burrill and Hersey, 1821), 21.

19. See, e.g., Robert F. Berkhofer Jr., *The White Man's Indian: Images of the American Indian from Columbus to the Present* (New York: Vintage, 1979), especially 86–96.

20. Brian W. Dippie, *The Vanishing American: White Attitudes and U.S. Indian Policy* (Lawrence: University Press of Kansas, 1982), 11.

21. Lepore, *The Name of War*, 191–226. The quotation is from 191. On *Metamora* see also Jones, "The First but Not the Last of the 'Vanishing Indians.'"

22. William S. Simmons, "The Earliest Prints and Paintings of New England Indians," *Rhode Island History* 41 (1982): 73–85.

23. Although Turano concludes that the Indians depicted were not in fact the last, the tone of her piece parallels the nostalgia of a time, people, and place past that is at the heart of romanticization. "Taken from Life: Early Photographic Portraits of New

England Algonkians, ca. 1844–1865," in *Algonkians of New England: Past and Present,* ed. Peter Benes, 121–43 (Boston: Boston University, 1993), no. 16, Annual Proceedings for New England Folklife. The quotation is from 121–22.

24. William Cullen Bryant and Sydney Howard Gay, *A Popular History of the United States, from the First Discovery of the Western Hemisphere by the Northmen, to the End of the First Century of the Union of the States, Preceded by a Sketch of the Pre-Historic Period and the Age of the Mound Builders,* vol. 3 (New York: Charles Scribner's Sons, 1882), 114–16.

25. Ibid., 114.

26. Ibid., 115–16.

27. Daniel Ricketson, *History of New Bedford, Bristol County, Massachusetts* (New Bedford: Published by the Author, 1858), 95–96.

28. Henry David Thoreau, *The Writings of Henry David Thoreau: Journal,* ed. Bradford Torrey, vol. 8 (Boston: Houghton Mifflin, 1868), 390–91.

29. Turano, "Taken from Life," and Simmons, "Earliest Prints and Paintings."

30. Turano, "Taken from Life," 133.

31. Samuel F. Haven, *An Historical Address, Delivered before the Citizens of the Town of Dedham* (Dedham, Mass.: Printed by Herman Mann, 1837), 63. This "last" story is repeated practically verbatim in another Dedham history published ten years later. Herman Mann, *Historical Annals of Dedham, from Its Settlement in 1635 to 1847* (Dedham: Herman Mann, 1847).

32. Bailey, *Historical Sketches of Andover,* 27.

33. Maurice B. Dorgan, *History of Lawrence, Massachusetts, with War Records* (Published by the Author, 1924), 9.

34. Stiles, *The History of Ancient Windsor, Connecticut,* 117–18.

35. Biglow, *History of the Town of Natick, Mass.,* 84.

36. Timothy P. Gillett, *The Past and the Present, in the Secular and Religious History of the Congregational Church and Society of Branford. A Semi-Centennial Discourse, Delivered July 7th, 1858* (New Haven: Morehouse & Taylor, 1858), 22.

37. George F. Daniels, *History of the Town of Oxford, Massachusetts, with Genealogies and Notes on Persons and Estates* (Oxford, 1892), 43.

38. Ledyard Bill, *The History of Paxton, Massachusetts* (Worcester, Mass.: Putnam, Davis, 1889), 45.

39. Porter, *A Historical Discourse,* 44. This passage is also referenced in R. Manning Chipman, *The History of Harwinton, Connecticut* (Hartford: Williams, Wiley & Turner, 1860), 125.

40. Windsor, Connecticut, *Report of the Centennial Celebration of the Anniversary of our Independence at Windsor, Conn., July 4, 1876* (Hartford: Case, Lockwood, and Brainard, 1876), 26.

41. Ellis, *The History of Roxbury Town,* 116.

42. Rev. James H. Means, *Dorchester, Past and Present: A Sermon Preached in the Second Church, Dorchester, December 26, 1869* (Boston: Moses H. Sargent, 1870), 17–18.

43. Rufus P. Stebbins, *An Historical Address, Delivered at the Centennial Celebration of*

the Incorporation of the Town of Wilbraham, June 15, 1863 (Boston: George C. Rand & Avery, 1864), 21–22.

44. Westfield, Massachusetts, *The Westfield Jubilee: A Report of the Celebration at Westfield, Mass., on the Two Hundredth Anniversary of the Incorporation of the Town, October 6, 1869, with the Historical Address of the Hon. William G. Bates* (Westfield, Mass.: Clark and Story, 1870), 21.

45. Earle, *Report to the Governor.* For a critique of Earle and the very real consequences of his problematic notions about Indianness, see Thee, "Massachusetts Nipmucs and the Long Shadow of John Milton Earle."

46. Emory Washburn, *Historical Sketches of the Town of Leicester, Massachusetts, during the First Century of Its Settlement* (Boston: John Wilson and Son, 1860), 48.

47. Thoreau, *Journal*, 251–52.

48. On modernity see Latour, *We Have Never Been Modern.* On Indians and modernity see, e.g., Deloria, *Indians in Unexpected Places*; Konkle, *Writing Indian Nations*; Noble, *Death of a Nation*; and Raibmon, *Authentic Indians.*

49. Jean M. O'Brien, "'Divorced from the Land,'" in Calloway, *After King Philip's War.*

50. Andrew H. Ward, *History of the Town of Shrewsbury, Massachusetts, from Its Settlement in 1717 to 1829, with Other Matters Relating Thereto Not Before Published, Including an Extensive Family Register* (Boston: Samuel G. Drake, 1847), 185.

51. DeForest and Bates, *The History of Westborough, Massachusetts*, 9. This assertion calls to mind the image of the famous George Catlin painting *Wi-Jun-Jon, the Pigeon's Egg Head (The Light), Going to and Returning from Washington* (1832). Berkhofer, *White Man's Indian.* On Indians and expectations about modernity see Deloria, *Indians in Unexpected Places*, especially the chapter titled "Technology," whose stories about Geronimo in an automobile wearing a top hat richly illuminate these themes.

52. On racial thinking at this moment, see especially Horsman, *Race and Manifest Destiny.*

53. Smith, *The History of Pittsfield, Massachusetts*, 98.

54. Caulkins, *History of Norwich*, 46.

55. *The Berkshire Jubilee, Celebrated at Pittsfield, Mass., August 22 and 23, 1845* (Albany: Weare C. Little, 1845), 39.

56. Collier, *History of the Statue*, 30. From the historical oration, Mason statue unveiling.

57. Ibid., 47–48.

58. Stiles, *History of Ancient Windsor*, 4.

59. Tustin, *A Discourse Delivered at the Dedication of the New Church Edifice*, 40–41.

60. Ibid., 46–48.

61. Ibid., 48–49.

62. Ibid., 50–51.

63. Ibid., 56.

64. Lynn, Massachusetts, *Proceedings*, 19–20.

65. Adams, *An Address on the Occasion of Opening the New Town Hall*, 84.

66. Barre, Massachusetts, *A Memorial of the One Hundredth Anniversary*, 42–43; John Gorham Palfrey, *History of New England* (Boston: Little, Brown, 1860). On the construction of whiteness see, e.g., Noel Ignatiev, *How the Irish Became White* (New York: Routledge, 1995); Matthew Frye Jacobson, *Whiteness of a Different Color: European Immigrants and the Alchemy of Race* (Cambridge, Mass.: Harvard University Press, 1998); and David R. Roediger, *The Wages of Whiteness: Race and the Making of the American Working Class* (New York: Verso, 1991).

67. George F. Hoar, *Address Delivered before the City Government and Citizens, on the Two Hundredth Anniversary of Worcester, October 14, 1884* (Worcester: Charles Hamilton, 1885), 29.

68. Ibid., 30.

69. Ibid., 31.

70. Ibid., 36.

71. Dedham, Massachusetts, *Proceedings*, 141–42 (emphasis added).

72. Denison, *Westerly (Rhode Island) and Its Witnesses*, 150.

73. Rochester, Mass., *Rochester's Official Bi-Centennial Record. Tuesday, July 22, 1879. Containing the Historical Address of Rev. N.W. Everett; the Responses by Lieut. Gov. Long, Hon. W. W. Crapo, M.C., Judge Thos. Russell and Others. Also, a Full Account of the Proceedings of the Day* (Bedford: Mercury, 1879), 15.

74. Ibid., 17.

75. Sheffield, Massachusetts, *Centennial Celebration of the Town of Sheffield, Berkshire Co., Mass., June 18th and 19th, 1876* (Sheffield, 1876), 72.

76. Ibid., 73.

77. Ibid., 89.

78. Surely, this is one of the things New Englanders have in mind in dwelling on the definitive nature of their "origins," which is all about "firsting."

79. See bradfordgenealogy.org. This is not to suggest in any way that the genealogical craze is the exclusive purview of New Englanders. The popularity of tracing roots is a widespread phenomenon, and the use of Internet resources such as ancestry.com is also common.

80. Bela Bates Edwards, *Address Delivered at Southampton, Mass. At the Centennial Celebration of the Incorporation of That Town, July 23, 1841* (Andover: Allen, Morrill and Wardwell, 1841), 3.

81. Palfrey, *A Discourse Pronounced at Barnstable*, 5.

82. Nathaniel B. Shurtleff and Henry W. Cushman, *The Proceedings at the Cushman Celebration, at Plymouth, August 15, 1855, in Commemoration of the Embarkation of the Plymouth Pilgrims from Southampton, England; Together with an Account of the Services at the Grave of Elder Thomas Cushman, August 16, 1855* (Boston: J. M. Hewes, 1855), 3.

83. Ibid.

84. Allen, *Myles Standish*, 55.

85. Ibid., 52–53.

86. Brace, *A Leaf of Milford History*, 10.

87. On this point see also Abrams, *The Pilgrims and Pocahontas*, and Fredric Gleach, "Pocahontas at the Fair: Crafting Identities at the 1907 Jamestown Exposition," *Ethnohistory* 50 (2003): 419–45.

88. Rev. Edward Peterson, *History of Rhode Island* (New York: John S. Taylor, 1853), 293–94.

89. Denison, *Westerly (Rhode Island)*, 29.

90. Medfield, Massachusetts, *Exercises at the Bi-Centennial Commemoration of the Burning of Medfield by Indians in King Philip's War, February 21, 1876* (Medfield: George H. Ellis, 1876), 50.

91. Hadley, Massachusetts, *Celebration of the Two Hundredth Anniversary of the Settlement of Hadley, Massachusetts, at Hadley, June 8, 1859* (Northampton: Bridgman & Childs, 1859), 13.

92. Brooks, *History of the Town of Medford*, 80–81.

93. S. T. Livermore, *A History of Block Island from Its Discovery, in 1514, to the Present Time, 1876* (Hartford: Case, Lockwood, and Brainard, 1877), 64.

94. Ibid., 65–66.

95. Ibid., 64–65.

96. Ibid.

97. Frederick Freeman, *The History of Cape Cod: The Annals of Barnstable County, Including the District of Mashpee*, vol. 1 (Boston: Printed for the author, 1860), 719, "extinct" (emphasis added), and 700–701 (Isaac Simon).

98. Joshua Bates, *An Anniversary Discourse, Delivered at Dudley, Mass., March 20, 1853, with Topographical and Historical Notices of the Town* (Boston: T. R. Marvin, 1853), 44.

99. Euphemia Vale Smith, *History of Newburyport; from the Earliest Settlement of the Country to the Present Time, with a Biographical Appendix* (Boston: Damrell and Moore, 1854), 3.

100. William Lincoln, *History of Worcester, Massachusetts, from Its Earliest Settlement to September, 1836; with Various Notices Relating to the History of Worcester County* (Worcester: Charles Hersey, 1862), 41.

101. Washburn, *Historical Sketches of the Town of Leicester*, 48.

102. Bates, *Anniversary Discourse*, 44.

103. Rochester, Massachusetts, *Rochester's Official Bi-Centennial Records*, 15 (emphasis added).

104. Cleaveland, *An Address, Delivered at Topsfield*, 70–72.

105. Livermore, *History of Block Island*, 162–63.

106. Horace A. Keach, *Burrillville; As It Was and As It Is* (Providence: Knowles, Anthony & Co., Printers, 1856), 19. On the transformation of New England see Cronon, *Changes in the Land*. On the link between the "last buffalo hunt" and the notion of the "vanishing Indian" see Jeffrey Ostler, *The Plains Sioux and U.S. Colonialism from Lewis and Clark to Wounded Knee* (Cambridge: Cambridge University Press, 2004), 128.

107. Keach, *Burrillville*, 17.

108. Ibid., 19 (Herring Pond); 21 (Wolf Hill); 23 (quotation). On the transformation of New England as a region, including changes in the landscape, and their connection to regional identity see Conforti, *Imagining New England*.

109. Daniel W. Teller, *The History of Ridgefield, Conn., from Its First Settlement to the Present Time* (Danbury: T. Donovan, 1878), 166.

110. Ibid., 172.

111. Cleaveland, *An Address, Delivered at Topsfield*, 16.

112. Salisbury, Connecticut, *Historical Addresses Delivered by Hon. Samuel Church*, 15. This address was initially delivered for the town's centennial celebration in 1841, and was published in conjunction with the national centennial.

113. Cleaveland, *An Address, Delivered at Topsfield*, 17.

114. Falmouth, Massachusetts, *The Celebration of the Two Hundredth Anniversary*, 138.

115. On Indians and the whaling industry see Daniel Vickers, "The First Whalemen of Nantucket," in Calloway, *After King Philip's War*, 90–113.

116. Henry A. Miles, *Lowell, As It Was, and As It Is* (Lowell: Powers and Bagley, 1845), 12.

117. William B. Hincks, *Historical Sketches* (Bridgeport, 1872), 22.

118. Samuel Francis Smith, *History of Newton, Massachusetts, Town and City, from Its Earliest Settlement to the Present Time, 1630–1880* (Boston: American Logotype Co., 1880), 538.

119. Rich, *Truro—Cape Cod*, 226.

120. Spencer P. Mead, *Ye Historie of ye Town of Greenwich, County of Fairfield and State of Connecticut* (Harrison, N.Y.: Harbor Hill Books, 1979), 153. This is a reprint of the 1911 reprint of the 1857 volume.

121. Edwards, *Address Delivered at Southampton*, 25.

122. Cohasset, Massachusetts, *Centennial Anniversary of the Town of Cohasset, May 7, 1870, Oration by Hon. Thomas Russell, Speeches by Gov. Claflin, Hiram Revels, Loring Lothrop, Solomon Lincoln, George B. Loring, and Others* (Boston: Wright & Potter, 1870), 51–52.

123. Russell, *Pilgrim Memorials* (1855), 51.

124. R. Manning Chipman, *The History of Harwinton, Connecticut* (Hartford: Williams, Wiley & Turner, 1860), 148.

125. Charles A. Nelson, *Waltham, Past and Present; and Its Industries. With an Historical Sketch of Watertown from Its Settlement in 1630 to the Incorporation of Waltham, January 15, 1738* (Cambridge: John Ford & Son, 1879), 104.

126. Staples, *Annals of the Town of Providence*, 229 (Gaspee); Braintree, Massachusetts, *Centennial Celebration*, 32 (last woman); Stiles, *History of Ancient Windsor*, 489 (last colored survivor); and Watertown, Massachusetts, *Address of William H. Ingraham, Esq., and Oration by Rev. J. F. Lovering, at the Centennial Celebration, White's Hill Grove, Watertown, Mass., July 5th, 1876* (Watertown, 1876), 6.

127. Mendon, Massachusetts, *An Address, by Rev. Carlton A. Staples, of Milwaukee,*

Wis.; A Poem, by Hon. Henry Chapin, of Worcester, Mass., and other Proceedings, in Commemoration of the Two Hundredth Anniversary of the Incorporation of Mendon, Massachusetts (Worcester, Mass.: Chas. Hamilton, 1868), 74. See also Allen, *History of Wenham,* 134, where the Fisk family had dwindled to a single family, "and more recently, it has become almost extinct."

128. Dedham, Massachusetts, *Proceedings at the Celebration,* 127–28.

129. Nason, *A History of the Town of Dunstable,* 270.

130. David D. Field, *A History of the Towns of Haddam and East-Haddam* (Middletown, Conn.: Loomis and Richards, 1814), 43.

131. Bronson, *The History of Waterbury, Connecticut,* 115 (emphasis added).

132. Fairfield, Connecticut, *Centennial Commemoration,* 50 ("last hope" in a poem); Samuel Sewall, *The History of Woburn, Middlesex County, Mass., from the Grant of its Territory to Charlestown, in 1640, to the Year 1860* (Boston: Wiggin and Lunt, 1868), 207 (Pigwacket Fight); Field, *History of the Towns of Haddam and East-Haddam,* 17 ("remembrance"); Joseph Willard, *An Address in Commemoration of the Two-Hundredth Anniversary of the Incorporation of Lancaster, Massachusetts* (Boston: John Wilson and Son, 1853), 90 (last great struggle); Jonathan Fay Barrett, *Concord: A Poem, Delivered before the Lyceum, Concord, Mass., January 22, 1851* (Boston: Ticknor, Reed, and Fields, 1851), 22 (red Philip's race); Phelps, *History of Simsbury,* 35 (last alarm); Rufus C. Torrey, *History of the Town of Fitchburg, Massachusetts, Comprising also a History of Lunenburg, from Its First Settlement to the Year 1764* (Fitchburg, Mass.: J. Garfield, Printer, 1836), 51 (last Indian warfare); and Joseph I. Foot, *An Historical Discourse, Delivered at West Brookfield, Mass., Nov. 27, 1828, on the Day of the Annual Thanksgiving, with Capt. Thomas Wheeler's Narrative* (West Brookfield: Merriam & Cooke, 1843), 65–66 (Brookfield).

133. Caleb Butler, *History of the Town of Groton, Including Pepperrell and Shirley, from the First Grant of Groton Plantation in 1655. With Appendices, Containing Family Registers, Town and State Officers, Population, and Other Statistics* (Boston: T. R. Marvin, 1848), 111 (last killed by Indian); Lincoln, *History of Worcester,* 41 (last Indian killed by white man); Wilder, *The History of Leominster,* 9 (last attack/Indian boy); Joseph Willard, *Topographical and Historical Sketches of the Town of Lancaster, in the Commonwealth of Massachusetts; Furnished of the Worcester Magazine and Historical Journal* (Worcester: Charles Griffin, 1826), 45 (Indian killed by Indian).

134. Judd, *History of Hadley,* 127–28.

135. Anson Titus, *Charlton Historical Sketches* (Southbridge: George M. Whitaker, 1877), 3.

136. Theodore S. Gold, *Historical Records of the Town of Cornwall, Litchfield County, Connecticut, Collected and Arranged by Theodore S. Gold* (Hartford: Case, Lockwood, & Brainard, 1877), 23 (quote); Kingsley, *A Historical Discourse,* 21; and Suffield, Connecticut, *Celebration of the Bi-Centennial Anniversary of the Town of Suffield, Conn., Wednesday, Oct. 12, 1870* (Hartford: Wiley, Waterman & Eaton, 1871), 32.

137. Daniel Hunt, *History of Pomfret: A Discourse Delivered on the Day of Annual Thanksgiving in the First Church in Pomfret, Nov. 19th, 1840* (Hartford: J. Holbrook, 1841), 5

(favorite residence), and Kiah B. Glidden, *A Centennial Discourse, Delivered in the First Congregational Church, Mansfield Center, July 1876* (Willimantic: Enterprise Printing Co., [1876]), 8 (full quota).

138. See, e.g., Benjamin Cutter and William R. Cutter, *History of the Town of Arlington, Massachusetts, Formerly the Second Precinct in Cambridge or District Menotomy, Afterward the Town of West Cambridge, 1635–1879, with a Genealogical Register of the Inhabitants of the Precinct* (Boston: David Clapp, 1880), 6.

139. John Warner Barber, *History and Antiquities of New Haven (Conn.), from Its Earliest Settlement to the Present Time* (New Haven: J. W. Barber, 1831), 25 (Quinnipiacs); Joseph Merrill, *History of Amesbury, Including the First Seventeen Years of Salisbury, to the Separation in 1654, from Its Incorporation in 1876* (Haverhill: Franklin P. Stiles, 1880), 314 (happy hunting grounds); and Mead, *Ye Historie of ye Town of Greenwich*, 53 (melted away).

140. Everett, *An Address Delivered at Bloody Brook*, 8.

141. Francis Convers, *An Historical Sketch of Watertown, in Massachusetts, from the First Settlement of the Town to the Close of Its Second Century* (Cambridge, Mass.: E. W. Metcalf, 1830), 25 (extinguished); W. H. Starr, *A Centennial Historical Sketch of the Town of New London* (New London: Charles Allyn, 1876), 5 (extinction); and H. B. Smith, *Transactions of the One Hundred and Fiftieth Anniversary of Greenfield, Ct., Congregational Church, Held May 18th, 1876* (Southport, Conn.: Chronicle Print, 1876), 12 (exterminated).

142. Abbott, *History of Andover*, 46.

143. William Allen, *An Address, Delivered at Northampton, Mass., on the Evening of October 29, 1854, in Commemoration of the Close of the Second Century since the Settlement of the Town* (Northampton: Hopkins, Bridgman & Co., 1855), 10.

144. Wright, *Historical Sketch of Easthampton, Mass.*, 5.

145. Samuel St. John, *Historical Address, Delivered in the Congregational Church, of New Canaan, Conn., July 4th, 1876* (New Canaan, Conn., 1876), 13.

146. Hawes, *An Address Delivered at the Request of the Citizens of Hartford*, 35.

147. Dorchester, Massachusetts, *Proceedings of the Two Hundred and Fiftieth Anniversary of the Gathering in England, Departure for America, and Final Settlement in New England, of the First Church and Parish of Dorchester, Mass., Coincident with the Settlement of the Town* (Boston: Geo. H. Ellis, 1880), 121.

148. Ibid.

149. Rev. C. M. Hyde and Alexander Hyde, *Lee: The Centennial Celebration and Centennial History of the Town of Lee, Mass.* (Springfield, Mass.: Clark W. Bryan, 1878), 122.

150. Bragdon, *The Columbia Guide to American Indians of the Northeast*, 154.

151. Peyer, *The Tutor'd Mind*, 82–88. On the complex history of Brothertown's formation and relocations in search of autonomy, see Jarvis, "Preserving the Brothertown Nation of Indians." On Occom's role in the Brothertown movement see Brooks, *American Lazarus*, 51–86. She has also collected and edited his writings in *The Collected Writings of Samson Occom, Mohegan: Leadership and Literature in Eighteenth-Century Native America* (New York: Oxford University Press, 2006). Johnson's writings have been ably

compiled and edited by Laura J. Murray in *To Do Good to My Indian Brethren: The Writings of Joseph Johnson, 1751–1776* (Amherst: University of Massachusetts Press, 1998).

152. Payson W. Lyman, *History of Easthampton: Its Settlement and Growth; Its Material, Educational, and Religious Interests, Together with a Genealogical Record of its Original Families* (Northampton: Trumbull & Gere, 1866), 20.

153. Thomas C. Simonds, *History of South Boston; Formerly Dorchester Neck, now Ward XII, of the City of Boston* (Boston: David Clapp, 1857), 228.

154. Jackson, *A History of the Early Settlement of Newton*, 85.

155. Newton, Mass., *The Centennial Celebrations of the City of Newton on the Seventeenth of June and the Fourth of July* (Boston: Rand, Avery, 1876), 52. He is quoting "the Rev. S. F. Smith."

156. Falmouth, Massachusetts, *The Celebration of the Two Hundredth Anniversary*, 47.

4. Resisting

1. Mandell, *Tribe, Race, History*, 203–4, 207–8, and 213–14.

2. Earle, *Report to the Governor*, 9. Earle's report is not without its problems, steeped as it is in the racial thinking of the time. For an analysis of the report as problematic in contemporary recognition cases see Thee, "Massachusetts Nipmucs."

3. Ibid.

4. Paul R. Campbell and Glenn W. LaFantasie, "Scattered to the Winds of Heaven—Narragansett Indians 1676–1800," *Rhode Island History* 37 (1978): 77.

5. Den Ouden, *Beyond Conquest*, 15.

6. Mandell, *Tribe, Race, History*, 2–5.

7. Ibid., 1–38.

8. Earle, *Report to the Governor*, 27.

9. Doughton, "Unseen Neighbors."

10. Mandell, *Tribe, Race, History*, 1–38; McMullen and Handsman, *A Key into the Language of Woodsplint Baskets*; and Wolverton, "'A Precarious Living.'" On the deleterious impact of indentured servitude on Indians, see Sainsbury, "Indian Labor in Early Rhode Island," and Herndon and Sekatau, "Colonizing the Children."

11. Silverman, *Faith and Boundaries*, 276.

12. Trudie Lamb Richmond, "A Native Perspective of History: The Schaghticoke Nation, Resistance and Survival," in Weinstein, *Enduring Traditions*, 107–11.

13. Mandell, *Tribe, Race, History*, 118–19.

14. See, e.g., Bragdon, *The Columbia Guide to American Indians of the Northeast*, 75–76; Den Ouden, *Beyond Conquest*; Jean O'Brien, " 'Our Old and Valluable Liberty': A Natick Indian Petition in Defense of Their Fishing Rights, 1748," in *Early Native Literacies in New England: A Documentary and Critical Analysis*, ed. Kristina Bross and Hilary E. Wyss, 119–23 (Amherst: University of Massachusetts Press, 2008); and Brooks, *The Common Pot*.

15. Earle, *Report to the Governor*, 89–99 (Hassanamisco); Campisi, *The Mashpee Indians*, 99–118; and Mandell, *Tribe, Race, Nation*, 18–19.

16. Silverman, *Faith and Boundaries*, 223–73.

17. John Wood Sweet, *Bodies Politic: Negotiating Race in the American North, 1730–1830* (Baltimore: The Johns Hopkins University Press, 2003), 172–79.

18. Chipman, *History of Harwinton*, 125.

19. For an account of the incident, and a discussion of the temporary rehabilitation of Michael Cresap's reputation from ruthless "Indian killer" to an icon during the Revolutionary era, see Robert G. Parkinson, "Notes and Documents: From Indian Killer to Worthy Citizen: The Revolutionary Transformation of Michael Cresap," *William and Mary Quarterly*, 3rd ser., 63 (2006): 97–122. Thomas Jefferson secured Cresap as Indian killer through his inclusion of "Logan's Lament" in his *Notes on the State of Virginia*, ed. William Peden (New York: W. W. Norton, 1954), 63.

20. Daniel K. Richter, *Facing East from Indian Country: A Native History of Early America* (Cambridge, Mass.: Harvard University Press, 2003), 213–14.

21. See chapter 2.

22. William Brigham, *An Address Delivered before the Inhabitants of Grafton, on the First Centennial Anniversary of that Town, April 29, 1835* (Boston: Light & Horton, 1835), 30.

23. Ibid., [37].

24. Frederick Clifton Pierce, *History of Grafton, Worcester County, Massachusetts, from Its Early Settlement by the Indians in 1647 to the Present Time, 1879* (Worcester: Chas. Hamilton, 1879), 28, 68, and 79.

25. Ibid., 79.

26. Ibid., 318.

27. R. H. Cook, *Historical Notes of the Island of Nantucket, and Tourist's Guide* (Nantucket: n.p., 1871), 19.

28. Folger, *Handbook of Nantucket*, 31–32.

29. Edward K. Godfrey, *The Island of Nantucket: What It Was and What It Is* (Boston: Lee and Shepard, 1882), 183–84.

30. R. A. Douglas-Lithgow, *Nantucket: A History* (New York: G. P. Putnam's Sons, 1914), 52–53.

31. George Faber Clark, *A History of the Town of Norton, Bristol County, Massachusetts, from 1669 to 1859* (Boston: Crosby, Nichols, 1859), 50 and 56.

32. Samuel Deane, *History of Scituate, Massachusetts, from Its First Settlement to 1831* (Boston: James Loring, 1831), 144.

33. Ibid., 145, and Clark, *A History of the Town of Norton*, 19.

34. New Bedford, Massachusetts, *Centennial Celebration: Proceedings in Connection with the Celebration at New Bedford, September 14th, 1864, of the Two Hundredth Anniversary of the Incorporation of the Town of Dartmouth* (New Bedford: E. Anthony & Sons, 1865), 110–11.

35. Martha Simon is also claimed as the last Indian of Fairhaven, Massachusetts, on the Web site of the town's library.

36. Earle, *Report to the Governor*, 9.

37. Old Dartmouth Historical Sketches, *Proceedings of the Old Dartmouth Historical Society, no. 51* (New Bedford: Old Dartmouth Historical Society, 1921), 33. On the Mitchell family, see William S. Simmons, "From Manifest Destiny to the Melting Pot: The Life and Times of Charlotte Mitchell, Wampanoag," in *Anthropology, History, and American Indians: Essays in Honor of William Curtis Sturtevant*, ed. William L. Merrill and Ives Goddard, 131–38 (Washington, D.C.: Smithsonian Institution Press, 2002).

38. Mary De Witt Freeland, *The Records of Oxford, Massachusetts: Including Chapters of Nipmuck, Huguenot and English History from the Earliest Date, 1630, with Manners and Fashions of the Time* (Albany, N.Y.: Joel Munsell's Sons, 1894), 31–32.

39. Ibid., 133.

40. Earle, *Report to the Governor,* lv–lix.

41. Caulkins, *History of New London,* 38.

42. Ibid., 51.

43. Cave, *The Pequot War,* 161–62. The text of the treaty can be found in Elisha R. Potter, *The Early History of Narragansett, with an Appendix of Original Documents, Many of Which Are Now for the First Time Published* (Providence, R.I.: Marshall, Brown, 1835), 177–78.

44. Caulkins, *History of New London,* 604.

45. Ibid., 604–5 (emphasis added).

46. Ibid., 605.

47. Ibid., 617.

48. Jack Campisi, "The Emergence of the Mashantucket Pequot Tribe, 1637–1975," in Hauptman and Wherry, *The Pequots in Southern New England,* 132–33. William Starna suggests that in the early seventeenth century, the Pequot seem to have reckoned kinship patrilineally with a tendency toward bilateral descent rules. William A. Starna, "The Pequots in the Early Seventeenth Century," in Hauptman and Wherry, *The Pequots in Southern New England,* 39.

49. Winsor, *History of the Town of Duxbury, Massachusetts,* 75.

50. F. W. Bird, Whiting Griswold, and Cyrus Weeks, *Report of the Commissioners Relating to the Condition of the Indians in Massachusetts* (Boston: Commonwealth of Massachusetts, 1849).

51. Ebenezer Clapp, *History of the Town of Dorchester, Massachusetts* (Boston: Ebenezer Clapp, 1859), 13.

52. Bacon, *A History of Natick,* 17. See Jill Lepore's excellent discussion of the attendance of a delegation of Penobscots to a performance of *Metamora; or, The Last of the Wampanoags* in her *The Name of War,* 212–15. As she points out, "real Indians" in the audience were a big draw. But the Penobscots were actually in Boston to petition the government for political autonomy.

53. Bacon, *History of Natick,* 17.

54. See, e.g., Stephen Badger, "Historical and Characteristic Traits of the American Indians in General, and Those of Natick in Particular; in a Letter from the Rev. Stephen Badger, of Natick, to the Corresponding Secretary," *Massachusetts Historical Society Collections,* 1st ser., 5 (1790): 43.

55. Jackson, *History of the Early Settlement of Newton*, 85; Worthington, *History of Dedham*, 29; and Mann, *Historical Annals of Dedham*, 39.

56. Gilman, *A Historical Discourse, Delivered in Norwich*, 7.

57. Ibid., 13–14.

58. Ibid., 87.

59. U.S. Department of the Interior, Office of Federal Acknowledgment, *Summary under the Criteria and Evidence for Final Determination for Federal Acknowledgment of the Mohegan Tribe of Indians of the State of Connecticut, March 7, 1994*, 43.

60. Canonicus Memorial, *Services of Dedication*, 9.

61. Ibid. (emphasis added).

62. Ibid., 27.

63. Ibid., 3.

64. Ibid., 17.

65. Ibid.

66. Society of Colonial Wars of Rhode Island and Massachusetts, *A Record of the Ceremony and Oration on the Occasion of the Unveiling of the Monument Commemorating the Great Swamp Fight, December 19, 1675, in the Narragansett County, Rhode Island* (Boston: D. B. Updike, 1906), 5–6.

67. Ibid., 6.

68. Ibid., 5–6.

69. Ibid., 53.

70. Rubertone, *Grave Undertakings*, 18–38. The quotation is from 34.

71. Rochester, Massachusetts, *Rochester's Official Bi-Centennial Records*, 109–10.

72. Recall that Charlotte Mitchell was identified as the last descendant of Massasoit in a 1921 history of New Bedford.

73. Rochester, Massachusetts, *Rochester's Official Bi-Centennial Records*, 12.

74. Ibid., 108.

75. Lepore, *The Name of War*, 231–35. She was also involved in property disputes in the 1850s that she lodged before the Massachusetts legislature.

76. Rochester, Massachusetts, *Rochester's Official Bi-Centennial Records*, 109.

77. Ibid., 108–14. The quotation is from 114.

78. Ibid., 121.

79. Massasoit Monument Association, *Exercises under the Auspices of the Thalia Club*, 34. The Mitchell family were also guests at "King Philip's Day" in Bristol in 1876. See Lepore, *The Name of War*, 234.

80. Massasoit Monument Association, *Exercises under the Auspices of the Thalia Club*, 34.

81. Ibid., 40.

82. Ibid.

83. Historical, Natural History, and Library Society of South Natick, Mass., *Proceedings at the Reunion of the Descendants of John Eliot*, 84 (honor guard), 106 (last Indian), and 109 (emphasis added).

84. Gage, *History of Rowley*, xiii.

85. Bridgewater, Massachusetts, *Celebration of the Two-Hundredth Anniversary*.

86. A revisionist footnote informs us that the rock still bears that name.

87. Bridgewater, Massachusetts, *Celebration of the Two-Hundredth Anniversary*, 46.

88. Ibid., 83–97.

89. Ibid., 46 and 47.

90. Ibid., 88 and 89.

91. Ibid., 136.

92. Ibid.

93. Ibid., 139–40.

94. Ibid., 140.

95. Earle, *Report to the Governor*. All totals up to 764.

96. Hine, *Early Lebanon*, 8–9.

97. Gilman, *Historical Discourse, Delivered in Norwich*, 7.

98. Ibid. While the acknowledgment of Mohegans at the celebration was part of the historical discourse (quoted on 13–14), an asterisk directed readers to note C on 87 for the passage quoted here.

99. Stone, *Uncas and Miantonomoh*, 171.

100. Ibid., 183–84.

101. Ibid., 187.

102. Gilman, *Historical Discourse, Delivered in Norwich*, 7.

103. Stone, *Uncas and Miantonomoh*, 84.

104. Ibid., 204.

105. Caulkins, *History of New London*, 604.

106. Ibid., 605.

107. Ibid., 617.

108. William C. Sharpe, *History of Seymour, Connecticut, with Biographies and Genealogies* (Seymour, Conn.: Record Print, 1879), 36. On the marginalization of the Schaghticoke in local histories, see Richmond, "A Native Perspective of History," 103–12. See also Richmond and Den Ouden, "Recovering Gendered Political Histories," in Calloway and Salisbury, *Reinterpreting New England*.

109. Teller, *The History of Ridgefield, Conn.*, 166.

110. Livermore, *A History of Block Island*, 64–66.

111. Oliver Payson Fuller, *The History of Warwick, Rhode Island, Settlement in 1642 to the Present Time* (Providence: Angell, Burlingame, 1875), 6. The author cites "Dr. Usher Parson's Account" for the 1861 numbers.

112. Peterson, *History of Rhode Island*, 293–94.

113. William Franklin Tucker, *Historical Sketch of the Town of Charlestown, in Rhode Island, from 1636 to 1876* (Westerly, R.I.: G. B. & J. H. Utter, Steam Printers, 1877), 68.

114. Ibid., 48–49.

115. Denison, *Westerly (Rhode Island) and Its Witnesses*, 81.

116. Ibid.

117. Ibid., 82.

118. Bates, *An Anniversary Discourse, Delivered at Dudley, Mass.*, 44.

119. Brigham, *Address Delivered Before the Inhabitants of Grafton,* [37]. On nineteenth-century Nipmuc history see Thomas L. Doughton, "Unseen Neighbors," and Baron, Hood, and Izard, "They Were Here All Along."

120. George Bliss, *An Address, Delivered at the Opening of the Town-Hall in Springfield, March 24, 1828, Containing Sketches of the Early History of That Town, and Those in Its Vicinity* (Springfield, Mass.: Tannatt, 1828), 25.

121. Frederic Denison, *Illustrated New Bedford, Martha's Vineyard, and Nantucket: Sketches of Discoveries, Aborigines, Settlers, Wars, Incidents, Towns, Hamlets, Scenes, Camp Meetings, Cottages, and Interesting Localities, with Maps of the Islands* (Providence: J. A. & R. A. Reid, 1879), 55.

122. Martin Moore, *A Sermon Delivered at Natick, January 5, 1817, Containing a History of Said Town, from 1651 to the Day of Delivery* (Cambridge, Mass.: Hilliard and Metcalf, 1817), 20.

123. Biglow, *History of the Town of Natick, Mass.*, 84.

124. Earle, *Report to the Governor,* 89–90.

125. DeForest and Bates, *The History of Westborough, Massachusetts,* 28.

126. Ibid.

127. Forbes, *The Hundredth Town,* 170–71.

128. Ibid., 180.

129. Westminster, Massachusetts, *Celebration of the One Hundredth Anniversary,* 62–63.

130. Clapp, *History of the Town of Dorchester, Massachusetts,* 13.

131. In addition to the texts cited in this section, see William H. Sumner, *A History of East Boston; with Biographical Sketches of its Early Proprietors* (Boston: William H. Piper, 1869), 506; Winsor, *History of the Town of Duxbury,* 75; Lynn, Massachusetts, *Centennial Memorial of Lynn,* 91; and Lamson, *History of the Town of Manchester,* 10.

132. Russell, *Pilgrim Memorials* (1851), 132.

133. Kingston, Massachusetts, *Report of the Proceedings and Exercises at the One Hundred and Fiftieth Anniversary of the Incorporation of the Town of Kingston, Mass., June 27, 1876* (Boston: E. B. Stillings & Co., Printers, 1876), 115.

134. Medfield, Massachusetts, *Exercises at the Bi-Centennial Commemoration of the Burning of Medfield,* 36.

135. Ibid., 40.

136. Ibid.

137. Ibid.

138. Freeman, *History of Cape Cod.* This volume is not included in my calculations because it is a county history, not a local history.

139. Donald M. Nielsen, "The Mashpee Indian Revolt of 1833," *New England Quarterly* 58 (1985): 400–20.

140. Brooks, *The Common Pot,* 163–97.

141. Freeman, *History of Cape Cod,* 1:703. It is unclear whom he is quoting. The narration of post Revolutionary War Mashpee is in volume 1, 689–719. The Mashpee Revolt itself (not called that by the author) is discussed on 698–714.

142. Warrior, *The People and the Word,* 26.

143. On Stewart see Lora Romero, *Home Fronts: Domesticity and Its Critics in the Antebellum United States* (Durham, N.C.: Duke University Press, 1997), 52–70, and on Walker see Peter P. Hinks, ed., *David Walker's Appeal to the Coloured Citizens of the World* (University Park: Pennsylvania State University Press, 2006).

144. Apess might be seen as part of "The Secret History of Indian Modernity": Deloria, *Indians in Unexpected Places.* The literature on Apess is immense and growing, much of it emanating from literary criticism, and building on the indispensable collected edition of Apess's publications with its essential introduction and bibliographic essay by O'Connell, *On Our Own Ground.* See also Barry O'Connell, "'Once More Let Us Consider': William Apess in the Writing of New England Native American History," in Calloway, *After King Philip's War,* 162–77; Warrior, *The People and the Word,* which demonstrates in compelling fashion Apess's significance as a Native intellectual whose experiential perspective continues to "speak to a contemporary intellectual agenda" (2); Brooks, *The Common Pot,* 163–218, who examines a long history of Native writing as instrumental in reclaiming Native space; and Konkle, *Writing Indian Nations,* who suggests Apess might even have been "notorious," for a richly historicized account of Apess's life that charts the development of Apess's "critique of racial difference" (104) that is attuned to his political projects. Konkle also provides an excellent review of the secondary literature on Apess (see especially 304–18). In addition to O'Connell, Warrior, and Konkle, most pertinent for my purposes are Anne Marie Dannenberg, "'Where, Then, Shall we Place the Hero of the Wilderness?': William Apess's *Eulogy on King Philip* and Doctrines of Racial Destiny," in Jaskoski, *Early Native American Writing,* 66–82, which illuminates the political dimensions of Apess's work and points out that "the complexity of his political project has not yet been fully appreciated" (79); and Lepore, *The Name of War,* who situates Apess in dialogue with the wildly popular play *Metamora,* which dramatized a fictional national story of Indian extinction in the wake of King Philip's War as part of a project of American identity formation. As Konkle has pointed out, Lepore and two other monographs use Apess as "the closer": Richter, *Facing East from Indian Country,* and Waldstreicher, *In the Midst of Perpetual Fetes.* I follow Barry O'Connell's spelling of Apess's name based on his conclusion that it was Apess's preference and because the scholarship on him has generally followed this practice. O'Connell, *On Our Own Ground,* xiv.

145. O'Connell, *On Our Own Ground,* 7.

146. My overview of Apess's life here and in the next several paragraphs is based on ibid., Introduction.

147. Warrior, *The People and the Word.*

148. O'Connell, *On Our Own Ground,* 177.

149. William Apess, "Eulogy on King Philip, as Pronounced at the Odeon, in Federal

Street, Boston," in O'Connell, *On Our Own Ground*, 286. In *Indian Nullification of the Unconstitutional Laws of Massachusetts Relative to the Marshpee Tribe; or, The Pretended Riot Explained*, Apess offers a slightly different take on the problem of commemoration: "I think that the Indians ought to keep the twenty-fifty of December (Christmas) and the fourth of July as days of fasting and lamentation, and dress themselves, and their houses, and their cattle in mourning weeds, and pray to heaven for deliverance from their oppressions; for surely there is no joy in those days for the man of color" (187). Sixteen years later Frederick Douglass sounded similar themes in his 5 July 1852, address commemorating the Declaration of Independence in Rochester, New York, "The Meaning of July Fourth for the Negro." pbs.org/wgbh/aia/part4/4h2927 (accessed 26 November 2008).

150. O'Connell, *On Our Own Ground*, [275]. Metacom actually died on August 12, 1676.

151. Ibid., 286n15. O'Connell notes that in addition, he seems to be consciously "echoing and disputing Webster's reverential reading both of the 'Fathers' and of the Pilgrims." See also Konkle, *Writing Indian Nations*, 132–39.

152. O'Connell, *On Our Own Ground*, 276.

153. Ibid., 277.

154. Ibid., 279. As O'Connell notes, Apess seems to have mixed up Thomas Hunt's misdeeds with Edward Harlow's 1611 slaving expedition.

155. Ibid.

156. Ibid., 304.

157. Ibid., 277.

158. The concept of Indians aiming to retain a "measured separatism" that stood at the center of treaty relations beginning in the nineteenth century and changing over time comes from Charles F. Wilkinson, *American Indians, Time, and the Law* (New Haven, Conn.: Yale University Press, 1987), 14–19. For a study that builds brilliantly on this insight and traces the deleterious impact of the failure of the U.S. Supreme Court to understand Indian peoples as modern from the nineteenth century onward, see Williams, *Like a Loaded Weapon*. Here my argument differs from Maureen Konkle's in *Writing Indian Nations:* she notes that Apess traces a history of legal transactions that are not quite the same thing as the formal treaty arrangements other tribes could draw upon in order to bolster their "more ambiguous position" vis-à-vis tribes such as the Cherokee (143). Konkle also suggests that Apess's use of "citizen" in a passage I quote later in this chapter is intended "in the general sense of human rights, to indicate human freedom and equality."

159. See, e.g., O'Connell, *On Our Own Ground*, and Konkle, *Writing Indian Nations*.

160. I would like to thank David Wilkins for helping me understand some of the complexities of citizenship. On the political and legal origins of citizenship see David Wilkins, *American Indian Politics and the American Political System* (New York: Rowman and Littlefield, 2002), 49–56. And I would also like to thank Robert Warrior for a conversation about Apess that helped me clarify the ideas I develop here about dual citizenship.

161. O'Connell, *On Our Own Ground,* 310.

162. Ibid., 294. Jenny Hale Pulsipher makes this point about Philip's insistence on negotiating with the king of England as his equivalent in *Subjects unto the Same King: Indians, English, and the Contest for Authority in Colonial New England* (Philadelphia: University of Pennsylvania Press, 2005), 99, part of her broader argument about contests over authority as structuring affairs in seventeenth-century New England. In the end, she argues that Indian sovereignty in New England ended with the end of the seventeenth century with the dramatic shift in relations of power, which effectively equates sovereignty with military resistance. She ends her book by suggesting that New England Indians today are seeking to regain the autonomy that antedated the arrival of the English (269–71). My position is that the particular dimensions of New England Indian autonomy have always changed in subtle and not so subtle ways in dialogue with colonialism, rather than having ended with a particular event shift in social, cultural, or political processes.

163. O'Connell, *On Our Own Ground,* 306. References to the Cherokee situation, often coded as the oppression of Georgia, abound in *Indian Nullification of the Unconstitutional Laws of Massachusetts Relative to the Marshpee Tribe; or, The Pretended Riot Explained* (which he refers to in the *Eulogy*), published the year before in 1835 in the wake of the Mashpee Revolt. See, e.g., 177, 196, 200, 205, 226, 238, and 239 (all page numbers refer to O'Connell, *On Our Own Ground*). As Robert Warrior has argued in *The People and the Word,* the Mashpee petition "expresses what it meant to be Native, specifically Mashpee, in New England in the 1830s" (34).

164. O'Connell, *On Our Own Ground,* 304.

165. Ibid., 115.

166. Warrior, *The People and the Word,* 3–4, 47, and throughout.

167. On this point see especially Simmons, *Spirit of the New England Tribes.*

168. My use of the term "termination" here should not be conflated with the federal Indian policy initiated in the 1950s of the same name, even though interesting parallels can be drawn between nineteenth-century southern New England Indian affairs and the later federal policy. It is important to maintain a distinction between state and federal actions because of their standing in Indian policy and law. On federal termination policy see, e.g., Donald L. Fixico, *Termination and Relocation: Federal Indian Policy, 1945–1960* (Albuquerque: University of New Mexico Press, 1986). Herndon and Sekatau make the point that "detribalization" of the Narragansett occurred without federal approval. Herndon and Sekatau, "Right to a Name," 114 and 134. It is important to note that one of the seven criteria for achieving federal acknowledgment under the guidelines of the Office of Federal Acknowledgment is that the tribe under consideration has never been terminated under federal policy.

169. See, e.g., Ann Marie Plane and Gregory Button, "The Massachusetts Indian Enfranchisement Act: Ethnic Contest in Historical Context, 1849–1869," in Calloway, *After King Philip's War,* 178–206; Silverman, *Faith and Boundaries,* 222–73; Mandell, *Tribe, Race, Nation,* 195–217; and Deborah A. Rosen, *American Indians and State Law:*

Sovereignty, Race, and Citizenship, 1790–1880 (Lincoln: University of Nebraska Press, 2007), 155–201.

170. On the federal acknowledgment process see, e.g., Renée Ann Cramer, *Cash, Color, and Colonialism: The Politics of Tribal Acknowledgment* (Norman: University of Oklahoma Press, 2005); Anne Merline McCullock and David E. Wilkins, "Constructing Nations within States: The Quest for Federal Recognition by the Catawba and Lumbee Tribes," *American Indian Quarterly* 12 (1995): 361–88; Mark Edwin Miller, *Forgotten Tribes: Unrecognized Indians and the Federal Acknowledgment Process* (Lincoln: University of Nebraska Press, 2004); and William A. Starna, "'We'll All Be Together Again': The Federal Acknowledgment of the Wampanoag Tribe of Gay Head," *Northeast Anthropology* 51 (1996): 3–12.

171. As of 2005, the United States has restored recognition to thirty-seven tribes that had been "terminated." Cramer, *Cash, Color, and Colonialism*, 44.

172. See Jedidiah Morse, *A Report to the Secretary of War of the United States, on Indian Affairs* (New Haven, Conn.: S. Converse, 1822), 24, as well as Jack Campisi, "The Emergence of the Mashantucket Pequot Tribe, 1637–1975," in Hauptman and Wherry, *The Pequots in Southern New England*, 117–40; Campisi, *The Mashpee Indians*, 99–118; James Clifford, "Identity in Mashpee," in Clifford, *The Predicament of Culture: Twentieth-Century Ethnography, Literature, and Art* (Cambridge, Mass.: Harvard University Press, 1988), 277–348; U.S. Department of the Interior, Office of Federal Acknowledgment, *Summary under the Criteria and Evidence for Final Determination in Regard to Federal Acknowledgment of the Eastern Pequot Indians of Connecticut as a Portion of the Historical Eastern Pequot Tribe, June 24, 2002*, 29.

173. For an overview of these relationships, see Wilkins, *American Indian Politics*, 21–23.

174. For a useful overview of the colonial roots of this situation see Dorothy V. Jones, "British Colonial Indian Treaties," in Wilcomb E. Washburn, ed., *Handbook of North American Indians*, vol. 4 (Washington, D.C.: Smithsonian Institution, 1988), 185–94.

175. See, e.g., Silverman, *Faith and Boundaries*, 258, and Earle, *Report to the Governor*, 39.

176. Campbell and LaFantasie, "Scattered to the Winds of Heaven."

177. Earle, *Report to the Governor*, 133.

178. Earle also lamented the state of record keeping, which hindered his task tremendously. He suggested that measures be taken to keep regular records regarding Indians, including vital records. Earle, *Report to the Governor*, 45 and 48. The final act didn't create a commissioner, but instead its fifth section called for "the clerks of the Districts of Mashpee and Gay Head and the guardians of the other tribes" to make registers of members and to keep vital records, land registers, and to keep track of any changes in land holdings. Massachusetts General Court, Council, *Acts and Resolves, Passed by the General Court of Massachusetts, in the Year 1862* (Boston: William White, Printer to the State, 1862), 150–51.

179. Earle, *Report to the Governor*, e.g., 19, 75, 101, 103–4, 114, and 117.

180. Ibid., 116 (emphasis added).

181. U.S. Department of the Interior, Office of Federal Acknowledgment, *Summary Under the Criteria and Evidence for Final Determination . . . Eastern Pequot*, 78.

182. Rosen, *American Indians and State Law*, 155, 170, and 176.

183. Silverman, *Faith and Boundaries*, 257.

184. For an important overview of this legislation and its relationship to the Indian community at Mashpee and race relations more generally, see Plane and Button, "The Massachusetts Indian Enfranchisement Act." Deborah A. Rosen has recently expanded upon this article in her wide-ranging and helpful book *American Indians and State Law*, 155–201.

185. Plane and Button, "The Massachusetts Indian Enfranchisement Act," 183.

186. Ibid.

187. Ibid., 181–82.

188. Ibid., 199–200.

189. Here is the language of the Indian Citizenship Act: "*Be it enacted . . .* That all non citizen Indians born within the territorial limits of the United States be, and they are hereby, declared to be citizens of the United States; Provided That the granting of such citizenship shall not in any manner impair or otherwise affect the right of any Indian to tribal or other property." Francis Paul Prucha, ed., *Documents of United States Indian Policy* (Lincoln: University of Nebraska Press, 1975), 218.

190. Massachusetts General Court, Council, *Acts and Resolves*, 1862, 149.

191. Ibid., 149–50.

192. U.S. Department of the Interior, Office of Federal Acknowledgment, *Evidence for Proposed Finding Against Federal Acknowledgment of the Wampanoag Tribal Council of Gay Head, Inc.*, June 25, 1985, 27.

193. Ibid., 28 (quoting from House documents).

194. Ibid.

195. Ibid.

196. Earle, *Report to the Governor*, 24.

197. Silverman, *Faith and Boundaries*, esp. 223–73.

198. Ibid., 270.

199. U.S. Department of the Interior, Office of Federal Acknowledgment, *Summary Under the Criteria and Evidence for Final Determination . . . Eastern Pequot*, 55. On the origins of the guardianship system in Connecticut, see Wendy B. St. Jean, "Inventing Guardianship: The Mohegan Indians and Their 'Protectors,'" *New England Quarterly* 72 (1999): 362–87.

200. U.S. Department of the Interior, Office of Federal Acknowledgment, *Summary Under the Criteria and Evidence for Final Determination . . . Eastern Pequot*, 61.

201. Some Mohegans protested the sale of lands at this time. U.S. Department of the Interior, Office of Federal Acknowledgment, *Summary under the Criteria and Evidence for Proposed Finding against Federal Acknowledgment of the Mohegan Tribe of Indians of the State of Connecticut*, 47. The membership list prepared for the land distribution that

occurred in 1861 ironically "now serves as the primary historic roll for the petitioning group," 90.

202. Fawcett, *The Lasting of the Mohegans*, 22.

203. U.S. Department of the Interior, Office of Federal Acknowledgment, *Summary Under the Criteria and Evidence for Final Determination . . . Eastern Pequot*, 61. Note that continuous state recognition is contested.

204. Ibid., 62.

205. Ibid., 63.

206. Ibid.

207. Rubertone, *Grave Undertakings*, xx, and Campbell and LaFantasie, "Scattered to the Winds of Heaven," 76–79. For an early study of Narragansett detribalization that bears the marks of terminationist thinking in the 1950s, see Ethel Boissevain, "The Detribalization of the Narragansett Indians: A Case Study," *Ethnohistory* 3 (1956): 225–45.

208. Denison, *Westerly (Rhode Island) and Its Witnesses*, 82. This text reproduces an account of these events published in the *Providence Journal* of Oct. 17, 1866.

209. Denison, *Westerly (Rhode Island) and Its Witnesses*, 83.

210. Ibid., 83–84.

211. Ibid., 84.

212. Paul Robinson, "A Narragansett History from 1000 B.P. to the Present," in Weinstein, *Enduring Traditions*, especially 85–86.

213. U.S. Department of the Interior, Office of Federal Acknowledgment, *Recommendation and Summary of Evidence for Proposed Finding for Federal Acknowledgment of the Narragansett Indian Tribe of Rhode Island Pursuant to 25 CFR 83*, 5.

214. Ibid.

Conclusion

1. The numbers are as follows: Golden Hill Paugussett, 74 and 190; Mohegan, 1,180 and 2,428; Narragansett, 2,137 and 4,342; Nipmuc, 666 and 1,484; Pequot, 1,283 and 2,797; Schaghticoke, 256 and 498; and Wampanoag, 2,336 and 4,594. Table 1: American Indian and Alaska Native Alone and Alone or in any Combination Population, by Tribe for the United States: 2000, released 9/19/02. www.census.gov/population/www/cen2000/briefs/phc-t18/index (accessed 10 November 2008).

2. O'Brien, *Dispossession by Degrees*.

3. See Omi and Winant, *Racial Formation in the United States*.

4. Wilkins, *American Indian Politics*, 41.

5. Ibid., 23. See also Kimberly TallBear, "DNA, Blood, and Racializing the Tribe," *Wicazo Sa Review* 18 (2003): 81–107, for an excellent discussion of the complex interplay of "blood talk," belonging, and the political determination of Indian citizenship.

6. Wilkins, *American Indian Politics*, 49.

7. Ibid., 23–24, and TallBear, "DNA," 82, 88–93, and 98–99. For helpful overviews on blood and identity see Melissa L. Meyer, "American Indian Blood Quantum

Requirements: Blood Is Thicker than Family," in *Over the Edge: Remapping the American West*, ed. Valerie J. Matsumoto and Blake Almendinger, 321–49 (Berkeley and Los Angeles: University of California Press, 1999), and Pauline Turner Strong and Barrik Van Winkle, "'Indian Blood': Reflections on the Reckoning and Refiguring of Native North American Identity," *Cultural Anthropology* 11 (1996): 547–76.

8. For a discussion of this process in Massachusetts see Plane and Button, "The Massachusetts Indian Enfranchisement Act," in Calloway, *After King Philip's War*. On the Narragansett see Campbell and LaFantasie, "Scattered to the Winds of Heaven." For an important corrective to Campbell and LaFantasie's interpretation of detribalization, see Paul A. Robinson, "A Narragansett History from 1000 B.P. to the Present," in Weinstein, *Enduring Traditions*, 85–87.

9. Earle, *Report to the Governor,* and Bird, Griswold, and Weeks, *Report of the Commissioners.*

10. U.S. Department of the Interior, Office of Federal Acknowledgment, *Summary under the Criteria and Evidence for Proposed Finding against Federal Acknowledgment of the Mohegan Tribe of Indians of the State of Connecticut,* 18, and *Federal Register,* vol. 54, no. 216, Thursday, 9 November 1989, 47136. Federal acknowledgment came in 1994. *Federal Register,* vol. 59, no. 50, 15 March 1994, 12140–144.

11. U.S. Department of the Interior, Office of Federal Acknowledgment, *Recommendation and Summary of Evidence for Proposed Finding for Federal Acknowledgment of the Narragansett Indian Tribe of Rhode Island Pursuant to 25 CFR 93,* 5.

12. Charles F. Wilkinson has astutely pointed out that "a central thrust of the old laws, shared both by the tribes and by the United States, was to create a measured separatism. That is, the reservation system was intended to establish homelands for the tribes, islands of tribalism largely free from interference by non-Indians or future state governments. This separatism is measured rather than absolute, because it contemplates supervision and support by the United States." Although measured separatism has varied in practice over the years, Wilkinson points to treaties and treaty substitutes as foundational to understanding Indian sovereignty. He also argues that decisions in the modern era have affirmed measured separatism as a promise the United States has guaranteed to the tribes (102). Wilkinson, *American Indians, Time, and the Law,* 14–18. The quotation is from 14.

13. Amy E. Den Ouden notes that she encountered feelings of bitterness and resentment over the process itself as dehumanizing and intrusive in her fieldwork with the Golden Hill Paugussetts and Eastern Pequots succinctly expressed by one man who said, "'I'm tired of people trying to tell me that my grandmother lied to me.'" *Beyond Conquest,* 228.

14. *Federal Register,* vol. 48, no. 29, Thursday, 10 February 1983, Notices, 6177.

15. Ibid.

16. On the highly contentious process of federal acknowledgment, see, e.g., Cramer, *Cash, Color, and Colonialism,* and Miller, *Forgotten Tribes.*

Index

Jean M. O'Brien (White Earth Ojibwe) is professor of history at the University of Minnesota, where she is also affiliated with American Indian studies and American studies. She is the author of *Dispossession by Degrees: Indian Land and Identity in Natick, Massachusetts, 1650–1790.*